D0933782

CONDOMINIUMS
AND COOPERATIVES

Real Estate for Professional Practitioners
A Wiley Series
DAVID CLURMAN, Editor

CONDOMINIUMS AND COOPERATIVES

SECOND EDITION

DAVID CLURMAN
F. SCOTT JACKSON
EDNA L. HEBARD

JOHN WILEY & SONS

NEW YORK • CHICHESTER • BRISBANE • TORONTO • SINGAPORE

Copyright © 1984 by John Wiley & Sons, Inc.

All rights reserved. Published simultaneously in Canada

Reproduction or translation of any part of this work
beyond that permitted by Section 107 or 108 of the
1976 United States Copyright Act without the permission
of the copyright owner is unlawful. Requests for
permission or further information should be addressed to
the Permissions Department, John Wiley & Sons, Inc.

This publication is designed to provide accurate and
authoritative information in regard to the subject
matter covered. It is sold with the understanding that
the publisher is not engaged in rendering legal, accounting,
or other professional service. If legal advice or other
expert assistance is required, the services of a competent
professional person should be sought. *From a Declaration
of Principles jointly adopted by a Committee of the
American Bar Association and a Committee of Publishers.*

Library of Congress Cataloging in Publication Data

Clurman, David, 1927–
    Condominiums and cooperatives.

    (Real estate for professional practitioners)
    Includes index.
    1. Condominiums—Law and legislation—United States.
2. Housing, Cooperative—Law and legislation—United
States.   I. Jackson, F. Scott, 1945–   . II. Hebard,
Edna L.   III. Title.   IV. Series.
KF581.C5   1984   306'.32   84-3643
 ISBN 0-471-89197-5

Printed in the United States of America

10 9 8 7 6 5 4 3 2 1

To
OUR SPOUSES and CHILDREN

SERIES PREFACE

Since the end of World War II, tremendous changes have taken place in the business and residential real estate fields throughout the world. This has been evidenced not only by architectural changes, exemplified by the modern shopping center, but also in the many innovative financing responses that have enabled development of new structures and complexes, such as multiuse buildings. It can be expected that real estate development will speed in new directions at an ever increasing pace to match the oncoming needs of our time. With this perspective, the Real Estate for Professional Practitioners series has been developed in response to professional needs.

As real estate professional activities have become divided into specialties, because of intensive demand for expertise at all stages, so has there developed an increasing need for extensive training and continual education for persons directly involved or dealing in business ventures requiring detailed knowledge of realty procedures.

Perhaps no field of business endeavor is more in need of a series of professional books than real estate. Working in the practical world of business and residential construction and space utilization, or at advanced levels of college training covering these areas, one is constantly aware that too little of existing creative thinking has been transcribed into viable books. Many of the books that have been written do not thoroughly enough encompass both the practical and theoretical aspects of complex subjects. Too often the drive for immediate answers has led to the overlooking of fundamental purposes and technical know-how that might lead to much more favorable results for the persons seeking knowledge.

This series will be made up of books thoroughly and expertly expounding existing procedures in the many fields of real estate, but searching as well for innovative solutions to current and future problems. These books are intended to offer a compendium of each author's wide experience and knowledge to aid the seasoned professional.

The series is addressed to professionals in all walks of realty endeavor. These include business investors and developers, urban affairs specialists, attorneys, accountants, and the many others whose work involves real estate creativity and investment. Just as importantly, the series will present to advanced students in many realty fields the opportunity to review professional thinking that will help to stimulate their own thoughts on modern trends in housing and business construction.

We believe these goals can be achieved by the outstanding group of authors who will create the books in the series.

DAVID CLURMAN

PREFACE

The first edition of this text appeared in 1970. At that time it was one of the few texts written on the subject in an emerging field. Its purpose was to provide a comprehensive survey of condomium and cooperative ownership for professionals and for the astute prospective purchaser who wished to learn the fine details of these new forms of real estate. Additionally, the book was widely used in college courses, including graduate programs.

The predictions set forth in the initial text have not only come true but are being dramatized everywhere to such a degree that these areas of real estate are not even considered novel by most Americans anymore. It is fair to conclude that by the end of the twentieth century the overwhelming number of new and converted units of American residential housing will be in the form of condominium, cooperative, or homeownership association. Therefore, this text now covers subjects that will touch the lives of most Americans in the near future.

While there has been a proliferation of texts in these fields, most are not comprehensive and have never really replaced the thorough study made in the first edition. However, new developments required a thorough revision of the original text, which has now been accomplished in this second edition. The new version includes new material on the Uniform Condominium Act, updated tax information, current California law, updating of federal housing programs and much more.

The second edition should be as useful as the first edition has been to professionals such as bankers, brokers, real estate developers, sales staff, planners, government agencies, and those others whose professions have carried them into the condominium and cooperative areas.

Once again, the text addresses the need for a thorough college-level text that is comprehensive in terms of history, policy, and technical expertise, to provide thorough training for those studying in this field as well as perspectives for the challenges of the future.

DAVID CLURMAN
F. SCOTT JACKSON
EDNA L. HEBARD

New York, New York
Newport Beach, California
Rollins, Montana
May 1984

CONTENTS

ONE

INTRODUCTION TO CONDOMINIUMS

ANOTHER WORD FOR HOME

The term *condominium* refers to a form of ownership in which more than one homeowner shares the ownership of, use of, and responsibility for certain common facilities. Essentially, it means to have control (*-dominium*) over a certain property owned jointly with (*con-*) one or more other persons. Therefore, each of those hundreds of thousands of people who now own condominium homes in the United States will have been deeded his or her own sole unit in a multiple-unit property, together with an undivided portion of ownership in areas and facilities that are shared with his or her neighbors. The co-ownership aspect directly concerns only a part of the owner's complete bundle of property rights, but the particular form of packaging or combination of these rights has come to be known in its entirety as a condominium.

The purchaser of a condominium receives a separate deed that gives him or her exclusive ownership of the particular home or unit and an interest in the so-called common elements associated with the building in which the unit is located. These common elements may include the underlying land, structural components of the buildings, amenities such as parking areas and recreational facilities, and other portions of the development that are not described as units. In some states, however, the unit may include an entire detached home and the land beneath it, as in those states where the Uniform Condominium Act (UCA) has been adopted. (See Chapter 5 for a discussion of the UCA.)

What separates the condominium life style from the life style of a home-owner in a standard subdivision of detached homes? It is the community association of which each condominium homeowner is a member. The association is an organization of homeowners (usually incorporated) wherein the ownership of a condominium requires automatic membership in the organization and the organization has the power and duty to assess (tax) its members to generate operating funds. The association is a form of business enterprise, as well as a form of mini-government, distinguishing it from voluntary civic or social organizations. (See Chapter 7 for a more thorough discussion of the rights and powers of a community association.)

Condominium homes may take a number of forms, including attached townhouses, midrise buildings, highrise buildings, garden apartments, and other forms of residential structures. Moreover, the condominium is also being widely used as a form of sharing ownership within mixed-use and commercial projects (offices, shopping centers, industrial buildings, etc.) Large planned communities have been created throughout the country, with neighborhood condominium projects being an integral form of ownership bound to other forms of ownership with a master or "umbrella" community association. Homeowners may find themselves members of two associations, one formed primarily to maintain the exteriors of their buildings and one to maintain parks and recreational centers common to several projects.

GROWTH OF THE CONDOMINIUM

During the past several years, the condominium form of ownership has become an accepted way of life in America. According to a survey of the Urban Land Institute, there were only 500 condominium projects nationwide in 1962, representing approximately 50,000 condominium units. Census data indicate that the number of condominium units in America grew to 436,000 in 1970. In 1975, the Department of Housing and Urban Development (HUD) identified 12,500 different projects representing more than 1 million condominiums in the United States. By early 1982, condominium sales had risen to 12 percent of total sales by real estate agents in America. Eighteen percent of all nonsubsidized, apartment-type, attached-unit projects being built in the United States are condominiums, and that percentage, compared to only 11 percent in 1973, is creeping up every year.

Condominiums are more prevalent in some areas of the United States than in other areas. By far, most condominium activity has occurred in Florida, California, Illinois, Michigan, the District of Columbia, and Hawaii, although every state in the Union has experienced some activity. In some areas of Florida, condominiums represent a majority of all new residential construction. In 1981, the California Department of Real Estate estimated that at least 2.5 million California residents lived in condominium-type homes.

Most condominiums have been created through new construction, but many projects are created through the conversion of rental apartment projects to the condominium form of ownership. The 1975 HUD study estimated that there were 100,000 condominium units created through conversion before 1975. However, the conversion boom became widespread in many metropolitan areas between 1975 and 1980.

A BIT OF HISTORY

The present usage of the Latin word *condominium* derives chiefly from its adoption in the Italian codes in the 1930s. The concept apparently had only the sparsest antecedents in Ancient Rome. Convincing evidence indicates that individual ownership of "stories" of property developed as a Germanic–Franco concept, probably as the result of a quest for living space in congested walled cities struggling with a growing urban population oppressed by the limitations of fortress living. In medieval times, many towns that later developed into some of Europe's largest cities were surrounded by walls to protect them from marauders. The great city of Paris was once a small town covering only about 675 acres and situated within high walls, the first of which had been erected between 1180 and the early 1200s.

If for no other reason, the sanitary conditions that prevailed in the multi-storied dwellings of medieval times would have been sufficient cause to abandon such housing. As the danger of attack became less threatening and the expanding urban population moved outside the city walls into the comparatively unrestricted expanses of the countryside, storied ownership tended to dwindle away, although recognition of the lingering use of this form of ownership was contained in various codifications of real property law, such as the Napoleonic Code of 1804. Finally, during the first half of the twentieth century, the condominium once again came into use in Western Europe. One form, the *coproprietaire* ownership, is a major form of ownership among the new housing in France today.

Long before the United States adopted the condominium form, the statutes of other countries, including Spain, Italy, Germany, Belgium, and France, denoted rights and obligations in such ownership. In South America, the statute books contain many condominium laws enacted before those created by American legislatures. While there was a Brazilian law enacted in 1928 and a Chilean statute adopted as early as 1937, most South American laws are products of the late 1940s and 1950s. Interestingly, most of these laws never employ the term *condominium* but adopt such names as *horizontal property* or similar attempts at descriptive terminology, most of which are just as poor. At the heart of all these statutes is the allowance of and protection for exclusive ownership of airspace, with essential concomitants of common ownership. In addition, these laws carry the tradition of storied property with emphasis on vertical division of space by horizontal planes in highrise buildings. There is a minimal concern for other uses of the concept. In Mexico during 1967, private banking sources announced the availability of hundreds of millions of dollars (American) for mortgage financing of condominium apartment purchasers. Such financing was probably the most readily available and the easiest to obtain of any financing in that country thereafter.

ENGLAND

Despite general omission from British law texts and rare and obscure consideration in court decisions and statutes, the condominium has become employed increasingly by the English as a form of ownership in the past sixty years. Occasional stringent housing conditions in crowded central locations and the popularity of owned apartments among their French neighbors might account for some of the growing popularity. Flats, as these apartments are commonly called, have given rise to very little litigation, despite the absence of a specific enabling statute. In a report written for the United Nations in 1963, a British government statistician classified flats into large blocks, small blocks, and adapted houses, the last referring no doubt to conversions of buildings not originally constructed as flats. Under one procedure, a separate legal entity is established by the flat owners to administer the common facilities, with the owners sharing in control of the board of directors. This procedure would appear superior to the other practice of sponsor–developer retaining the common elements as trustee for the owner. The successful use of the condominium form also has been attributed to the recognized artfulness of English conveyancing practice, although this is more an implementing than a causative factor. It must be assumed that skilled drafting and the development of custom have been of enormous value in avoiding the courts.

CONGRESS AND PUERTO RICO

Section 234 of the National Housing Act was enacted by the U.S. Congress in 1961 for the avowed and almost exclusive purpose of extending Federal Housing Administration (FHA) insurance to mortgage loans issued to residents of Puerto Rico. Because of population concentrations, Puerto Rico was distressingly in need of highrise and other middle-income developments in urban centers at that time. In view of the limited success of upper middle-class and luxury condominiums already built, it was felt that this form of ownership would receive acceptance at lower income levels. Moreover, it was hoped that lending institutions, which had balked at making condominium mortgage loans to the island's middle class, might be willing to channel funds into this area under a guarantee umbrella.

As of the middle of 1968, Section 234 insurance had been of limited direct importance on the American mainland, having been utilized only in the District of Columbia, California, Florida, and Michigan for individual unit financing. The law, as indicated in Exhibit 1-1, had been implemented substantially in Puerto Rico but on a far from massive scale. The exhibit, however, demonstrates the early history under Section 234.

Exhibit 1-1.   Cumulative as of June 30, 1968, Title III, Section 234, Condominium Housing Operations; Summary of Condominium Individual Units Insured

State	Number	Amount
District of Columbia	3	$ 505,350
California	156	2,181,150
Florida	20	421,400
Michigan	131	2,002,750
Puerto Rico	818	16,573,500
U.S. Total	1,163	$21,684,150

Source: Federal Housing Administration.

Importance of Section 234

Regardless of the minimal use of Section 234 following enactment, its passage by the Eighty-seventh Congress in 1961 was a significant step in condominium history in the United States, representing as it did a declaration of confidence in this form of ownership by Congress and federal housing officials. Certainly, any radical departure in ownership form in a field as hard-bedded as real estate needs every possible authoritative support.

With federal insurance at stake, a great deal of attention was directed to research and development of safeguards for lenders, sponsors, and purchasers. Because the law was passed at a time when the conventional home mortgage market was experiencing "easy money," most sponsors successfully avoided the added bureaucracy of the federal program. Nevertheless, the federal program remains a reachable pump for funds during periods when institutional lenders may decide that mortgage insurance is desirable or when property development is being encouraged by national policy but is lacking a degree of security deemed adequate for uninsured loans by ordinary appraisal standards.

The most significant result arising from the passage of Section 234 was the impetus given state legislatures to enact condominium-enabling legislation. Nearly every governor who signed such a bill into law noted the value of securing the benefits of Section 234 for residents of his or her state. While the pretext was honorable, few builders and lenders have shown interest in these laws from the standpoint of utilizing Section 234. Even though usage of Section 234 has been insignificant in the United States thus far, it is dubious whether more than a handful of states' condominium laws would have been enacted if Puerto Rico had not fought for the enactment of Section 234. Fortunately, Section 234 authorized FHA insurance on a nationwide basis rather than merely as a trial testing of the program in Puerto Rico as some had urged.

THE CONDOMINIUM IN DECISION MAKING

To any passerby, a highrise apartment building looks exactly the same whether or not it is condominium owned. Clusters of row townhouses, except for advertising signs, do not ordinarily expose any particular mark that proclaims condominium ownership. Apart from current financial and other practical considerations, which are fully explored later, it would be well at this point to examine the underlying motif for garnering this relatively new format into the category of important subjects for future decision making.

Random examination of only three of the newest concepts in land utilization should demonstrate how great a potential exists in the condominium form of ownership. Much has been written in planning literature on three topics:

1. Multiple-use improvements
2. Construction over platforms
3. Utilization of areas now unsuitable for construction

If each of these new ideas is considered carefully, it becomes apparent how the condominium can help in their fulfillment.

Multiple-Use Improvements

The rapid population growth since World War II has forcibly brought to the attention of city planners, builders, businesspeople, and the general public the fact that land must be used more wisely in the future than it generally has been used in the past. The scarcity of economically desirable land necessitates not only a better selection of uses for the land but also a more intensive use of much of it. Hence, multiple-use improvements are receiving considerable attention. Such improvements can successfully include the use of condominium ownership, as the following case illustrates.

A municipality plans to construct a twenty-story building with only five floors to be retained for municipal use as an elementary school. The initial capital cost for land acquisition, tenant relocation, and building demolition cannot be rapidly recouped by the mere rental of unneeded areas. The same can be said for the cost of the remainder of the structure, assuming that rental is decided to be the best procedure. In addition, it is quite possible that the entire site might be removed from the tax rolls because of its municipal ownership.

However, if a condominium alternative were considered, a better solution quickly becomes apparent. Such a solution would grant exclusive ownership to commercial, residential, and educational users for specific areas, with an undivided interest in commonly used facilities. The municipality, by contributing only a portion of the construction and acquisition costs or by outright sale of the unneeded areas after construction, expends much less on the venture. Each area, including the land, would bear the obligation inherent in separate tax assessments.

In order to have flexibility, it need not always be assumed that in multiple-use ownership the overall condominium arrangement requires that all residential facilities must also be internally condominium. The residential (or even commercial) area may be a separate condominium project distinct from the overall building, if the building is subdivided into several horizontal lots in jurisdictions that authorize three-dimensional planned unit developments (PUDs). Alternatively, the residential (or commercial) area may be divided into specific units within the framework of the overall condominium, and the entire residential (or commercial) unit could itself be employed alternatively for rental or cooperative apartment purposes within the overall condominium.

Formulated before the enactment of a condominium law in New York, the United Nations Plaza buildings opposite UN headquarters are comprised of two parallel luxury cooperative apartment buildings rising from a common lower-level office building. Each cooperative apartment building, as well as the office building, is independently controlled. The legal problems involving this landmark structure were resolved finally by a reciprocal agreement of several hundred pages that covered easements and mutual rights and obligations. While local authorities did agree to three separate tax bills, it is hard to believe that such solutions must always involve so complicated a procedure. Difficulties in drafting the reciprocal agreement, although reasonable and unavoidable, expensively delayed the culmination of the cooperatives for many months. Almost certainly, use of a statutorily sanctioned overall condominium arrangement would have been preferable. Nevertheless, this undertaking evidenced great imagination and courage in employing realty in these new arrangements. In the event that present statutes impose restrictions on the simplification of such solutions, then amendments must be considered.

Platform Construction

In recent years the principal uses of platform construction have been as follows:

1. To build over ground-level facilities that need only limited height for operations, such as railroad yards and trackage, bridge approaches, and highways.
2. To construct buildings over rocky terrain unsuitable for ordinary methods of economic development because of otherwise prohibitive foundation expense or the impracticality of providing utilities, water, and other sources of essential services.
3. To erect tall structures over one or more smaller buildings, in order to superimpose office buildings or highrise apartment buildings, even though this has seldom contributed toward ennobling the grandeur of older buildings.

The condominium's legal format can contribute substantially to the solution of many platform problems that frequently arise in the above situations. With the condominium, financing costs can be shared and legal problems of divided ownership can be solved.

To date, in most cases of divided ownership of airspace and land, some form of leasing grant of the airspace combined with a conveyance of special ground easements has been employed in creating the legal and financial basis for platform construction of improvements. In a few situations, tiny portions of land on which to rest the platform foundations have been sold to the builder, with specific ownership of these fractions of land conveyed by a separate document. In other cases, a complete sale of land and inherent air rights was made, subject to the reservation of a long-term lease held by the user of the lower facilities. It must be said that many of these solutions were remarkable improvisations (especially in view of the property disposition restrictions on the railroads, which pioneered such solutions), enabling the owners to obtain maximal income from valuable property that was being underutilized for ground transportation alone.

But solutions based on railroad problems need not restrict simpler devices for joint ownership in cases where the special restrictions that bar solutions when railroad property is involved do not exist. Nevertheless, to date, railroad solutions have prevailed in most nonrailroad situations. In any event, the condominium looms as an important new and perhaps universal solution for the near future.

Heavy expenses, building codes, and zoning laws have limited most platform construction to massive undertakings that require special approval by planning boards, often as part of redevelopment plans. With new technology alread indicating the feasibility of inexpensive trusses and platforms for substantial load-bearing duties, greater consideration will be given in the future to the construction of small blocks or rows of buildings on platforms over ground utilized in any of the ways already mentioned and in many other situations. Covered parking areas extending into the air may become common parts of such condominiums. Cost, though reduced, will still require joint effort for which condominium ownership is well suited.

Utilization of Areas Now Unsuitable for Construction

Massive underground recreational, parking, industrial, and even housing areas can be expected to emerge as commonplace in future decades. Being literally a form of layer ownership, these structures will require common usage of lower and side platforms and braces, and common air and utility systems. Division of ownership of space carved downward can be facilitated by the condominium form as readily as ownership of space in a finite or infinite upward direction.

The condominium is the only form of ownership that permits exclusiveness in the traditional sense of individual fee simple ownership while still allowing for almost any type of physical arrangement. The vast sums of money that have been spent on research (even though much more concerned with the moon than the earth) are expected to provide sudden breakthroughs in our knowledge of soil and subsoil, rock formation, and water and power availability, with the result that the population of tomorrow may be living on the sides of jagged mountains and other presently uninhabitable sites. Single, narrow foundation shafts and platform coverings can be expected to support groups of separate homes with common foundation, underlying land, elevator shafts, and utilities. The practical legal format for marketing construction of this type is unquestionably the condominium.

Although much less spectacular, the pressure of population growth and economic expansion will force into the housing market in the near future land now considered unsuitable for housing construction because of the rough contour of the land, swampiness, or some other objectionable feature. Land that was skipped over in the early rush to the suburbs will take on a new desirability for apartment and townhouse developments. The high cost of preparing such land for development will not prove to be economically intolerable in the case of condominium housing.

FLEXIBILITY IN SOLUTIONS

The excitement generated by the condominium motif is primarily the result of the wide extension of housing solutions made possible by its existence. More imaginative and realistic decision making can be expected from those who fully understand the potential here.

The Different Kinds of Condominiums

Many persons have singular notions regarding the actual physical nature of a condominium development. Unfortunately, their views generally are based on a limited experience with a particular building or group of buildings or on a limited utilization of the condominium form of ownership in a specific community or neighborhood.

The real estate business has always been enlivened by the creation of entirely new ideas for space utilization. The condominium concept emphasizes this important aspect, and in the potential uses of this new medium there is a rather wide variety of purposeful and creative possibilities.

The condominium form can be adapted to any of the following kinds of housing:

1. Single high rise apartments in an entirely residential building.
2. A single highrise apartment building with a mixed condominium ownership of residentially and commercially utilized space.
3. Single highrise apartment ownership consisting primarily of residential areas under condominium ownership with commercially utilized space owned by the condominium residents but operated by commercial tenants under leases.
4. Single highrise apartment condominiums with only the residential areas under condominium ownership, with commercial areas reserved for the sponsor or other owner, with various easements and other reciprocal obligations existing between the condominium and the other owner or owners.
5. Groups of highrise apartment-type buildings utilizing any one of the aforesaid distributions of ownership rights.
6. Attached townhouse-type, single-family homes distributed in rows or clusters in various arrangements.
7. Groups of townhouses divided into groupings that include detached one-family condominium homes.
8. Groups of detached one-family condominium homes.
9. Groups of garden-type apartment condominiums with each of the floors owned by separate owners of condominium units.

10. Commerical condominium buildings of various sizes and arrangements, including office buildings, industrial plants, lofts, industrial parks, shopping centers, parking structures, grain elevators, horse stables, boat marinas, and similar uses.

11. Varieties of recreational developments, such as ski resorts, golf courses, beach clubs, and other types where housing or space is owned in the condominium form with the principal utilization being the usage and ownership of recreational facilities.

12. Educational or government-used facilities shared in usage and ownership by several independent localities.

Within each of the above classifications are countless possibilities for different arrangements, special common facilities, and primary purposes. A highrise condominium can provide homeownership to the wealthy in an expensive land location just as well as housing for the poor in more modest surroundings. A whole block of new housing may go condominium to facilitate the combined use of a leased or owned computer. Townhouses can be principal residences or second homes occupied on a limited seasonal basis. Two school districts together can own an educational complex of lower elementary grades or any number of other combinations. A school district may sell or lease excess land to a developer for residential condominium development purposes and perhaps lease back condominium units for its school purposes.

Within a short space of time, firsts in the condominium field have been arising in all parts of the United States. An interesting example is a New Jersey condominium—the first shopping center condominium in the eastern United States. The first phase of this development is reported to include parking space for 250 cars and nine stores, which utilize approximately 16,-800 square feet. When all phases are completed, the center will contain 61,-000 square feet and parking for 410 cars. Thus, the separate ownership of stores within a shopping center has become an actuality.

The choices and potentials for successfully utilizing the condominium form of ownership are varied and numerous, with many complex problems still to be resolved. Truly, all those concerned with the economic and social problems of space distribution in the future cannot escape the need for a full understanding of the techniques of condominium. Most of the remainder of this book attempts to convey a basic understanding of the essentials of this new frontier of real estate.

TWO

BASIC LEGAL STRUCTURE OF A CONDOMINIUM

THE DECLARATION OR MASTER DEED

In order to make the condominium concept meaningful, simplicity must be invoked with respect to the form of declaration of legal right, title, obligation, and immunity for those who participate in condominium ownership. In the United States, this legal feat is accomplished by preparing and filing a document with the appropriate local government registry. Depending on the terminology of the particular state's condominium act, the document can be called a declaration or master deed or other similar term. The declaration contains fundamental ownership covenants that "run with the land" so that it binds every person who becomes a property owner in the project. In essence, this document provides for dividing ownership—a veritable declaration of independence for the separate units created by this process as well as affirmation by unit owners of the shared obligation for commonly used areas or common elements. In some states (e.g., California) the unit location is shown on a separately recorded drawing called a condominium plan.

AN ENABLING STATUTE

To provide the mortar and trowel for giving legal structure to the declaration, condominium statutes have been enacted that bestow legislative sanction on the effectiveness of this document among participating owners and between them and outsiders.

Perhaps the most important functions of such statutes are the following:

1. To provide for recognition of divided ownership and the utilization of conveyancing instruments that adequately and clearly demonstrate ownership and its transferability.
2. To establish a form of binding contract (the declaration) among the participants, which cannot be avoided or altered to the detriment of the others without adequate consent.
3. To avoid otherwise uncontrollable legal means for partitioning property intended for common use.
4. To mandate recognition by government officials of the need to file documents in official places, to assess units separately and fairly for real property taxes, and to allow one unit to relieve itself from a blanket judgment or mechanics lien by satisfaction of a pro rata portion of the entire obligation.
5. To provide adequate safety and thus impel institutional lenders to issue mortgage loans secured by the separate units and their respective interests in commonly owned areas.

Before the enactment of such statutes, there were occasional attempts to form condominiums by complex agreement among residents. The files of the Veterans' Administration show projects planned or built as nonstatutory condominiums in Detroit, Chicago, New Haven, the District of Columbia, New York City, and Stamford, Connecticut. Without statutory enactments, the condominium form in the United States would have been relegated to the status of an historical curiosity.

Although every state has a condominium enabling statute, usually based upon the model of FHA in 1961, many (first-generation) statutes are deficient. Some do not provide for expandable (phased) or contractable condominiums, and they provide the drafter and the homeowners little guidance in creating and operating the association. Gradually, states (e.g., Georgia and Virginia) are adopting second-generation condominium acts to deal with problems that have been recognized through several years of experience, and the Uniform Condominium Act (UCA) discussed in Chapter 5 is an example of such a flexible, innovative statute.

DURATION OF CONDOMINIUM

Most statutory condominiums involve property ownership in fee simple (outright homeownership) form without the residual rights typically imposed by a landlord–tenant relationship. While in several states leasehold condominiums are permitted, this discussion will emphasize the fee form, which more truthfully embodies the essential motif of the condominium instrument. (In Chapter 11, the special aspects and problems of the leasehold type are discussed.)

The duration of the fee form of condominium is covered carefully in the declaration. The occurrence of any one of the following six eventualities could result in the defeasance, elimination, or severing of an individual's ownership in a condominium:

1. Fire or some other physical hazard may destroy the premises or its usefulness, and it may not be feasible to rebuild.
2. An arm of government, including the myriad of authorities and subgovernments, may seize the property by exercise of eminent domain.
3. Violation of condominium rules or other contractual obligations may result in forceful loss of ownership rights.
4. A lienor may foreclose on the unit with a consequent change in ownership.
5. The unit may be transferred voluntarily by an owner to a purchaser.
6. By unanimous or other required vote, the owners may decide to terminate the condominium.

The mechanics attending such contingencies, subject to the breadth and detail of the specific statute, should be set forth in precise details in the master documents. Second-generation condominium statutes such as the UCA cover each of these contingencies well and beg for briefer documents.

OWNERSHIP AS OF FILING OF DECLARATION

In most states the sponsor of a condominium (usually the owner of the land) subdivides his or her ownership of land and airspace when he or she declares his or her intention to form a condominium, although in some states (e.g., California) the land and airspace is not divided until the first condominium is transferred by deed. As of the moment of the filing of the declaration, all property ordinarily remains in the ownership of the sponsor. In order effectively to transfer ownership of the separate units, a form of deed consistent with the enabling statute and the terms of the declaration must be used for each unit.

BAR ON SEPARATION

The condominium statutes uniformly prohibit the severance of the two aspects of ownership—the unit and the undivided interest in common elements. Thus, each owner of a unit and each succeeding transferee bears the obligation of contributing to the maintenance of the commonly owned areas for that period when ownership of the unit itself is legally exercisable. Acceptance of a condominium deed automatically places on the owner all rights and obligations imposed by a validly filed declaration and the particular condominium statute, including many powers (including the power of sale on default) in the association. For these reasons, a condominium deed should always be signed by the new purchaser.

BAR ON PARTITION

Ordinarily, persons who share an undivided percentage interest in real estate ownership can maintain a court proceeding physically to divide or partition the land. This lawsuit is commonly available in almost every state and is known as a partition action. If it is greatly prejudicial to the other owners to so divide the owned realty, a court may order, as an alternative, the sale of the entire property involved.

It can be seen that the undivided interests of condominium owners in their common areas would be jeopardized by the existence of such a court remedy as partition. For this reason, condominium laws expressly bar partition actions by condominium owners seeking to divide the common areas of their condominium except under extraordinary conditions (e.g., obsolescence or substantial destruction of the project).

CONVENIENCE OF THE DECLARATION

The declaration, besides containing a detailed description of each condominium unit, gives a number or number–letter identification to each unit. In addition, the specific percentage interest in the common areas that belongs to such unit is almost always specifically stated. This interest assigned to each unit is usually based on relative value, square footage, or equality. Some states (e.g., Ohio) require that common area interests be based on value, causing several problems of computation in expandable, multiphase projects built over several years. Because these facts are incorporated in the declaration, the condominium deed most often can be a simple document that describes space location by the reference numbers and letters contained in the declaration:

> All that certain piece or parcel of real property with the improvements therein contained, situate and being a part of a condominium in the City of _____, County of _____ and State of _____, shown and designed as unit no. _____, together with the undivided _____ interest in the common elements constituting real property of the condominium hereinafter described as the same as defined in declaration of condominium herein referred to.

Where there are unique reservations or exclusive easement grants (called limited or restricted common areas), for such areas as patios, balconies, and parking spaces, accompanying the conveyance, the description will be expanded, but these complications are not different from what would be experienced in any real estate conveyance with such reservations or easements.

DESCRIPTION OF AIRSPACE

When the condominium does not involve individual units cut out of space (such as highrise or lowrise apartments), ordinary terminology for describing units sometimes can be utilized to a large degree. However, even attached clusters of separately owned, two-floor townhouses can be the subject of filed plans and descriptions quite dissimilar to noncondominium housing of the same physical appearance. But what about units composed of airspace not directly attached to land?

Many statutes directly or implicitly direct solution to these problems. For example, the imposition of a floor plan description requirement, used in some states, presents a formula for confining residency in space, so long as the height and bounds of each residence are also contained in such separate plans or as an adjunct to building plans. The declaration should specify narratively the formula for unit determination. The next section on unit bounds contains a discussion of the need for precision in defining each particular unit.

Besides the basic floor plan method of dividing airspace, it is also possible to divide an entire building into cubes of air or to render a survey by specific heights above focal levels. But the less mathematical "floor plan–building plan unit bounds" method offers fewer problems arising from such contingencies as the building settling or the rebuilding of damaged areas. Some statutes, as in California and Florida, do not set a specific formula for description; any description is acceptable if certified as a correct representation by an authorized architect, engineer, or surveyor.

UNIT BOUNDS

Many state statutes contain definitions of unit boundaries that will apply
unless the declaration has a different definition. Before entering into a discussion of the possible alternatives for setting the physical bounds of a condominium unit, let us examine a typical condominium declaration
paragraph for a lowrise condominium:

> *Dimensions of units.* As shown on the floor plans to be filed simultaneously
> with the filing of this declaration in the office of the Clerk of the County of
> _____, each unit home consists of the area enclosed at its sides by
> the unexposed faces of the dry walls at the unit side of the dry walls dividing
> the unit from other units. Above and below, each unit consists of the space
> between the underside of the finished floor of said unit and the unexposed face
> of the dry wall ceiling thereof. Above and below, on each of its two stories,
> each duplex unit consists of the space between the underside face of the fin-
> ished floor and the unexposed face of the dry wall ceilings.

Descriptions are by no means uniform, even if they achieve somewhat
similar results, as evidenced by the following:

> *Dimension of homes.* Each home is measured horizontally from the interior
> surface (but not including such surface) of the masonry block of all walls to
> the interior surface (but not including such surface) of the masonry block of
> all opposite walls and vertically from the lower surface (but not including such
> surface) of the roof rafters, structural members, and sheathing, as the locations
> of such walls, floor, and roof members are set forth in the building plans filed
> simultaneously with the recording of this declaration.

The subject can become a bit complex at the formative stage. But care at
that point will avoid burdensome complexities later. After all, it is the answer to the key question, "How much do you own?"

It is possible under the laws of several states to have units consist solely of
air without ownership of a speck of tangible boundary. In such cases, the
precision of measurements designed to bound each unit exactly by hypothetical lines in space would appear to be quite an undertaking. Alternatively, physical borders may be delineated, with the units to be comprised of
all airspace within such bounds but not including the physical borders.

Quite often the unexposed side, or skin or facing, of a dividing wall or
floor serves as one or more of the boundary lines enclosing a unit. Use of the
simple word *side* avoids many unnecessary complications that might ensue
from new paint skins or changed facings. In one of the examples above, the
border of the unit was the unexposed side of a dividing dry wall.

In some situations, especially where convenient for the separation of two highrise units (or units from an external wall covering), midpoints are selected in dividable structures such as fire walls. Care must be taken to avoid including space that also houses commonly owned items, such as pipes, ducts, cables, and wires serving more than one unit, although sometimes this is unavoidable. In those instances, such equipment is reserved from inclusion within unit ownership. In many declarations, all such equipment serving more than one unit is made part of the commonly owned elements, whether located centrally or on the edge of a particular unit.

Another boundary method that is practical in some cases is to encompass space in some directions to include all walls, with the exclusion of a defined covering such as brick veneer.

In a detached one-family house that is part of a condominium, it might be adequate to include within the unit the entire house; that is, everything but areas and properties defined as common areas. The UCA authorizes such a description, although some states do not.

To avoid legal problems regarding sufficient characteristics of co-ownership so as to constitute a fee condominium, underlying land usually should be made a common element, even if restricted to a particular unit owner's use. Many condominium statutes are vague on the basic elements that must be co-owned, with the result that the historical derivations and legislative intention tend to become the most important considerations. As the concept traditionally has presupposed landownership participation in common, there should be little veering from the basic characteristic in the absence of express legislative permission (as would be the case to some degree if leasehold condominiums or vertical subdivisions were permitted).

The notable exception in condominium statutes is the Michigan law, which states, in part, that the unit may include fee simple title to all the land underneath the given structure, provided a permanent easement is granted to the condominium for repair and maintenance of the exterior of the structure and the external improvements. It is believed that this provision resulted from builder desire to win FHA approval for condominium home financing under Section 203–B of the National Housing Act. But, regardless of other considerations, it is imperative that unit boundaries cover horizontal and vertical directions, and the boundaries should be finite.

Doors, windows, and terraces are often given special treatment. Typically, they are made common elements subject to the exclusive use of the unit to which they are attached. Terraces that are part of a unit have created awesome problems in description where they are attached to outer walls that are common elements and where the airspace between terraces is a common element.

Purchasers should be wary of disclaimers by a sponsor for responsibility, if unit dimensions as built are not in accordance with the declaration and building plans. The only disclaimer allowable would be for insubstantial and inconsequential variations, but the purchasers are protected with title insurance in most jurisdictions.

The unit owner ordinarily carries the sole responsibility for the maintenance and repair of his or her unit, with common responsibility remaining in the commonly owned areas. The boundary, then, serves more than a descriptive function. It may set the legal responsibility for maintenance, although this is not necessarily the case if the declaration carefully provides otherwise.

Restricted or limited common elements sometimes upset the last mentioned rule. For example, the doors and windows that are restricted common elements are often the responsibility of a unit owner for painting on the inner sides and the responsibility of the condominium association for external painting.

SPACE PROBLEMS TO BE SOLVED INITIALLY

Defining ownership in space present serious questions concerning future events, which may alter the exactness of original descriptions. When constructing new units, one must assume that some settlement may take place even where the best construction methods are utilized. During the course of ownership, fire or other hazards may partially or fully destroy the unit, requiring limited new construction that could alter the structure or even the location of boundaries of the unit involved, and perhaps of the adjoining units as well.

At some particular time, a unit owner may seek to redecorate his or her apartment and intentionally or inadvertently remove or replace the boundaries marking the space limits of his or her unit. Of course, such an occurrence might happen occasionally even when a new owner makes preliminary decorating innovations.

One must also be cognizant that original faults in construction or ordinary wear and tear may in time result in the need to rehabilitate the inner or outer portions of a building. The sponsor himself or herself may have to make such changes at an early stage in order to accommodate present and future purchasers and to comply with his or her undertakings. Termite damage could literally eat unit boundaries away.

In an actual case, the owners of a highrise condominium, within a year after their original purchases, decided to redecorate their lobby with a marble material that would increase attractiveness and be largely maintenance-free. What if such changes impede upon a particular unit owner's boundary line?

The three underlying premises that follow affect the security of a unit and must be thoroughly dealt with in the condominium instruments:

1. Ownership cannot be permitted to evaporate by the full or partial disappearance of the unit or one of more of its determinant boundaries.
2. Ownership cannot become confused and indefinite through the encroachment by or upon other units or commonly owned areas.
3. Ownership should not become clouded by ordinary expectable alternatives or replacements, such as new wiring systems, replaced or rehabilitated walls, or the use of wall paneling rather than overpainting.

Condominium, as with any form of ownership, does not permit uncontrolled incursion upon the rights of neighbors, especially in the form of seeking to capture ownership rights or possession beyond the bounds of legal entitlement.

If such incursion takes place while a unit owner is decorating, for example, the other condominium owners are entitled to enforce their ownership rights individually or as a group, if commonly owned areas are involved. Under some statutes, the group administering the condominium may act if a minimum number of other unit owners are affected. However, the condominium customarily provides for reasonable easements in the event of contingencies that do not materially alter ownership rights, but which easements actually add to the stability of ownership.

Some declarations use language such as the following:

> *Encroachments.* If any portion of the common elements encroaches upon any unit upon completion of construction, or if any unit encroaches upon any other unit or upon any portion of the common elements upon completion of construction or if any encroachment shall occur thereafter as a result of (1) settling of the buildings, (2) alteration or repair to the common elements made by or with the consent of the Board of Managers, (3) as a result of repair or restoration of the buildings or a unit after damage by fire or other casualty, or (4) as a result of condemnation or eminent domain proceedings, a valid easement shall exist for such encroachment and for the maintenance of the same so long as the buildings stand.

While this is a fair beginning, attorneys usually enlarge the scope of such paragraphs.

GOVERNMENT OF A CONDOMINIUM

Because of the co-ownership aspects of condominium, special rules must provide for administration of many activities materially affecting the occupants, specifically and generally, as well as for exclusive supervision over the properties in which each owner possesses an undivided interest only. These tasks are concentrated in an elected board, directorate, or group, depending on the particular statutory designation. In this text the governing body will be referred to as the board, whose precise functions are discussed more fully in a later chapter.

As with any government, a bill of rights is called for in the condominium in order to ensure minimal interference with the daily living of its occupants. For example, the key rights might be:

1. Unrestricted accessibility to one's home
2. Maximum privacy
3. A voice in the choice of an elected governing body
4. Adequate provision for hazard and liability insurance affecting units and common elements
5. Right to finance, refinance, and transfer the unit with a minimum of restrictions
6. Personal veto over any major change in status

Bylaws and house rules, in addition to the declaration, must provide for such basic rights or clearly depict any attenuation of them. The bylaws provide the procedural guidance for governing the day-to-day operation of the association. Each of these rights requires ample discussion and is covered later in this book, together with the specific provisions of bylaws and other relevant topics. It should be noted at the very outset that a governing statute imposes the format for administration of a condominium, giving legislative sanction to condominium government.

THREE

ASSESSING A COMMUNITY

PLANNING AT THE OUTSET

The market reception to condominium development is predictably more difficult than usual to assess than the market reception to a standard subdivision. Many times the builder or other sponsor himself or herself is confused or unsure of how extensive a development to build or what type of units to offer. In effect, such a builder begins his or her offering to the public without an educated awareness of what the final results might be if they were based on meaningful analysis. While the builder may have induced an institutional lender to provide an informal commitment for a construction loan on land that has been optioned by the builder, there is a planning deficiency by builder and lender unless independent steps are taken to honestly evaluate the available market.

THE DECISION FOR CONDOMINIUMS

Thus far in the United States, there are six direct routes that have brought many, if not most, builders into the condominium field.

First, members of the real estate profession and the construction industry tend to be well traveled. During their travels, they seldom miss an opportunity to investigate new building designs and techniques. Examination of condominium sales methods and results in states and countries other than his or her home base frequently has captivated the more imaginative builder. Whenever this was the case, he or she may have photographed, copied, or secured advertising and design layouts on which to fashion a program of his or her own.

Second, the building industry is undergoing revolutionary changes in the design and grouping of buildings. Coupled with these changes are new concepts of landscaping and environmental design. Developers are giving greater attention to conservationists' pleas for preservation of natural beauty and unspoiled landscape. A more efficient use of the land is often the result. Townhouses and highrise apartment buildings of interesting new designs are clustered together in attractive, parklike settings. The condominium form of ownership, of course, lends itself exceptionally well to this type of development. News stories describing these new condominiums constantly stir builders, especially the younger ones, into an enthusiastic investigation of the concept with a view toward utilizing it in their own operations.

Third, many communities have already adopted the condominium concept, with this new form of ownership being taken for granted as a logical alternative for home buyers. It is an idea that touches a basic emotion of many people—the seemingly inherent desire for homeownership. The condominium satisfies two strong desires of many families today—the longing for actual ownership of a home with its present-day income tax advantages, and the preference for an attached house or an apartment unit free from all of the responsibilities of a home such as yard maintenance. However, as will be discussed in Chapter 7, the maintenance responsibility will be assumed by the association, and the association must be run by volunteer homeowners. Builders, faced with constantly rising costs and land availability difficulties in constructing and marketing traditional housing, have welcomed this new trend. Most have been quick to recognize the condominium as a potential savior for their industry.

Fourth, the nation is experiencing a long-term energy shortage, evidencing itself in continual searches for alternative sources to traditional fossil fuels. As a result, home builders and homeowners are encouraged to conserve energy wherever possible. It has been proven that one way to maximize energy consumption consistent with conservation of energy in home building is to build attached homes that lose less heat and cooling in the aggregate than detached homes. Hence, condominiums and other forms of co-ownership tend to be more energy-efficient than separately owned homes, because most condominium projects are attached home developments.

Fifth, as the nation is learning to conserve its energy, it is also learning that the government cannot solve all of its problems. Taxpayers do not wish to pay for the growing appetites of mushrooming government. The trend toward less government is forcing cities and counties to look to the developer to design communities that are capable of maintaining properties (e.g., slopes, parkways, parks, monuments, streets, etc.) that historically have been the responsibility of the local government to maintain. The condominium is a logical form of ownership to assume these responsibilities.

Last, but most important, the condominium offers the first genuinely effectual opportunity since the mid-1930s to provide an adequate supply of middle-income housing. Because nearly every town and city has a heavy backlog of unsatisfied demand for such housing, all that is needed is simply for the building industry to be able to construct housing that can be marketed at prices suitable for the middle-income groups. Consequently, economic realism indicates that, with cheaper housing practically impossible to create without some kind of subsidy and with luxury housing often a dangerously speculative undertaking, the intelligent builder of acceptable middle-income housing should have a better than even chance to flourish. There has been a clear trend during the past decade or so toward communal living and smaller units to meet an increasing demand by those who have been priced out of the housing market by rapid inflation.

TYPE OF BUILDING OFFERED

Experience has shown that new builders in this field seem to be able to formulate their plans more readily in connection with highrise condominiums than with sprawling townhouse projects. Even so, greater success might be achieved with the highrise type of development if projections were presented to the public before the finalization of floor plans in an attempt to muster adequate changes that would result in more effectively meeting the demand for particular types of room distribution and amenities.

In many states, initial offering material has been submitted to the public before a specific number of townhouse condominiums have been finalized in detailed plans and in the selection of the physical location on the site. In fact, it is fairly common for builders to make offerings to the public based on pictures consisting merely of artists' renderings and providing for the builders' option of returning deposits if they should decide not to proceed with the developments. Frequently, a prospective buyer is unable to ascertain even the most fundamental information, such as the total number of units that will be finally offered. Furthermore, it is not unusual for a sponsor, who has determined in his or her own mind that the sales will be adequate, to go so far as to promise recreational facilities, such as swimming pools, meeting halls, and even medical facilities.

Some states are taking steps to protect the prospective buyer and to require the developer to provide the buyer with more detailed and reliable information regarding the proposed project. Leaders in California and New York have been noteworthy in this respect in enacting laws requiring significant disclosure of facts pertaining to any condominium offered to the public in that state. Under these statutes, vague deliberations like those indicated must give way at a very early stage to specifics. In California, the builder may not legally promise any amenity unless it is completed when the unit sale closes or a bond or other assurance has been posted to ensure its completion.

NEED FOR EARLY PLANNING

It easily might be assumed that the entire course of events and the success or failure of a condominium (however much they may be controlled by statute) are largely in the hands of the builder, who is capable of protecting himself or herself against faulty estimates of public response. However, this may be far from the actual case.

A builder would be wise to plan carefully at the earliest possible stage in order to have a specific and firm offering to present to the public and, thus, avoid the pitfalls that result from indecision and uncertainty, which cause many astute prospective buyers to turn away because they refuse to bind themselves on the basis of vague projections. Programming by the builder should include a maximum effort at the very outset to determine the availability and effectiveness of the market and to eliminate the possibility of expenditures and losses caused by the recall of the project development.

BASIC CONSIDERATIONS

Regardless of the type of condominium being promoted, the builder should emphasize the special considerations and amenities involved. In his or her own mind the builder should be aware of the fact that purchasers will be interested in buying condominiums rather than other types of available housing, if the condominium offers something better than something that is just different and novel.

Location

As in the great majority of housing investment decisions, the factor of location is of greatest importance. Often, the price of land for single-family homes or the rentals of offered apartments are prohibitive to a major segment of the population desiring the particular location. On the other hand, the condominium form may make it possible to offer people housing in these neighborhoods. Such locations do not necessarily have to be in heavily urbanized areas. It may be possible to take advantage of settings of trees and woodland areas that cannot be utilized for more conventional housing. Thus, the scenic location and the central location constitute different considerations for the builder.

Frequently, areas that appear to be marginal because they are undeveloped and surrounded by shoddy houses or commercial eyesores and are consequently not particularly appealing to the prospective homeowner, may be utilized profitably by careful condominium planning. Examination will show that if a new condominium development is large enough and broad enough in its scope, it can create a community-like atmosphere that will cause the onlooker to disregard much of the surrounding area. This kind of development is even more important if it is also possible to obtain new schools and other facilities that will serve the new community.

Price

Price is also a factor of primary significance. A person who is being offered facilities in a condominium, where he or she must share some responsibilities with others, must decide whether or not it is acceptable to him or her financially. An available rental apartment of equal value, when compared to an apartment-type condominium, would be for many people the better choice in view of the substantial sum required to purchase the condominium, even though it can be demonstrated that the latter may still be more economical because of taxes and other benefits. Price can be the decisive factor in comparisons of detached or attached one-family homes that are sold in fee simple as against the attached or even detached type of condominium development. Unquestionably, price must be considered as an overriding essential, and the offering should be made with the basic premise that a related price has to be made available to the public in order to attract those who will make comparisons with the other available facilities. It should not be forgotten that the person who is going into a condominium does give up some absolute rights of ownership typically associated with single-family homes.

In one case, a condominium developer sought to sell a cluster of row houses in competition with a developer of detached one-family homes whose site was a short distance away and within easy viewing by prospective purchasers of both developments. The offering prices were almost the same, and yet the better location of the condominium property would have prevented any competitive pressures from the other seller except for one overlooked factor: The detached one-family home developer built a garage within each of his homes, while the condominium developer merely provided a common parking area with rather limited facilities. Even though the condominium developer did eventually sell out, great difficulty was encountered in many instances because of the lack of planning to provide some special considerations to purchasers to offset the competitive factor that was missing.

Uniqueness

From several years of condominium development experience, it is possible to gain helpful insight into the public receptivity of this new form. People who consider the condominium for purchase are generally most eager to emphasize unique features that just are not available in any other type of housing at equal price. The unique feature might be a swimming pool, recreational facilities, the availability or ownership of a golf course, an adjacent lake or ocean with beach facilities, an adjacent marina, or similar additions for relaxed living. The developer must be able to provide the answers for the condominium purchaser when his or her friends ask, "But why do you want to buy a condominium?" In order to have a successful experience with condominium development, a sponsor is almost compelled to provide something different, something extra, or something outstandingly attractive.

Size of Units

The actual size of facilities is important. Today in this country, many persons are finding a need for smaller units that are relatively carefree. A greater proportion of the population than ever before consists of people between the ages of twenty-five and thirty-five. These millions of young men and women do not have the financial ability to purchase luxurious housing but nevertheless are interested in a good location and adequate facilities, even though limited in space, as long as the price does not exceed their ability to pay.

At the other end of the age spectrum, the number of persons sixty-five years old and over has also been increasing at a rapid pace and will continue to do so. These people make up the retired group, an important segment of society. With many years of active life remaining and with more or less substantial incomes from pensions and investments, this age group requires comparatively small housing accommodations that are safe, convenient, and free from maintenance problems, and include some recreational facilities, such as golf courses, game rooms, and so forth. Having been conditioned to single-family homeownership throughout most of their lives, a condominium frequently appeals to them. In many so-called retirement villages throughout the country, small condominiums of good quality designed to fill the needs of older couples have met with much success.

The condominium developer must consider the surging and varied demands of the 1980s and 1990s. He or she must recognize the different needs of the groups that make up the market for housing. He or she has a form of ownership in the condominium to apply to the wise utilization of space.

As indicated previously, there remains a tremendous demand for low-

and middle-income housing in this country, and in many of the larger states the matter is becoming a real problem. Demand for such housing ranges from larger units for family living to small efficiency units for working couples without children or for unattached individuals. Because of its economical utilization of space in addition to its potential for providing attractive housing in scenic modern settings, the condominium concept could very well offer housing to the middle-income groups that is not available in any other form at suitable prices.

At the same time, the condominium concept can be so grandiose as to encompass the most luxurious type of living facilities. There are already many examples of condominiums for which buyers have paid enormous prices, even though the housing was in attached rows, because it afforded them the luxury of their own golf course, private areas, and scenic settings. Undoubtedly, the individual builder or developer will have to choose one aspect of the condominium form designed for a particular economic group as his or her initial entry into the field and then may possibly develop into a specialist in that particular form.

Carefree Aspects

Another important feature that has to be considered initially by the builder is the freedom from care that he or she may offer as a characteristic of the condominium form of ownership. It is almost axiomatic that the American people are becoming more and more desirous of doing as little as possible in connection with homeownership, so that cutting grass and the difficult work of carpentry, painting, and other time-consuming chores are largely disposed of by others. The developer is obliged to provide the means whereby the condominium owner can be relieved of some of the otherwise normal responsibilities of homeownership. However, the condominium owner has a responsibility to serve on the board of directors or governors of the condominium association toward the end that the project runs smoothly. If the condominium project is large enough (usually more than fifty units), the members may choose to hire an onsite or offsite manager to assist the board. Consequently, the type of management available in a particular community, the possibility of organizing new types of management companies if they do not already exist, and providing them with facilities for the acquisition of adequate specialized training are all important considerations for a condominium developer. More and more management companies have condominium training or experience, and many companies specialize in condominium management. There are even organizations, such as the Community Association Institute, the Institute of Real Estate Managers, and the National Association of Home Builders, that offer training courses for those interested in becoming condominium managers. To a large extent, the initial management problems can be disposed of by careful planning for management at the same time as the initial concept of the condominium is being formulated and projected.

PRELIMINARY TESTING OF COMMUNITY INTEREST

Perhaps the easiest and most direct way to gauge the marketability of proposed units is a procedure followed by several builders in some states, including New Jersey and New York. Nonbinding unit reservations and token good-faith payments are received following a newspaper advertisement that solicits interest. In the majority of cases where this procedure has been adopted, the immediate response correctly foretold the eventual success or failure of the planned property and was helpful to lending institutions in determining mortgage financing.

Builders utilizing this procedure have employed three methods of demonstrating their wares:

1. In a few cases, the builder has constructed one or more model homes.
2. Sometimes a temporary special building is erected on the site, with room cutouts built within for demonstration purposes.
3. Often, an office building is constructed that merely contains colorful descriptive layouts, floor plans, and basic information on pricing.

In New York and California, all funds obtained through this procedure must be placed by the builder in a special bank account and held in trust. The actual form used to record reservations and receipts in California, which can be adapted to the requirements of other states, is as follows:

RESERVATION INSTRUMENT   State of California
                              Department of Real Estate

RE Form 612 (Rev. 9/30/81)

_____

_____

THIS IS NOT A CONTRACT NOR AN OFFER TO PURCHASE OR SELL

_____ (hereinafter subdivider)
acknowledges receipt from _____

(hereinafter potential buyer) of _____
                                          (Address)
_____ of the sum of $_____
for the reservation of _____
                                    (Lot or Unit Number)
in _____,
                                  (Name of Subdivision)
County of _____, State of _____.

Subdivider hereby reserves the above-identified lot or unit for potential buyer and represents that he or she will immediately place the deposit and a signed copy of this document in the following neutral escrow depository:

_____
                                        (Name)

_____, _____, _____
         (Address)   (City)   (State)

1. THIS INSTRUMENT DOES NOT CREATE A CONTRACTUAL OBLI-
GATION TO BUY OR SELL ON THE PART OF EITHER SUBDIVIDER OR
POTENTIAL BUYER. EITHER PARTY MAY AT ANY TIME CANCEL THIS
RESERVATION INSTRUMENT WITHOUT INCURRING LIABILITY TO
THE OTHER. IN THE EVENT OF CANCELLATION BY EITHER PARTY,
THE DEPOSIT SHALL BE IMMEDIATELY RETURNED TO POTENTIAL
BUYER WITHOUT ANY DEDUCTION EXCEPT AS PROVIDED IN (2)
BELOW.

2. If potential buyer so requests by completing appropriate instructions below, subdivider will make arrangements with the escrow depository for the earning of interest on potential buyer's deposit. $_____ will be deducted by escrow depository from interest earned on the deposit as a charge for providing the service to potential buyer. The balance of the interest earned will be paid to potential buyer or credited to his or her account.

3. By initialing here _____, potential buyer agrees to the payment of charges as set forth above and requests that the deposit be placed into an interest bearing account as follows:

Name as Account is to be Held
_____
Taxpayer Identification No. (Social Security No.)
_____

4. CAVEAT: If the deposit is to be placed into an interest-bearing account:
(a) Escrow depository will not deposit funds into the account on potential buyer's behalf -- and therefore interest will not accrue -- until escrow depository has been notified that potential buyer's check has cleared.
(b) There may be a delay in returning the deposit to potential buyer on his request.
(c) There may be an interest penalty in the case of an early withdrawal from the account.
(d) If after potential buyer has received a Final Subdivision Public Report for this subdivision, he enters into a contract with owner to purchase the reserved subdivision interest, the deposit plus interest earned on the deposit, if

any, may be applied toward the purchase of the subdivision interest with the express authorization of potential buyer.

5.   THE PRICE AND OTHER TERMS OF PURCHASE OF THE SUBDIVI-SION INTEREST WILL BE THOSE SET FORTH IN A PURCHASE CON-TRACT IF POTENTIAL BUYER ENTERS INTO ONE AFTER RECEIVING A COPY OF THE FINAL SUBDIVISION PUBLIC REPORT.

Subdivider _____

By _____

(authorized agent)

Potential Buyer(s) _____

_____

Dated _____, 19____

RE Form 612 (Rev. 9/30/81)

ZONING

New forms of real estate ownership must slink into an accepted category within local zoning and other permissive land use restrictions. Otherwise, they will remain only hypothetical forms of ownership. In the case of the condominium, the best and the worst of a community's land use restrictions become markedly apparent.

Land use restrictions tend to be of three kinds: (1) the historical legisla-tive precedents set to limit physical neighborhood change or population in-flux, (2) the more recent emergency legislative changes or authorization to expand further such restrictions or liberalize rules on a limited or overall basis, or (3) the largely subjective safeguards adopted by a planning com-missioner or board having wide powers to deviate from entrenched patterns, which are usually applied on wide tracts of vacant land or sites subject to demolition.

The look-alike rule generally prevails in condominium zoning in most of the United States. That is, zoning qualifications ordinarily are met if a simi-lar-appearing building could be built for other purposes. A highrise condo-minium can, therefore, be built in an area zoned for rental apartment houses. But not every type of projected condominium always finds a look-alike area.

At present, those builders planning condominium construction usually face one of the three following land use enabling situations where (in most cases) there is no specific condominium zoning.

1.   The local land use agencies will or will not sanction the particular form of housing as falling within permitted land use restrictions,

based on a strictly look-alike comparison. The builder will argue that
two-story attached condominium townhouses should be considered
with a garden apartment zoned area. Look-alike will generally be the
theme.

2. A locality has already considered, or may be willing to consider, a
   special administrative or ordinance ruling expressly authorizing the
   particular condominium. This has often been the case with respect to
   open-space, cluster-housing condominiums that would be at variance
   with local requirements and prohibitions. The recall power of localities makes the first condominium experience of wide significance to
   the entire local building and financing community.

3. The locality may issue permits and withhold injunctive action in
   order to build a precedent by administrative action or inaction, rather
   than raise a hailstorm by ruling on the need for new ordinances or
   variances that require public hearings for what will not produce
   look-alike housing. Sometimes this attitude is occasioned by confusion and lack of expert knowledge on the condominium concept.

Conformity and Mediocrity

The ubiquitous repetition of look-alike housing should not be extended into
the condominium field, even though a typical vista of American landscape
exposes the unhappy fact that housing officials, financial institutions, and
builders have together created a look-alike atmosphere in the past thirty
years, and brings a worrisome concern to anyone who may be thinking
ahead to the almost certain massive increases in population projected for the
immediate future. Constant repetition has deterred and corrupted aesthetic
development of homes, apartments, offices, and shopping areas in the
United States. Little argument is needed by those who inhabit the metropolitan areas and their suburbs to support the contention that there is a crying
need for economic and beautifying conservation of precious landscape. Old
conformity-prone arguments about public demand and construction economics can be dispelled by the new tool for financing, construction, and
community-involved living that is presented by the condominium concept
now available.

Our present prototyped single-family zoning districts are not permitted to
encompass multi-family or group dwellings, attached, patio, terrace, court,
town, or similar houses. Most typically, a single gridlike pattern is created by
zoning codes that call for mandatory setbacks and lot sizes of drab and re-
petitive standards. The result is conformity and look-alike appearance, regardless of how devotedly an architect or developer might strive to alter the
prevailing similarity and monotony of a community.

Localities tend to impose multi-family zoning in less attractive districts, sometimes in the worst places possible, such as those backing onto industrial complexes, railroad sidings, highways, and similar locations. In addition, there is often the pernicious attempt to locate such developments on the rim of old or expanding ghetto areas as a buffer zone rather than to bring about the creation of good housing.

The fundamental concept lacking in the present zoning approach is one that involves the utilization of multi-unit housing in various forms in an effort to raise the standards of housing, both in better areas and in middle-class and low-income neighborhoods that have become dregs of decaying conformity. Depressed areas have suffered a great misfortune as a consequence of the continuing appointment to housing positions of those people who gained their experience devising and managing massive public housing horrors. Novel approaches are necessary if the eyesores of conformity are to be erased and the look-alike attitudes changed.

Zoning is sometimes used by those who would inhibit growth to preclude reasonable densities or intensities of land use. Of course, the infrastructure must be in place to accommodate increased traffic congestion and noise associated with further building. However, some communities use the zoning code as a shield against any further development, evidencing a selfish "I've got mine and I'm on board, so pull up the plank" attitude.

Community zoning regulations should expressly cover condominium housing, and many communities now have such zoning. Such rules would emphasize clusters and the use of multi-unit developments in original and interesting patterns, which include attached houses, lowrise housing, and highrise housing. The variations and combinations that are possible would assist the community in providing decent housing, would cut construction costs, and would conserve elements of beauty in the existing terrain or even create beauty where there has been a deterioration or lack of concern for aesthetics in the past. Therefore, there is a real need for drafting special zoning to include a variety of multipatterned condominiums or to provide for condominiums only. Such zoning should permit size, height, and setback differentials to help achieve interesting, unusual, and varied structures.

Many economic and social goals can be achieved through condominiums. Large and small units could be put into one grouping so as to attract families of different sizes and income levels and thereby more effectively integrate the community both economically and socially.

Another but less bold approach might be an interim zoning pattern lying somewhere between the ordinary one-family type and the small rental unit. This would permit condominiums of various types to be built that would be specifically covered by a zoning code, thus avoiding the necessity of adhering to typical one-family home or traditional apartment house appearance.

Still another approach could be available where new cities or large developments, which are intended to house essentially new communities, are under consideration. Here, since the builders would not be bound by pressures from surrounding areas for ordinary zoning standards, there can be a greater freedom to adopt wise planning practices that encompass various types of houses. In such cases, the condominium concept can be utilized to great effect.

The Builder's Zoning Dilemma

Realism necessitates that a builder be permitted to construct condominiums that, in the event of a difficult selling experience, could be utilized on a temporary rental basis. This leeway would apply equally to the financial institution involved in giving the mortgage loan and to the builder himself or herself. This problem has resulted in condominiums being built in rental areas, even though in many cases they have been designed primarily for single-family home purposes. By including in zoning standards the right to sublease on a reasonable basis, greater encouragement would be given to novel approaches that have been untried and untested in the past but that are, at least, secured by the knowledge that rental on a temporary basis could be carried on as a program before complete and final purchases are made by way of condominium. Furthermore, in order to avoid possible deception on the part of a builder, a community should require a careful appraisal and study of the area before such construction is commenced, and it would also seem advisable to require a reasonable direct market test as a prerequisite to approval of any proposed development of this kind.

FOUR

INSTITUTIONAL FINANCING OF CONDOMINIUMS

THE ESSENTIAL ELEMENT OF SECURITY

Statutory enactments have widened the scope of institutional lending powers in the last forty years. One of the most innovative of these new laws has added the condominium to the real estate classifications permissible for bank, savings and loan association, and insurance company lending. Important and far reaching as such laws appear to be, their effectiveness depends on the quality of security of condominium collateral for mortgage investments. In addition to the ordinary concepts that pertain to the appraisal of real estate for mortgage purposes, the lending institution must comprehend that substantial differences in lending techniques and analyses are involved in condominium lending. Many lenders have already found the need for special condominium formats for the traditional type of title insurance policies and documents, such as mortgages and deeds. However, there has been a noticeable tendency in the United States for lenders to employ standard forms prepared by the agencies in the secondary mortgage market with short riders attached in an attempt to conform to unique requirements of the particular condominium.

THE TWO KEYS TO CONDOMINIUM FINANCING

There are two basic considerations on which the future of condominium mortgage financing must rest:

1. State and federal legislation empowering such activities
2. Basic lending and appraisal policies of individual lenders

Legislative Attitudes

On examining the extent of present operations and the future outlook for commercial banks, savings and loan associations, mutual savings banks, insurance companies, and other sources of mortgage funds, we find it hard to believe that most are less than fifty years old and that the particular grouping itself goes back at the earliest to the first decades of the nation's history.

Once such lenders had weathered early fiscal hardships, the emerging profitable footholds tended to become recognizable, with real estate playing a prime, if not always dominant, role. It was in the midst of the stress, panic, and expansions of the nineteenth and twentieth centuries that many of these new institutions were organized, relying typically for initial capital on a little cash and a small reserve of valuable real estate mortgages, and striving to profit from economic opportunities developing out of such financing problems as widespread industrial plant expansion and a severe shortage of residential real estate mortgage funds. Many successful financial institutions speculated quite heartlessly as they invested in new industry, land development, and housing, in order to realize, in addition to immediate profits, two basic objectives—respect for their issued paper and public trust in their respective safekeeping functions.

Legislatures finally concluded that the public interest in such entities required some control over their activities. Not only did these controls provide for the exclusion of new institutions that did not meet minimum tests of reliability, but, for our purposes, the most important of the controls was related to limitations on investments.

In effect, the lawmakers in the field of permissive lending legislation have been acting as authoritative investment advisors by specifying the types and limits of real estate loans in order to protect the institution's stability. Because by statute such investment limitations customarily carry no expiration date, they constitute an effort to freeze the needed restrictions of a particular economic period into continued existence. Such a practice would presuppose periodic reevaluation. Changes in economic and social conditions might require either a liberalization or a further tightening of lending restrictions. But the removal or amendment of laws and, to a lesser degree, even of mere administrative rulings, usually awaits new pressing problems rather than wise foresight. And the field demonstrating the slowest movement for change in economic structure has been the field of real property.

As the result of well-founded reaction to the economic difficulties of the 1930s, legislatures bombarded the statute books with severe lending restrictions placed on institutional lenders. However, in the period beginning in the 1950s, the pressing need for wider and newer forms of lending power generated some initial reactions from legislative bodies. Since then, federal and state laws have broadened lending powers into such fields as urban renewal projects and housing for the aged. Such legislation also liberalized attitudes toward larger loan-to-value ratios, leasehold mortgages, and similar subjects. The most promising of the new legislation consisted of an overwhelming response to proposals for condominium housing.

Thus far, condominium legislation typically classifies this form of ownership as real estate in the same sense as the term is employed in banking, savings and loan, and insurance legislation limiting investments. Consequently, the condominium format is placed under all existing financing prohibitions, with some minor exceptions contained in the respective condominium statutes.

BASIC LENDING AND APPRAISAL POLICIES OF LENDERS

The Fundamental Traditions of Real Estate Finance

Before analyzing the lending and appraisal policies and techniques of institutional lenders as they particularly concern condominiums, it would be well to examine the underlying traditions that are consciously or unconsciously present in the lender's attitude, for it is impossible to divorce condominium lending from the general strategies prevalent in all real estate lending. If special techniques are needed, we must first be sure that fundamental changes in attitudes do not violate the good sense of well-founded tradition.

Maximum Community Protection

Until recent times, landownership was historically the chief criterion for measuring wealth as well as social and economic power in almost all western and eastern civilizations. In past eras, it proved to be the most secure, indestructible, and inheritable form of wealth. Ownership rights evolved and solidified as a consequence of growing custom and whatever formalized protective law came to exist. Upon this basis was formed the continually confirmed attitude that realty presents the best community-protected security for financing, and the seemingly inbred reluctance of courts and legislatures to disturb or alter the rights of owners and lenders has appeared to substantiate this opinion.

More recently, a growing concern has developed about those aspects of land use that should be entitled to continued absolute protection from government interference. The answer often depends on weighing abusive uses against their overall effects on the general land inventory as well as the social and economic climate. The principle of maximum community protection of its landed property owners is reaffirmed in rigid zoning laws and building codes, even though the latter were originally a product of the early twentieth century's overcrowded and unsanitary conditions in urban areas.

Minimum lot sizes and other restrictive attempts to obtain community exclusiveness are under assault by the overburdening of existing sources of property taxes, increases in population, and community planning techniques that involve the clustering of homes amid attractive green areas. The emerging wider scope of government takeover under the right of eminent domain is the greatest single challenge to the principle of community protection of private property ownership, although the concept of fair payment upon condemnation does, in fact, reflect respect for this principle.

The condominium concept did not become important in the United States until its features received community protection under statutory declarations granting the same protections already guarding other real estate ownership. This was most easily obtained by defining the condominium as real estate.

Except to the pure conservationist, the current conflict between grid zoning and open-space development, on which much of the future of the condominium depends, is to a large extent an argument about the best way for a community to protect or enhance its economic and social benefits from individual property ownership.

The dream goal of homeownership is so entrenched in American life that tremendous emotional forces work against major occupancy of tenanted highrise buildings over the lifetimes of maturing generations. In addition, sharp inflationary tendencies make such an outlook, even among advocates not eager for grass-cutting chores, a hazardous one. A growing number of young Americans will almost certainly seek to remove the profit factor attending a landlord–tenant relationship. In addition, planning boards, zoning codes, and the like are up against the basic principle of community protection of existing property ownership, which in many cases means opposition to any further development, particularly development of projects with high density and intensity of land use.

The condominium technique, which can be used to produce modest or massive housing additions, while still maintaining and protecting the concept of full homeownership, presents itself as a much more acceptable solution in communities that have traditionally emphasized homeownership. Because condominium owners are separately assessed for property, school, and similar tax burdens, there is a community of interest between them and the one-family homeowner.

Thus, a technique exists that is flexible enough to cope with some of the problems of population growth and, at the same time, is capable of providing basic protection to the principle of community concern for bolstering and shielding homeownership.

HIGH LOAN-TO-EQUITY RATIOS

Ever since colonial days, loans secured by residential real estate have traditionally been treated by lenders as the safest kinds of loans. And in early America there was good reason. In a society where the landowner and the tenant tended to remain for most of a lifetime on a specific parcel, the compulsion to remain imparted a curious coloring to such collateral. In reality, the very lives of individuals, their families, and even their tenants and workers, were the security for the land loan. What greater safety could there be than a pledge that was almost tantamount to offering the lifetime of a human being to secure that pledge? Heavy loans on land and crops were made not because of the primarily profitable agricultural nature of the community but because of the incomparable safety aspects of the security when judged against other possible loans.

The tradition of realty loans being customarily large and presumably safer then other loans came into being. This tradition of high loan-to-equity-value loans, even though usually short-term, was tested, refined, encouraged, and brought into modern times by laws that moved a heavy store of public deposits and savings held by many banking and other institutions into loans secured by residential and nonresidential real estate by the means of limiting a large percentage of investments to real estate. Of course, what appeared to be heavy financing in one economic period might be considered highly conservative at another time. Thus, a 60-percent-of-value loan in 1880 on excellent residential real estate security would have been considered at that time very speculative. Today, when 90- or 95-percent-of-value loans are frequently sought, 60 percent might be called a fairly conservative ratio.

Experience in the past few years indicates that institutional lenders have regularly issued to condominium owners maximum loan-to-equity loans of the same percentage that is prevalent for ordinary one-family detached or attached homes. For example, in New York State in 1966 most condominium loans were 90 percent loans, and in 1981 and 1982 they were primarily 80 percent loans; in both cases, they were in consonance with the typical highest loans made on other forms of residential real estate. It may be expected that the condominium form will generally not result in the diminution of maximum real estate financing for the particular category involved.

There is still another important point to be made on loan-to-equity ratios. Up until the present time, where highrise or garden-apartment-type housing has been utilized in the United States for the creation of condominium ownership, the individual loans on the condominium homes (and sometimes even the construction loan to the builder) tend to be of a higher percentage (loan-to-value ratio) than if the development had been built for rental purposes. Thus, the builder of a highrise apartment house intended for tenanted use might be able to obtain only a 75 percent mortgage with a large balloon payment of principal coming due over a short term of years. But, if he or she built a condominium, it is quite possible that an institutional lender, possibly the same one, would give all condominium purchasers 80 percent mortgages that would be self-liquidating over a considerable period, such as twenty-five or thirty years.

The lender receives greater protection by eliminating the single large loss coming from the default of one overall large mortgage, as compared to the safety of a large number of individual smaller mortgages. In addition, in many American localities it is customary for large commercial mortgages to rest for security exclusively on the land and improvements, rather than the security of individual personal responsibility. Corporate responsibility has often actually represented a dummy obligation requiring extra care in appraisals of value by bankers. But in condominium ownership, individual personal responsibility on mortgages is already an established concept. So, on considering the division of risk into many mortgages, and adding individual liability, the lender's decision to finance a highrise or garden-type condominium might be far wiser than one to make a similar but smaller loan on the same kind of real estate designed for tenanted investment, regardless of the increased administrative burden associated with servicing multiple loans.

And if the lender is careful and worries about the security's physical longevity, the condominium is far more preferable on the basis of its preservation factor. Owners tend to preserve and enhance premises to a greater degree than tenants do. Owners holding the security deposits of tenants rarely do more than minimal rehabilitation when leases end—despite their withholding of funds from repayment of security to the tenants. More and more tenants, as was not the case before World War II, must make their own decorations and internal repairs. With construction quality also off, lenders have never before seen their security jeopardized to such an extent from the physical deterioration standpoint. But inflationary trends and an increase in young households have so far protected quickly aging apartment houses and garden apartments, which are largely occupied by more mobile, short-term tenants.

When one walks through lobbies, carpeted hallways, and many apartments of similar building constructed contemporaneously—in some cases condominium and in others tenanted—it is apparent that resident abuse is markedly lower in the condominiums. This conclusion also is reached from visible examination of outside lawn and planted areas. To condominium owners the residence is not only his or her deeded home, it is also realty which he or she may have to sell someday. The logic of simple economics seems to be a self-operating force in effecting adequate care of internal and external premises.

On the other side of the ledger, short-term balloon mortgages covering commercial real estate permit periodic reevaluation of the investments and an adjustment of interest rates in accordance with the then current money markets. However, danger lurks in the possibility that, in a period of constant or lower rates and easy money, another institution will gain a financial foothold in valuable property and that the original interest rate will be lost.

However, there will also be a continuing refunding factor in the condominium development. Owners will sell their properties in normal turnover, thus affording lenders opportunities for liquidation or revision of interest rates.

REACHABILITY OF DEBT SERVICE

Most of us take for granted the real estate tradition that assumes that most residential lending must be long-term. But actually, it was not until the 1930s that this important financial tradition gained wide acceptance, born of government-insured mortgages that added safety to mortgage investing and placed homeownership within the reach of millions of Americans because of the low monthly payments resulting from long-term self-liquidating loans.

Up until the mid-1960s, the most important factor affecting grouping was the FHA (and, later, VA), which, beginning in 1934, converted a nation with a majority of people living in rented quarters to one in which by 1966 more than 60 percent of the population were homeowners.

This concept of longer loans might be called the principle of reachability. The greater the hardship in purchasing or the greater the inflationary trends, the greater the likelihood that the length of time required to repay the loans is extended in order to make them "reachable" by large numbers of citizens. Changes liberalizing lending attitudes toward the duration of loans tend to come in sudden spurts, attended by worrisome comments by those appraisers who lived through the Great Depression. But, to date, inflationary movements in resale housing prices, spurred by growing population demands, usually safeguarded most such investments. The severest threat arising from mortgage delinquencies is posed by a leveling, or receding, economy where housing prices remain constant or move downward over a period of more than one year. However, except for some localities beset by overbuilding as a result of incorrect projections of population absorption, this has not often been a problem. The solution seems to be in institutions making wise predictions of population density and demand in the areas they service.

The long-term mortgage not only makes new housing reachable but also would seem to provide better opportunity for resale and, at the same time, tends to prevent a constant resale turnover of the resulting supply of new bank funds.

Because of the need for making purchases reachable in rising markets hit by inflation, lenders, even though using uninsured conventional financing, also adopted the long-term loan. Today, this practice is an established underlying factor in all real estate finance that involves residential lending. However, the use of creative financing techniques during the recession of 1980 to 1983 has led to the widespread use of variable rate mortgages to protect long-term mortgage lenders from the effects of severe interest rate fluctuations.

The condominium concept can add several factors to further accentuate reachability. Price reductions, which mean smaller mortgages, can be obtained through the wise clustering of housing, thereby reducing overall development costs for utilities, roads, sewage, and water drainage. Second, smaller areas, which are not feasible for detached one-family home development, can be used residentially in the condominium form of fee simple ownership and, thus, can provide the security necessary for long-term mortgage loans on terms most favorable for homeownership.

Current census data disclose that there are large numbers of single, divorced, or widowed persons in the nation's growing population. Medical advances and health programs have increased the number of active, fruitful years to be expected by the average American and in doing so have created a need for thousands of additional units of small, convenient housing for the elderly. A tremendous growth in the number of young adults—both single and married—with limited financial resources has accounted for an important source of demand for small, functional apartments and townhouses rather than full-sized detached houses during the decades of the 1970s and 1980s.

Third, commercial income from stores or multiple-use premises can offset current mortgage costs for individuals. If commercial space is co-owned in condominium form by some business firm and the residents, well-located residences may be obtained at reachable mortgage and maintenance costs that are impossible to achieve in other forms of real estate ownership. And, finally, government-aided programs can make homeownership more reachable for various economic classes of citizens who would otherwise have to accept tenant status, which lacks the feeling of personal responsibility and attainment resulting from use of the condominium.

MARKET TESTING IMPORTANCE

Especially in connection with construction of attached or series buildings, lenders are often concerned about the possibility that condominiums may violate certain traditional rules of lender control. The main vexations are the large number of units, all dependent on one another because of the pooling of common interests, and the limited use of security (especially remaining vacant land) upon foreclosure because of the condominium's dependence upon a filed declaration or master deed. Because of the latter factors, most lenders are urgently insistent that the condominium development be no less than 100 percent successful. In the absence of careful planning, disclosures, and modern legislative authority, once units are constructed and sold after filing of the declaration, the builder and the lender no longer have the customary alternative of assigning unsold areas and abandoning construction lending commitments for land that can be severed from the rest of the development.

One may consider the lender's thinking to be somewhat as follows. Suppose a builder of a forty-unit, attached-house condominium fails to complete more than four units. Titles to the four have been passed, and the entire tract has been submitted to the condominium act of the particular state. The owners of the four completed units have acquired, under their individual condominium deeds, a one-fortieth undivided common interest in the land and other common elements in the rest of the uncompleted tract. Because condominium laws ordinarily require all construction liens to be eliminated before conveyance, the completed buildings are no longer security for the loan. But much more importantly, the interest of the four owners in the rest of the common areas jeopardizes the use of such areas upon foreclosure. And so, the lender can be expected to conclude that no condominium declaration should be permitted to be filed until a high degree of success is absolutely assured.

In single-family homes or clusters of lowrise housing, some lenders require 50 to 90 percent of the proposed units to be under contract before the release of any construction funds. Most construction loan commitments set the 50 percent presale condition.

If the same lender issues construction as well as unit mortgages, it is usual to insist on an intensive selling campaign by the sponsor before release of initial funds. The same early sales program is sought by take-out mortgagees who set contract percentage conditions. For instance, the presale requirements of the Federal Home Loan Mortgage Corporation (Freddie Mac) and the Federal National Mortgage Association (Fannie Mae) vary between 50 percent and 70 percent. However, the guarantees required in take-out mortgages by initial blanket lenders as conditions for construction funds often force firm decisions by permanent lenders at an early stage.

Where permanent mortgage commitments are less than firm, construction lenders may be expected to continue the practice of not releasing any finished units before a specific number of units are under contract or the permanent lender agrees to pay over all or a great portion of the entire building loan. One of the reasons for hesitancy by the blanket lender in such instances would be the practical elimination of possibilities of alternative tenanted occupancy once the declaration is filed and the first unit is released.

It is advisable for the same institutional lender to give both the construction loan and the permanent financing for at least three reasons: (1) to better protect the security of incomplete areas by subjecting condominium management decisions to lender approval through restrictions in unit mortgages, (2) to take advantage of an existing market for permanent financing, and (3) to avoid problems from the construction loan which is not only earlier in time but also not subordinated to the master declaration, except for released units.

Preliminary market testing techniques and division of large developments into stage condominiums must be considered of more than ordinary importance to lenders when they are considering financing condominiums. Some devices are discussed in Chapter 15 for literally tying together otherwise separate condominium developments to achieve lower costs and greater benefits from the sweep of a planned community, swimming pools, and such additions as a common parking area.

Traditionally, market considerations have received lender attention, but always with the knowledge that poor judgment would be largely negated by selling and constructing separate homes one by one. On the other hand, market considerations are of much greater importance in financing condominiums than in financing homes in a standard subdivision.

SHORT SUMMARY OF CONSTRUCTION LENDING

Meaningful histories of construction practices by lenders are as rare as those few bankers who question their validity. With the advent of the condominium, a reevaluation is beginning of the methods and procedures that historically have been accepted with almost religious fanaticism in banking finance and are enormously important to planning strategies, even though they are rarely the subject of college-level courses in banking and related subjects.

Banks, savings associations, and insurance companies almost single-handedly guided the creation of the American construction industry. The roots of the financial creative process have left some customs that bear examination in terms of their current validity to our subject.

Even as late at 1910, the builder of new housing rarely undertook more than one house per year. Looking at the ornate outer and inner facings of older city buildings, it seems certain that time could not have been of the essence. Actually, the early builders generally were really brokers, who contracted with specialty tradespeople for the multitude of awesome construction tasks. Contractor experts at the banks supervised the planning and culmination of the slow-process housing. The patterns of colonial towns and the farm simplicity in construction established easy designs to copy. Red schoolhouses, fire stations, barns, and farmhouses were almost always one style or pattern within particular communities. The few original creative designers were widely copied, as may be noted in the simple, evocative towers and rectangular porches emphasized by Alexander Jackson Davis as early as 1830 and copied by careful craftspeople with a few mild variations for another fifty years. Cheap immigrant labor permitted the long, drawn-out process of more complicated building, so that a great deal of such construction had to be built in the larger cities in which the newcomers settled. Many of the skills of carpentry and other trades emanated from Old World apprenticeship methods and never achieved an equal excellence among native-born Americans.

In early years, many laborers camped on the construction premises in tents, shacks, and other makeshift structures. When it was possible for the immigrant construction force to move by means of early trolleys and elevator trains to new construction sites, cities began to expand outward along the routes of mass transit as well as inward to the more concentrated cores. Prestige locations for business and fine townhouses tended to be concentrated in focal areas of the cities. Contractors and carpenters whose names have long since been forgotten did much of the early lender-supported design of American buildings. It was not until 1865 that the first American school of architecture was established in Massachusetts. General recognition of the profession took at least another twenty-five years.

With the notable exception of those owned by the extremely wealthy, the greatest number of American buildings constructed in the nineteenth and early twentieth centuries was financed by banks, savings associations, and insurance companies. Actually, they were more than financed; they were planned, promoted, supervised, and inspected by them as well. It was institutional know-how that brought the plans and trades together.

Mortgage banking, therefore, was really the process of rounding up tradespeople to put new structures together. Yet somehow, real estate financing was adequate to support the tremendous growth in population taking place in the United States at the turn of the century. Immigrants began to fill major cities, such as New York, Boston, and Philadelphia. One of the results was the birth of new lending institutions in large numbers. The slow process of financing and constructing real estate in the traditionally homely manner did not lend itself to massive banking operations by just a few institutions. Consequently, hundreds of new institutions came upon the scene. Most were limited in resources and almost universally geared to simple one-family home construction.

The slow process of building lent itself to periodic scrutiny by the lender at various stages of construction, so that monies were paid out as the building's constituent parts came into being. The practice developed wherein the trades were not paid in advance. As there was no need for the full cash payout of the building loan initially, there was really little impediment to construction by this type of stage-payment technique. Tradespeople agreed to delays in payment from the building contractor on the assumption that monies would be made available at graduated levels during construction as the lender indicated satisfaction with the progress.

Foundation work was so unscientific and groping an experience that fear of collapse was the chief concern of the lender. Lack of an even elementary knowledge of subsoil capabilities made most nineteenth century foundation work a matter of hunch judgment based on topographical appearances. Marginal land, swamps, soft soils, and similar nightmarish resting beds were avoided by all but "swamp rats," the very poor, and naturalists, who solved their problems by tenting or building prayerfully on crude elevated stilts. Much of the huddling of the masses in cities and suburban towns was the result of merely following careful rules for resting housing foundations. Many a green belt, supposedly only recently forsaken, was land not considered appropriate for buildings in earlier periods. In addition, foundation materials were formidable more because of size and depth than because of sturdiness of constituent materials. It can be observed that land edging on bays and channels has recently been developed for luxury housing, where once only the shacks of fishermen and squatters rested on the fearsome sand.

As custom developed, the lender usually began to pay out his or her construction loan after the foundation was dug and set, with subsequent payments coming in stages while the lender's eye remained primarily on the foundation.

Close supervision by the lending institution was also necessitated by completely different attitudes toward the topic of credit than those typical of today's lenders. No central credit rating system existed. The inadequacy of communications meant long delays for processing inquiries, recordkeeping was flimsy, and most of the documents were handwritten and hard to decipher in later years by other persons. Most lending was localized to well-known, knowledgeable contractors. In addition, the accounting profession waited for the income tax amendment to the U.S. Constitution to gain widespread recognition as the asset–liability confirmation authority. The result was that the existence or nonexistence of an unencumbered particular bank account or material collateral, such as a mortgage assignment involving improved property, together with successful past efforts by the borrower in construction, was the type of basis guiding the decision to give a building loan. Rarely was primary reliance placed on the mere personal credit rating of the contractor because of the stringent controls attached to the transaction by the bank, which really was acting as the true overall contractor in the transaction.

Surprisingly, there has been little real change in construction lending procedures even though the original reasons for such procedures no longer have their earlier validity.

LENDING DISCRIMINATION AGAINST CONDOMINIUM BUILDERS

Except for the use of highly trained independent architects and other technicians, as well as the adjustment to power technology, construction lending techniques have not changed in their essentials during the past sixty years. Bank application forms call for new credit information (such as verified balance sheets) but rarely is it either given or requested. Much spoofing involves shell corporations. Even where urban renewal regulations require certified historical accountings, compliance is a rarity, with the government agency substituting itself for bank personnel in the old stage-payment procedures. One must concede, however, that general credit information could be made more available if it were demanded and that decisions to lend are often tuned to immediate management pressure for or against the investment of funds. But once the general attitude toward lending at any one time is formed and is reinforced during recessionary times, many lenders and government agencies still slumber with the notion that such credit information is secondary to the fanatically pursued stage-payment technique.

During the 1980 to 1983 real estate recession, hundreds of condominium projects were lost by developers to their construction lenders through foreclosure. In virtually all of these cases, lenders had praisingly approved construction funds, during the double-digit inflationary period which preceded the recession, to rather speculative builders. Although most of these projects were brought to completion finally, it was more because of the watchful eyes of state agencies, regulatory sales, the Federal Deposit Insurance Corporation, the Office of the Comptroller of the Currency, the Federal Savings and Loan Insurance Corporation, the Federal Home Loan Bank Board, and the applicable state lending regulatory agencies, than because of the wisdom of banks or savings and loan associations.

The fallacy of the stage-payment technique is its inadequacy of financing for speculative builders—a substantial and needed section of the building industry—especially the younger and more imaginative groups. If banks put up funds from the beginning and supervised stages, problems other than poor site selection would be rare. But banks take shelter in practices that put heavy financial burdens on builders in the initial stages, before payments are advanced in substantial amounts that are usually more than sufficient for total construction. This pressure can force solvent builders, in the case of unforeseen events, into seeking outside financial arrangements and entering into various deals with other builders and contractors that can jeopardize any later needed financial involvement by the builder. This technique continues to be used with condominiums, and great attention is given to credit, balance sheets, and the escrow of initial development funds for the reason that banks appear to expect greater builder outlays and more initial project work before making the first payments, in view of the prerequisite assurance of 100 percent project completion. The greater strain on condominium builders is unreasonable and actually jeopardizes more than it protects the lender.

It would be hard to ask lenders to change their techniques for single high-rise developments; custom is just too entrenched. But in the case of row houses, cluster housing, and the like, the following procedure would seem to provide the means of expediting construction, assuring 100 percent completion, and safeguarding purchaser deposits:

1. A modern credit check should be made that is factual rather than puffed-up fiction. Honest analysis would demonstrate that many promising builders who formerly looked good on paper are in thin financial condition.

2. When a builder is selected, no commitment should be given until the market has been thoroughly tested for a successful effort in accordance with our previous discussion.

3. A detailed evaluation should be made about whether a combination of purchaser deposits, the builder's own funds, and expected bank payouts will complete all structures under all reasonable contingencies.

4. After the above requirements are met, substantial funds should be paid out directly for land clearance, foundation work, and other initial construction. These funds could be paid directly to subcontractors to assure proper usage.

5. From this point forward, the lender could adhere to the stage-payment technique, if it wished. The principal effect would really be to

protect against substitution of materials not permitted under the commitment rather than to assure completion.

More modern building techniques and factory preassembly of entire, interlocking interiors and exteriors—long held back—will make stage-payment methods less inspective and more academic.

CONSTRUCTION LENDING AND THE CONDOMINIUM

The extreme degree of control by lenders in the construction field has been noted. Their concern over the tendency of condominium ownership to remove the independent nature of ordinary mortgage security has also been recognized. However, modern methods of credit analysis would seem to offset this concern somewhat by aiding in the selection of builders whose experience, credit standing, and attitude might also be considered important security factors. Large loans based on credit standing are made in just about every other American business, with some risk regarding collateral value, especially in the field of personal property loans (a field into which many lenders have been seeking wider entry). The condominium is leading to a reevaluation of outmoded construction techniques in all of real estate, techniques that are slow, plodding, and scarcely aimed at producing the massive housing solutions required in today's society. However, many construction lenders still pass the buck to the condominium unit lenders by requiring permanent mortgage loan commitments with respect to most of the condominiums before they will fund construction monies.

PERMANENT CONDOMINIUM FINANCING—THE PRACTICAL ALTERNATIVES

In considering the final, "permanent" financing loans to individual condominium owners, the lending institutions have a few major areas for consideration, each of which must be carefully evaluated. These can be divided into five groupings:

1. Priority of lien right
2. Decisions on escrow funds
3. Management controls
4. Relations with other lenders
5. Techniques for liquidating security

From the subsequent discussion of the above topics, it will become apparent that the condominium mortgagee loses some traditional rights but, at the same time, gains a voice in ownership and control.

Priority of Lien Right

The two usual questions that are posed at the take-out time in every case when permanent financing must be obtained also have to be answered in connection with condominium financing: Have prior liens been removed or adequately bonded? Will the permanent mortgage have prior rights over all subsequent liens?

For the first question, there is little choice under the laws of most states, because the laws expressly provide that all blanket mortgages must be removed before the condominium conveyance can be made. The blanket mortgage would probably not be issued in the first place, unless a commitment for a take-out mortgage existed. But a construction lender may insist on the sale of a minimum number of units before the lender will release any unit from the blanket mortgage.

Removal of a unit and its common element from a blanket construction loan does not of itself solve the problem involving possible interference by the construction lender. Even though the unconveyed area is subject to undivided common interest ownership by those owners who have taken title and secured release from the blanket mortgage, there is still a lurking problem. In the event of foreclosure on the unfinished areas, a court might grant a severance of ownership rather than force completion of the development as planned. This possible reduction in the size and facilities of the condominium could result because the construction loan was earlier in time than the filing of the master declaration. Statutory bans on partition relate to owners who are subject to the declaration, and the construction lender would not be subject to the declaration.

There are three ways for the permanent lender, who does not also issue the blanket mortgage, to seek protection in this instance. The take-out mortgage should be conditioned on the recorded subordination of the blanket mortgage to the declaration or master deed.

Alternatively, the builder could be required to concurrently close enough condominium sales to generate adequate funds to satisfy the entire unpaid balance of the blanket loan at one time. In small projects or larger projects with small, subdivided phases, this option may be feasible, but it is difficult to delay closings in most condominium projects.

In other situations, especially where single, highrise housing structures are involved, the blanket mortgage could be entirely eliminated and satisfied at one time before the conveyance of any condominium units. In such case, the permanent lender would take over the cover mortgage on unsold areas. For the protection of the permanent lender, the sponsor, and the purchasers, the declaration should be filed before the permanent lender issues its takeover money.

Will the permanent mortgage have priority over all subsequent liens? The condominium statutes generally do not interfere with other state laws and judicial precedent applicable to the priority of mortgages. It should be noted, however, that some condominium statutes or related laws limit certain institutional investors to first mortgages on residential condominiums. In these cases, the laws themselves impose as a prerequisite the elimination of prior mortgage liens.

But, if a bank were to stop at this point, it would be oversimplifying the problem. Priority should be considered on the basis of other factors and not from the point of view of lien laws alone. Contractual rights exist in the condominium that can endanger collateral almost as much as undiscovered encumbrance. That is, even a first mortgage is subject to the provisions of the declaration that could empower action detrimental to a bank's collateral. The solution to this problem is strikingly clear: The declaration must be carefully read and analyzed in order to assure the adequacy of its terms with respect to the protection in the form of collateral.

In current methods of analysis used by banks, the declaration or master deed is looked upon as the essential document protecting the condominium and those lenders resting on it for security. The declaration is so important to the bank that it is considered essential to include in the unit mortgages a provision stating that if terms of the mortgage are inconsistent with those of the declaration, then the declaration shall prevail. In effect, such a mortgage incorporates all terms of the declaration into its provisions. For this reason, it can be expected that lenders will attempt to prohibit any changes in the declaration without their prior approval, or to provide for foreclosure rights based on that contingency.

There would appear to be at least three underlying reasons for placing the terms of the mortgage subject to the declaration. First, the very validity of the condominium and its effectiveness as security depend on compliance with the statutory requirements pertaining to the contents of the declaration. A mortgage with inconsistent requirements can jeopardize the validity of the condominium form, a primary element of the security. Second, there seems to be an awkwardness in formulating artful language without incorporating the declaration. And, of course, such a procedure tends to bring about a greater consistency and uniformity where several lenders separately participate in permanent financing. The personal experience of the authors of this text indicates that subordination to the declaration is accepted by many lenders because they note it in the mortgages of other lenders or because they observe that the original draft declaration itself states this fact. Nevertheless, their conclusions are otherwise well founded.

Decisions on Escrow Funds

The principle underlying the concept of bank collection of key charges in addition to mortgage interest and principal is to provide for the absolute insurance against defeasance of the lender's security. Defeasance could come about from the failure to make insurance premium payments on an adequate policy, from real property tax foreclosures, or from the failure to meet municipal water, sanitary, school, or similar charges that could result in proceedings endangering lender security. Therefore, the question arises: Should all condominium maintenance charges, including the cost of heating, common repairs, and such items as swimming pool or garage operation, be collected by the bank?

For various reasons, individual banks, savings and loan associations, and insurance companies have gone different ways in deciding those costs that must be funded through the condominium unit owner's escrow payments to his or her mortgage.

Where the principal loan amount exceeds 80 percent of the value of the home, most lenders insist on property taxes being included in the monthly escrow payments that cover mortgage principal and interest. In cases where the condominium's board must rebuild, either by statutory or declaration requirements, some lenders still insist that insurance escrow payments be made to themselves or to an insurance trustee; others merely require escrow payments to the managing board. But it should be noted that the collection of escrow in these cases does not relate to individual policies, since most hazard insurance policies are carried by the overall condominium. Thus, the existence of other lenders or some unit owners owning free and clear would confuse payment schedules. Eventually, the lender must turn over premiums to the board. As long as a special trust bank account is set aside by the board or its managing agent, with duplicate statements or other accurate reports being sent to the lender in order to provide adequate notice of potential default, the lender would seem to be substantially protected. A lender should insist on receiving a copy of the master hazard insurance policy, which should contain the requirement for adequate notice of default, with a reasonable time to cure.

It might also be possible for a lender holding all or most of the mortgages to require an initial escrow deposit from each new mortgagor, which taken together can constitute a continuous escrow deposit representing the major portion of the cost for a year's premium as security for any default in payment by the board of managers. This fee would also be continuous protection for unit owners against possible management lapses.

Some institutions (notably savings and loan associations) have insisted on monthly payments of all maintenance charges to unit owner escrow accounts. In some highrise condominiums, this would not include utility charges directly billed to each owner, such as for telephone service and possibly gas and electricity; in others, where most utility charges are made by means of a single bill, some of the costs for these services would be included in the escrow account. In townhouse developments, where utilities are usually individually billed and where heating costs are an individual problem, the remaining maintenance charge paid to the lender by escrow is small indeed.

It seems a rather questionable practice for a lender to collect maintenance charges that include budgeted heating costs, management salaries, minor repairs, and other expenses lying largely within the discretion of a board for allocation. On the other hand, if the condominium requires a special reserve for a previously unforeseen major contingency that may jeopardize bank security, the lender may wish to be assured of the collection, at least from its own mortgagors. If a lender holds very few mortgages, extensive escrow treatment of maintenance costs would be more of a headache than a practical means of protection.

In addition, a lending institution that collects as escrow more than tax payments and insurance premiums might involve itself in needless lawsuits arising from a question about the proper application of other escrow proceeds when problems develop such as whether or not bylaw authority is vested in the board of managers with respect to making repairs.

The benefit to owners from full escrow collection rests largely in the simplicity of payment made to a single entity. Usually, where boards collect their own escrows for maintenance costs, these charges are collected on a monthly, quarterly, semiannually, or (rarely) yearly basis. This procedure places heavy bookkeeping responsibilities on the managing board or agent. However, to do otherwise would require heavier financial burdens on the owners at special times during the year, thus possibly endangering security. A lender should at least review the board's own escrow procedures so as to assure the least possible burdening of unit owners. Furthermore, the time for the collection of maintenance charges by the board should give sufficient time for the lender and the board to appraise the availability of funds and any default problems.

Management Controls by Lenders

Holders of unit mortgages ordinarily impose controls on major management decisions by condominium boards. This strategy begins when they receive the initial demand for their prerequisite approval of the original drafts of condominium documents suggested by the sponsor, especially the master declaration and bylaws. The control advances beyond this stage by various means, either through the use of language inserted in individual mortgages or by formulas for change set forth in the declaration or bylaws.

The most common form of check on board decisions is the unit mortgage clause that provides for the right of foreclosure where approval by certain classes of mortgage lenders (usually those holding mortgages on 25 percent or more of the units) has not been obtained before any amendments to the declaration or bylaws that offset the rights of the mortgagees are voted into effect. Sometimes mortgages provide that any unit owner's individual vote for such amendments must be approved by the mortgagee, under threat of foreclosure. Interestingly, the actual effect of certain clauses used might be to provide for the right of foreclosure even though the particular unit owner involved did not participate in voting for amendments.

Experience proves that the fearful threat imposed by such clauses as these eliminates some board initiative that would typically produce amendment. However, the lenders usually act reasonably in granting consent or in denying approval on grounds that actually protect the interests of most unit owners as well as the lender. The problem is acute chiefly in instances where lenders and their counsel do not peruse proposed documents carefully enough, or where unreasonable restraints were placed on ordinary management decisions.

In most states, direct voting controls by lenders should not be placed in the declaration or bylaws because of possible inconsistency with the freedom of voting that is intended by the statutes. Where controls exist in unit mortgages, they should be asserted with the greatest restraint, in order to avoid undue interference by banks and other institutions with condominium operations that pose no threat to security.

The declaration or bylaws might, however, expressly permit any unit mortgagee ready access to condominium financial records, require notices of annual meetings (with stated purposes) to be sent to lenders who notify the board of their holdings, permit lenders to attend meetings of the membership or board, require notification of lenders about the names of all current board members, give adequate notice of intended changes in insurance policies and appointments of managing agents, notify the lenders of defaults under the documents by their mortgagees, notify the lenders of significant condemnation or casualty loss, and further require that a copy of each year's budget and audited report be sent to each mortgagee who requests such information. A significant majority of first mortgage lenders should consent before the unit owners or the condominium association terminates the projects (unless incident to destruction or condemnation), materially changes the scheme of regulation of the project, sells or encumbers a significant portion of the association's property, or changes the ownership interests in the common areas or the relative obligations for paying assessments. Apparently satisfied with drastic controls over the amendment of basic documents, many institutional lenders have overlooked simple procedures that could forewarn them of impending problems. The foregoing concerns have been addressed thoroughly by the agencies in the secondary mortgage market, and the function of such agencies will be discussed later in this chapter.

An underlying question must be faced by each mortgagee: How much interference with management is reasonable? The answer suggested is as little as possible. Controls that tend to be overreaching might be found to be invalid by courts concerned about protecting this form of homeownership. Too much continuous rule by one lender might give rise to lawsuits against the lender by third-party unit owners, or outsiders, concerned with damages that resulted from the board's decisions or failure to act.

Without bank personnel competent to evaluate condominium problems, most checks on management imposed by lenders could not be applied intelligently. Special training programs undertaken by lending institutions should include visits to annual meetings, review of budgets, and analysis of special insurance techniques and reserve adequacy.

Relations With Other Lenders

As a rule, the primary lending institution involved in a particular condominium development will make some attempts to place financing restrictions in the original bylaws. Before this stage, commitment letters to builders on occasion have provided that take-out financing must be obtained only from the same lender, or else the construction loan will not be released for the particular unit. Take-out lenders sometimes directly or indirectly condition continued issuance of unit mortgages on builders' insistence to buyers that only one particular lender be used and only on specific terms.

The case for institutional mortgagees is probably based on (1) the use of projected lender-to-lender cooperation in the myriad of foreseen and unforeseen possibilities, (2) the more humanistic attitude toward the entire project by a usually locally based lending institution, (3) the ability to effectively weather minor financial defaults, and (4) their need to protect their local or national reputation. A bank or savings and loan association can be expected to solicit savings deposits or other business from individual mortgagors. Life insurance companies have even been known to condition mortgage loans on the unit owner's purchase of a required amount of life insurance. In any event, the uncontrolled lender would be almost certain to include foreclosure clauses that could have a harsh effect on the life of the condominium community.

Second and third mortgages tend to spur the overpricing of units because of the ease of purchase permitted by the heavy leverage. The resulting over-valuation can lead to higher property tax assessments based on market value, as evidenced by the purchase price. Higher mortgage charges on second and third mortgage money may endanger the solvency of purchasers. In addition, junior lienors tend to be less constrained to avoid foreclosure, even though they cannot wipe out the prior first mortgage and thereby add to the greater turnover of the property and the concomitant problems of short-term residents.

It has been argued by eminent banking officials of institutional lenders that second mortgages are welcomed by some institutions as backups in home financing, because they add security to the first loan. This is because the second mortgagee cannot permit default by unit owners to go uncorrected, with the resulting foreclosure by the first mortgagee and the almost certain wiping out of subsequent lienors.

The Federal National Mortgage Association (FNMA) and the Federal Home Loan Mortgage Corporation (FHLMC) have developed uniform mortgage forms. Copies of the FNMA or FHLMC Uniform Note and Deed of Trust (or mortgage) are available from those agencies for most jurisdictions. These instruments assure the primary mortgagee that all mortgages ever issued conform to his or her own. In addition, they encourage uniformity in management notifications to lenders and foreclosure procedures, while at the same time not restricting interest rates that tend to change frequently.

Techniques for Liquidating Security

In order to determine the effectiveness of techniques available for liquidating its mortgage security, a lending institution must review the adequacy of existing laws and contractual bases, such as the mortgage instrument and declaration. From the standpoint of possible liquidation, there is nothing more foreboding or dangerous about the risk involved in the condominium than there would be in the case of an ordinary homeownership mortgage, in most cases. Elimination of the individual mortgage loan could be either voluntary by prepayment of mortgage principal or forced by means of foreclosure.

A discussion of voluntary prepayment must necessarily relate directly to other types of mortgages as well as the condominiums mortgage, because they are governed by similar factors. Economic conditions create a mortgagee or mortgagor market that can result in either stringent or liberal prepayment terms in the original unit mortgage. Persons not conversant with the more fully tested mortgage fields may shudder at the lack of unit mortgage clauses that provide for the waiver of prepayment penalties when fire levels the building or a government body exercises its right of eminent domain. In spite of some peculiarities or individual characteristics, it is unrealistic to center this discussion on the condominium, because the question cuts across the entire gamut of real estate lending.

We have surmised that some institutional lenders have sought substantial restrictions on prepayment in order to assure that new institutions will enter the same condominium at the slowest possible pace. Such an attitude and similar ones are so rarely expressed in words or writings that persons studying this field from written documents and erudite bibliography alone can easily be led far afield of actual motivations. In any event tough prepayment penalty clauses are not always based on the mere quest for more funds in the future or the maintenance of high interest rates. Fortunately, the prospective concern for higher interests rates on turnover in the future has often neutralized such attitudes.

Perhaps greater consideration should be given to prepayment clauses that permit unconditional prepayment of unpaid principal but are conditioned on the mortgagee's right of first refusal. If the laws of a state permit, the primary condominium lender should evaluate the advantages inherent in such a clause.

PROTECTION AGAINST HAZARD LOSSES

Hazard losses arising from occurrences such as fire and windstorm present interesting questions for a mortgagee's review when he or she is contemplating initial condominium financing.

For example, it would be entirely impracticable to permit three of twenty mortgagees to collect insurance funds and apply them in the reduction of unpaid mortgage principal. Such practice would not only seriously imperil the interests of other unit owners, but would also fly in the face of the investments of other lenders in the same condominium. Moreover, whether as a result of the mandates of some statutes or the requirements of the declaration, the condominium board is ordinarily obligated to rebuild using the proceeds of the policy that named it as beneficiary under the same requirements.

The holder of the largest number of unit mortgages, the prime lender, who does not initiate (in the declaration) restrictive requirements that prohibit any mortgagee's retention of insurance proceeds, is the most seriously affected by such failure for at least two reasons. First, if a different mortgagee can retain fire proceeds, the primary lender would have the most to lose, because of the jeopardy of its larger security. Second, existing mortgagee payment clauses should make it more difficult for prospective unit purchasers to find other lenders willing to finance resales; the potential ravages of their small condominium investment through the reckless use of the mortgagee clause might be considered controlling.

Unless limited to payovers after decisions on the part of boards or unit owners not to rebuild, repair, or restore, the standard mortgagee clause should have only a limited place in condominium financing. But bankers are so conditioned to its inclusion in most other financing that it has sometimes been inserted in individual unit mortgages even though this may be inconsistent with the declaration. Again, it is urgent to recognize the reason why each unit mortgage should specifically subordinate itself to the declaration.

Still another fact should be kept in mind. It would be as dangerous to name unit owners as policy beneficiaries, perhaps even more so, even if there were a payover requirement in the declaration or bylaws. Since the board should be made responsible for rebuilding, it should be named as the recipient of the insurance proceeds for the owners and should act as trustee for all of the owners to negotiate claims.

But the primary lending institution must not be relegated to a position from which it can merely speculate about whether or not the insurance proceeds will be properly applied. The declaration should, as it often does, expressly name the particular institution or another selected institutional nominee as insurance trustee armed with authority to pay out funds for specific building purposes (usually after satisfactory architectural confirmation of completion schedules). Conservative practice requires the naming of such an insurance trustee in the policy, even though the real beneficiary is the board. Consideration should also be given to a formula empowering the trustee, with board approval, to reimburse all lienors to the extent of their interest upon the failure of the required number of unit owners to vote for rebuilding, if a certain percentage of destruction has occurred. Problems of inaction by unit owners or the board in such instances might be dealt with by time limitations in the statute, declaration, or insurance policy itself. Some declarations and mortgages do not adequately cover enough contingencies here.

Acting as insurance trustee, a primary lender is actually empowered to act in disbursement decisions that affect the security of other lenders as well. In comparison, if four noncondominium homes were fire-gutted on one street block, and the same four were mortgaged to the same lender, the holders of the mortgages on the other six houses on the block could not safeguard against the first bank's walking away with the insurance money and leaving behind a dangerous deterioration in real estate values of the other homes.

MAINTENANCE PAYMENTS DURING FORECLOSURE

Generally, condominium statutes have been silent on the payment of maintenance charges incurred by the lender during any stage of foreclosure proceedings. But see Chapter 5 for a discussion of the Uniform Condominium Act (UCA), which provides for a limited priming of the assessment lien to first mortgages. It would appear that any owner, regardless of the source, should pay upkeep charges for preserving common elements and proper operational maintenance. The only exclusion to this rule would be the condominium board, if it were to take title to a unit.

Nevertheless, lenders typically insist that the lien of the condominium association be subordinate to the lien of a recorded first mortgage. The declaration usually will have priority over the mortgage because of its earlier recording date, and the assessment lien basically derives its priority from the recorded declaration. Hence, the declaration usually will provide for a limited exemption of first mortgage lien holders from the assessment obligations. The mortgage insurers and the agencies in the secondary mortgage market require such subordination, with respect to assessments that accrue before the date on which the lender acquires title to the home by foreclosure or by other means.

Many lenders require assessment lien subordination, because they are reluctant to be placed in the position of a collection agent for the condominium association, to the extent that their mortgagors are delinquent in paying assessments. Although modern loan documents usually provide that failure to pay assessments constitutes a default under the mortgage, the remedies available to the lender are involved and time-consuming. The assessments could accumulate to a significant sum while the lender is enforcing its rights under the mortgage, and lenders generally prefer not to foreclose unless the borrower is also in default on his or her mortgage payments.

However, subordination of assessment liens to first mortgages does not appear to be in the best interest of the development. A lawsuit for money is generally not as effective as the assessment lien to the association. Moreover, whenever the lender takes title to the home following foreclosure of the mortgage, the other homeowners (including other lenders in possession) must collectively absorb the loss of income to satisfy the ongoing common expenses of the homeowners' association. Quite probably, such subordination discourages homeowners' associations from using the assessment lien remedies to enforce assessment collections from their defaulting members. Nevertheless, until the agencies in the secondary mortgage market and the mortgage insuring agencies recognize the extent to which the development suffers as a result of such subordination, lenders will continue to insist upon at least limited subordination of the assessment lien to the first mortgages.

Of course, the legal documents should always require a lender to pay regular assessments accruing during the period of time that the lender is holding title to a condominium in the development.

OTHER SECURITY PROBLEMS

In the initial review of drafts of condominium documents, attention also should be given to the possibilities of condemnation under existing state and federal laws and judicial determinations; the need for supplemental foreclosure clauses in the unit mortgage or declaration; and property alteration techniques permitted under the declaration and bylaws. Particularly significant is that a lender should consider the insertion of language in the unit mortgage with respect to the identification of all major alterations that will be deemed reasonable.

Some unit mortgages provide that a lender may foreclose a unit mortgage in the event that a particular unit owner does not vote to rebuild or restore the premises if there has been damage to or destruction of the premises of which the mortgaged property is a part. Many such clauses are vague and do not differentiate between reasonable and unreasonable motions to rebuild. The literal meaning of some of these phrases is that the maker of any motion to rebuild, under any conditions and in whatever manner, would be assured of an overwhelming vote. But what if another motion formulating a different approach to the expenditure of funds for rebuilding is made thereafter at the same meeting? In such an event, in addition to ordinary decisions to alter the premises where there has not been sudden destruction, mortgagees should be able to rely for protection on language asserting reasonable provisions rather than unenforceable implied all-inclusiveness that defeats the purpose intended.

In the absence of contrary intention, the many foreclosure statutes that exist in all states have the effect of governing foreclosure proceedings involving mortgages on condominiums because of their general classification as real estate.

IMPORTANCE OF SECONDARY MORTGAGE MARKET

The Federal National Mortgage Association (FNMA, also known as Fannie Mae) was formed by the federal government, but it has been owned by private shareholders since 1968. Fannie Mae was formed to purchase conventional and government-insured loans on individual condominium and cooperative units through competitive bidding, thus providing liquidity for lenders so that they can make more loans and facilitating the development and financing of new condominium projects. As the nation's largest purchaser of residential mortgages, Fannie Mae held a mortgage portfolio of $61 billion in December 1981. Fannie Mae is quasi-governmental, because the president of the United States appoints five of its fifteen directors, and the secretary of HUD exercises significant powers over its operations. As of 1983, the maximum whole loan or participation portion of a loan that Fannie Mae would purchase was $108,000, but this figure is adjusted upward from time to time.

The Federal Home Loan Mortgage Corporation (FHLMC, also known as Freddie Mac) was formed in 1970 for purposes similar to those for which Fannie Mae was created. Freddie Mac is under the direction of the Federal Home Loan Bank, and it may only purchase loans from financial institutions meeting prescribed criteria. Freddie Mac purchases new loans and existing loans, in whole or through participation with other lenders. It obtains funds to finance its purchases through the sale of mortgage certificates which it guarantees.

The Government National Mortgage Association (GNMA, also known as Ginnie Mae) is wholly owned by the U.S. government and has its offices in HUD. Ginnie Mae was created in 1968 principally to assist Fannie Mae in purchasing government-insured or guaranteed mortgages. Ginnie Mae guarantees a form of mortgage-backed security called a pass-through. Payments of mortgage principal and interest are passed along to the security holder, and these payments are fully guaranteed by the federal government.

The Veterans' Administration (VA) guarantees loans made by private lenders on individual condominium units created by new construction or conversion. The guarantee is provided free of charge where the loan is made to an eligible veteran of the U.S. armed forces. The VA reduces the lender's risk by guaranteeing a part of the loan, so the lender can safely offer the veteran low down payments and long repayment terms. During the period from World War II to 1983, the maximum VA guarantee on any condominium home loan increased from $2000 to $27,000.

The Federal Housing Administration (FHA) was created by the National Housing Act of 1934, and it is an agency within HUD. The FHA operates a variety of loan subsidy and insurance programs designed primarily to stabilize the home mortgage market. The secretary of HUD sets certain rules on FHA-insured loans, and the borrower pays an annual insurance premium to FHA. The maximum loan amount which FHA would insure on a condominium home changes regularly with the new statutory enactments.

The entire secondary mortgage market has been buttressed by the considerable involvement of Fannie Mae, Freddie Mac, Ginnie Mae, FHA, and VA, because these agencies lend credibility to the condominium concept and provide necessary funds and protection to lenders who otherwise might not be interested in loaning on units in condominium projects. A condominium task force was created in 1976, consisting of Fannie Mae, Freddie Mac, FHA, and VA. The task force was formed for the purpose of creating uniform policies for management and other documentation centering around the creation of condominium projects, so that the developer would not be faced with conflicting requirements from these agencies, all of whom could be participants in a large condominium project. Proposed policies (with several dissenting opinions) were published in the *Federal Register* in February 1977, and final policies (with dissenting opinions) were finally published by HUD in December 1980. See Appendix 1 for the text of the final condominium policies of the task force. The task force has now reconstituted itself to focus on the creation of uniform policies for legal management documentation for planned unit developments.

CHECKLIST FOR THE APPRAISER

More than anything else, an experienced real estate appraiser relies on intuition and judgment once he or she has covered the ordinary operating procedures necessary for the determination of value. No definitive lesson can be given that will adequately cover the artfulness of evaluation of facts so as to be meaningful in a field that will in the future test the breadth and ability of even the best appraisers. Nevertheless, the following checklist is offered as a running notation of topics that should not be overlooked, regardless of the initial approach that a particular appraiser may take.

A. How much are you appraising?
   1. Extent of land area.
   2. Minimum and maximum size limitations of total condominium.
   3. Improvements to be built only if specific number of sales take place (recreation center, medical building, etc.).
B. Will the condominium be all-inclusive?
   1. Prospective tie-ins with existing or proposed condominiums.
   2. The obligations of unit owners under precontracted lease or club memberships for the benefit of the sponsor or others.
   3. The number of separate condominiums to be built in surrounding or adjacent area by same or other builder, their prices, and attractiveness.
   4. The adequacy of easements among unit owners themselves and between unit owners and others.

C. Are all commonly used areas readily governable?
1. Control by the condominium board.
2. Separate government districts to be established.
3. Deeding title to surrounding municipality.
4. Adequacy of assessments for maintenance care.
D. Is there adequate linkage of condominium units and facilities?
1. Necessity of crossing heavy traffic streets to reach facilities?
2. How are separate highrise buildings linked (e.g., who owns intervening property)?
E. What are the particular facilities?
1. Parking (whether adjacent to units, centralized parking areas, off-street parking, and adequacy for proposed condominium owners, visitors, and delivery traffic).
2. Sewage facilities (sanitary and storm).
3. Police and fire-fighting availability.
4. Adequacy of warranties from manufacturers and contractors (especially self-operating elevators, roofing, heating, plumbing, electrical work, carpeting, basements, and other concrete work).
5. Air-conditioning (central systems versus noisy window units, especially in close areas).
6. Quality of equipment furnished by builder within units, potential longevity, and warranties.
F. Does size of condominium and range of assessments permit employment of professional management company and resident superintendent?
1. Availability of management companies in particular area.
2. Will residents live relatively carefree (grass, snow, etc.)?
G. Does the community accept the condominium form of highrise or other format?
1. May hostility result in higher property taxes or other discrimination?
2. Experience of other existing condominiums.
H. Do physical layouts permit privacy?
1. Ingress and egress.
2. Individual garbage disposal or incinerator.
3. Fencing.
4. On-floor, in-apartment, or basement laundry facilities.
I. Zoning of particular tract and surrounding area.
1. Threat from surrounding area.
2. Threat from builder's retention of surrounding land for speculative development.

3. Threat from inability to develop condominium as large as originally planned.
4. Future of zoning and planning patterns in particular community.
5. Pending industrial and commercial construction in community and pending applications for variances.

J. Comparisons.
1. With other condominiums (including features of other condominiums that sold readily or increased in value, as against aspects of prior slow movers).
2. With other types of available housing inventory in the community.
3. With market price structure of community (apartments, homes, cooperatives, and other condominiums).

K. History of condominium resales in the community.
1. Price fluctuations.
2. Has particular state law and have ordinary condominium documents permitted mobility and easy transfer of units?

L. Unique features.
1. Special facilities (swimming pool, golf course, private beach, recreation center, medical building, and so forth).
2. Special design (lighting effects, cluster layout of homes or highrise building, landscaping, wooded areas, children's modern playground, and others).
3. Special layout of apartments internally.

M. Size of units.
1. Floor space dimensions (including evaluation of borders of unit beyond inner walls).
2. Will units appeal to young households, single persons, retired persons, or large families?
3. Population statistics and variants in area.

N. Are variations of price ranges and maintenance charges for different units reasonable?
1. Should the differential carry over to financing?
2. Will the variations carry over on resale?

O. Adequacy of proposed initial budget.
1. Prospective future cost increases and effect on market value.
2. Extent of unit owner's personal responsibilities for internal painting and repairs.
3. Collection of reserve funds for major future alterations.

P. Commercial income of condominium (stores, garages, retaurant, etc.).

Q. Adequacy of transportation.
    1. Internal elevators.
    2. Buses, railroads, highways, airports.
R. Alternative uses of property by builder.
    1. Adequacy for tenanted use.
    2. Whether temporary tenanted use will damage value of premises.

THE LENDER AS CREATOR

In the patterns that are reshaping society in the coming decades, lenders may expect to experience inroads on their freedom of choice. This should come about because of all-level government experimentation in the struggle to improve the social and economic directions of the realty inventory. Having the heaviest financial stake in the financial decision, the lender nevertheless can expect to rely less than in the past on mechanical, moribund loan guideposts that reflect the comforts of practices typical of earlier eras.

A current factor that must be accepted as a challenge to the real estate profession is the pressure to develop total population solutions. Attached to this purposeful concept is the opportunity for creativity by the enlightened lender. Under the new trends, responsible financing solutions will not come without a satisfactory balance between the investor and the community interest.

The community planning structure will lack clear direction and purpose to the extent that there is disagreement, ineptitude, or lack of coordination by fragmented local governing bodies.

Moreover, the mere fact that some overall or wide area planning exists or is initiated does not of itself mean that some particular collateral has necessarily been safeguarded. Experimentation is only experimentation even if huge outlays of funds are budgeted. In fact, the more the outlay, the more rigid and irrevocable the experiment often tends to be.

In newly developed or redeveloped areas, there is just as much need for the lender to evaluate the space immediately adjacent to the building as for him or her to appraise the structure itself. With the expected growth and the wider, forced acceptance of planning concepts in future years, the new buildings comprising future competition will offer more open space around the building structures. Landscaped recreational areas, reflecting pools, fountains, rows of trees, and soothing and relaxing outside lighting effects may well keep a building competitive for considerably longer than the mere quality of its facing materials.

The aesthetic demands of a better educated, more urban, more cosmopolitan, and more integrated population will press for government implementation of their desires and tastes. In the future, the successful lender will have to judge the inherent value of new artistic forms. But let the lender beware of the curse of conformity even if the style is modern. There is hope that the responsible lending institution will encourage creative diversity in design for aesthetic as well as business reasons, although the two may very possibly be closer than they appear at first.

GROWTH OF THE PLANNING FUNCTION

A new profession has zoomed in on the real estate establishment in recent years and may become a dominant factor by the end of the twentieth century. This is the profession of planning, sometimes nominally tied to its origins by being called city planning. The birth of this new group can hardly be said to represent a tribute to the lack of manifest interest in community development shown by other segments of the real estate profession, including management, brokerage, and appraisal organizations, as well as institutional lenders. Whatever has been the degree of neglect of such basic considerations before, it may be conjectured that in the years to come no appraisal for lenders will be deemed to be complete without a community planning analysis that will involve a scrutiny of master plans, a study of pressures for zoning variances, and the analysis of potential support by the electorate for overall and particular planning strategy. A thorough understanding of the reasons for population shifts as well as population growth in specific areas is essential. Large lending commitments might be conditioned on overall community planning, just as present urban renewal allocations are so conditioned. This basic interest in community direction will demonstrate a similar concern for community protection of collateral.

There is currently an intensive argument being waged against continuation of simplified zoning patterns that create group setoffs and heavy property tax burdens, and the subsequent sudden changes involving decay in community makeup. In effect, it is in the long-term lender's interest to promote planning that supports well-balanced communities containing residential, industrial, and educational opportunities for different classes together with built-in leverage for betterment, and that also provides a means for rehabilitation of any developing deterioration.

It is to be hoped that much of the deep concern for self-justification now evident in planning literature will disappear as the profession approaches maturity. In addition, the customary grouping of the planning profession into sociology and technical layout design thus far has not provided enough breadth in this budding profession. Perhaps the weakest link to date has been the tendency to ignore the importance of the field of real estate and its many contributions to and linkage with community development and wise land utilization. This is particularly true with respect to the lack of emphasis on the need to formulate new financing patterns to carry innovative theories into fruition. The planner should stop looking askance at the world of financing as if it were an establishment that never can reach his or her intellectual heights. The imagination and innovation of major private money sources, if understood, must be respected and utilized. And, conversely, the lender should master the art and strategy of the best planning concepts in formulating his or her lending decisions. The lender's participation is absolutely indispensable to large-scale, long-range, successful restructuring and development of communities in tomorrow's world.

FIVE

BASICS OF THE UNIFORM CONDOMINIUM ACT

In 1978, the American Bar Association approved the Uniform Condominium Act (UCA) for submission to the various state legislatures for adoption. The UCA was drafted to provide uniformity on a national basis to the morass of state statutes that governed the creation, sale financing, and management of condominiums in the various jurisdictions. Although HUD has drafted a National Condominium Disclosure Act, the constitutionality of that act is questionable, and it has not yet been adopted by the federal government. One very positive aspect of the UCA is the fact that it leaves regulation of condominiums at the state rather than the federal level.

As of the date of this writing, only the states of Maine, Minnesota, Pennsylvania, New Mexico, Rhode Island, and West Virginia, Missouri, Nebraska, Oregon, and Connecticut had adopted versions of the UCA, although the District of Columbia and the states of Virginia, Georgia, and New Hampshire have condominium statutes that contain key aspects of the UCA. Those states with extensive statutory regulation of condominium development, such as California, Florida, Illinois, Michigan, and Hawaii, will probably adopt only certain piecemeal provisions of the UCA. On the other hand, states with little current regulation may deem it highly desirable to adopt the UCA in its entirety.

An overriding concern will be the reaction of lenders to the UCA. For example, the Condominium Task Force composed of the United States Department of Housing and Urban Development, the Veterans Administration, the Federal National Mortgage Association and The Mortgage Corporation (formerly the Federal Home Loan Mortgage Corporation) have expressed some approval of the UCA but have taken no official position with regard to recommendation for or against its adoption by the states. However, a serious concern expressed by lenders toward the UCA is the degree of flexibility it grants the developer. If various lending institutions eventually oppose the UCA, its proponents will face an uphill battle in their attempts to have it widely accepted.

FLEXIBILITY OF UCA

The UCA is designed in part to maximize the flexibility of the developer in creating a condominium project. This important characteristic significantly differs from most state condominium statutes, which usually try to fix common element interests, voting powers, and assessment obligations. The act provides for flexible condominiums, allowing condominium projects to expand by the addition of real estate and to contract by the removal of real estate. To protect the consumer, the builder remains liable for all expenses relating to real estate retained by the builder for future development.

The definitions of *unit* and *common element* may be altered by the developer from the definitions provided in the UCA, so that the developer may tailor his or her documents to the needs of his or her particular project. For example, the unit may consist of a cube of airspace in which an entire building containing one or more apartments is located, and that unit may be subsequently subdivided or converted by the declarant into more units and common elements. This is a particularly desirable feature for those involved in the creation of commercial condominiums where the developer or the purchaser needs the ability to further subdivide and sell portions of the building not separated by common walls or the flexibility to consolidate existing units by removing, in whole or in part, partitions separating those units.

The UCA allows for the creation of fee condominiums, leasehold condominiums, subleasehold condominiums, and any combination of the foregoing. Hence, the developer under the UCA has the flexibility of leasing an undivided interest in the ground together with the airspace unit for a long term while selling in fee an undivided interest in the improvements to the purchaser for tax and marketing reasons.

The UCA also distinguishes between common elements and limited common elements, providing further flexibility for the developer. Although common elements and limited common elements would be owned in common by all of the unit owners, any of the common elements may be designated as limited common elements when the use is restricted to fewer than all of the owners in the project. Thus, parking spaces may be designated as parts of each unit, as separate units, as limited common elements, or as common elements, at the discretion of the developer. The developer, therefore, has the discretion to assign the use and the expenses for maintenance of the parking spaces to one or more owners, depending upon the needs of the project.

A unique aspect of the UCA allows the condominium to be created with noncontiguous parcels of real estate. Hence, several noncontiguous apartment buildings along a city block could be included within one condominium project. On the other hand, each such building may constitute a separate condominium, subject to an umbrella association, at the discretion of the developer. (See Chapter 16.)

Common element interests and expense liabilities may be allocated on any basis under the UCA. This is an important feature, because common element interests should be allocated based on the relative values of the units, but the common expense liabilities should be allocated based upon the relative degree of services available to the particular unit, and these concepts may not correspond with one another. The voting power within the owners' association also may be allocated equally or based upon the relative common expense liability or its relative common element interest, depending upon the particular project.

DISCLOSURE PROTECTIONS

The basic premise of the UCA regarding consumer protection is that full disclosure of the product is the best way to balance the interests of the seller and the buyer. However, the condominium form of ownership and the community association process complicate the bundle of rights and obligations that are sold with the condominium home.

Except for single-phase projects with fewer than thirteen units, the UCA requires a list of information to be provided for each purchaser in the public offering statement before that purchaser consummates his or her purchase of the unit. This statement includes not only information in the recorded management documents but also other important materials such as reports on the progress of the development. For example, the developer must disclose whether additional units may be rented or marketed to investors rather than owner–occupants, copies and explanations of the legal management documents, the current financial condition of the owners' association, projected common expense assessments, future expenses that might arise upon completion of the development, any problems involving the condominium title, financing arrangements, warranty provisions, pending legal actions, and any other unusual circumstances affecting the condominium. Certain information also must be disclosed by each unit owner upon resale of his or her unit.

As new units are added to the condominium project, the relative interests in the common elements, voting power in the association, and common expense liabilities will change, and this could significantly affect the relative liabilities of the purchasers in the condominiums' early phases of development. The UCA requires disclosure of the conditions under which a flexible condominium may be developed, and this development must occur within a seven-year period. However, the ability of the developer to withdraw real estate from the condominium imposes potential problems. Simply by declaring that certain property is withdrawable, the declarant may, for example, designate recreational facilities as withdrawable real estate and hold them as such until the last sale. Under the UCA, the developer then could withdraw these facilities as long as the action occurred within the seven-year option period.

If a developer does not provide the detailed public offering statement to a purchaser before conveyance of the unit or fails to update the information periodically, he or she will be penalized for such noncompliance; that is, the purchaser may recover 10 percent of the sale price of the unit from the declarant. The UCA further provides a substantial cooling-off period, essentially allowing the purchaser fifteen days following the receipt of the public offering statement in which to cancel a sales contract. The UCA also creates both express and implied warranties of quality, which for the most part are patterned after the warranties contained in the Uniform Land Transactions Act.

The offering statement and the required accurate labeling of promotional literature are particularly important parts of the UCA. Many condominium buyers are attracted by advertising literature, elaborate models, and sales presentations. They frequently fail to review written documents such as the legal management documents or the public offering statement. The UCA requires that promotional literature and models describing the developments must represent what will be available after closing or clearly reflect if the facility is not a part of the offering.

CONVERSION CONDOMINIUMS

The principal problems in the area of condominium conversions center around (1) the quality of construction or refurbishment and (2) displacement of low- and moderate-income tenants from their rental homes. The conversion of a building to condominium ownership can increase the property value of the building. Also, the conversion of rental units in urban areas to individual ownership may stabilize a neighborhood because the occupants now have a pride of ownership that the tenants may not have. In attempting to balance the competing interests of the developers, tenants, and prospective owners, the UCA provides the tenant with a sixty-day right to purchase his or her rental unit at a price and on terms offered by the developer to the public. The act also requires that the developer give the tenant 120 days' notice before eviction so that the unit can be sold to someone else.

The UCA requires the public offering statements for residential conversion projects to include a description of the condition of the structure and its mechanical and electrical systems. The converter must also estimate the expected useful life of each component of the building, along with a list of notices detailing violations of building codes or other regulations and the estimated cost for making the required repairs. Otherwise, the developer must state that he or she makes no representations about the condition of the building.

WARRANTIES

Regardless of whether the condominium is new or was created through conversion of an existing rental property, the UCA requires the developer to offer implied warranties of quality. These warranties cover both units and common elements and assure that they "are suitable for the ordinary uses of real estate of its type." Any improvements made before the creation of the condominium must be free from defective materials and constructed in accordance with applicable law and sound engineering and construction standards, in a professional manner. The UCA allows buyers of commercial property to waive the implied warranties of quality if the waiver uses such terms as "as is" or "with all faults."

A developer may also make express warranties of quality, such as that a new shopping center is going to be built near the project or that tennis courts will be located near the unit. The UCA requires that models or brochures that include maps or improvements must create an express warranty that the finished product will conform to the model, drawings, or description. If the developer warrants that the condominium will only be sold to adults, then the sale of a unit to a family with children would violate that warranty. All warranties of a developer are transferred to the new owner when the unit is resold. The warranty provisions are among the most controversial in the UCA.

CONDOMINIUM MANAGEMENT

Most developers insist upon controlling the community association that manages the condominium project at least during the initial sales period. Since the developer has the greatest investment in the project, he or she should have the greatest voice in the way in which the association is managed. However, control can lead to abuse, and the association must continue to operate effectively after it loses the helping hand of the developer.

The UCA contains provisions relating to the organization, operation, and other important aspects of condominium associations. Among other things, the article contains provisions relating to the contents of bylaws and meetings of the association, and even goes so far as to set forth a quorum requirement. Additionally, the UCA contains provisions relating to assessments for common expenses and the liens that attach to the units to secure them.

Under the UCA, the maximum period of declarant control is generally three years following the first conveyance of a unit (five years for flexible condominiums), although a declarant may surrender control at an earlier point if he or she so desires. The UCA further provides that following the conveyance of 25 percent of the units, the unit owners have the right to elect 25 percent of the executive board; following the conveyance of 50 percent of the units, they may elect 33 percent of the executive board; and declarant control automatically terminates following conveyance of 75 percent of the units. To avoid overreaching by developers, the unit owners may terminate certain recreational leases, contracts for services, and management contracts following ninety days' notice.

One excellent provision of the UCA is a dramatic departure from existing practice. It provides that an association's lien for common expenses has priority over first mortgages on the units up to a maximum of assessments due for six months immediately preceding any action to enforce the lien. The purpose of this provision is to strike an equitable balance between the need to enforce the collection of unpaid assessments and the necessity of protecting the priority of security interests of mortgage lenders. As a practical matter, mortgage lenders will probably prefer to pay the six months' assessments demanded by the association rather than permit foreclosure. In reality, such lenders are not only in the best position to collect such debts, but also their own best interests are served by having the assessments paid so that the association remains solvent. However, since this requirement may conflict with statutes pertaining to the priority of institutional mortgages, appropriate amendments would have to be made in the affected jurisdictions.

DEVELOPER LIABILITY

The UCA imposes a very high fiduciary standard of care on board members appointed by the seller. This standard has been imposed by courts in some states (e.g., California), and it holds the developer liable as a trustee for self-dealing or negligent acts. For example, the UCA makes the seller liable to the association for financial losses not covered by insurance while the seller was in control of the board, even if the seller was not at fault.

Most policy and management decisions are made by the board of directors of the condominium association. These include the power to enforce rules and to collect assessments from the members. However, the UCA reserves some rights to the membership at large, such as amending the declaration and terminating the condominium.

ADMINISTRATION AND REGULATION

An agency may be created to administer and regulate condominiums at the state level as an option. A state agency would approve the legal documents for projects containing more than twelve units and would generally oversee and enforce the UCA. Some states are opposed to the creation of any additional administrative agencies, while others may determine that the agency set up to enforce the UCA would not be strong enough. As a general matter, however, in those states where there is a substantial amount of activity in the condominium field, a state agency having some enforcement powers is desirable.

DESIRABILITY OF UCA

Every state has a condominium act, but most such acts are antiquated and need substantial updating. Uniform legislation would allow those involved in condominiums in more than one state, especially lenders, to understand the law regardless of where the project is located.

The UCA balances the interests of the buyer, the seller, the lender, the community association, and others involved in the creation and operation of condominiums. Therefore, many states are actively considering adoption of at least portions of the UCA.

SIX

SHOULD A HOME BUYER PURCHASE A CONDOMINIUM?

This chapter is written chiefly for persons seeking housing for themselves. It may also prove equally useful for their attorneys and for builders and sales-people interested in the presentation and other factors that may affect the prospective purchaser's decision either to buy or not to buy a particular condominium home that is to be constructed or offered for resale. Chapter 10 contains a detailed consideration of the tax benefits and problems involved in the purchase of a condominium.

THE FUNDAMENTAL QUESTIONS

A home buyer usually emphasizes one or all of the following three points in determining the best housing available to him or her at a cost and method of financing he or she can afford:

1. *Cost.* The cost of the unit, both to buy and to maintain, must be within his or her reasonable ability to pay. This includes considering not only the sales price, down payment, and closing costs, but also the costs of financing the acquisition.
2. *Living Environment.* The promotional literature of the developer has promised to create a community with certain specified facilities and

other amenities and a certain appearance. An important element of the purchaser's decision to buy will be based upon his or her desire to live in the type of atmosphere and under the conditions represented. These include the kind of neighborhood in which he or she wishes to live, his or her essential demands for the size of housing and for internal and adjacent facilities, and his or her personal taste regarding external and internal decorative appearance or the capability for redecoration, layout, and materials.

3. *Value.* The purchaser expects to obtain reasonable value for his or her investment. This particularly relates to the manner of construction and the facilities actually supplied by the developer. The purchaser does not want the value of this investment depreciated by subsequent activities of the developer.

The decision for or against a particular condominium is, therefore, not a decision that can be made outside the context of personal needs by merely reviewing a particular development's legal and governing structure. The particular condominium must stand up against the competition of other types of housing, as well as against other condominiums. Buying a home is a most personal decision. At most, it is possible to evaluate some of the factors that many persons might consider important, once they become curious about the possibility of buying a condominium, and perhaps some of the factors that the ordinary lay person may often overlook.

THE ORDER OF CONFRONTATION

One will probably first learn about a new condominium development while conversing with an acquaintance, reading a newspaper or mailed flyer, or scanning a roadside sign advertising the new housing.

Unfortunately, in most condominium offerings, a copy of the declaration and bylaws or even an adequate summary of them never gets to the purchaser until after he or she has signed a binder or has actually executed a full contract to purchase, or until the time of final settlement and delivery of the individual deed. Some builders never make such delivery but merely represent that these documents are available to be read at an office by the prospective purchaser or his or her attorney. In only a handful of states does it appear to be regular builder practice to give extensive information before the signing of the contract.

The California and New York regulations are among the most comprehensive in protection afforded investors by states. When FHA financing is employed, an adequate set of basic explanatory documents must be issued to purchasers. Unfortunately, as of the date of the printing of this book, only fourteen states had regulations of varying effectiveness governing the sale of condominiums.

Precedent for the lack of public protection in this field can be found in the almost universal lack of disclosure standards in the sale of homes and rental of apartments, as well as in the practice of selling homeowner association memberships by the mere reference to a filed master agreement.

The prospective condominium purchaser is usually given a sheet of paper similar to the ordinary one-family home offering. On it he or she will find a projection for mortgage charges, fire insurance premiums, property taxes, and common-element maintenance charges per unit. These figures can be expected to be typically unreliable as in the case of one-family home sales. Review of actual offerings outside California and New York has led to the conclusion that, in a large number of cases, the property tax projection should be about 20 percent higher than the builder's estimate and fire insurance about 40 to 50 percent higher, and that the projection of common maintenance charges is regularly divorced from reality. One common delusion practiced is either to provide for sponsor management for one year, at little or no cost, without projecting the sizeable increase in management costs almost certain to occur thereafter, or to state management costs as being unreasonably low or even nonexistent.

In a landmark California case, *Raven's Cove Townhomes, Inc.* v. *Knuppe Development Company, Inc., et al.,* 114 Cal. App. 3d 783 (1981), the court held that the developer and his representatives in control of a residential community association breached their fudiciary duty by failing to properly determine operating cost and to fund a maintenance reserve. There are other cases in which associations have successfully sued developers for misrepresenting the true costs of operating the association in the initial budget. This is called lowballing. For guidance in developing a pro forma budget for a condominium association, one may turn to the detailed *Operating Cost Manual* published by the California Department of Real Estate.

A sponsor will sometimes predetermine limits on common charges in order to make the purchase more attractive. He or she will then arbitrarily reduce or eliminate necessary services from the projected budget. In one case, the sponsor projected a $150 annual cost for snow removal, grass cutting, and shrubbery maintenance for a twenty-nine-unit condominium. The project was advertised as carefree. Nevertheless, regardless of such selling techniques, the figures and accompanying representations have appeared to be more truthful than those for most of the competitive one-family home offerings reviewed, probably because buyers of condominiums are more inquisitive.

Before a prospective purchaser signs anything, he or she should have his or her attorney find out the actual combined tax rate and also the assessment ratio for the community. The purchaser should check with his or her insurance agent on the actual cost of a hazard policy, as well as the charges for other needed insurance coverage, including liability and theft. He or she should ask the proposed managing agent of the property whether that agent has examined the budget for common expenses and whether he or she has certified the reasonableness of the projection. The purchaser should be sure that the management contracts provide for periodic renegotiation to avoid sweetheart deals. In any case, he or she should get a budget breakdown that covers all essential expenses. In California, any developer who wishes to sell five or more condominiums must submit the proposed common expenses to the State Department of Real Estate for review and approval before the condominiums may legally be sold.

LIMITATIONS ON NEGOTIATION WITH SPONSORS

By the time the prospective purchaser is offered his or her condominium unit, the essential framework of contractual relationships that will be binding on all future occupants has probably been worked out by the sponsor. In most instances, the sponsor will have met the primary lending institution's requirements concerning the contents of the declaration, bylaws, and rules, if any. However, the purchaser should ask whether the documents have been approved by the Federal Home Loan Mortgage Corporation and the Federal National Mortgage Association to ensure that the condominium unit will be financeable on resales.

The other important participant in the transaction who must be satisfied is the title insurance company (or other source of title insurance), in order to make certain that the lender will be able to obtain title insurance that is satisfactory. As of the date of printing of this book, only the state of Iowa did not permit title insurance companies to do business in the state. Both the lending institution and the title company naturally are primarily interested in the protection of their own positions. Except in a very few jurisdictions, there is no agency of government that is especially concerned with the initial problems of the condominium purchaser. The VA reviews documents with the purchaser's interest in mind, but the VA is not asked to guarantee initial sponsor sales of condominiums in most projects.

Local building departments that administer builder codes that govern all types of housing, in the overwhelming number of instances, will be the only governmental agency passing on any protective aspect of the new condominium, and then only in a most limited way will be conditioning the issuance of certificates of occupancy upon compliance with local ordinances.

Some, but very few, sponsors have appointed independent local attorneys, other than the sponsor's attorney, for the express purpose of representing unknown future purchasers during the drafting of the major documents. While at first blush this might smack of self-dealing by the sponsor, it must be remembered that the ordinary sponsor should have no real objection to the careful drafting of legal management documents that will protect the internal affairs of the condominium not directly related to the sponsor. If the historical precedent for the use of such interim attorneys (which was established in promoting cooperatives) is an indication, such attorneys in many situations will play a restraining role on the sponsor's over-reaching on matters in which he or she is concerned. But the existence of such an attorney should never be considered as a substitute for a purchaser's own counsel.

The prospective buyer should start, then, with the assumption that the legal management documents that will govern his or her condominium must be either accepted or rejected in their entirety. Therefore, the necessity of reading a fair summary and of being represented by counsel early cannot be emphasized too strongly. The traditional use of a lawyer at the time of contract and title closing is inadequate when buying a condominium. No attorney can be expected to be able to digest these documents thoroughly if he or she is confronted with them for the first time at contract closing. The primary underlying documents should be in his or her hands at least several days before the buyer's contract appointment.

SAFETY OF THE CONTRACT DEPOSIT

The dangers of the buyer losing his or her deposit on a condominium are, practically speaking, almost as great as those of the purchaser of a one-family home. Perhaps it may be argued that the greater precautions taken by the lending institution to assure success in the case of the condominium actually creates a situation in which there is less chance for the loss of a deposit because of a sponsor's failure. But the buyer may not know whether a lender has even given a construction commitment as yet and what the conditions are for such an undertaking.

If it is not already required by state or local law, the purchaser should attempt to limit the use of his or her deposit to the construction of his or her unit and the common elements. Unfortunately, the common-element feature weakens the protection of such an agreement or statutory requirement. The sponsor could not possibly segregate an undivided interest in the common elements so as to achieve a realistic application of the deposit. This feature results in further enlarging the risk of the condominium purchaser.

The FHA sometimes requires that the deposit be retained in an escrow account until delivery of title. But this provision is very difficult to obtain from builders during the negotiation of uninsured transactions, just as it is rarely obtained in the purchase of a one-family home. It should be remembered that, as in the case of one-family homes, the contract deposit often will be subordinated to the blanket mortgage obligations of the builder. California is an exception, in that the deposit must be placed in a neutral escrow depository until title is delivered to the buyer, unless a bond, letter of credit, or other assurance is posted to insure the return of the deposit if the unit is not eventually completed. New York has a similar statute for condominiums and cooperatives.

Perhaps the best protection for the deposit (short of a full escrow until delivery of the title) will be a requirement that no part of the deposit may be expended for any purpose until a specific number of units has been sold. Quite often, the declaration or condominium plan refers to such an eventuality as the effective date of the plan. Be cautioned, however, that such a clause would not be of much effect unless a lending institution has already issued a commitment to the sponsor. The addition of a specific use clause to an effective date clause would provide substantial protection, if a commitment has been issued that is tied to the exact requirements for the number of units that must be sold in order to make the commitment effective.

The purchaser should attempt to revise the sales agreement to eliminate any liquidated damages clause, unless the purchaser wishes to limit his or her damages and is willing to lose the deposit in the event of the purchaser's default.

Regardless of the above discussion, the most important protection of a purchaser's deposit is the reputation and experience of the builder. The buyer should ascertain whether or not he or she was ever a principal of a corporation that went bankrupt and whether he or she has material lawsuits now pending against either him or her or the corporate names under which he or she built. One wonders at the naivete of the purchasers and some of their attorneys in not even getting representations of such material information.

From the point of view of the developer, the sales agreement is the key document in the development and marketing of the condominium project. One of the purposes of the sales agreement is to grant the developer as much flexibility as possible in pursuing the project. This flexibility is manifested in several ways:

1. The minimum number of units to be sold before the developer is committed to the project. This provision may be dictated by the terms of the developer's construction loan commitment, as well as the overall economics of the project.

2. The developer's ability to amend or modify the project documents and the proposed sizes, locations, and layouts of units at any time before or after the first closing of a sale of a condominium. This reflects the developer's desire to make changes dictated by the general response to his or her marketing program. (In New York, this may result in a rescission offer to all prior purchasers under contract.)

3. Specifying a date for closing far enough in the future to allow for a full marketing effort, giving sufficient time for construction or refurbishment (as applicable), and providing for additional delays for events beyond the developer's reasonable control.

EFFECTIVE DATE OF PLAN

While in the purchase of a home a buyer ordinarily would be much concerned with an outside date for the actual completion and delivery of the house, this particular outside date represents the second outside date frequently encountered in condominium purchases. In many instances, contracts provide that the deposit is returnable if a specific number of units has not been sold by a specific date. This clause may be a prerequisite for all contracts entered into by the builder, or it may have been independently negotiated. Even when the builder represents an outside date for declaring a plan effective, the purchaser might want the date to be earlier for the purpose of his or her own contract and future plans.

A fair plan for declaring the condominium plan effective is helpful to the purchaser as well as the sponsor. The sponsor need not go ahead with his or her program if contracts have not materialized by a specific date. The purchaser, with the protection of a minimum number of sales required to be made by the effective date, need not worry about being the sole inhabitant of the condominium and having to gaze at the surrounding empty space for many months.

THE COMMON INTEREST

The percentage of a buyer's interest in common facilities should be specified exactly in the contract and not merely alluded to by reference to some filed or unfiled declaration. It is important for the buyer to know this figure, because on it will ordinarily depend his or her assessment for maintenance charges, possibly his or her voting rights, the extent of local property tax assessment, and even his or her participation in the income or proceeds from some future condemnation of the condominium property. But such a figure would be insufficient by itself, unless the buyer were also shown a reasonable projection of the condominium budget and a listing of the percentages of common interest that were applicable to all other units of the condominium. A copy of the legal management documents should be compared with the percentage in the contract before the purchaser signs. The buyer may expect common interests to be calculated on the approximate ratio of the basic purchase price to the total price of all units (excluding extras). Sometimes the determination is based on floor area ratios, and sometimes the interests are equally apportioned. In some instances, statutes give leeway for computing the interests, but most plans follow the price or floor area formulas.

It would seem that a purchaser should be entitled to a representation that, where the master documents have not been filed, no change in the allocation of common interests may be made by the sponsor without the written permission of the purchaser. Even where the declaration has been filed and statutory requirement for unanimous consent for any change in percentages is required, the sponsor may be the sole owner of units until he or she conveys actual title to the purchaser.

Checking the exactness of the purchaser's common interest and its consequences is probably the one feature that most clearly distinguishes condominium contractual negotiations from the purchase of a one-family home.

ADEQUACY OF TITLE INSURANCE

The purchaser should obtain title insurance covering all of the property purchased in fee or by leasehold and over which he or she has an easement for his or her exclusive use. The standard forms of title insurance policies issued on individual condominium units should protect the unit owner against damages resulting from a judicial declaration to the effect that the condominium had not been validly formed pursuant to the particular state's statute.

The buyer of a one-family home bases his or her title on the validity of the title to the underlying land. But the condominium homeowner bases his or her title not only on a good title to the land but also on a good title to the unit itself. The unit title, or title in space, depends on the validity of the condominium in which it is located and which purportedly was formed under a state law. The totality of the unit owner's title basis should carry adequate title insurance, and the policy providing such insurance should expressly insure against damages resulting from two eventualities:

1. Failure of the underlying land title
2. Invalidity of the condominium under the state law under which it purportedly was created

Many institutional lenders require such dual title insurance for their permanent loans and will not issue mortgages without such protection for themselves. But only in a few states, such as California and New York, is the full-coverage policy considered to be standard. Some astute attorneys in other states have, in individual cases, obtained a letter from title companies stating that the policy to be issued shall be construed to cover both such eventualities and any ensuing damages.

If such adequate title policy is available, the purchaser will be making a good investment. If only a more limited policy is available, every attempt should be made to obtain a letter declaring that the language of the policy is to be construed as covering the second eventuality.

If units are being closed before expiration of all lien periods, endorsement should be obtained covering any mechanics liens that may be created after closing of the condominium unit sale.

APPROVAL OF BUILDING OCCUPANCY

In localities requiring certificates of occupancy, it is important to make certain that a permanent certificate of occupancy has been issued for the unit. This is relatively simple to do when highrise condominiums are involved, because ordinarily the entire building will have had to be completed before any permanent certificate is issued. Certainly, the person who takes title when all that exists is a temporary certificate for only a specific part of an unfinished building takes on a substantial risk that some contingency may result in work stoppage during construction. Unlike a tenant who is somewhat inconvenienced, the unit owner is a homeowner who is left stranded with a substantial investment, a personal obligation on a usually heavy mortgage, and a separate obligation to pay property taxes. If the highrise condominium is not completed when a unit owner's occupancy becomes possible and necessary, consideration should be given to temporary, alternative tenancy.

In cluster housing or in row, attached, and similar forms of strewn-out housing, another problem is sometimes faced by the purchaser who would prefer the issuance of a permanent rather than temporary certificate of occupancy. This comes about because the locality may take the attitude that an overall permanent certificate, or separate permanent certificates, should only be issued when the entire development has been completed. Argument in favor of this position is made on the basis that the common elements attached to each unit have not been completed even though the individual units are habitable.

It would seem preferable for a community to issue individual certificates of occupancy for each unit, thus recognizing separate fee ownership. The power of a community to cancel certificates because of a violation of law by an occupant or for any reasons applicable to the activities of a single owner should not result in the cancellation of certificates for neighboring units, just as is the case of an innocent neighboring single-family homeowner who would not be affected by the cancellation of a neighbor's certificate. If cancellation of the entire venture were required in the public interest, this would merely require the additional bookkeeping involved in canceling a group of certificates rather than an overall permit.

Different communities take different views regarding the number of certificates and the timing of their issuance. Wherever possible, local ordinances should be enacted to specifically cover the problem rather than to leave it to random administrative opinion.

California by statute allows a builder to phase closings of condominiums in a manner that does not correspond with lot lines. A builder in that state may create two or more construction phases on one lot and obtain final certificates of occupancy on each grouping of units as they are completed. Nevertheless, it is still advisable to subdivide each development into as many lots as reasonably possible to allow the builder flexibility to choose not to build part of the planned project; to meet presale requirements of the lender; to avoid construction or permanent loan commitments for the entire project; to test the market and make reasonable modifications to the units and common elements to meet changing technology, laws, and market desires; to stage association assessments; and to treat each phase separately for accounting purposes.

WARRANTIES

Warranties available to the purchaser of a condominium unit fall into the same categories as in the purchase of a one-family home. Some will be the direct warranty of the builder, while others are guarantees by manufacturers or contractors. The latter are rarely read until title is obtained. At the least, the purchase contract should provide for their delivery at closing. It is interesting to note that the warranties most frequently omitted from the provisions of the contract or through the failure to deliver separate written guarantees are those for kitchen cabinets, bathroom vanities, flooring, air-conditioning ducts, wrought-iron work, roofing, siding, concrete work other than foundations, electrical systems, and painting. While more reputable builders obtain effective warranties from subcontractors covering defects in such materials or their installation, the terms and applicability of such obligation are rarely expressed in the purchaser's contract or made expressly in favor of the purchaser.

Warranties from well-known appliance manufacturers seldom pose any problem, although their limitations should be recognized. In addition, many builders will give some warranty against leakage and seepage in the foundation. There is often a guarantee that heating and air-conditioning facilities meet specific temperature requirements.

The Magnuson–Moss Warranty Act became law in 1975. The act is primarily a disclosure law, based on the idea that if warranties are written in simple language and made available for consumers to examine before they buy certain components of a home, they will shop around for the best deal available. The act affects the form in which warranties are written, and it only applies to consumer products such as appliances and furnaces.

But the purchaser of a condominium should not limit himself or herself to his or her own unit when considering the question of warranties. The purchaser should be assured that there is adequate warranty for commonly used facilities such as swimming pools, private roads, elevators, hallway carpeting, parking lots, lawn sod and shrubbery, decorative walls, privacy fencing, and other commonly used facilities, where applicable. The early deterioration of such facilities might place burdensome assessments on owners or create the alternative unattractiveness that might reduce the value of their investments.

Information regarding the age and physical condition of the structure should be reviewed very carefully to determine whether or not substantial repairs will be required within the near future.

As in all real estate purchases, the purchaser of a condominium should be wary of undefined terms, such as "structural defects," that are used occasionally in limited guarantee clauses. The purchaser should examine each of these clauses carefully and ascertain the nature and extent of their coverage. For example, when reviewing the provision for painting of units, the purchaser should determine whether closets are included.

Condominium developers may be liable under either an express warranty or an implied warranty theory of liability. For a discussion of warranties under the Uniform Condominium Act, see Chapter 5.

Although as recently as 1970 the view of most state courts was the traditional *caveat emptor* (let the buyer beware), at least forty-two states plus the District of Columbia have now imposed on the builder an implied warranty of habitability to the purchaser. This warranty is a promise to correct defects that interfere with the unit's use as a residence. This trend toward the creation of an implied warranty reflects the changing public awareness now that a home buyer is entitled to be protected against defective work by the builder, similar to the protection that the purchaser of a new automobile enjoys. However, only eight states protect resale purchasers in the same way that they protect the first purchaser. In any event, the purchaser should obtain as many representations in writing as possible regarding quality, services, and future plans.

FLOOR PLAN AND LAYOUT DIAGRAMS

Great care should be taken by a purchaser of a condominium to define the area limits of his or her unit. Some of the more questionable practices of builders with respect to the diagrams of room layout that are shown to purchasers of condominiums (as is also true in the case of one-family housing) are the following:

1. Marking the dimensions of a room to include closet space, patios, or balconies without so disclosing.
2. Using outside overhangs, such as those on many garages, as additional room footage.
3. Omitting entirely dimensions of areas that might be considered inadequate.
4. Marking off rooms to be separated by dividers rather than walls.
5. Changing room sizes in the model house without changing the diagram given to purchasers.
6. Using a florid description of space that implies inclusion of items not to be included. (For example, an "atrium garden" sometimes turns out to be merely sand or dirt where, at the purchaser's additional expense, a miniature garden can be installed.)
7. Planning to reverse the plans for room layout in a manner that might make the housing unattractive to certain purchasers.
8. Failure to locate leaders and gutters on diagrams.
9. Failure either to give any dimensions or to affix accurate dimensions to space areas in the front or rear of the structure.
10. Failure to specify the heights of all rooms.

Almost all of the above and similar problems are even more pronounced when no model house or model unit exists, and purchase is made from mere drawings or simulated room cutouts. Because of bank blanket financing restrictions, condominiums are often sold in such a manner. In states where full disclosure rarely occurs—and that means most states—extra care is essential in such situations in order to be fully apprised of the exact dimensions and limitations relative to floor plans.

Because of the division of responsibility for upkeep, a purchaser should obtain a definite description of the space and facilities where he or she has personal responsibility for upkeep. The purchaser should ask such questions as: Must the unit owner paint just the inside of all doors and windows within his or her unit, or both sides? Where does the unit owner's electrical and plumbing line responsibility begin and end?

In addition, the condominium owner has problems with respect to floor plans. Recreation rooms, swimming and sauna areas, parking areas, hallways, and similar common areas are not usually delineated in the detailed diagram layouts presented to purchasers. For example, the actual dimensions of a swimming pool may make the difference between comfort and overcrowding. Yet many persons do not inquire about dimensions. Such an inquiry should be considered essential.

Many condominiums include substantial numbers of compact units. In such instances, where models are used, the prospective purchaser should be wary of model houses that utilize miniature bedroom and other furniture. Such devices create an illusion that masks the actual dimensions. Too often, tiny wooden crates are covered with handsome bedspreads in a room visible to but chained off from the public. The same or similar techniques are also sometimes employed in the sale of one- and two-family homes.

REMOVAL OF LIENS

In most states, the condominium statute provides for the removal of all liens on any unit before its first conveyance. Regardless of this built-in protection, the purchase contract should specifically impose the obligation on the sponsor to remove all liens at title closing time. The title insurance search or other title search will serve to confirm the fact that the buyer hasn't been given a deed that is defective because of existing liens.

CONTINGENT FACILITIES

Key features of many condominiums are the special recreational or other facilities not ordinarily available to the purchasers of one-family homes. Advertising programs for condominiums emphasize such features so as to accentuate the extra that weakens competition. The purchaser must be on guard to make certain that he or she understands any contingencies attached. These usually fall into at least one of the following patterns:

1. Unfinalized local zoning approval for the special facility.
2. Discretion retained by the sponsor not to construct if total sales are inadequate.
3. Lack of specification of a definite date by which such facilities must be completed.
4. Unavailability of specific plans and layouts that give the units' location, size, and materials used in construction.
5. Contingent increase in assessments if sales are inadequate.
6. Unavailability of all or a portion of the recreational facilities to all of the owners for a period of time during which the developer is appropriating the facilities for its sales program.

As far as the last problem is concerned, the builder usually will not contractually represent the actual number of units he or she will build. If the builder fails to complete the number anticipated, after a recreational facility has been turned over to the condominium, maintenance charges might have to be increased considerably. (This would be the case even if the land were abandoned to the construction lender, unless the lender or its successor assumed full responsibility for all maintenance charges. During interim defaults and before foreclosure, no mortgagee responsibility can be expected to exist.)

There are two other situations that must be considered carefully in connection with contingencies. One may arise when a sponsor constructs a substantial facility that will remain the initial size or will be enlarged when other separate condominiums are built later on surrounding land and are given the right to participate in the facility. In such a case, two questions must be answered: Will the enlarged facility be adequate? If the other condominiums are not built, will maintenance charges be too high? If the builder chooses to subsidize the charges or to maintain the facility during the initial sales period, the charges initially may appear to be reasonable but may increase dramatically after the subsidy expires.

A purchaser of a condominium unit should try to find out the zoning limitations on land immediately surrounding his or her particular unit. A certain group of condominium owners threw tantrums when a huge shopping center with a 2000-car parking lot was built directly behind the dividing fence about a year after completion of the condominium. While some residents liked the added shopping facilities, many others were furious with themselves for not having paid attention to the surrounding zoning.

SPONSOR'S OBLIGATIONS FOR UNSOLD UNITS

The buyer should inquire about the sponsor's obligations for any unsold condominium units; that is, whether he or she agrees to pay full maintenance charges for completed units while they remain unsold. Furthermore, it is just as important to show concern for maintenance obligations where units have not been built. Some initial formula should exist for the buyer's protection against unreasonable waiver of maintenance responsibility by the builder after the first few units have been conveyed. Construction warranties usually protect the builder against heavy repair costs, even if he or she is required to share fully in such costs involving any unbuilt or unsold units. As for charges for management and for maintenance of common parking areas, private roads, recreation areas, common utilities, elevators, cleaning, and other forms of maintenance, any expenditures resulting in common charges are of maximum benefit to the sponsor as well as the residents. In fact, maintenance charges could be heightened by the trampling and other abuse inflicted upon the behest of and for the benefit of the sponsor. Therefore, it would not be unreasonable for the sponsor to bear fair initial costs representing a proportionate share attributable to unsold or even unbuilt units. As a practical matter, it is almost essential for the preservation of an attractive appearance so necessary for a successful selling experience that the sponsor participate in the maintenance of the condominium. This has been a protective factor in many situations where the builder substantially exonerated himself or herself from responsibility for carrying charges for unsold or unbuilt units. It would seem to be clearly evident why a blanket mortgagee should insist on the payment of adequate maintenance charges by the sponsor in such cases.

As in one-family home construction, the more successful builder of condominiums also tends to be more courteous and more cognizant of the need for customer satisfaction. In a slow-moving venture, there is the greater possibility of an assignment of the entire venture and of scrubbing around for cheaper subcontracting work. It should be remembered that most builders operate through a shell corporation in order to protect themselves from personal liability. Wherever possible, attempts should be made to secure the builder's personal guarantees for completion and for major warranties. Unhappily, the latter are not always easy to obtain.

Once again, it cannot be emphasized too strongly how important it is for the purchaser to insist upon an investigation of the background, experience, and reputation of the builder.

MORTGAGES

Most of the same factors applicable to mortgages on one-family homes should be examined by the prospective condominium purchaser. The right to prepay some or all of the mortgage principal with or without penalty, the interest rate, the grace period, the amount of mortgage available, and the requirements for advanced payments for escrow accounts are some of the matters to be considered.

One should exercise great care in assuming second or third mortgage obligations. It should be recognized that sometimes the price of the unit could have been inflated because of the ease of attracting purchasers because of high leverage. Noninstitutional lenders frequently follow a less sympathetic approach when circumstances may result in delayed payments. Of greater danger is the tendency to place balloon mortgages, which require a large repayment of principal in a short number of years. Such mortgages proved catastrophic during the Great Depression, caused many homeowners to lose their homes in the early 1980s, and should never be contracted except after the most astute examination of all alternatives available for housing and financing. (A purchaser interested in a more detailed study of condominium mortgagee considerations should read Chapter 4.)

PARKING SPACE

Most condominium developers have found a satisfactory solution to parking problems. The more luxurious types invariably provide individual garages; others rely on carports, lots, or numbered spaces that may be either on or off the immediate site of the unit. The purchaser should not limit himself or herself merely to an evaluation of where he or she will park one car. Several other matters should be examined, including these factors:

1. Adequacy of parking space for guests.
2. Parking for delivery vehicles.
3. Provision of parking space for a unit owner's second car.
4. The distance of the parking space from the unit and the convenience of loading and unloading a car from the various units.
5. Adequacy of lighted areas between parking space and unit.

Sometimes yearly contracts for parking space are signed by unit owners with the condominium management. If so, the purchaser should determine if he or she can keep the original space as long as he or she remains an owner, or if the exact space or availability of some special parking facility is renegotiable each year. It is also essential to learn about the possibilities for confirmed parking space for any eventual purchaser of any particular unit. It is generally preferable to have the parking space or spaces irrevocably assigned in the deeds to the owners of certain units, rather than to allow the board of directors of the association to assign and reassign the spaces among the owners from time to time.

PROJECTIONS OF MAINTENANCE CHARGES

One of the more dangerous features of buying a condominium is the general lack of awareness that advertised carrying charges may not include some essential carrying charges.

In highrise condominiums, some utility charges and most heating expenses are usually collected through common maintenance assessments on all unit owners. In row housing and similar types of condominiums, heating and utility costs are usually paid individually and are not assessed as part of the common maintenance charges. Generally, special garage and parking charges are collected as maintenance charges in both kinds of condominiums.

The cost of outside painting and decoration is almost always collected as common maintenance, but charges for internal painting and decoration are most often paid by the individual unit owner.

However, there are no absolute rules on the above costs. Each prospective purchaser should ask for a breakdown of each condominium sponsor's projected carrying costs.

The largest part of the carrying charges will consist of mortgage principal and interest and property taxes. Therefore, most of a unit owner's carrying costs will be paid directly or to the bank escrow account, rather than through the condominium board.

Purchasers should be wary of projects that include subtractions of tax deductions from carrying charges. The extent of a buyer's tax deductions should not be subtracted when he or she is figuring the cost of the unit. The following factors must be borne in mind. First, the figure for the deduction (of interest and taxes) has little meaning unless the buyer's highest tax bracket is first injected. Second, the buyer's taxes have no connection with his or her obligation to pay the full carrying charges. Third, the same deductions are also generally allowable when a one-family home or a cooperative is purchased. If a buyer is comparing costs with the latter and injects the tax saving factor, then he or she must do the same in all three cases.

RESTRICTION ON OCCUPANCY

The condominium purchaser should inquire about any restrictions on the use of his or her premises that might limit exercise of full ownership. The following types of restrictions must be explored:

1. *Restrictions on Leasing.* Such restrictions may preclude leasing altogether or may require that leases have terms of a designated duration.

2. *Approval Required for Transfer of Units.* Some condominiums impose the right of first refusal (right of the unit owners as a group to purchase any unit at the best outside price offered) in the board when notice of a proposed sale is given by the unit owner. Because of doubts existing in some states concerning legal impediments to transfer good title that might result from the outright requirement of board approval of all sales, the right of first refusal has become standard there. Purchasers should be on guard against any limitations on profit from sales or any requirements that a part of the profit must go to either the board of managers or a state or local agency formed to ensure continued affordability of units.

3. *Restrictions on the Number of Occupants and Their Family Relationships.* For example, an aunt may not be permitted as a resident occupant in instances where bylaws limit regular residence to children and parents of the unit owners.

4. *Limitations on Business or Professional Use of Premises.* These restrictions may preclude a unit owner from using a portion of his or her unit as an office.

5. *Tailored Restrictions.* Sometimes unusual restrictions are imposed so as to comply with some direct or indirect mandate of planning or zoning boards or in order to superimpose a specific character on the housing. In at least one situation, a condominium required all purchasers and repurchasers to agree that the units would be used only as second homes, and that none of the unit owners would seek to send their children to local schools.

6. *Restrictions on the Number of Units That Any One Person May Own.* FHA-insured condominiums limit ownership to three additional units for any resident owner of a single unit. Bylaws of most condominiums correctly impose requirements that the units be essentially

occupied by owner–residents. The real problem usually relates to the inventory of unsold units owned by the sponsor or his or her assignees. Unit owners ordinarily are not satisfied with a large number of tenancies in their condominium. In one case, it was found that sloppy practices in the laundry room of a highrise condominium could be traced almost entirely to tenants of the sponsor's units. Sometimes the sponsor will attempt to hold back the best-located units in order to gain a continuous rental income and eventual sales at higher prices.

7. *Restrictions on Pets.* Such restrictions should be taken quite seriously by condominium purchasers. The situation with respect to the condominium differs somewhat in that whereas a cooperative owner can forfeit his or her lease by a violation, the likely relief against a persistent condominium unit owner violater can be expected to be a court injunction.

8. *Restrictions on Recreational Vehicles.* These restrictions may preclude a unit owner from using a van or other recreational vehicle for daily transportation to or from his or her unit.

9. *Age Restrictions.* Restrictions limiting occupancy of units to adults are enforceable in most states, and there are landmark cases upholding age restrictions in Arizona and Florida. However, in California such restrictions have been stricken down as contrary to the Unruh Civil Rights Act.

THE NEED FOR COUNSEL

No matter how much faith the purchaser has in a sponsor, he or she must have noted already how important an able lawyer can be. There is just as much reason, if not more, to engage counsel when purchasing a condominium unit as when buying a one-family home.

Most condominium sales do not involve purchasers who are represented by legal counsel. The explanation might lie in the typical mental characterization associated with townhouses, which are considered to be more like one-family homes, and with highrise units, which are looked upon as being closer to rental apartments. In addition, salespeople tend to convince prospective condominium unit purchasers that all documents are the same for everyone and cannot be changed by a lawyer. Of course, such an argument cannot apply to purchase agreements, provisions for extra appliances, escrow receipts, and documents other then the declaration, bylaws, and house rules. Unquestionably, every purchaser needs advice about what all the documents, both changeable and unchangeable, mean for his or her future.

The purchaser needs a lawyer to represent him or her. A purchaser should never let any fast sales talk deter him or her from retaining qualified counsel.

RESALES

If a purchaser is buying a resale unit, most of the areas of study contained in this text are applicable. However, some differences may exist. For example, the purchaser will probably not have a few years of free repairs available for his or her unit, appliances, and common elements as a consequence of contractor or manufacturer warranty. In addition, the purchaser's interest in the common elements cannot be adjusted as a result of a higher or lower purchase price. He or she should not consider signing anything until the seller furnishes an up-to-date copy of the declaration, bylaws, and house rules, a certification of the common charges, the current budget, and the last tax deduction statement for the unit, and until after he or she has turned these documents over to a lawyer for review and counsel. The purchaser should also talk to someone on the board of directors of the condominium association to determine whether or not there are any management problems in the project or if the homeowners are getting along with one another.

THE CONDOMINIUM PURCHASER'S DECISION

At the beginning of this chapter the basic factors involved in formulating a decision with respect to housing were set forth. In the future, in addition to traditional kinds of housing, most prospective purchasers will also be offered the choice of housing in the form of a condominium. This will necessitate a decision about whether or not the condominium being considered will satisfy the individual's housing needs at costs he or she can afford. In the next chapter, the management functions that make the condominium viable will be discussed. These, too, must be examined before a final decision can be made.

SEVEN

OPERATION AND MANAGEMENT OF CONDOMINIUM REGIME

MEETING SOCIAL REQUIREMENTS

In 1975, Dr. Carl Norcross conducted for the Urban Land Institute (ULI) an extensive national study of the likes and dislikes of residents of townhouse (PUD) and condominium projects. The survey included residents of forty-nine projects in California and the District of Columbia. Subjects explored in the study included parking problems, recreational amenities, owners' association responsibilities, density factors, pets, and quality of construction.

Dr. Norcross developed an Owner's Satisfaction Scale. Three-quarters of the residents surveyed said they were reasonably satisfied with the condominium-type life style. Those who were dissatisfied indicated that, if their very specific complaints were changed, they would be content with condominium living.

It is commonly said that the principal problems associated with condominium-type living center around the three Ps—pets, parking, and people. However, the principal topics of complaint in the referenced survey among unhappy residents were as follows:

1. Crowdedness (living too close together)
2. Noisy neighbors (especially children)
3. Neighbors' dogs

4. Renters
5. Parking
6. Management (by association)
7. Poor construction
8. Dishonest salespeople

According to the ULI report, there is a close inverse relationship between density and satisfaction. There are close-quartered townhouses with porches provided for relaxation that do not violate the privacy of neighbors. On the other hand, there are condominiums whose builders have been inconsiderate of privacy. Unfortunately, models or room layouts do not provide visitors with an appreciation of conditions or a realistic feeling of cramped living or overhanging neighbors. The solution rests with wise architectural design, which considers privacy as well as outside appearance.

Among the most satisfied condominium dwellers are those living in units that contained a small back yard hidden by six- to eight-foot fencing. At first glance, this might seem like stockade living, but the privacy features were welcomed by the residents, many of whom were former apartment dwellers.

In the search for cluster housing, builders sometimes seek an inexpensive solution to drainage problems posed by ridges and slopes. For instance, in some developments land lies between groups of units that are laid out in a V shape so that enormous pools can accumulate during rains.

In one condominium there is an immense runoff of water from the front of the roof, a situation that is ordinarily solved by using gutters and leaders. The builder stated that he had initially installed such equipment but found that the design of the buildings was marred by the metal hangings. He removed them to achieve aesthetic values, but in so doing he created water problems that would prove most uncomfortable. However, his sales did increase.

Builders who have developed one-family homes, highrise apartments, and duplex garden-type rental space too often find their usual architect or construction engineer incapable of solving or even foreseeing condominium problems. Over the years, however, better training and more experience has helped to provide the solutions to many problems for condominium housing.

INTERNAL MANAGEMENT

Getting people to serve on the boards of managers of condominiums has not been much of a problem. Many residents are interested enough to be willing to serve in the representative capacity. However, getting the overwhelming majority of residents to be interested in carefully assaying the merits of candidates in the first place is another matter. The greatest concern in condominium ownership generally appears about a full year after the first election of management by residents. It is said that the first three things that unit owners do when the developer loses control of the association are to fire the developer-appointed manager, hire an attorney, and sue the developer. This concern generally has three targets:

1. To get rid of the developer's influence, sometimes including his or her controlled managing agent.
2. To thoroughly assess the record of incumbent board managers against major and petty grievances of individual owners.
3. To unify unit owners in their quest for repairs and replacements by the sponsor of facilities and equipment that have been found faulty or inadequate. Sometimes this incudes the outright failure to furnish additional equipment promised.

In the majority of cases, the most pleasant atmosphere appears in condominium developments during the second year of full unit occupancy. Generally, there is less concern for petty problems, more friendliness among neighbors, a more experienced board and managing agent in operation, and a general awareness that there are few problems that cannot be solved by intelligent action by the unit owners themselves. In addition, the success of the few owners who have sold their units has tended to reassure the remaining residents that their homes have real and even increasing value.

TYPICAL DEVELOPER MISTAKES

There are several mistakes that condominium developers commonly make in creating and managing the association framework. An awareness of these mistakes may help developers to avoid these pitfalls. The success or failure of the association is important to the developer. Expensive and lengthy litigation may be brought about by disgruntled unit owners who blame the developer for unworkable management document structures. Even if they are not exposed to liability for badly structured associations, developers may avoid disputes if transitions are smooth and if the unit owners are given vehicles through which they can effectively manage their affairs after the developer leaves the community.

Fines and Due Process

Good legal documents usually establish a right in the board of directors of the association to levy fines against homeowners who damage common facilities or otherwise violate the use restrictions. Any fine (assuming fines are not prohibited in the local jurisdiction) is enforceable only if the accused homeowner is afforded due process of law. The legal documents should entitle each homeowner accused of violating the use restrictions to:

Adequate notice of any default with a right to cure the default
An opportunity to defend himself or herself against allegations of default
An opportunity to cross-examine witnesses
An opportunity to receive a formal hearing before an impartial forum
A penalty reasonably proportionate to the offense

Although the documents of many projects provide that no fines shall be levied unless the accused individual is afforded reasonable notice and an opportunity to a hearing before the board, few documents spell out the details of notice and hearing procedures. In the absence of such details, the developer is likely to be accused by confused board members of failing to create the framework needed to operate the association effectively.

Guiding the Homeowners' Association

Frequently, the declaration authorizes the board of directors of the association to adopt rules and regulations regarding use of the common area. However, developers often neglect to assist the board by preparing proposed rules and regulations for adoption by the board. When rules are adopted, they are often not distributed or otherwise adequately communicated to the unit owners, thus jeopardizing their enforceability and subjecting the developer to the wrath of angry homeowners.

Some legal documents do not provide for their own amendment, and too many documents provide for amendments or easement grants only if the signatures of all or practically all of the homeowners are placed on the instrument to be recorded. It is practically impossible to obtain written consent of all of the unit owners on any proposed action. Far preferable is a requirement that the vote or written consent of 51 to 75 percent of the members is adequate to permit amendments and easement conveyances. This eases administration of the association, and, in multiphased condominium projects, it facilitates the development of annexable property. The declaration also should provide that it may be amended by a written, recorded instrument signed by two officers of the association, which certifies that the requisite majority of the members has consented to the amendment or to the proposed easement grant.

Maintenance and Insurance Clauses

The developer often fails to analyze and allocate the responsibilities for maintenance and insurance between the unit owners and the association. Significant problems develop if the legal documents are unclear and ambiguous on these points or do not conform with local law. Moreover, few documents specify the level of maintenance of common areas. The absence of maintenance standards is the source of later conflicts and misunderstandings.

Rights of the Owners

All legal documents should provide for enforcement rights in the individual homeowners as well as in the association. The legal documents also should provide, to the extent authorized under local law, for the recovery of attorneys' fees by the prevailing party in the event that a lawsuit is filed to enforce the provisions of the management documents. Such rights are vital to the success of the project and to the goal of leaving self-reliant homeowners to manage their own affairs.

In all cases, the documents should be as flexible as possible so they will not be outdated when the homeowners assume control of the association.

Marketing the Development and the Association

Many developers are paranoid where associations are concerned and delay their formation. Developers find it difficult to sell the value of the association to prospective purchasers. For marketing and other reasons, they are reluctant to point out the purchasers' responsibilities for the ongoing operation of the association.

Unit owner apathy is a major problem faced by associations. The developer must not present the condominium project as a form of maintenance-free property ownership that has none of the normal responsibilities of homeownership. On the contrary, each homeowner owes a duty to the association to become involved in its affairs. The sales force should stress the advantage of the association as a vehicle through which the nature and character of the project will be preserved.

In addition, sales and marketing personnel working for the developer usually do not have adequate understanding of associations. Yet the association must be sold by them to unsophisticated purchasers as a part of the package along with the home and the common amenities. The failure to explain how and why the association was created is the cause of subsequent liabilities for negligent or willful misrepresentations. Copies of the legal documents, together with an easily understood disclosure brochure, should be given to the prospective purchasers before the sale so that serious misunderstandings may be avoided.

It is always difficult for the developer to control sales personnel, particularly if the salespeople are employees of the developer's broker–agent and not the developer's direct employees. The development team should try to ensure that the sales force understands the purpose and effect of the homeowners' association and the documents creating the association. The more the seller and purchasers understand about the legal documents and their responsibilities in connection with the association, the greater the chances are that the community will succeed.

Other problems may arise during the marketing phase that may later plague the association. For example, many developers fail to control speculators and investors adequately. Unless at least 80 percent of the homes in a development are owner-occupied, the developer runs the risk that permanent mortgage financing may not be available because FHLMC and FNMA will be reluctant to purchase loans in the development. The existence of "for lease" or "for sale" signs in the windows of the first homes sold can seriously hamper the developer's continuing sales. Furthermore, nonresident homeowners may not be as responsive to the needs of the development or the association as resident homeowners.

Another problem is the attempt of some developers to change the specific project in the middle of the sales program. Such a change, such as the addition or deletion of an age restriction, can result in substantial developer liability to those individuals who purchased their homes before the change. Express or implied promises contained in the development documents concerning land use restrictions are generally enforced by the courts.

Many developers fail even to recognize the existence of the association until they are ready to turn over the association to the homeowners. The turnover date generally occurs when the developer loses voting control of the association. A developer recently declared that he was ready to turn over the association to the homeowners and to commence assessment collections. It was disconcerting to learn not only that the last home in the development had been sold, but also that the sale had been consummated more than one year previously.

An unincorporated association exists from the date on which the first home is sold. An incorporated association, on the other hand, exists from the date on which the articles of incorporation are filed. Formation of the association is only the first step in carrying out the responsibilities of the developer. After that point, many developers fail to hold required regular meetings, they fail to enter into contracts with third parties on behalf of the association, they fail to maintain separate books and records for the association, they fail to file tax returns and other mandatory filings with governmental agencies, and they fail to educate the homeowners who must operate the association after the developer has left the scene.

Many developers also fail to convey in a timely manner the common area to the association, free of mechanic's liens, even when they are required to do so by the legal documents. If the association will own any of the common area in fee simple, then it usually should be conveyed by grant (or warranty) deed to the association, before the sale of the first unit in that phase of development. This action makes the lenders happy, because a proportionate value of the common area is usually included in the value of each home for purposes of loan appraisal.

Each developer should furnish the association with a policy of title insurance, reflecting lien-free title to any common area it owns. A title insurance policy covering a parcel of common area property usually can be obtained for a nominal premium with a maximum liability of about $1000. Secondary mortgage market agencies, such as FNMA and VA, require such assurance of title in the association.

The development team should set realistic dates for the completion of common area amenities. Although the common amenities need not be completed at the time of conveyance of the first home, completion of the facilities should be guaranteed within a reasonable period of time following conveyance of the land to the association. The development team should arrange to make building plans available to the association with respect to any improvements constructed on the common areas.

Developer's Responsibility for Assessments

A recurring problem during the transition stage is the failure of developers to commence and enforce the collection of assessments at an early stage during the development. The developer may choose to subsidize the operating portion of the association's budget during the initial stages in accordance with local law, because the developer probably can accomplish the necessary tasks at a lower cost than the association can. However, at least the reserves should be collected from all homeowners. (The developer should pay its pro rata share of assessments while it owns any unsold lots in the particular phase of development.) Lowballing and highballing of assessments as a marketing technique will cause problems when the homeowners belatedly become aware of the true operating costs.

Developer's Representatives on the Board

Many developers fail to recognize the fiduciary position of the representatives on the board of directors of the association. Each representative of the developer wears two hats, one as an employee of the developer and one as a member of the governing body of the association. These responsibilities frequently conflict with each other. The developer's failure to recognize the conflicts of interest is the main cause of later liabilities. The developer's representatives may not vote for resolutions benefiting the developer's interests to the detriment of either the association or the unit owners.

The developer should therefore avoid self-dealing in entering into sweetheart contracts and leases on behalf of the association. Hence, the developer should avoid contracts with his or her own subsidiaries or affiliates and should always refuse kickbacks. The developer should ask himself or herself: Is the contract commercially reasonable? Is the contract negotiated at arm's length?

INTERNAL MANAGEMENT—PERSONAL LIABILITY TO CONTRACTORS

Several attempts at an analysis of the potential liability of unit owners and their boards both on contracts and for damages by negligence or otherwise to third parties and other unit owners have appeared in print. But there is little really pertinent advice available to unit owners concerning the means of protecting themselves, outside of some general suggestions to seek adequate hazard and liability insurance, which will be discussed later in this chapter. The source of and protection against liability may be identified as follows.

Contracts by a Unit Owner to Make Internal Repairs within a Unit

The declaration or bylaws should provide that a unit owner bears full personal responsibility for his or her own unit repairs, and that neither the board nor other unit owners or their interests in common elements are in any case responsible or assessable for nonpayment. The declaration should provide (if not already in the statute) that in no case shall any lien ever exist against the common elements. Recording of the declaration and bylaws should constitute adequate notice to all persons of these limitations.

Contracts Made by the Board in Behalf of the Condominium

It would appear that in most situations the board is absolved from personal responsibility if the condominium statute clearly intends that they act merely as agents. But this is not adequate protection. A specific written statement should be contained in the bylaws to this effect, and a statement disclaiming all personal liability for nonperformance should be included in all contracts executed by the board in behalf of the condominium owners. In addition, and just as important, specific insulation from contractual liability should be given to unit owners in cases where an interim corporation is not used. This could be done by a contractual clause excluding all liability (as some writers have implied is necessary), but the effect probably would be that no major work would be done under contract by any sane contractor dealing with the condominium. Instead, a limited liability clause along the following lines is suggested:

> There shall be no personal liability by any unit owners or board of managers, except that the common charges shall constitute a trust fund for and until payment of the obligation in the event of a default in payments; and in no case shall any lien be created or exist against the common elements, any unit, or interest in common elements.

Most contractors who have been asked to do work for condominiums indicate that they do not understand the consequences of state laws or the management documents. It is suggested that the above recommendations may offer some solution to their problems.

Consideration should be given to regular use by management of a stamp and stamp pad containing a simple clause, such as "Subject to bylaws and declaration" or some other clause pertinent to the above problems, which will serve to insulate unit owners, the board of managers, and common elements.

INSURING UNIT OWNERS AND THE BOARD

Separate or Package Policies

Condominium ownership involves unique insurable risks. Special consideration must be given to insurance problems that might be created needlessly either by the failure to provide adequate protection for all aspects of ownership, separate or co-owned, or special coverage for board members.

Nearly every condominium regime has taken a package-type policy covering at least property hazard in addition to personal liability of the unit owners resulting from their ownership of the common elements. A chief error committed in such policies is a confusion about the named insured. For example, the properly named insured for a fire policy might be inadvertently applied overall on the package policy, without clarification, even though, as shall be known, the named insureds on a liability policy should be different. While there is no reason why a package policy cannot be adopted adequately for a condominium, it should be made up of two separate policies serving two separate purposes.

Except in full disclosure states, the individual unit owner and his or her mortgagee are given a certificate of insurance, while the policy itself is filed with the board. Such a situation leads to the uniform assumption by the unit owner that there is adequate coverage.

Because package policies provide economy and are in almost universal use, this discussion describes what such policies and riders covering condominiums should specifically contain to provide for hazard and liability insurance. In any event, the policy should be written by an insurance carrier that is acceptable to the secondary mortgage market. If possible, the company should have a very high rating by A. M. Best Company, Inc. (XI or better in Best's financial category).

Named Insured—Hazard Part

It is important for the hazard portion of the policy to name as the insured the board or association of managers, wherever the board has the obligation to rebuild, repair, or restore unit and co-owned premises in the event of a casualty. The statute, declaration, and bylaws should state the terms of relationship between the board and unit owners with respect to the disposition of insurance proceeds on such occurrence; however, it would be clearer to expressly name in the policy, as additional insureds, all of the unit owners. The secondary mortgage market prefers that the name of the insured be set forth substantially as follows:

> Association of owners of the _____ Condominium for use
> and benefit of the individual owners (designated by name if required by law).

It would seem best, in order to avoid technical reservations for payment by the insurance company, that contractual relationships between the board and unit owners not be spelled out in the policy through the use of such words as *agent* or *trustee*. An exception is those cases in which there is an independent insurance trustee who should be covered by a special endorsement providing for payover to the trustee. In this situation, a separate insurance trustee agreement should exist between the board and the trustee (usually not changeable without mortgagee permission). The specific contract terms do not belong in the policy.

Note that it is customary, because of board obligation to rebuild, to fully blanket all property made up of units and common elements into one policy, rather than to separate the units and common elements for hazard insurance purposes. However, the difficulty with this approach is that various contents within the unit (e.g., personal property, upgrades in carpeting and drapes, etc.) must be separately scheduled in separate unit owner policies, unless arrangements are made for individualized endorsements to the master policy.

The hazard policy should be written to cover 100 percent of the insurable value (based upon full replacement cost) of the property covered following partial or total damage. Lenders frequently require that the amount of the insurance must equal or exceed the aggregate mortgage amounts (presumed to be 80 percent of the appraised valuation of the project) in the project. However, in areas of the country where the value of the land exceeds 20 percent of the value of the project, this requirement may result in over-insuring the project and unnecessary costs. Thus, the lenders should be encouraged to accept full replacement guarantees for the insured improvements (i.e., excepting land, foundation, and excavation), and such guarantees are acceptable to the agencies in the secondary mortgage market.

The association should also obtain a single-entity blanket insurance policy rather than a "bare walls" blanket policy. A single-entity policy insures fixtures (regardless of whether they are part of the common elements), building service equipment and supplies, and other personal property owned by the association. As might be expected, a bare walls policy is not as comprehensive as a single-entity policy. Room-dividing walls should be covered in all policies, as may not be the case with a bare wall definition covering only the perimeter of a unit.

Named Insured—Liability Part

That part of the package policy covering liability should name the following as insured:

1. The board of managers
2. Each unit owner, to cover his or her liability as co-owner

Because of the general refusal of insurance companies to issue liability policies that cover both occurrences in units and in common areas together, the liability part of the package policy covers only responsibility for events that take place in common elements. Individual unit owners usually must obtain separate liability policies covering occurrences within their own units. They should secure binders for unit coverage before taking title.

Insurance companies like to limit board coverage to liability incurred during the time the members are acting within the scope of their duties. Preferably, the coverage should include activities believed to have been done in good faith within such scope.

Essential Condominium Endorsements

Condominium management should consider it wise not to accept or continue any package policies that have not provided all-risk protection with any or all of the following endorsements, which are felt to be essential:

1. A unit owner's insurance for his or her personal property sometimes overlaps with the association's blanket policy. If the association's policy comes into contribution with the owner's policy, then the association's policy could be reduced by the overlap. Separate insurance obtained by any unit owner should not reduce the insurance in the package policy, so the association's policy should be written to not be brought into contribution with insurance of the unit owners or their mortgagees.

2. Adequate written notice to the named insureds (as well as primary mortgagees) should be given before any cancellation can take final effect. Thirty days' notice should be the minimum, although many insurance companies are more easily convinced that it is acceptable to provide ten days' notice.

3. The insurance company should waive its right of subrogation against any unit owner, including members of his or her household and the board of directors because they are the true beneficiaries of the insurance. For example, if a unit owner were to negligently start a fire that destroyed a portion of the project over which the association had insurance, then the waiver of subrogation would preclude the carrier from suing the unit owner for the loss. This clause takes on an additional urgency if bank or government officials or other non-unit-owners serve on the board regularly or under specific conditions.

4. The insurance should not be prejudiced by any act or negligence of any insured or other person or firm (including employees and managing agent) when such an act or neglect was beyond the control and knowledge of the board.

5. When the state law permits, the insurance company should waive its right to repair fire damage or other destruction where the condominium owners elect to terminate the regime because of the damage.

6. Fire and other hazard coverage for buildings should include all condominium real property (e.g., steam boilers) and personal property used in connection therewith. (If some kinds of personal property, such as decorative flower pots and lamps, are not considered

within the meaning of such terminology under state law, an additional property endorsement is essential.)

7. Settlements can be delayed because of disputes between owners of damaged units. Therefore, regardless of the naming of an insurance trustee other than the board, all losses under the package policy should be adjusted by the board (assuming there is no restriction in any mortgagee loss-payable clause).

8. If the project is in an area designated by HUD as a flood zone, then the association should insure against damage that may be caused by flood. This insurance should be in the form of a blanket policy insuring all of the common property.

9. Regardless of a provision for an insurance trustee to receive claims and payout, small losses should be paid directly to the board, in order to avoid delay and needless red tape. Some policies provide for direct payment of claims not exceeding $20,000. Such a figure should be evaluated on the basis of the size of the particular condominium.

10. In some cases, it is not in the best interest of the members to repair the loss, and the association may decide to take a cash settlement to be used for some other purposes. The policy should contain a waiver of the right of the insurer to require reconstruction, so long as a requisite percentage of the unit owners and their mortgagees elect not to reconstruct.

11. Cross-claims by coinsured unit owners for damages against the board or other unit owners should be permitted in the liability portion of the policy. (Thus, an individual owner injured in common areas could collect on the basis of some negligence of the board that was the causative factor.)

12. Deductibles can be shared by all of the owners pro rata or paid solely by the owners of the damaged units. Deductibles can be charged on a per-occurrence basis or on a per-item basis. The board should determine who should be responsible for payment and how the deductible should be applied to losses.

13. The association should attempt to obtain, where available, an agreed-amount endorsement and an inflation-guard endorsement. If the condominium is subject to a construction code provision that would become operative after partial damage to the building, then the association should obtain construction code endorsements to protect against the risk that rebuilding costs are excessive.

14. The association board also should consider such additional endorsements as host liquor liability, comprehensive automobile liability,

personal injury (libel, slander, false arrest, etc.), medical payments, cross liability (where one unit owner sues another for injury on the common elements), garage keepers' liability, watercraft liability, umbrella liability, products liability, and contractual liability, as applicable.

Other Condominium Policies

The nature of extended coverage in the package policy should be evaluated thoroughly even though it is more of a general insurance problem than a condominium problem.

The condominium that employes service workers must comply with state workers' compensation requirements and may need an adequate policy applicable to such purpose.

It would seem wise to provide fidelity bonds covering association officers and directors, the managing agent, and any other employees who should be bonded, and naming the association as an obligee. A reasonable amount of coverage recommended is the estimated maximum of funds, including reserves, in the custody of the association or the managing agent at any given time. A good rule of thumb is an amount equal to three months' aggregate assessments on all units plus reserves. If the board acts as an insurance trustee, the amount of the bond should be reevaluated before receipt of funds. The bond should contain a waiver by the insurer of all defenses based on the exclusion of persons serving without compensation.

If condominium employees ordinarily will operate automobiles in the course of their employment, adequate insurance coverage should be either tacked on to other policies or separately provided, in accordance with local practice and laws.

The Insurance Trustee

Where an insurance trustee is required, it is common practice for the primary institutional lender to serve in such capacity. However, under state laws, certain savings institutions are barred from so acting, thus creating the problem of the selection of an alternative trustee. Usually, the alternative choice is another institutional lender or the board of directors of the association. In any event, the insurance trustee should have exclusive authority to negotiate losses with the carrier on behalf of all interested parties.

Individual Policies Held by the Unit Owner

With the exception of personal property owned entirely by a unit owner, the blanket provisions of the package policy taken by the board ordinarily will cover protection of both the unit and the undivided interest in common areas. There are at least three problems posed by this relationship:

1. An individual personal property (contents) hazard policy should be obtained by each unit owner.

2. Additional or separate hazard policies for the unit are unnecessary, except as special extensions of the blanket policy covering expensive additions to the real estate and other property within the coverage of the master policy. In some states, it may be possible to increase individual maintenance charges caused by the need for additional insurance on some units; in others, some method of direct payment by the unit owner to the insurance company might be found, so as to avoid assessment limitations otherwise strictly based on the percentage of common elements owned by a particular unit owner.

3. Notice of structural or physical changes within units and bylaw requirements for permission to make such changes are essential; otherwise, coinsurance requirements might jeopardize claims by limiting recovery. The master policy should not be invalidated by the failure of the board to comply with percentage requirements of coinsurance clauses.

An individual comprehensive liability policy is essential for each unit owner because of the custom of not including such coverage in the master package policy. However, liability for co-owned property is generally included in the overall policy and need not be insured against in the unit owner's policy.

It would appear wise to use the same insurance company that has written the master policy on all individual policies. This would avoid intercompany feuding with respect to definitions or the extent of policy coverage.

Novel Policies Needed—Maintenance and Living Expenses

Insurance companies should formulate new policies or endorsements to cover several eventualities rarely covered in the policies heretofore discussed.

A unit owner should be insured for some portion of his or her living costs that result from the destruction of his or her premises and that continue until such time as his or her unit is either restored or rebuilt by the board. Such destruction may be caused by any of the hazards previously discussed or by termite infestation, which usually affects an entire building. Such insurance should also cover maintenance expenses payable during that time, unless the bylaws provide for their waiver during such periods.

The condominium regime itself should determine the need for and the availability of common charges insurance to cover defaults by unit owners in residence and to provide for charges attributable to units that have been abandoned. Rent insurance is well established in commercial rental practice, and this concept can be extended to the condominium. Rent insurance policies generally cover one year of rentals, and the same coverage might be made applicable to unpaid or uncollected common charges for a similar period.

Theft insurance should be added to the overall package policy taken by the board. Sponsors often neglect adding such insurance, in order to cut projections of maintenance charges. In addition, each unit owner should consider adding such coverage to his or her own personal property hazard insurance.

Of course, the need for or practicality of such additional forms of insurance depends on the cost and availability of policies. Unfortunately, most insurance companies and state insurance departments have given little thought to special condominium problems. But the growth of condominium ownership will make this lack of attention a rather uneconomic attitude and, therefore, will force all those concerned to give special consideration to condominium insurance problems.

NONINSURANCE PROTECTION FOR UNIT OWNERS

Another typical method used in cutting cost projections is the elimination by the sponsor of any contingency fund covering both unit owner arrears in maintenance payments and unit owner damages either to the common elements or their own units.

Many sets of declarations or bylaws provide that no structural changes may be made internally by unit owners without the board's consent. Some go beyond the restriction and only allow the board to make applications to local building departments for permission to make any structural addition, alteration, or improvement to units wherever such government permits are required. But such rules will not take care of the immediate monetary needs arising in situations where a unit has been substantially damaged either intentionally or as a result of an inordinate lack of maintenance and repair with the result that its own saleability and the market value of surrounding units are seriously jeopardized.

It is recommended that an initial reserve or security fund be established to self-insure against the effects of such damages. The right of the board to dip into the fund and to surcharge individual abusive owners would have salutary effects, especially if the security deposit is returnable in full to each unit owner upon termination of his or her ownership or if it is deposited in an interest-bearing account with all interest credited individually.

The custom in some condominiums of providing for the prepayment of common charges two or three months in advance is not adequate for the above purpose. An initial deposit by all new owners of at least three months' common charges for security purposes would provide an immediate warning to all new owners of their obligations to the other owners. The overall fund also would provide immediate reserve funds for unforeseen contingencies, and it should be so represented with clarity to purchasers. But a high-percentage vote by owners should be required before such funds could be directed from their essential security purpose or could be borrowed subject to repayment through increasing maintenance assessments.

All prepaid or reserve funds should be established as the individually owned and so allocated monies of unit owners in a form as required to avoid characterization as association income.

Regardless of the existence of a willing buyer on resale by a unit owner, the board always should inspect the unit for unnecessary or intentional damages and violations of the use restrictions in the declaration, bylaws, or house rules. Security deposits should be returned, subject to reductions for damages and to the use of the retained funds in making possible repairs.

One of the great dangers in condominium ownership is the resale of deteriorated units to buyers who will not restore the premises, while the other owners remain either oblivious or unconcerned about the condition of the interior of the premises. People tend to worry more about the outside appearance of the neighboring houses and seem stunned when units are occasionally resold far below the market price. Such occurrences, even though they may be somewhat rare, can have a massive deteriorating effect on the resale value of other, well-kept units.

Moreover, such contingency funds could be made available when an inspection before a foreclosure, by either a bank or other lienor, discloses the inattentiveness to physical maintenance that is typical of many distressed owners. Lenders will fight any obligation on their part to make repairs to premises damaged by mortgages. Regardless of the bank's gain derived from the condominium regime's own repairs, the right to repair at such time should be reserved in the condominium's board for the benefit of the other unit owners who will be indirectly aided by the increased price that the unit will bring, and who understandably might be wary of persons who are of a character to be attracted by shoddy premises, since the existing unit owners will have to assume common responsibility with them.

LEASING RESTRICTIONS

It is advisable to require all leases of units to be in writing and to be subject to the declaration and bylaws. Tenants do not have the same pride of ownership as do homeowners, so a natural antagonism has developed over the years between the two types of occupants. If the number of tenants in a condominium project exceeds 20 percent of the occupants, problems usually begin to surface. These problems are exacerbated when the tenancy is transient in nature.

In recognition of this problem, three members of the task force of secondary mortgage agencies (VA, FHA, and FNMA) agreed that unit owners should be prohibited from leasing their units for an initial term of less than thirty days. However, it is usually inappropriate to require such leases to have initial terms of longer than six months.

APPROVAL OF UNIT TRANSFERS

Because of the traditional fear on the part of legislators regarding unreasonable restraints on free transfer of ownership that may result from an unlimited longevity of general powers to approve new owners in the future, some condominium statutes have been explicit in defining the limits imposed on the board's right to approve new owners. In other cases, the laws either are vague on the subject or employ "iffy" language that is being tested by litigation. For example, a New Jersey statute, creating a rebuttable presumption of unconscionability regarding provisions in master deeds and bylaws giving the developer or the association a right of first refusal to buy a condominium upon resale, was recently upheld by the state supreme court. Nevertheless, it is fairly safe to say that a well-drafted and carefully exercised right of first refusal in the board will generally satisfy statutory limitations in the overwhelming number of states. Although a large number of condominiums now in operation adopt the right of first refusal as the form of new owner approval to be used by the board, the use of this device is dwindling in new condominium projects. In some situations, the board has the alternative of purchasing a unit itself at the best offer presented or obtaining a different buyer on the same terms. A usual exception to requirements for any form of approval or first refusal is the heir or devisee who takes by will or intestacy. However, it is customary to retain restrictions in the case of mere inter vivos gifts (that is, those made during the lifetime of the unit owner).

It is disturbing to find that in a large number of condominiums the residents hold mistaken beliefs concerning restrictions on the transfer of units. The usual error consists of believing that the approval of the board was required rather than that notice of the intended sale subject to the right of first refusal or of buyer substitution must be given by the unit owner to the board before any sale could be made. Managing agents easily delude unit owners who made inquiry, through the use of such language as, "Well, you can sell after you get the board's approval." The lower the income levels, the easier such delusion appears to be. This result may stem from the fact that many purchasers do not employ attorneys and that managing agents sometimes seek to promote their own interests by obtaining brokerage commissions on sales arranged through their efforts.

The trend of the case law is to construe provisions containing rights of first refusal very strictly, and community associations may be liable for heavy punitive damages if the right is discriminatorily exercised. In fact, the task force of the secondary market agencies (VA, FHA, FNMA, and FHLMC) published a report in December of 1980, which said that the agencies will not involve themselves in any condominium project where the right of a unit owner to freely sell or rent his or her unit is subject to any right of first refusal or similar restriction.

BOARD OF MANAGERS

Qualifications of Board Members

Care should be exercised in the selection of board members. Certain types of persons are most undesirable in such positions. For example, the hothead types can cause a good deal of trouble and annoyance for unit owners. Such individuals can be seen placing stickers on every car parked in guest parking areas warning against constant parking, even though the cars involved were not owned by persons parking repeatedly in those areas. However, since the unit owners have control over the selection of board members, it is possible for them to demonstrate their dissatisfaction with such action at the next owners' meeting by replacing the objectionable board member, and this is considerably more than owners of single-family homes can do if they are unfortunate enough to have a cantankerous neighbor who believes he or she owns the street in front of his or her house and expresses displeasure with cars parked there, sometimes by going to such lengths as to deflate the tires.

Experience indicates that business executives and other professionals, such as lawyers and accountants, make effective board members, although mere occupation does not mean automatic infallibility. In one case, the president of the board, an attorney, defied the board's own counsel, sent out a notice and proxy to unit owners pertaining to an important meeting, and came close to obtaining a vote that would automatically have been cause for foreclosure by every mortgagee holding a mortgage on the condominium. Only the most spirited last-moment argument persuaded the president to withdraw his plan, which he had very forcefully convinced the other board members that they should follow.

Voting

The tendency toward equal-weight voting is much stronger in the condominium than in cooperatives. In this connection, the usual single-vote-per-resident rule in homeowner associations may have been influential.

There is much discussion to the effect that responsibility for higher carrying charges should carry greater weight in any decision making that is largely concerned with lifting those charges. On the other hand, where carrying charges are not equated with unit costs, there would be less reason for weighted voting on many decisions, but the owner of a more expensive unit still has a greater financial interest in all decisions, regardless of whether they are for budget approval, restoration of damaged facilities, leasing of commercial facilities, or the selection of a managing agent. It would seem that equal voting is logical in many condominiums because the extent of cost differentials is not heavily disproportionate to voting interest. However, especially in luxury condominiums, purchasers of units whose costs are not even closely comparable to most other units should be wary of equal voting. This is even more true when several units are combined for one owner, or when the condominium is composed of middle-income apartment blocks interspersed with luxury townhouses.

In government-subsidized housing or other condominiums that deny or restrict profits arising from appreciation in value of the units on resale, there is less reason for weighted voting.

Drafters of condominium documents usually provide for voting rights based on the percentage interest held in common elements or on one vote per unit owned. Bylaws then provide for different minimum percentages of votes that are necessary for ordinary or special decisions. The statutes themselves also generally superimpose minimum vote requirements for major decisions, such as amending bylaws or declaration, voting to terminate the regime, and important questions involving the disposition of insurance proceeds. Occasionally, a statute will evidence legislative concern for critical decisions by requiring that a specific percentage of both unit owners and owners of common interests be represented in the voting. Regardless of state law, the latter type of requirement might be considered for bylaw adoption.

Voting by unit owners, with the exception of requirements of statute or bylaws for critical decisions, is principally concerned with the election of a board of directors. Such election ordinarily takes place at an annual meeting.

Conducting the Annual Meeting—The First Meeting

The primary lender should insist that the developer (or his or her nominee for unsold units) undertake to call the first meeting of unit owners. Even more appropriately, the specific obligation to summon the owners initially and the conditions therefore should be inserted in the management agreement with any agent who contracts with the controlling sponsor to service the condominium.

Unfortunately, most bylaws vacillate with respect to the first meeting, leaving it almost up to the mere discretion of the sponsor. Stating that a specific number of owners are entitled to call a meeting leaves the matter up in the air. Instead, specific requirements that set responsibility for calling the meeting should be set forth in the bylaws, as for example:

1. That the managing agent (or developer) shall give notice of an annual meeting on the premises of the condominium at least ten days after 25 percent of the units are occupied by unit owners.
2. Regardless of the other conditions for calling a meeting, the sponsor must summon owners to such meeting at least by the end of six months following the date on which the first unit owner is given title and possession.

The notice of such meeting should specify its chief purpose—the election of a board of directors.

In most cases, developers provide for continued control or representation with respect to the board, at least for that period when units remain unsold. While developer representation is reasonable for unsold or controlled units, the unit owners should be free of any developer veto once they represent 51 percent of all sold and occupied units. However, one of the worst failures in developer disclosure in many instances has been failure to disclose adequately the extent and conditions of developer control after units are conveyed.

The Community Associations Institute (CAI) is a national nonprofit organization that was formed in 1973 to assist in the creation and operation of community association (condominiums, stock cooperatives, homeowners' associations on PUDs, etc.). GAP Report No. 3 is an in-depth report on transition from developer control published by CAI in 1978. This report lists five basic approaches to the evolutionary process of shifting control of the association from the developer to the unit owners:

1. Add one or more unit owners to the board of directors at specified levels of sales.
2. Use an interim or advisory board or committee of unit owners to work with the developer-controlled board to make decisions.
3. Transfer the full board control to the unit owners and reserve to the developer a review and approval (veto) power over certain basic types of action.

4. Use a weighted voting approach in which the developer has a weighted vote (usually three votes for each unit owned) for each unsold unit.
5. Use some combination of the above.

Notice of Meeting

The occasional practice of meeting notice requirements by just posting signs in elevators or bulletin boards should not be accepted as a substitute for actual notice by mail. Perhaps the best method of giving notice is personal delivery to each owner, with a short conversation dealing with the need for the unit owner's full participation in the affairs of the condominium. In addition, it may be pointed out that attendance can be a good way for owners to get to know their neighbors better.

It is possible that subjects in which unit owners have an interest but of which they are given no notice might be discussed at the meeting, if the notice is permitted to include such language as, "and such other business which will be brought before the membership."

Every attempt should be made to give notice of meetings that are informative. Notices should include:

1. The date, time, and place of the meeting (preferably the same each year, so that owners can plan to attend).
2. The specific subjects to be voted on (with no general clauses).
3. The specific subjects to be discussed, as far as they are known, with allowance made for topics to be introduced by members present.

If it is necessary to vote on important topics that do not specifically pertain to the subject of the specific notice, then it would be better to consider calling a special meeting for this purpose rather than merely to circulate petitions. In the latter case, it is less likely that full discussion will be available. Such problems should not be too bothersome, because it is the board and not the membership that will supervise immediate operations.

It has become customary in many condominiums to give ten days' notice of meetings to unit owners. If this is so, then mailings should be sent twelve days before the date of the meeting, in order to avoid all argument about a full ten days' notice. Some bylaws prohibit a long period of notice because of the possibility that the matter will be forgotten by unit owners. Where ten days' notice is required, it might be good practice to limit notice to a mailing made fifteen or eighteen days before the meeting.

Meeting are usually called for the same date as the original organizational meeting. But this date can sometimes be a problem. The sponsor may have used an initial date in the summer or around holidays when attendance could be expected to be poor. If such a date had been used, consideration should be given to a new date. Most people seem to be available during periods when the weather is temperate and when major holidays do not occur. In many parts of the United States, October 1 seems as good a date as any for the annual meeting.

Unit owners seem to dislike weekend meetings, and many prefer a day early in the week, usually Tuesday at 8:00 P.M.

Though the secretary of the board will be responsible for transmitting notice, the preparation of the notice and actual notification in many instances will probably be done by a managing agent, under the secretary's general direction.

Annual Meeting Agenda

Sometimes bylaws specify the agenda to be followed at annual or special meetings, and sometimes the matter is left largely to the discretion of the board or its president. In any event, a recommended procedure, based on actual practice might be as follows:

1. Roll call of unit owners present.
2. Submission by the secretary of proof of notice of the meeting or waivers by members of such notice.
3. Reading or waiver of reading of the minutes of the preceding meeting.
4. Financial and business reports of the managing agent and board members.
5. Reports of committees of board members or general membership.
6. Election of election supervisors.
7. Election of the board (when such must take place).
8. Business unfinished and postponed from the previous meeting.
9. New business.

Number and Term of Board Members

The board should consist of any uneven number of members in order to forestall, as far as possible, the likelihood of deadlocks. The most common and manageable number is five directors, and other unit owners should be encouraged to get involved in the association operations by serving on committees established by the board.

Some condominiums provide for new elections to fill all vacancies annually. Other bylaws provide for three-, two-, and one-year terms for different members initially. The latter formula does have the merit of permitting continuity of seasoned members. But it also permits a developer to extend control and influence into future years of operation through the device of appointing his or her representative to the longer term. Perhaps the answer might be a bylaw provision that limits all board member terms to one year until such time as the bona fide resident unit owners have taken title to more than half of the units (or more than half of the common interests) whereupon they will possess a voting majority.

Ample provision is usually made for filling board vacancies by the calling of a special meeting. But care should be exercised that the time allowed will give sufficient opportunity for the unit owners to express their preferences and opinions.

Many bylaws provide for the automatic removal of a board member at such time as he ceases to be a unit owner. Although there is generally some provision for the removal of members of the board by unit owners for "cause," it is questionable whether or not this will be adequate as far as those board members are concerned who have leased their units for extensive periods or those who have contracted to sell units a substantial time in advance of conveyance of title.

Quorums

Most bylaws specify the number of board members who must be present personally (usually three out of five) in order to constitute a quorum at annual meetings and at board meetings. It would seem that board decisions should be based on a majority of the required quorum. Many bylaws refer to decisions of the board without making any mention of the effect of votes by the board that are not unanimous.

Many bylaws are completely silent on the quorum of unit owners necessary for a valid board election. A quorum for the election of the board should be the presence in person or by proxy of no fewer than 25 percent nor more than 50 percent of the total voting power of the association. If a quorum is not present at a meeting of the members, then those present should be authorized to adjourn the meeting in order to acquire the requisite quorum.

CHECKLIST FOR CONDOMINIUM MANAGEMENT AGREEMENT

The following basic subject matter should be covered by or at least considered for inclusion in the original management agreements by the condominium board and the proposed managing agent. If the developer negotiated or controlled negotiations for the original contract, the board may wish to appoint a committee to review its adequacy, and in that case, too, the outline shown below might serve as a helpful initial checklist.

1. The contract should state explicitly just what the managing agent is supposed to manage. He or she should be given copies of the building plans, all warranties, the initial association budget, all management documents, and all tax records of the association. Is it just the commonly used areas or the restricted common areas as well? In many agreements, there appears to be a fear of declaring the agent as the manager of the entire property, subject to the rights of unit owners as stated in the declaration, bylaws, and house rules. Yet the managing agent is only an agent employed by the board on behalf of all of the unit owners; therefore, the agreement should not read as if the owners were giving up ownership in hiring an agent.

2. The managing agent may reasonably be expected to properly require an agreement making him or her the exclusive managing agent for the property. Unless an onsite permanent employee of the association is hired, the manager clearly should be hired as an agent of the association, and no employment relationship should be established.

3. The agreement should specify how, when, and by whom instructions are to be given to the managing agent. Generally, one or more specific board officers are authorized to instruct the agent. When no such officer is available, a deputy should be empowered to make emergency decisions. When no major emergency exists, the agent should await the return of the board official who has been properly designated to instruct the agent.

4. The managing agent's functions should be differentiated and enumerated. The agreement should specify that the agent will make himself or herself available at all reasonable times and for whatever periods necessary to properly fulfill his or her management duties, including board meetings, inspecting the property, supervising emergency repairs, collecting common charges, and hearing and disposing of complaints. This is particularly important if no resident agent is to be employed. The question of whether complaints by unit owners relative to common areas go to the board or directly to the agent should be answered in the agreement.

5. The term of the agreement, the conditions for accelerating the termination of the agreement, and the notice, if any, required for its renewal should be specified. Both the managing agent's and the selling agent's functions might be treated separately in the agreement, but it is customary for the same firm to act in both capacities. Commissions on initial sales and on resales should be set forth in detail, including the possibility of splitting commissions with other brokers and the consequent effect on selling com-

mission limitations. Some managing agents also like to charge a fee (often $50 to $150) for processing applications of prospective purchasers on resales that are payable by the seller. If a full broker's commission will also be payable, the condominium board should give careful consideration to this additional charge to unit owners (and to the board when it must be the seller). It would not be advisable to appoint the agent as an exclusive selling agent for resales. In fact, a representation of full cooperation with the selling owners for required processing by management should be obtained, even when the agent will not receive a broker's commission.

6. The agreement should specifically authorize the agent to spend funds. All funds should be spent in accordance with budgetary projections, which should be presented to the board and unit owners at least sixty days before the beginning of the new fiscal year and preferably before the annual meeting. The managing agent should do nothing that will be at a substantial variance from the budget without express board approval. Any overrun of expenditures beyond the budget figures should promptly be brought to the attention of the board, whether or not authorized by the general language of the management agreement.

A limit may be placed on the authority of the managing agent to spend more than a specific amount for any one item of repair or alteration ($500 or $1000, perhaps) without the written authorization of the president or treasurer of the board. However, authority to make immediate emergency repairs involving the safety of the unit owners or their property or the termination or suspension of vital building services should not be conditioned on any limitation of the amount of expenditure or any unnecessary delay in securing written authority to act. Such emergency clause should not be subject to the condominium statute and declaration and bylaws for a most important (but regularly overlooked) reason. Provision for emergency action sometimes conflicts with the clause governing major destruction in the state statute or controlling documents. The latter usually require a special unit owner vote for rebuilding or restoration when a heavy percentage of the facilities has been destroyed.

It is a good idea to require the agent to segregate condominium funds by opening and maintaining a special bank account for the deposit of such funds, with monthly statements and canceled checks available for inspection by the board.

The contract also should require disclosure by the agent of instances where services or supplies are obtained from companies in which the agent has a financial interest. In addition, a specific clause should outlaw the receipt of commissions and require such payment of money to the agent to be treated as the reduction in price, with the possible exception of insurance commissions resulting from the placement of condominium insurance.

7. Monthly statements, supported by bills and disbursement vouchers, should be delivered to the board treasurer within a few days after the end of the month covered. Such a statement should include:

A. The amount collected during the previous month.

B. Disbursements during such period.

C. Compensation retained by the agent.

D. Funds withheld as reserves to cover later expenditures for which then-current income may be insufficient.

E. Any amounts expended beyond budgetary predictions, with an explanation of the causes and specification of the authorization for making such expenditures.

8. The agent should assist the association in preparing and filing all tax returns and other such forms in connection with unemployment insurance, franchise tax, income tax, social security, and disability benefits.

9. The agent's duties and pay in the event of major destruction of the condominium property, termination of the condominium, or total or partial condemnation of condominium premises are rarely included in management contracts. At the very least, the contract should provide that responsibilities arising from such contingencies shall be determined by the board of managers, including the right to cancel the management agreement, so long as there is no mere replacement.

10. The agent should agree to lecture the board and management on condominium management techniques and unit owner responsibilities at the first annual meeting, or at successive annual meetings at the request of the board, and to attend regular and special meetings of the members of the board on request.

11. It should be made the agent's duty to coordinate and supervise the moving in and out of unit owners and tenants, arranging dates, times, and procedures so as to minimize interference with or inconvenience of other owners.

12. The agent should be required to bill unit owners, commercial tenants, concessionaires, and others owing money to the condominium for common charges, rent, fees, and so forth. Where required by local law, the agent should be licensed to conduct such collection activities.

13. The agent must prepare and file all forms made necessary by the employment of personnel by the condominium, including unemployment insurance, withholding taxes, and social security taxes for permanent or temporary employees.

14. The agent should report changes in tax assessments to the board of

managers and the unit owners involved and should outline the proper procedures for appealing such determinations when requested to do so by unit owners and the board.

15. The agent should agree to maintain an inventory list of all condominium property, including furniture, gardening equipment and supplies, typewriters, and fuel, on the premises.

16. The agent should arrange for and acquire all permits required for ordinary operations, such as tree planting, garage licensing, and so forth.

17. At the direction of the board, the agent should send out all notices of unit owner and board meetings, tax deduction reports for unit owners, and all reports, recommendations, and other notices the board requests to be sent.

18. The agreement should include a statement of the terms of compensation for the agent. The amount might be conditioned on the number of units completed, the number occupied under title or lease, the number of onsite employees who must be hired and supervised, and similar factors.

19. Whether or not liability insurance in the name of the agent shall be carried by the condominium should be set out in the agreement.

20. The managing agent should be responsible for procuring and reviewing adequate hazard and liability insurance policies applicable to the common elements, even if one or all of such policies blanket unit owners as well. In the latter case, a provision for making the policies available for inspection by unit owners should be made where they receive only a certificate of insurance that incorporates the policy by reference. In addition, all other forms of insurance considered necessary should be recommended by such agent, who must continually review the adequacy of the coverage. The board should be apprised of insurance requirements and the existence of specific policies to cover the problem. Office and other direct employees of the agent who handle condominium funds should be bonded.

21. The management agency contract should specify the method to be employed during condominium contracting in order to assure limitation of liability on the part of unit owners and board members.

22. The agreement should provide for the suspension of the contract after a period of time deemed sufficient to test the performance of management. Contracts can be for one, two, three, or four years, but it is rare that a contract should bind the association for longer than one year. The developer should not bind the association to any management contract unless the association may terminate the contract, without penalty at any time after transfer of control, upon not more than ninety days' notice to the agent.

23.   The agent should maintain in careful fashion copies of all condominium documents, a library of the minutes of meetings, the books of account of the condominium, special account checkbooks relating to the condominium, correspondence relating to the condominium (including bids), applications to sell and buy units after the condominium is formed, a record of mortgagees holding mortgages on units, and similar records.

24.   Where service employees engaged by the managing agent also may be employed directly by unit owners, it may be useful to fix the charges, availability of such employees, and priorities for internal unit work. For example, owners with emergency problems could be serviced first, especially when the other units also might be imperiled. One of the difficulties in mixing luxury with middle-income units or middle-income with low-income units is the unfair and unequal use of service employees that may be resorted to by those able to pay more.

25.   The managing agent should process requests to exercise or waive the right of first refusal in accordance with current board policy. The review of prospective purchasers' backgrounds and references might be aided through the use of an application form. A prompt and convenient procedure should be adopted. The agent must represent that all financial and credit information, as far as possible, will be kept confidential, so as to avoid undue embarrassment of future unit owners and to attract more applicants for resales. The broader the agent's authority to pass on new owners, the more reasonable should be the use of applications containing detailed financial condition. But no matter what procedure is adopted, the time involved should not burden the seller or buyer needlessly. The contract also might require prompt reporting by the agent of resale requests to the board or a new-applicant committee of the board.

WASHING MACHINES, TV ANTENNAS, UNIT AIR-CONDITIONERS

Condominiums that supply washing machines and dryers in each unit, or adequate space and plumbing for their installation, will avoid the customary confusion that arises from community-used machines, especially where the machines are commonly owned by the unit owners instead of coin-operated by a concessionaire. Commonly used machines should be available in sufficient numbers to avoid delays by their users. Furthermore, the terms of any concession should require the provision of a minimum number of machines and should not leave the decision concerning that important matter up to the discretion of the concessionaire, expecting that he or she will furnish enough to meet the demand. When a large number of tenancies exists, greater abuse of the machines may be expected. And if the machines are coin-operated, there tends to be an even greater abuse by both owners and tenants.

Typically, failure to provide central air-conditioning and master TV antennas or cable TV service invariably results in the imposition of restrictions that can be distasteful to the unit owners. The sponsor and the selling agent should make clear to the buyers the limitations and responsibilities involved where these facilities are not furnished and should inform them of any additional maintenance charges that result from individual installations. At the very least, the method of installation, the materials used, and the approval of final work should be made subject to either the board's or the managing agent's acquiescence, in order to safeguard the appearance and safety of the condominium.

USE OF RECREATION AREAS

In a large number of condominiums already observed, there is a clustering of housing with the resulting open areas utilized for play or landscaping. Quite obviously, the amount of open space interwoven and surrounding highrise condominiums often exceeds similar areas set aside for the typical tenanted buildings in the immediate vicinity.

Play areas for children, easily visible from individual units, generally are preferred by owners. The greatest hesitation on the part of prospective buyers has resulted from parklike or woodland allocations of space in the condominium development, probably because many city and suburban dwellers are apprehensive about open areas with concern for their children. Time seems to bring about an adjustment to and realization of the desirability and advantages of such land use. It may be advisable for management to initiate children into an appreciation of the condominium's buildings and grounds by means of a carefully led tour of the premises, accompanied by a discussion of the proper utilization of the facilities.

Except for decorative strips of grass and shrubs immediately adjacent to buildings or directly fronting on a main entrance, "Keep Off the Grass" signs do not belong in most cluster housing developments. The quality of grass in such areas should be tough and durable enough for ordinary play. In winter, snow games and possibly ice skating should be organized in selected locations, where the condition of the lawn is not considered of paramount importance. The board of directors and the managing agent should emphasize maximum opportunities for residents to benefit from condominium living.

If a swimming pool is included in the condominium, the following basic problems that require management's decisions are presented:

1. Meeting local health regulations
2. Utilization of lifeguards
3. Posting adequate warning and notice signs
4. The problem of unsupervised children
5. Limitations on use by neighbors and guests
6. Arranging for repairs and implementation of warranties

Wading pools for children add an important feature to a pool area. In housing for the elderly, all outside swimming pools are sometimes entirely heated, or special pools are set aside for those residents requiring heated water.

The managing agent should be made responsible for reporting persistent violators of bylaws and house rules to the board. If no managing agent is employed, owners can expect to have many more personal arguments with other owners on rule violations.

Many condominiums have separate recreation rooms or buildings that double as meeting rooms and space for family gatherings or parties. In such a situation, an additional duty of the managing agent would be to keep a reservation book controlling the use of the room. A cleaning charge is often assessed against owners as a condition for making such reservation, in order to assure that no additional cost will accrue to other owners. A portion of such charges could be used to defray the cost of repainting and decoration of such a room. Sometimes the original concrete or unfinished wallboard rooms built by the sponsor for such a purpose have been paneled and otherwise pleasantly decorated by the condominium. Some larger developments run educational courses or a lecture series, sometimes with the cooperation of a nearby university. In a small number of condominiums, the recreation room is rarely used by residents, especially when it is located below ground in a highrise structure. The best locations for recreation rooms have been on or above ground level with a well-lighted entrance. If possible, the room should be located away from residential areas, or at least it should be soundproof, to avoid the problem of noise and the disturbance of sleeping residents.

EFFECTIVENESS OF LARGE OR SMALL CONDOMINIUMS

In many situations, the size of the condominium contributes to its success or failure as a provider of pleasant, relaxed living.

Larger condominiums appear to offer several advantages that cannot be overlooked, although the degree of advantage depends largely on the good sense and cooperation of the owners themselves.

The large condominium is able to retain a professional managing agent and, possibly, other resident personnel, such as a building superintendent, a guard, and seasonal gardening employees. The most important is the managing agent, who will relieve the board of the burden of dealing on a person-to-person basis with unit owners when collecting maintenance charges and of hearing and weighing all complaints and requests for service. After reviewing the duties of a managing agent, it is easy to foresee the heavier duties imposed on the board in the absence of such an agent. In some condominiums of fewer than fifty units, the boards have operated without a managing agent quite effectively. However, the president of the board has devoted enormous energies to the venture and has been able to secure amazing cooperation from unit owners who are interested in keeping costs at a minimum. But many smaller condominiums that started their existence without professional management later found it advisable to acquire some degree of such management.

Often, the larger condominium contains facilities that are neither practical nor possible in smaller groupings. The immediate retort to such a statement might be that many small condominiums do possess swimming pools and recreation rooms. The answer to that is, "Yes, but look at their size." While in some cases a sponsor has provided minuscule recreation facilities, or even none at all, in large condominiums, on the whole the facilities in larger developments are generally more substantial. There are many persons who prefer a larger pool, even if more crowded, to a limited swimming area that restricts distance swimming and does not have graduated depth levels that serve as a form of protection for growing children. Moreover, the smaller condominium is less likely to be able to afford some form of lifeguard or pool supervision.

A large condominium, especially one widely allocated over substantial acreage, presents a more self-contained community atmosphere. Such an arrangement tends to add pride to the community and intensify the cooperative spirit so helpful to the solution of common problems.

It is generally conceded by management experts that larger groupings of units, both highrises and cluster, can lead to lower unit operating costs. In the case of highrise or large blocks of units, this could mean lower heating, utility, and maintenance costs. For clustered housing, joint contracting can cut gardening, painting, and other expenses. These are only examples. Elevator cost operation certainly diminishes (after a minimum cost is reached) with the number of floors serviced.

In a larger condominium, there is less likelihood of oppressive tactics in the form of board positioning being used by individual unit owners or by small cliques against other unit owners. Some condominiums have only two units, thereby requiring unanimous votes on all matters. In some small condominiums there have been complaints that individual owners are constantly being reelected to the board by tiny majorities, even though there may be a major split within the ownership on essential policies. There would seem to be a greater opportunity for adequate representation of viewpoints in larger groupings. It also appears that courts, when faced with board proceedings against individual owners, would be more responsive to the cause because of the larger group represented by the board. Where just a few owners make up the entire condominium, a court might be more hesitant to upset ownership rights and might hurriedly conclude that the issues are more a case of personal squabbling than a real violation of rules. In addition, where there are few owners, the owner of a greater segment of the property interest is being challenged by the board, a most important practical consideration regardless of the merits of the case.

Larger condominiums represent a larger voting block in a community, either new or old, a fact that elected government officials tend to recognize rather quickly. This is not to say that special dispensations will be expected from government. More than likely, the condominium would prefer to be the recipient of no special penalties or discrimination in current government allocations. For example, initial and later tax assessments should be levied reasonably, not for the purpose of dissuading future condominium construction.

EQUITABLE ALLOCATION OF COMMON CHARGES

Allocation of common expenses in most condominiums in the United States is made as if they were rents computed on the basis of unit value. This is achieved by basing charges on a percentage interest in common elements attached to the particular unit. In turn, the percentage is most commonly determined by reference to the price of the units that exists at the time the master declaration is filed. Where units do not exist at the time of filing, the percentage is based on the contemplated value of the units that would apply if they actually did exist, although this relationship is rarely expressed.

It is largely a fiction that the common expenses in a condominium are borne by unit owners in accordance with the operating costs that are applicable to the owners. But the formula is more understandable when the precedent established in other forms of housing is examined.

In the case of ordinary tenancies, those tenants who rent better facilities than other tenants in the same apartment house are willing to pay more rent because of the higher value and the greater satisfaction accruing to the occupant during the tenancy, a fact that would be more obvious if property tax assessments and blanket mortgage charges were broken down by apartment.

A similar concept attaches to cooperative apartment ownership, where higher rentals are paid for more costly apartments. Justification for such a scaling of charges may lie in the necessity in most cooperatives of allocating fairly the single tax assessment on the entire cooperative and the payments in interest and amortization on the overall blanket mortgage, which together make up the major portion of costs.

But in the typical condominium, property taxes and mortgage payments are not included in maintenance charges. Nevertheless, common charges usually are prorated based on the original unit cost. The effect of creating such a relationship in the case of the condominium is to permit a mix of economic levels of ownership, by means of injecting into the concept of maintenance charges the factor of use value of the premises, thus lowering carrying charges for less costly units.

If units are approximately the same in value, subject to minor price differentials, then it is simpler to apply the exact interest in common elements to each unit rather than to devise some complicated but more precise formula.

Floor space formulas for determining responsibility for common charges are sometimes allowed by law but are used only occasionally. This method might be used to eliminate the use-value factor, unless the space method will be conditioned by the location of the floor being measured.

Some states permit wide discretion in allocating condominium common expenses, but many provide for limiting formulas within the enabling statute.

The use-value concept should be eliminated for housing that has no wide range of economic levels represented by potential purchasers. That is, minor differences in price levels should not be perpetually enlarged by pro rata differences in carrying charges. On the other hand, if the use-value concept were eliminated from an economically integrated development offering radically different housing for different monetary levels of buyers, it might not be possible to achieve the integration.

It must be understood, however, that for purposes of dissolution of the condominium regime, payout of insurance on destruction, condemnation awards, and other payments based on unit value, the measure of payments should be appropriately equated with relative then-current unit values. Unfortunately, the formulas most widely used at the present time relate to a single day (the day on which the declaration was filed) rather than to the much more pertinent later date applicable to such occurrences. This is so even though the funds received relate in most instances to an existing valuation. Applying the common interest percentage (calculated on the basis of initial value) to the payment of a lump sum representing current value actually confuses the concept of return of investment with the concept of payment at current market value.

TIE-INS AND CO-OWNERSHIP WITH OTHER CONDOMINIUMS

The original size of a condominium may undergo substantial or even radical change during the period of its existence. This may come about for several reasons, including the following:

1. The sponsor retained power to fix the limits on the number of units. This power may be unlimited, may be subject to a maximum limitation, or may involve the determination to extend the number after an earlier decision to cut back.
2. The original condominium is subject to a cross-easement agreement with the sponsor covering any separate condominiums he or she may build in the future, which may join the usage of common facilities or may even be so broad as to, in effect, tie together two, three, or even more condominiums.
3. Common facilities may have been deeded to a local government as a condition for approval of the condominium. Requirements imposed might change the character of the development.
4. Common facilities or parts of the common areas may have been placed in the ownership of a separate corporation in which outside parties have an interest. These may be the sponsor, other landowners, or nearby condominium owners, cooperative owner–tenants, or a homeowner association. The vote of condominium owners may not be enough to control corporate policies that could change the character of commonly used areas.

Any of the above possibilities could result in a housing development that conceivably might be quite inconsistent with the desires of original condominium purchasers. Density strategies proposed are often designed to maximize the sponsor's profits, but planning commissions and zoning officials should be very cautious of bestowing overbroad powers to cluster additional housing through the elimination of needed green belts and play areas essential to offset initial density zoning. Where the construction involves broad discretionary powers vested in the builder as well as large numbers of potential units, the local planning commission may wish to reserve the right of approval of future additions encompassing more than a reasonable number of units based on the adequacy of open areas, the sufficiency of street approaches, and the effects on local traffic.

If the plan of development is adequately specific and the planners feel that they have had an opportunity for review, at least the purchasers and planners know what is coming. For planning commissions to leave too extensive a discretion in developers could very well result in construction that would be quite different from the planning strategy.

Another major problem for planning officials should be the mere leasing to the condominium by the developer of swimming pools or other recreational facilities. Sometimes the sponsor places a contractual lease arrangement in the preliminary agreements made by the condominium while controlled by the developer. The effect could be required maintenance charges by unit owners to provide an annuity to the sponsor and his or her heirs. In one case, each unit owner was supposed to pay $10 per month for use of a leased swimming pool under a ninety-nine-year lease by the condominium, with no requirement for replacement imposed on the sponsor. Each successive unit owner would not have been required to make such payments as part of the maintenance charges.

Planning officials should be wary of such arrangements because of the potential deterioration of premises that might not be adequately replaced. Such leasing arrangements are frequently found only in Florida condominium projects.

EIGHT

CONDOMINIUMS FOR LOW- AND MODERATE-INCOME RESIDENTS

SUITABILITY FOR LOW- AND MODERATE-INCOME HOUSING

A thoughtful examination of the condominium form of ownership will disclose its suitability for low- and moderate-income housing. Instead of the stereotyped and tasteless living accommodations so typical of massive public housing projects, the condominium can be used to provide reasonably priced, attractive housing for those in the low- and moderate-income groups. The 1968 Housing and Urban Development Act, with its provisions for mortgage interest rates below the market, made the condominium one of the most important tools by which government assistance could be offered to the poor and lower middle class.

Condominium ownership affords the opportunity for families with low incomes to acquire an apartment home having some of the same benefits and ownership characteristics as the traditional single-family detached house—a more or less permanent occupancy, a responsibility for its upkeep and maintenance, a pride and sense of fulfillment in actually owning the unit, income tax deductions for real estate taxes and mortgage interest, a chance to benefit from any appreciation in its value, and a share in the management of the condominium itself. Most of these factors are not present in rental housing. However, there is no assurance that the low-income occupants of the publicly assisted condominiums will automatically avail themselves of these advantages.

To say that the condominium gives pride of homeownership is merely begging the real question: How can the lower-income groups be brought to an appreciation of the responsibility and pride of homeownership through the use of the condominium? In many poor households, these are concepts with which they have never had any experience in their long history of occupancy of dilapidated and outmoded rental housing. A special approach will be necessary if the unworkable aspects of earlier solutions are to be eliminated. This approach must make special use of the condominium form, in a fashion somewhat different from the case of other condominiums.

SOME FORMATS FOR SOLUTION

To date, most housing intended for the poor has been in one of the following forms:

1. Massive highrise public housing projects.
2. Large and small lowrise public housing developments.
3. Spotted public housing that involves limited numbers of units interspersed in middle-income areas.
4. Rent supplement payments for publicly assisted residents of privately owned housing.
5. Conversion of public housing developments to limited-equity cooperatives.
6. Sale of public housing units to tenants.
7. Various rehabilitation housing programs to improve existing quarters of the poor.
8. Below-market mortgage assistance.

The condominium is flexible enough to be substituted for or fitted into any of the above formats. Before examining a federal program that has made some strides in that direction, it will be helpful to survey the existing social and management problems associated with some of the above solutions, as well as the arguments against viewing the condominium as a panacea.

OWNERSHIP AND THE RIGHT TO PROFITS

If the condominium form is to be used to instill the pride of ownership, a practical aspect of ownership must accompany the condominium deed—the right to profit on resales. Without this right, pride of ownership is virtually impossible. This concept would be directly opposed to the purpose expressed in most of the programs that are essentially publicly assisted. Even middle-income cooperatives, constructed or financed under federal and state housing and urban renewal programs, generally limit the apartment owner to either the return of his or her original investment or the depreciated book value of the unit, even though the unit is permitted to be resold at substantially higher prices. In order to prevent immediate resales at higher prices, profit should be allowable only after a purchaser has resided on the premises for an extensive period, say five years.

Let us forego a consideration of the well-argued assumptions of planners concerning the need to eliminate profiteering by the low-income groups who have benefited from tax abatements, below-market mortgage financing, planning subsidies, land cost writedown, government mortgage guarantees and loans, and the elimination of slums and deteriorated buildings through the special powers of condemnation. It is really not without justification that profits have gone either to the government that gave the tax abatement or subsidy or to the board of directors of the association who would thus be able to cut additional requests for government funds.

There is one major housing area in which disillusionment with such restrictions in FHA–213 cooperatives was of tremendous help to the sponsor of a large private condominium development who stressed that condominium ownership included the right to resell at a profit rather than being required to turn over any profit to the board or to sell at a price set by government decree. The condominiums sold at least three times faster than the FHA–213 cooperatives.

What should this country's aim be—to uplift the poor or to create a perpetual inventory of housing for the poor? If the latter is the case, there should be no attempt to mislead by offering public housing condominiums. On the other hand, if low-income people were to be given a deed to their own homes with the understanding that their care of those homes and any neighborhood improvements could give them personal profits on resale, the fertile seeds of pride of ownership would be planted and could be expected to grow.

Should the poor be permitted to retain such profits? Yes, they should. Public assistance in housing should be a first step toward elevating a family, if possible, from a difficult economic status that has led to disarray and lack of attention to the cleanliness and durability of its environment.

Such a right to profits should be extended to subsidized middle-income developments, where several thousand dollars can be expected to be placed in down payment for the unit. If we are looking for practical rather than paper solutions, let us not overlook the profit motive, a most forceful factor in all classes of society.

CAN LOW-INCOME RESIDENTS DIRECT THEMSELVES?

It would be impossible from an analysis of actual experience to comment on how well low-income persons govern their own housing. There have been just too few examples. Regardless of the eyewash descriptions of such purported efforts, it is either the government or its chosen sponsor who has been calling the shots. From all appearances, there seems to be a great fear of letting these people run their own business affairs. While such an attitude might seem reasonable at first, it is hard to understand the general failure to educate and train residents of low-income housing for some management duties even after the passage of many years.

Many of the persons in government and allied with the sponsor have all too frequently shown tendencies to perpetuate the status quo of residents, to becloud errors in the original planning, and to turn from facing current sensitive problems that jeopardize the housing development.

Management of a publicly assisted cooperative or condominium should be divorced from the sponsor's control as soon as possible, just as it would be from the builder's control in ordinary private housing. One of the difficulties in public housing that has some of the same aspects as private housing (cooperatives, condominiums, etc.) is the retention as managing agent of the same firm that sold the units. (While such a relationship often also exists in private developments, it is rare that the selling–managing agent is also controlled by the developer.) In many situations, the developer retains substantial representation on the board of directors by contract or even by the mandate of government regulation. With the required representatives of government regularly added to the board (that is, those who chose the sponsor in the first place), it is amazing that any original errors are ever corrected.

One ray of hope has been the turnkey program that has been started in some localities, whereby private professional management takes over the responsibility for assisted housing from government housing authorities. In some cases, pleasantness of outside decor, change of name from public housing to a more sophisticated project designation, and added services and courtesy to tenants have resulted in a less drab and downtrodden atmosphere than one ordinarily finds in public housing. Such an attitude is essential if the federal program designed to spin off deeds conveying public housing units to residents for permanent homes can be effective. Section 15(9) of the Housing Act of 1937, as amended in 1968, now permits public housing units that possess sufficient individual identity to be sold to tenants as condominium units.

A more realistic and promising spinoff program was also authorized by Congress in 1968 pursuant to new Section 23(g) of the same statute. That section permits public housing agencies to purchase and resell to occupants privately owned one-family structures being used for public housing accommodations under direct leasing by the public agency. If the structure is multi-family, the transfer can still be made so long as the assisted tenants to whom the structure is to be sold occupy units aggregating (in value) 80 percent of the structure's total value. With the new authority to sell public housing units directly as condominiums, it is presumed that the condominium form of ownership is also permissible under Section 23(g), which provides for a method that can facilitate joint management and guidance for occupants of attached, detached, highrise, or lowrise dwellings. A supervised trial program is suggested in most cases, during which time low-income residents can adjust, but a program that, in effect, amounts to converting the private housing in which they were living with assistance into a public housing project is cautioned against.

Most importantly, a low-income condominium should not be budgeted so that it cannot afford a good independent managing agent.

It would appear reasonable to expect continuing government approval of large budgetary allocations by the board, but it would be desirable to have less delay in decision making.

In many private condominiums, the units must be decorated internally by the unit owners, with only outside portions considered as common elements. In low-income condominiums, painting and other decoration should be the responsibility of the unit owner, but such maintenance should be arranged and paid for by the common assessments in order to assure proper care of the premises.

SECURITY FOR DAMAGES

Earlier it was proposed that some form of security deposit be required in private condominiums. This requirement should also be instituted in government-assisted condominiums. A security deposit to insure against damage to common areas might be considered. There should be a regular payment of interest to the unit owner from his or her trust account for such purpose as both an annual token reminder and a warning of the financial risk involved if he or she fails to respect the premises and the rights of neighbors and to teach his or her children accordingly. Continual reminder of the profit potential to each owner should be communicated.

SWITCHING FROM LEASE STATUS

Low-income condominiums should be initially constructed as such, or an entire block of units should be rehabilitated on a condominium basis. If, for example, only a few units in a public housing project are converted to condominium, the program could not possibly hope to gain the full benefits of pride of ownership in surroundings foreign to the concept and even hostile to the participants. Moreover, under such circumstances, the questions arise: What is the new owner to gain, and who is to manage the segment of property suddenly given to him or her? Unless a major portion of tenants convert, the problems seem overwhelming. The atmosphere and characterization of existing public housing would not be the best means by which to attempt a new turn of events for uplifting the poor and instilling the pride of ownership. It does not appear that the condominium can function effectively as the means for piecemeal liberation of public housing tenants whose income has increased.

REHABILITATION HOUSING

A major highrise or a series of lowrise rehabilitation programs may be conditioned on the conversion of a large grouping of residences to full condominium status. But the availability of a competent resident manager might be severely limited if such program randomly selects only a few units for such purpose. In other words, even mere experiments designed to determine the effectiveness of condominiums in rehabilitation housing should be on a sizeable scale.

RESIDENT MANAGEMENT

Low-income condominiums require resident management. It would be too much to ask for absentee management to serve as a cost-cutting device. Management should arrange talks and educational programs to explain the personal and community benefits that can flow from condominium ownership.

DECOR

The layout of future highrise, detached, and row housing units should not be reminiscent of drab public housing of the past. In some public housing developments, venetian blinds were banned from windows in order to avoid the suggestion of any semblance of affluence to taxpayers. It is hard to understand why government-assisted developments must be subjected to the display of huge signs blatantly proclaiming government aid and the names of a host of politicians.

FEDERAL LOW-INCOME PROGRAMS

Section 235, added to housing legislation by the Housing and Urban Development Act of 1968, provides for mortgage assistance payments as an aid to low-income purchasers of condominium units. The assistance is in the form of payments made directly to the unit mortgagee. The permanent mortgage in such case generally must meet the specifications of Section 234(c), but funding for the Section 235 program has at least been temporarily halted by HUD.

Since 1968, Section 221(i) of the National Housing Act has authorized conversion of 221(d)(3) rental projects to condominiums. The interest rate for the permanent take-out mortgages is subject to the 3 percent below-market interest limitations that govern Section 221(d)(3). Section 223(e) would also appear to be applicable to such housing.

Section 223(f) provides federal mortgage insurance to facilitate the purchase and refinancing of existing apartment projects. These projects may later be converted to condominium projects. Under the 223(f) program, HUD insures mortgages to purchase or refinance existing multi-family projects originally financed with or without federal mortgage insurance. HUD may insure mortgages on existing multi-family projects under this program that do not require substantial rehabilitation. The project must contain at least five units and must be at least three years old.

THE UNCAP CONCEPT

In the late 1970s, HUD endorsed a program called Urban Neighborhood Community Association Project (UNCAP), which is designed to develop housing opportunities for people who reside in urban neighborhoods and want to improve their residential environment. The following paragraphs on this subject are taken from the introduction to the UNCAP manual:

The many housing market forces now shaping the face of urban neighborhoods are beyond the control of most low- and moderate-income residents. Instead, politicians, landlords, bankers, realtors, and others determine what housing options will be available.

Ownership—as a means of control—is at the base of the UNCAP concept. Renters traditionally cannot influence the quality or costs of housing, and are more vulnerable to market fluctuations than are owners. In addition, renters cannot decide how much an owner will invest in their building, control how much they must pay for space, or monitor the sale of their building to another owner. Despite efforts to regulate the rental market to the advantage of tenants (through rent control, rent stabilization, and conversion ordinances), renters remain relatively powerless to affect their housing environment. This situation has become more critical as landlords, faced with inflationary housing and maintenance costs, are forced to raise rents or decrease investment levels in order to maintain comparable profit margins.

Ownership, on the other hand, offers residents several benefits. Tax laws offer a large subsidy to owners by allowing income tax deductions for property tax and interest payments. In addition, owners—as opposed to renters—establish equity with their monthly housing payments. For those who desire it, then, ownership is the more advantageous housing choice; the urban neighborhood community association (UNCA) is one method of expanding ownership opportunities for residents who are normally not able to buy a house.

OBJECTIVES OF UNCAP

The first objective of UNCAP is to help people to learn to help themselves. Past efforts to halt housing deterioration in the central city areas have often ignored the importance of encouraging resident participation. Unless residents are involved in housing improvement programs, complex subsidy schemes and physical improvements will prove unsuccessful. Formation of a community association provides the framework through which residents can build their capacity to manage their housing environment.

The process of setting up a community association also can have a positive supportive effect on the neighborhood. Thus, the second objective of UNCAP is to contribute to community stabilization by offering residents the opportunity to remain permanently in the neighborhood as owners. By creating the opportunity for existing residents to stay as others move in or out, economic and racial diversity can be promoted. The physical improvements of property resulting from community association conversion contribute to the long-term maintenance of housing stock—a critical city resource.

The goals of improving the quality of urban housing for low and moderate-income residents and building the capacity of neighborhood-based organizations go hand-in-hand. The last decades have shown that quality housing cannot exist when social problems or physical decay eventually overwhelm direct attempts to improve housing conditions. The formation of neighborhood groups which can identify specific problems and propose solutions will prove useful long after the phase-out of local or Federal neighborhood assistance. By its very nature, the association form of ownership unites good housing with concerned residents; with the establishment of such organizations, a neighborhood will be watched, guided, and directed by those who have a stake in its future.

UNCA FUNCTIONS

A community association (UNCA) functions to maintain and enhance the property of its owner-members and to enforce democratically adopted rules of behavior. A community association is a "common interest community"—living units held together by a common interest in and ownership of a significant portion of the property.

Created in accordance with State or local law by a recorded declaration of covenants, the association's legal documents make it a private organization with many public powers and obligations. An UNCA may set and collect assessments, make and enforce rules and regulations, and enter into business transactions. These powers represent a unique advantage because they give the property owners both the responsibility and the ability to administer their own affairs without interference from outside parties.

Membership in a community association is mandatory. Upon taking title to his or her home, a purchaser automatically becomes a member of the association. Although the form of an association and the type of housing may vary, the practical differences among associations concern scale rather than function or design. All UNCA's perform the same fundamental roles.

In its first role, the community association is a service-oriented business, providing maintenance, repair, and security services to its members who are its "owners." The association also acts as a private government, performing public functions. It has a taxing power (via assessments) and rulemaking and enforcing authority. Its documents and the applicable State statute establish its business and regulatory framework and support its operating functions.

OPERATING ASSUMPTIONS

An UNCA can be defined in terms of properties, people, and neighborhoods involved. This concept is based on several assumptions. First, in the first phases of the project, it is assumed that existing rental properties will be converted to a community association form of ownership. These rental properties can be highrise multifamily buildings, attached rowhouses a group of flats, or detached single family houses. The scope of each project is limited only by the fact that the property owners must agree to the creation of the association and allow the imposition of the covenants.

Secondly, it is assumed that the UNCA will be available to the people who cannot easily afford to purchase housing in the regular market. As the costs of housing continue to escalate rapidly, the number of people who cannot afford to buy increases. Condominiums and cooperatives are often the least expensive form of ownership housing because of the economies of the common space. Therefore, developing these alternative forms of ownership is a logical method of increasing housing opportunities.

Resident income levels will likely differ in each UNCA according to the scheme of financial development. The more cost savings achieved through the use of subsidized loans, secondary market programs, or commitments of lower interest mortgages, the lower the cost of each unit. Because a down-payment and ability to support monthly mortgage payments are necessary for ownership housing, an UNCAP as currently described is a moderate-income program. This assumption is not meant to preclude the possibility of designing an UNCA with substantial public housing subsidies for low-income families. However, the concept is used to define the most realistic range of income required to support the costs of developing a nonsubsidized UNCAP.

Common interest ownership housing can be beneficial to moderate-income residents in either a declining neighborhood or a neighborhood undergoing renewal. In a deteriorating neighborhood, the process of UNCA conversion and rehabilitation will help to stop further decline by motivating residents and/or owners to invest in housing renovation on other properties.

Conversely, an inner-city neighborhood may become an object of renewal by higher income residents because of convenient location, attractive housing stock, or affordable prices. When builders and owners invest in rehabilitation, the general appearance of the neighborhood improves; however, displacement may occur when rents increase or units are converted to ownership. Conversion of units to condominiums or cooperatives, or creating an HOA [homeowners association] which offers housing at lower prices are strategies for filling such housing shortages.

UNCA DEVELOPERS

UNCAP is neither a program designed to stimulate the production of housing units nor a financing mechanism. Rather, the Urban Neighborhood Community Association Project was designed to outline a plan of action for those people working in neighborhood housing. This process: (1) must be adapted to each situation; (2) will demand the energies of a committed group of people; and (3) is an avenue through which neighborhood residents can build their capacity to design and manage their housing environment. The authors of this manual envision that each UNCAP developed will be the product of a team effort—a partnershhip of residents, lenders, government, attorneys, and developers involved in putting together the project. The UNCAP sponsor will initiate and oversee each component of the process. Possible sponsors may include:

- a community development corporation;
- a neighborhood-based organization;
- a group of tenants who are investigating housing ownership opportunities;
- a local housing or redevelopment authority; and
- a lender or group of lenders holding deteriorating properties.

The UNCA team (UNCAT) may include professionals from the real estate and development industry, the lending institutions, or a local technical assistance organization. The UNCAP Action Manual is available at the Office of Policy Development and Research of HUD.

USE OF SECTION 8 IN CONVERSIONS

Perhaps the most successful program to date to provide affordable housing is the one in which the local municipality approves a proposed conversion and purchases approximately 20 percent of the units back from the developer at bargain prices. These city-owned units are then rented to low-income families who qualify for Section 8 subsidies.

Section 8 is a program of HUD called Low-Rent Public Housing Assistance. Each tenant family must pay approximately 25 percent of its income toward rent and utilities. Then the remainder of the fair rent is paid directly by HUD.

CONVERSION OF RENTAL HOUSING TO CONDOMINIUMS

In the context of this book, *conversion* means a change in the legal form of ownership of a multi-family rental property from single ownership by a landlord to multiple ownership, usually by the occupants. Very few rental properties were converted to co-ownership before 1970. During the ensuing thirteen years, about 1 million rental housing units were converted. According to a survey published by HUD in 1980, 260,000 units were converted between 1977 and 1979, the conversion boom years. The HUD study indicated that conversions have been most numerous "in metropolitan areas characterized by strong and growing market demand for homeownership."

The conversion phenomenon, however, is not associated with distressed rental markets. Conversions tend to be most numerous in areas in which the mean household income is in the middle to higher levels. Only about one-third of the tenants in a typical rental building can be expected to purchase a unit in the project.

There are several factors that contributed to the conversion mania of apartment buildings that swept the country in the late 1970s. These factors included skyrocketing land costs and costs of construction; general shortage of housing; declining returns on apartment investments because of high operating costs and low rents; threats of rent controls, eviction controls, profit controls, and price controls; limitations on adult-only apartments that did not apply to condominiums; high interest rates and land use policies, both of which discouraged new construction; growing number of single member households; increasing number of people reaching home buying age; tax benefits of homeownership, including a chance to get a foothold on increasing inflation with nondiscretionary money; and high profit margins on conversions where very little builder expertise was needed.

General Procedure

The building owner should follow the same basic methodology that has been described in the creation of a condominium through new construction. The failure of many conversions is often attributable to the failure of developers and their consultants to properly understand and evaluate the problems inherent in the design, financing, sales, and transition of such complex projects. Hence, an advisory team of experienced professionals should be selected at the onset to assist the seller. Otherwise, the converter could be legally responsible for creating an unworkable structure, because most converters are far less experienced in this type of work than are most builders of for-sale properties.

Vesting Rights

Ambitious cities and counties may argue that a conversion occurs whenever an existing building is built pursuant to a rental permit and is later divided into a condominium project, whether or not the project has ever been occupied by tenants. However, a conversion probably occurs in most jurisdictions when a building that was originally created as a rental project and occupied by tenants is later divided into a form of common interest ownership. In some jurisdictions (e.g., California), a condominium project does not technically exist until the first unit is conveyed to a purchaser. However, in other jurisdictions (e.g., Virginia), a condominium project is created upon recordation of the declaration for the project. This factor can be very important in determining when a vested right to sell condominiums is created. Moratoria bills have been introduced in some state legislatures from time to time which preclude the sale of condominiums and conversions occurring in those local jurisdictions. Any such enactment would probably preclude sales of condominiums in conversion projects, unless the converter has previously vested his or her right to sell condominiums in the project.

Income Tax Considerations

The Internal Revenue Service has taken a very hard look at conversions of apartment projects to the condominium form of ownership, and the rulings and cases pertaining to residential conversions probably will apply to commercial conversions. Hence, it will be very difficult for an owner of a rental building to convert the building to condominiums and obtain capital gain treatment of the income without very careful tax planning. If an organized tenants' group or a converter approaches the owner–investor to purchase the building, the resulting bulk sale of the project has a better chance of being classified as a sale of a capital asset than if the sales are made piecemeal. However, the result depends largely on the taxpayer's intentions from the time he or she originally acquires the property, which intentions are sometimes difficult to prove objectively.

Owner–Converter Relationship

Aside from the usual considerations that must be addressed in the acquisition of a rental building (such as title matters and cash flow concerns), there are some unique factors that affect the convertibility of the building to the condominium form of ownership. In the first place, the prospective converter should cause a thorough inspection of the physical condition of the property to be conducted. A building might not be suitable for conversion because its design does not meet requirements imposed by city or county ordinance, and it may be impossible or extremely costly to meet such requirements. In addition, the cost of other necessary renovations and repairs to make the units marketable might be too high. Some buildings may be so dilapidated that no reasonable amount of renovation can convert them into readily marketable condominiums. It may be too expensive in an attractive building to separately meter the utilities (e.g., electricity), and such metering may be necessary to make the building marketable as a condominium project.

Each purchaser of a unit in a converted project should be given a written statement, listing all substantial defects or malfunctions in the major systems (such as roof, heating, air-conditioning, plumbing, and electrical systems) or disclaiming knowledge of any such substantial defects or malfunctions. This precaution should protect the converter from later claims of the purchasers that they were sold units that they thought were new but were defective and merely camouflaged by the converter with cosmetic repairs. Of course, a marketing study should be conducted to determine whether the condominiums will sell on an "as is" basis.

If the price to be paid for a convertible apartment is greater than its fair value as income property, then the purchaser–converter should assure that the principal obstacles to the conversion are addressed as contingencies before closing the sale. In most cases, the converter will not wish to close until final approvals of the city or county have been obtained. However, neither the cities or counties nor the converter are immune from lawsuits that may be brought by disgruntled tenants even after such approvals have been granted. Some cities and counties may require a conditional use permit to be obtained before a condominium can be created, so local zoning laws must be checked carefully.

Perhaps an option can be purchased by the buyer and a memorandum of the option can be recorded. This would give the prospective converter an opportunity to process the project with the proper authorities, who must approve the proposed conversion, without obligating the converter to purchase the building if the requests for approval are denied. Use of an option might help to preserve the capital gain treatment of income to the building owner and compensate the owner for holding the property off the market until all approvals have been obtained by the converter.

The converter should attempt to obtain copies of the original building plans, because such plans will help (1) the converter in making his or her inspection of the property, (2) the engineer in creating the condominium plan showing the location of the units, and (3) the association in operating and maintaining the project. The converter should secure the owner's consent to contact the building tenants to inform them of the conversion plan. The converter should obtain the names and addresses of all tenants and surrounding property owners, so that he or she and the city or county will be able properly to notify these interested parties when the application is ready to be heard.

The seller should deliver to the buyer all operating records for at least the past three years, if they are available. The seller should warrant the accuracy of these records, because they will be relied upon by the unit purchaser. The seller should also deliver all occupancy permits and repair records with a warranty of their accuracy. The converter should review all long-term leases so that they will not preclude or delay the conversion and sale of the condominiums. All new leases should have short-term cancellation provisions. Prospective tenants should be provided advance special notice that the building is being converted.

The seller and existing lender must cooperate with the converter in executing documents and maps to consummate the conversion. If the underlying lender will not sign the subdivision or plat map, condominium plan, and the declaration and release units for sale, bridge financing usually must be obtained to accomplish the conversion. This issue is particularly important when the existing lender, such as an insurance company, has a lock-in provision in its note and mortgage. See Chapter 4 pertaining to institutional financing of condominium projects.

Procedural Checklist

Anyone who is considering a condominium conversion should follow a procedural checklist to ensure that no important step is missed. The checklist that follows is not comprehensive, but it can be used as a beginning for a converter in most jurisdictions:

A. Examine Applicable Laws
   1. Statutes
      a. Subdivision or plat map act
      b. Condominium sales act
      c. Securities and Exchange Acts (federal), as applicable
      d. State Securities or Subdivision Offering Law, as applicable
      e. Environmental Quality Acts
   2. City and County Ordinances
      a. Zoning code
      b. Subdivision code
      c. Conversion ordinance

       d. Building code

       e. Rent control ordinance, if any

B. Evaluate Project
1. Determine developer team.
2. Physically inspect project against plans.
3. Establish conversion goals.
4. Obtain demographics of project.
5. Analyze market area and competition.
6. Check political issues in local government.
7. Review all existing leases.
8. Determine master timetable for conversion.
9. Determine form of ownership (condominium, planned development, co-op, etc.).
10. Check stability of businesses in area.
11. Check extent of refurbishment needed.

C. Tax Considerations
1. Tax basis
2. Capital gain versus ordinary income
3. Stage of Depreciation
4. Tax-free exchange possibilities
5. Installment sales

D. Financing Conversion
1. Check bridge financing sources
2. Obtain accurate appraisal as rental and as conversion
3. Check presale requirement
4. Negotiate release provisions
5. Commitments from take-out lenders

E. Public Relations
1. Tenant relocation plan
2. Businesses of tenants
3. Notices to tenants
4. Rights of first refusal to tenants
5. Tenant discounts
6. Communication with public
7. Effect of unit consolidation on tenant rights

F. Map Processing
1. Civil engineer duties
2. Role of legal counsel
3. Timing of approval

Converter–Unit Purchaser Relations

It is advisable to provide disclosures in the sales documents to the unit purchasers, in order to reflect the unique type of offering and the age and condition of the building, if known. It is important for the buyer to understand that, in most cases, he or she is not buying a new condominium and that the costs of maintenance and replacement may escalate rapidly. Most tenants already know the basic condition of the building, but outside purchasers may be fooled by refurbishment.

Whenever remodeling, refurbishing, or renovation work is planned but not completed at the time that the units are offered for sale, the converter should assure that the work will be completed before the first closing of a sale takes place. Unless the converter desires expressly to warrant the condition of the unit, "as is" language should be inserted in the individual conversion sales documents. The converter may choose to use language similar to the following:

> This condominium is a portion of a condominium conversion of an existing structure that was not constructed by the seller. Seller does not make, and is hereby relieved of any responsibility for, any warranty, express or implied, as to the condition of the condominium or of the improvements conveyed in connection therewith. Buyer agrees for himself or herself and his or her successors in interest, that he or she is purchasing the subject property and improvements in their "as is" condition and is accepting all defects thereon, whether known or unknown, presently existing or that may hereafter arise, if there be any.

Legal Documents

The legal project documents for a conversion are basically the same as the documents for a new project. The principal difference lies in the creation of the condominium plan (or subdivision map or plat, if project is a PUD) by the civil engineer. In one respect, the preparation of the condominium plan is easier for a conversion than that for a new project. If a new project, the condominium project might not be completed when the plan is initially recorded. Depending upon how closely the initial condominium plan approximates the actual construction of the units and the degree of tolerance required by the title insurance company, the plan might have to be amended before the first condominium sale closing.

On the other hand, the units in a conversion already exist, so a definitive plan can be created at the outset. The engineer may attempt to follow the building plans (if available) and actually survey only a few typical units. However, the engineer should take care to discover any bootleg units that may have been created without government approval, subsequent to the initial approval of the plans by the local government. Also, communication and coordination with the tenants is vital, so that some (if not all) of the occupied units can be measured by the engineer without unduly disturbing the tenants.

The condominium, if not stripped of its characteristics of real homeownership, can help effectuate a revolution in the provision of housing for the poor and middle-income families. The great deterrent thus far has been the lack of incisive knowledge of the potentials of this flexible new form of ownership. People talk of the condominium as a means of salvation without spelling out what they want to save or change and how. Others condemn it as another mere fiction intended to hide the misery of the poor. Notwithstanding such extremes of opinion, it is generally believed new federal legislation, if wisely administered, may initiate a healthy beginning. A continuing study of the condominium as a source of low- and moderate-income housing can have fruitful results.

NINE

RESORT AND SECOND-HOME CONDOMINIUMS

LOCATION OF SECOND HOMES

In Hawaii, a $6 million resort condominium presently seeks purchasers who will syndicate the construction and then retain ownership of units in a luxury hotel that may be occupied seasonally or rented to others. In Lido Beach, New York, a condominium seeks to attract Florida residents who want a second beach home for summer occupancy on the north Atlantic coast. In Aspen, Colorado, ski enthusiasts purchase condominium units in chalet-type developments to which they may fly in winter months. A sixteen-unit condominium overlooking a private golf and country club in the Marin Bay area of San Rafael, California, is within convenient distance of residents of other California cities who drive to their two-car-garage condominium second homes on weekends. In Spain, Switzerland, Israel, France, West Germany, and the Bahamas, vacationing Americans are offered literature advertising second-home condominiums for continued vacationing enjoyment or investment.

In the western United States, many unit owners of second-home condominiums live within two to four driving hours of their primary homes. Continuous pursuit of economy in air fares and jet speed has encouraged the ownership or rental of distant second homes that provide relief from severe temperatures in places like Florida and the Bahamas, or unique sport facilities in Colorado, Switzerland, and other fashionable ski resorts. This is not just an American trend; it is worldwide.

WHY OWN A RESORT HOME?

The great increase in numbers of middle-income people throughout the world, together with the speed and efficiency of transportation, has generally accelerated the demand for both travel and resort housing. Longer vacations are becoming commonplace in business and industry and are increasingly an important factor in employment competition. Ordinary hotel facilities are becoming more crowded and commercialized, if they were ever adequate. Where luxury is pursued in such accommodations, the prices are top-heavy for long sojourns. Crowding of existing facilities and problems arising out of the urgent need to plan sufficiently ahead of time have also increased the desire for privacy and easy availability of resort facilities free of the above problems. More and more persons welcome the idea of their own second home for resort use or just plain relaxation and getaway atmosphere.

The tax deductions of mortgage interest and real estate taxes that are ordinarily available to a homeowner can substantially reduce the carrying costs, especially for high-bracket Americans, as will be pointed out later in greater detail. (However, the Internal Revenue rules permitting deferral of taxes on sale are limited to the replacement of the principal residence of the seller by another home, cooperative, or condominium intended as his or her principal home.)

DIFFERENT KINDS OF SECOND HOMES

Resort and second homes fall into different categories that widen the choices available to persons interested in such housing.

By far the most important grouping is the alternative second home that is conveniently accessible throughout the year. Some homes are seasonable, in that access or facilities are not capable of being maintained except during certain months. Some second homes are purchased on the basis that needed improvements will be made over a long-term period, in order to satisfy retirement needs in the distant future. In the latter case, land alone may constitute the initial purchase.

Condominium second-home communities are generally offered in relatively completed condition. It would seem dangerous to sell merely raw land that would be subjected to a master declaration, because the declaration would have to serve as a community building code or would have to specifically set forth the only plans that would be used in construction. It is entirely probable that tastes in housing may change five or ten years after a purchase of land that was accompanied by the right to build under condominium ownership. Such offerings should at the very least require construction of improvements within a limited time.

A condominium might include land restricted to particular unit owners, in order to permit maximum recreational privacy. Thus, parts of a shoreline or woods might be restricted to the use of individual unit owners, with maintenance arranged on a common basis, while the units and the restricted common elements are organized on a condominium basis.

Various devices have been attempted to prevent the use of second homes as principal residences. In New Jersey, the purchasers of one condominium had to agree not to send their children to local schools. Complete seasonal closing of facilities also tends to accomplish this purpose.

Sometimes second-home communities attract persons interested in utilizing the residences as permanent homes. In such cases, there is bound to be some kind of a clash because of the different interests involved. An example would be the demand for heavy snow removal expenditures in a community that had been organized chiefly as a second home for summer resort living.

SIZE OF UNITS

Second homes tend to be compactly built, more so than similar homes built for principal residential use. Nevertheless, in many cases the compact detached or attached second home is more comfortable and spacious than the apartment residences of the unit owners. Size comparisons lose much significance when the environment encompassing the dwelling takes on a sharply different character. Most people are thoroughly satisfied to live in a one-room, cold-water cabin in the woods, but would adamantly refuse to occupy such space in the middle of a city.

LEASING A SECOND HOME

A larger percentage of occupants of second-home developments can be expected to be tenants of unit owners than in the case of ordinary principal residence communities. This fact poses several problems, namely (1) lack of concern for outside and inside appearance, (2) careless or abusive use of facilities, and (3) less attention to community rules. The latter factors are more prevalent in second homes than in ordinary condominiums because of weaker controls over the approval of tenants. Many second-home and resort condominiums emphasize potential profits from leasing and have only a weak provision for controlling lessees. In addition, where there is substantial absentee ownership, the right of first refusal or approval can lose significance through lack of attention.

Many second-home communities are not constructed for year-round use and durability. If owners overtax facilities by their own or lessee occupancy during all seasons, the repair and maintenance costs may suddenly soar. A condominium whose owners contemplate the wide use of short-term leasing to transients is an even more dangerous investment for a person seeking a second home.

In some countries in Europe and in the state of Hawaii, highrise homes are built by a syndicate of investors who are given first choice to purchase condominium units upon their completion. This procedure encourages speculation in units, which results in the leasing of units on a wide scale. Under such circumstances persons seeking a residence should be aware that many of their neighbors, being tenants, are not going to protect the premises because of any pride of ownership. Such syndications constitute securities under SEC and many state laws.

THE CYCLE OF RESORT HOUSING

In the past decade it has become evident that a cycle involving hotel and motel styles of construction has emerged. This cycle is affecting second-home condominium styling patterns at the present time and gives promise of influencing them even more dramatically in the future.

It appears that motel and hotel construction patterns that generally represent radical departures in styling at the time they are implemented tend to reappear in residential developments in five or six years and sometimes sooner. The newly constructed cluster-type housing development with its central swimming pool, small units, and adjacent parking is a more or less faithful reproduction of the then-radical styling of new motels and motor hotels five or ten years ago that made obsolete the old-style square and strip-type designs of previous motels.

This cycle in styling is extremely important, regardless of whether or not any scientific formula governing such results can be worked out. Of paramount concern must be the almost certain acceleration in the changes occurring in architectural design of resort motels and hotels with concomitantly more rapid changes in styling of housing types for which the condominium probably will provide the chief form of ownership. Value depends on comparable market conditions, and swift changes in styling can affect prices on resale.

Two factors most likely will determine the future application of this cycle. One is the attractiveness of the facilities, including pleasant appearance and atmosphere, as well as fundamental recreation facilities. The other factor concerns the characteristics of the people seeking new housing. The existence of many singles, retirees, small families, and the growing proportion of the population that is below thirty years of age should provide substantial demand for late-style compact facilities surrounded by contemporary recreational opportunities.

Developers of second-home condominiums will no doubt keep a cautious eye on new major resort offerings that attract vacationers, so that they will be able to forecast the probable offerings in second homes a few years later.

There may come a time when the most important competition offered to resort motels and hotels will be in the form of second-home clusters. In addition, huge hotel-like developments might be built widely on a condominium basis, creating further competition. But obsolescence can develop quite suddenly in such housing. In addition, some method of financing major alterations in later years must be considered because of the problems that would be involved as a result of individual mortgages. It would seem that major reserve funds are a must.

MANAGEMENT

Second-home condominiums that are shut down seasonally must consider special closing and reopening expenses as well as security problems. In addition, the problem of a constantly changing seasonal management or resident superintendent can be bothersome and even critical, depending upon the locality.

As second-home units approach resort status, there is greater need for management that is experienced in operating resort-type facilities. The cost of management, including resident employees, can be expected to rise considerably with each addition of extensive recreational facilities. In order to lighten the unit owners' burden of costs of operating heavy overhead items such as golf courses, tennis courts, bowling alleys, and marinas, consideration might be given to limited public subscription from outsiders to allay some part of the costs. If the latter program is adopted, it would seem logical not to include the shared facilities as common elements. Preferably, a separate nonprofit corporation could be organized in which the condominium board would hold either a majority of stock or all the voting stock, or both, on behalf of the condominium.

PRIMARY FACILITIES NEARBY

The purchaser of a condominium home who is seeking the use of nearby public or private recreational facilities should make certain of their continued availability beforehand. A prospective purchaser should have been accepted as a new resident member of a golf club by the time he or she takes title. Permanent, transferable membership investments provide a greater safety than mere annual fees for use of facilities. Unless memberships are transferable, the unit owner might experience a substantial reduction in his or her unit's resale price as compared to what it was at the time memberships were open. This is one case in which persons other than the board members and unit owners can seriously affect the condominium unit's resale value.

BUILDING CODES

Many outlying resort areas combine rustic appearance with nonexistent or inadequate building codes. In most states, buyers are strictly on their own in determining the adequacy of the method and quality of construction. Poor building codes often permit fire-prone construction, overloaded wiring insufficiently insulated, and minimum standard sewage disposal systems. Because of this problem, second-home buyers must exercise great care, regardless of bank financing. Institutional lenders eager to make loans often are satisfied if local minimum standards are met. Because condominium resort housing may include innovative styling, a builder may find it simple to hide poor quality under the guise of modernistic or unusual design.

STORAGE SPACE

The adequacy of storage space is a problem heightened by compact quarters that do not feature spacious closets. Where temporary leasing takes place, the condominium owner may wish to store furniture, bedding, and utensils on the site in order to avoid massive moving problems when he or she returns to his or her second home. In the case of units located above or below ground level, sufficient space should be provided for children's bicycles and the like. So long as gardening and snow removal are performed by maintenance personnel, the degree of necessity for nearby enclosed storage space is considerably lessened.

WATER AND UTILITY PROBLEMS

Availability of a potable water supply recurs as a constant problem to many purchasers of second homes. The problem has two essential aspects—present supply and future supply. If a well must be dug, an evaluation of its cost and the longevity of its usefulness must be made. If an unusually limited supply exists, some concern should be shown for future needs. One benefit of using the condominium form can be the pooling of resources to create a better engineered and lasting water supply that might otherwise be overly expensive for an individual homeowner. If a water company services the community, the prospective unit owner should learn of the existence or nonexistence of government regulation of rates, the trend of rate changes, and any existing applications for rate increases.

A problem unique to second-home owners involves all of the water and utility companies that service the condominium; that is, the custom of charging minimum rates even if there is no use of utilities. For this reason, condominiums that are basically seasonal but nevertheless open much of the year would probably fare better if certain utility charges were billed to the condominium as a whole, rather than individually to each unit owner. But solution of this problem depends on the local utility procedures as well as the nature of the condominium.

LAKES AND RIVERS

A few years ago a second-home community was created in the northeastern part of the United States by felling all of the existing woodland and constructing homes around an artificially created scenic lake. No boating or swimming was permitted. Nevertheless, the noncondominium development sold out. Apparently, the proximity to a harness racing track was attraction enough to overcome the lack of shade and swimming.

Such developments are rare, and sites on water are more attractive if there are no limitations on boating, swimming, and ice skating. In any event, the purchaser should be made aware of any such limitations whether they arise from community restrictions or private deed reservations.

In addition, many purchasers do not make sufficient inquiry into the present bacteria level of nearby waters. An exceedingly high percentage might lead to state or local prohibition of certain uses, such as swimming, in future years.

If boating is an important condominium feature, the depths of water adjacent to the shore as well as in channels that must be traversed is most important. Physical observation at different times of day for tide and depth problems should be considered. State and federal agencies might have essential information available for potential builders and purchasers.

Title problems to land on navigable waters have been quite troublesome. Qualifications in title policies that eliminate protection from federal use or takeover should be carefully explained to and understood by purchasers.

THE LENDING DECISION

A lending institution tends to employ two financial standards in judging mortgage applicants for ordinary home ownership:

1. Net worth to total value ratio
2. Ratio of present income to required debt service

Such formulas must be adjusted for second-home ownership. In the luxury field, generally the loans are made to persons of such high financial standing that the ratios are even better than the average ratios for one-family homeownership. As a rule, mortgage rates on second homes exceed average market rates for one-family homes or principal residence condominiums.

The danger inherent in such lending practices results from the computation of value attributable to status symbol and other intangibles. As noted before, such increases in valuation might be only short-lived. Although lenders have given many long-term, high-leverage mortgages on such property, the equity required is ordinarily higher than in the ordinary home transaction.

The term of the mortgage is another critical problem, because of the high obsolescence factor.

POLICE AND FIRE PROTECTION

Because many second homes are located in outlying and even remote areas, it is essential for a purchaser to learn of available police and fire protection. Police protection is usually less of a problem than the existence of fire companies and adequate fire-fighting equipment. Frequently, fire alarm boxes are located far from the condominium, with reliance being placed primarily on telephone communication. Better protection involves sponsor installation of fire alarm boxes at regular locations throughout the community.

A large condominium should attempt to acquire and store minimum fire-fighting equipment. It should require a protective water system, even if it is necessary to install private hydrants. When the size of the development permits, a good practice is to establish the condominium's own voluntary fire units. If this can be worked out with the local government, a large part of the cost and training of fire-fighting personnel will be borne by the government.

Anyone who buys an expensive condominium unit should be most concerned about the distance from fire-fighting equipment. This factor can be expected to have a definite relation to the imposition of high insurance rates in the locality.

The police problem is generally not so acute, because of the growing practice of regular cruising tours by motorized police units. The larger condominium, however, might do well to consider private guards to assure privacy as well as protection.

TIME-SHARING

Time-sharing is a generic term used to describe the interval ownership of an interest in real property. This interest can take different forms—a fee simple estate, an estate for years, or, in many cases, a license to use or exclusive right of occupancy during a prescribed period of time and/or under specified conditions. To date, most real estate time-sharing has involved recreational or resort property.

Time-sharing is a relatively recent phenomenon, first appearing on a significant scale in the mid-1970s. However, since that time the sale of time-shares has undoubtedly been the fastest-growing segment of the real estate industry. According to an article in the April 1982 issue of *Mortgage Banking* magazine, the number of time-share projects in the United States increased from approximately two dozen in 1975 to 425 in 1980. More than 100 new time-share projects initiated sales in 1981, despite a faltering economy and record high interest rates. It is estimated that the volume of time-share sales for properties located in the United States approximated $1.5 billion in 1981.

Time-sharing offers significant advantages to both consumers and the development industry. For consumers, it can provide an opportunity to largely fix future vacation costs without incurring the substantial expense associated with purchasing a full unit of real property. For developers, time-sharing can result in an enlarged target market and the opportunity for an increased profit margin.

The substantial and recent growth of the time-sharing concept has been largely unfettered by legislative and regulatory controls at the state level. Only a few states have enacted specific laws, and these are generally first-generation statutes that are not comprehensive in their treatment of this phenomenon. Several states have attempted to regulate time-sharing through administrative regulations. Apart from these scattered efforts, the only regulatory constraints placed upon time-share development apply to those projects that are required to register public offering statements under federal or state securities laws or under the provisions of the Interstate Land Sales Full Disclosure Act.

The lack of legislative or regulatory controls, coupled with the potential for significant consumer abuses, has raised a growing concern on the part of consumer and development groups. In response to this concern, two model acts have recently been promulgated. The Model Time-Share Ownership Act was jointly drafted by the Resort Time-Sharing Council of the American Land Development Association (ALDA/RTC) and the National Association of Real Estate License Law Officials (NARELLO). The Model Act was adopted by both organizations in October 1979. In August 1980, the National Conference of Commissioners on Uniform State Laws adopted a Model Real Estate Time-Share Act.

There are significant differences between the two model acts. In general, the act promulgated by the uniform law commissioners is of much greater length, addresses more issues, and provides more detailed provisions when compared to the RTC–Narello act. Perhaps the most substantive difference is the inclusion within the uniform law commissioners' act of many consumer protection provisions that are not contained in the RTC–Narello version. The proposed legislation covers the creation, warranties, termination, and management of time-shares, including the allocation of voting rights and expenses.

TEN

CONDOMINIUM INCOME TAX FACTORS

IMPORTANCE OF COMPARATIVE DEDUCTIONS

Condominium advertising proclaims the tax-saving benefits of condominium ownership to an audience already conscious of the importance of tax saving in homeownership. The itemized deduction has become a fine science to better-educated citizens who are continually pressured by increasing prices. The higher the tax bracket, the more attractive the deductibility of expenditures. Initially, real property taxes and interest on the mortgage loan secured by an individual condominium home can be expected to represent 50 to 70 percent of the condominium carrying charges. The right to deduct such charges often looms large in the decision to purchase the condominium. For lower-income taxpayers who utilize the standard deduction, the deductibility of such items is of no immediate help, except that prospectively it may be a welcome point or benefit when itemization gives a larger total deduction because of property tax increases or large medical or other deductible expenses.

GENERAL AUTHORITY FOR DEDUCTION

Section 163 of the Internal Revenue Code permits an itemizing taxpayer to deduct interest on home mortgage indebtedness. Section 164 of the same law permits such taxpayer to deduct real property taxes. While the application of such provisions to a unit owner of a fee condominium is implicit in the statutory language, the rule was expressly enunciated with respect to condominium owners in Revenue Ruling 64–31, which stated that such a "taxpayer may deduct, under Sections 163 and 164 of the Code, respectively, the interest on the mortgage indebtedness and the taxes assessed on his interest in the property which he pays each year, provided he itemizes his deductions in filing his Federal income tax returns."

If a locality's form of assessment involves the levy of an annual tax on the value of personal property of the condominium owner, such tax would appear to be deductible under Section 164. In addition, the deduction for casualty losses to homeowners would seem available to such taxpayer under Section 165 of the code.

If the condominium unit owner rents his or her unit, deductions for repairs and maintenance permitted under Section 162 might be utilized for those expenditures applicable to such period of time. And depreciation allowances under Section 167 also should be within the entitlement of such unit owner for the period of rental use.

EFFECT OF FORM OF COMMON INTEREST

In most condominiums in the United States, the unit owner is deeded his or her own unit plus an undivided and indivisible interest in the areas held in common with the other owners who hold similar ownership rights under separate and individual deeds.

The question might be posed: What if the common areas are placed under a separate corporate cloak, with only stock representing such interest distributed to the unit owners? Many condominium statutes might be held still to require that a separate tax assessment be levied against the unit and the interest in common elements, regardless of the form in which the common areas are attached to the units. In view of such direct obligation for property taxes covering unit and interest in common areas, it may be argued that the corporate cloak should be disregarded in awarding the deduction for property taxes assessed on the entire ownership of the condominium owner, so long as the stock is allocated strictly on the basis of the statutory formula for dividing interests in the common elements.

EFFECT OF A BLANKET MORTGAGE

In those rare cases where a condominium unit owner, at the time he or she purchased his or her individual unit, assumed in his or her deed a specified dollar amount of the obligation under a blanket mortgage on the entire project, which amount of such mortgage was equal to the unpaid balance of the purchase price, under Revenue Ruling 64–31, the mortgage interest is deductible by the condominium owner who itemizes deductions. The obligation to pay interest by one who assumes a mortgage in purchasing a home is adequate basis for supporting a deduction of such interest actually paid.

LEASED AREAS

The specific tax problems of leasehold condominiums and their unit lessees are discussed in Chapter 11. However, unit purchasers in a fee condominium still can be involved with leased facilities, either reserved by the sponsor or owned by someone other than the condominium regime. For example, these facilities could involve garages or recreational areas. The part of the carrying charges attributable to such facilities is merely a payment of rent, even if the regime has the contractual burden to pay mortgage indebtedness or real property taxes applicable to such outside-owned property from the collections of carrying charges paid by unit owners. As a general rule, rent paid for residential occupancy or use of property is not deductible by the resident.

REFINANCING INDIVIDUAL MORTGAGES

One of the chief tax advantages of the condominium unit owner stems from the customary practice of issuing individual, separate mortgages on each unit (including the interest in common elements). Because of this feature in most condominium ownership, the prospective benefits from future mortgage refinancing inure to the condominium unit owner. Such purchaser will gradually be paying back his or her mortgage loan through amortization payments. Even though the constant charges on long-term mortgages include a disproportionately high percentage of interest payment during the first six or seven years, increases in the market value of the condominium unit serve as a hedge against inflation without the need to sell. Having a greater value, the unit may serve as security for an increased or new and larger mortgage loan. And even without sale or refinancing, the unit's increased value adds to the credit standing of the unit owner who wishes to borrow otherwise.

The increase in an existing mortgage or a new mortgage obligation to replace an existing mortgage probably does not constitute a taxable event but only a loan transaction. Upon the sale of the property, the unpaid additional mortgage balance will be added to the selling price received.

HOME IMPROVEMENT LOANS

Federal and state programs for financing improvements in residences are generally tailored more favorably to the homeowner than to the short-term tenant or cooperative lessee who cannot give fee ownership as security for the loan. The condominium homeowner should be able generally to benefit from such home improvement financing aids.

DEFERRING TAX ON SALE OR EXCHANGE

As a general rule, a taxpayer who sells or exchanges his or her principal residence may defer any taxable gain if he or she meets the requirements of Section 1034 of the Internal Revenue Code concerning purchasing or receiving in exchange a different principal residence during the required period of time. Such rule would apply if the new residence is a condominium or if the relinquished condominium is the principal place of residence. As in the case of the sale of an individual dwelling used as a residence by the seller, no loss is allowable where it is incurred on the transaction because the property is not used in a trade or business.

TAXABILITY OF ASSOCIATION RECEIPTS

Under Section 7701(a)(3) of the Internal Revenue Code, the term *corporation* is defined to include an association. To determine whether the income of an unincorporated condominium association is taxable under the Internal Revenue Code, the IRS examines such factors as whether the association has such corporate characteristics as associates, a business purpose, centralization of management, continuity of existence, transferable interests, and limited liability. Generally, organizations formed to operate and maintain property for the benefit of the project have associates and seek to carry on business and divide any gains therefrom. Accordingly, the unincorporated association need only have more corporate characteristics than noncorporate characteristics to be taxed as a corporation. Most, if not all, unincorporated condominium associations possess a sufficient number of these characteristics, and double taxation may result to the unit owners unless an exemption is available.

Some very large homeowner associations that perform public functions (e.g., maintenance of public streets, sidewalks, parks, monuments, slopes, etc.) may be successful in obtaining a complete tax exemption under Section 501(c)(4) of the Internal Revenue Code. However, the IRS scrutinizes applications under Section 501(c)(4) very carefully, and it will not issue such an exemption to a condominium association because the association primarily contains private property.

Section 528 of the code permits most residential condominium associations to file an annual election with the IRS which would allow the associations to be treated as tax-exempt organizations with respect to their exempt function income. Basically, exempt function income means membership dues or assessments received by the association. Hence, interest received from monies held in reserve would be taxable to the association as nonexempt function income.

To qualify for favorable tax treatment under Section 528, at least 85 percent of the total square footage of all of the units in the project must be used for residential purposes or for residential-related purposes (e.g., laundry or storage rooms). Therefore, commercial condominium associations and associations that manage mixed-use condominium projects containing less than 85 percent residential space are not permitted to file elections under Section 528 of the code. Moreover, at least 60 percent of the association's income must be exempt function income, and at least 90 percent of the expenditures must be used to acquire or maintain association property.

Some associations with a lot of nonexempt function income that would qualify under Section 528 (such as large associations with considerable reserve requirements) may choose not to file the election under Section 528. This is because the tax rate on nonexempt function income received by an association that files its election under Section 528 is *higher* than the tax rate on income received by an association that does not file an election.

If the condominium association does not choose to file under Section 528, then it may avail itself of certain techniques to minimize its tax liability. Regular assessments are generally included in the gross income of an association, and the association will take deductions for the expenses of operating the association property. If, at the end of any fiscal year of the association, there are excess assessments over expenses, the IRS has ruled that the excess will not constitute taxable income if the excess is either returned to the unit owners or applied against the following year's assessments. Otherwise, the excess will be taxable to the association. Hence, a large condominium association that is establishing or increasing its operating reserves would be well advised to be taxed under Section 528; and after the reserves have been funded, the association would probably be better advised not to file under Section 528.

Special assessments used for the construction of new capital improvements or for extensive repairs to existing capital improvements are not included in the association's gross income. These capital assessments are treated either as nontaxable receipts of the association pursuant to Section

61 of the code or as nontaxable contributions to the capital of the association pursuant to Section 118 of the code. The tax rulings os the IRS indicate that the members should vote for such special assessments, the special assessments should be specifically earmarked for a particular capital improvement, and the funds should be segregated and not commingled with the general funds of the association.

Therefore, those responsible for the preparation of the federal income tax returns of the condominium association should carefully consider, on a year-by-year basis, whether any advantage exists in the election of Section 528 of the code. Unless the association is accumulating operating reserves or is a relatively small association, the association will in most cases be well advised to forego the Section 528 election and file its tax return instead as a corporation.

MISCELLANEOUS TAX BENEFITS

Some states provide for partial real property tax exemption for veterans, the infirm, or the aged. Similar reductions in cost of housing often are not available to ordinary tenants or even owners of cooperative apartments who are classified as lessees under state laws.

ELEVEN

THE LEASEHOLD CONDOMINIUM

THE CONCEPT

Thus far, the chief concern of this text has centered on the division of property ownership by issuance of package deeds to units tied to undivided interests in common facilities. It is possible for a developer to reserve ownership of part of the property and to charge rent for its use by unit owners (as might be the case for a garage or parking area under or over the units). When the developer or his or her assignee reserves ownership of the entire land area, or of the land and building in entirety, the underlying principles of condominium are strained indeed if the tenant–residents are still to be called condominium owners. Instead of deeds, unit leases (including an undivided leasehold interest in the improvements and land) are issued which resemble proprietary leases issued by leasehold cooperative apartment corporations that do not own the underlying land. Unlike the leasehold cooperative, condominium characteristics, such as individual unit tax assessments and separate unit leasehold mortgages, are present in the condominium leasehold. Government of the condominium leasehold regime is similar to its fee counterpart.

DERIVATION OF LEASEHOLD CONDOMINIUM

The modern American leasehold condominium, typified by Hawaiian developments, does not have the direct European and South American antecedents of the fee condominium. While it is true that the English have employed the long-term lease in the sale of flats, we cannot credit them with the American leasehold condominium. Instead, we must conclude that such condominium has been composed out of the experience of Americans in commercial leasehold mortgage financing of major properties since World War II. Anyone reading a condominium leasehold mortgage and unit lease who is familiar with major realty financing through leaseholds immediately notes that one has given birth to the other.

Section 234 of the National Housing Act permits federal insurance of condominium unit mortgages secured by leaseholds. Hawaii, the first state to pass a condominium statute, found the public receptive to leasehold residency when accorded the protection of the condominium statute and learned that major insurance companies and banks, which were accustomed to writing major leasehold mortgage financing, were at home with the concept. Much of those islands can only be developed through the use of the long-term leasehold.

Because most American states ostensibly enacted condominium statutes to permit use of Section 234 insurance, many initially or later authorized some form of leasehold condominiums in purported consonance with Section 234. Sometimes the format of allowed leasehold is restricted, as is the case in New York, where only certain nonresidential leasehold condominiums are allowed.

JUSTIFICATION FOR LEASEHOLD CONDOMINIUMS

Before discussing specific mechanics, let us try to evaluate the economic justification for the technique. Any method that accomplishes a helpful result not otherwise obtainable is not to be turned aside. And in areas where valuable land cannot be purchased outright, any development housing solutions must conform to such restrictions.

A long-term leasehold involves 100 percent financing of the cost of the land. If the technique substantially reduces the cost of acquiring a condominium unit, the argument of economy has substance. In the 1950s, leasehold cooperatives in Florida sold for prices averaging one-third less than comparable apartments in fee cooperatives. On the other hand, many leasehold cooperatives and condominiums have sold for prices nearly equal to those for comparable fee cooperatives. However, when periodic rental adjustments occur, the leasehold prices tend to drop dramatically. The leasehold condominium technique should bring to the market units below the cost of fee units and at the same time can be economically feasible.

The condominium in leasehold form may, on the one hand, be a speculator's dream. On the other hand, it may be the key to affordable homeownership in a tight credit market. The speculator may break up his or her ownership into parts and sell off land to another. The developer may combine a leasehold condominium with an option to purchase the fee in a time of high interest rates. This affords below-market financing of the land (by way of lower rent payments) until the purchase option is exercised when (it is hoped) interest rates have declined. Sometimes the landowner refuses to deal directly with the condominium owners or the seller believes he or she can charge a premium rent above that charged by the landowner. In either case, the seller might create a sandwich lease between the owner and the condominium owners that, in effect, relinquishes only a sublease to unit owners.

The complexities of this form of ownership lend themselves to misrepresentation and sharp practice. At the same time, its very flexibility also might be used to create realty interests permitting housing that would not be available otherwise. The test of success of leasehold condominiums will be the availability of reasonable financing and public demand.

AVAILABILITY OF TAX DEDUCTIONS

The owner of a unit in a fee condominium may deduct mortgage interest and real property taxes, both of which are the obligations of a fee condominium owner payable directly to lender or government.

The extent of the availability of such deductions for unit lessees in the leasehold condominium has not yet been clearly established. In evaluating the proper treatment, the standard of difference may be whether the interest and taxes are to be considered as direct personal charges, rather than payments made via the landlord's requirements of rent. In California, taxes may be directly assessed on the unit lessee, but the tax is "a lien solely on the interest of the owner of the fee" (California Revenue and Tax Code, Section 2188.3), thus adding another confusing factor. What is important is that the tax or interest is the obligation of the taxpayer and not someone else. A residential unit owner would not be entitled to a deduction for real estate taxes if the taxes are the obligations of the landlord, which are reimbursed to the landlord in the form of additional rent.

Interest paid on a separate unit leasehold mortgage should be deductible as an interest deduction. Pro rata payment of interest through monthly maintenance charges on an overall leasehold mortgage blanketing all units may be deductible, if the Treasury Department continues the same rationale it employs for leasehold cooperatives covered by a blanket mortgage. This theory seems to indicate that the tax deduction capacity of individual interest payments is not violated merely because it is paid by an agency of the controlling owners.

The deduction for real property taxes may prove a more difficult problem. The leasehold cooperative stockholders are cut off from the right to deduct the entire payment of land and building taxes on acquired existing property (Revenue Ruling 62–177), because the tax is the burden of the landowner, regardless of any contractual arrangements requiring cooperators to pay the tax. On the other hand, through arbitrary determination by the Treasury (Revenue Ruling 62–178), cooperators may deduct that portion of the taxes paid by a cooperative on a building erected by the cooperative on land leased for a term running beyond the useful life of the building.

Where separate assessments are required by law and the tax burden is directly placed on a condominium leasehold unit lessee, it would seem that the deduction is available. But if the landowner's own tax must be paid directly by the condominium lessees or through escalated ground rentals, such additional tax payments would not seem to be deductible by the individual unit owners. Once a payment is characterized as rent, with the burden of the tax payment imposed directly on another by government, it is unlikely that the deduction will be permitted in the absence of a permissive ruling.

The use of a separate leasehold for each unit on which taxes are directly levied would be the best format to protect a tax deduction for income tax purposes. If the unit owners are really sublessees under a developer's overall leasehold, it is questionable whether direct tax deductions will always be available, but no doubt litigation will solve this problem eventually. It would seem to be an imposition on local tax authorities for any statute to be so construed as to require separate assessments on many layers of ownership. If the sublessee condominium unit owner is to be assessed separately, then an intermediary primary lessee must also be assessed separately, even though the latter might not ordinarily be assessed directly under local law. An intermediary independent owner of the master leasehold is not the owner of any form of condominium. The purpose of the condominium statute was to bring separate assessments to unit owners, not to leasehold subdividers.

There are two items to discuss. First, we must distinguish a leasehold condominium used by its owner as a personal residence from the same condominium rented out to another person or a nonresidential leasehold condominium used in a business or held for rental income. Where there is a business purpose behind the ownership, the taxes and interest, if paid as a rent reimbursement or directly, would be deductible as a business rental expense under Internal Revenue Code Section 162 or deductible as taxes and interest under other sections of the code.

The other item involves the limitation on the deduction of investment interest. Where the leasehold unit is held for business or rental purposes, interest may not be deductible if the investment interest limitation is exceeded under Section 163(d) of the code. This limits a deduction for interest where the unit is subleased to another under a net lease or where the sublessor is guaranteed a specific return on investment by the sublessee.

THE DEVELOPER'S POSITION

Sponsors of leasehold condominiums begin in one of several positions when contemplating such a development. The sponsor may presently own vacant land, or he or she may own land from which present structures must be cleared in order to make way for the condominium.

A developer is sometimes faced with the problem of wanting to develop an attractive site that cannot be purchased outright. The owner may not wish to sell the land because of the tax bite that will be taken out of the proceeds of the sale. In other cases, the present owner desires to retain the property in his or her family and pass it on to his or her heirs. The owner may be required to reserve an important use of the land, such as railroad passes, and, therefore, may consider selling only air rights in the form of a long-term leasehold.

As distinguished from such cases where the land may never be purchased, the developer may not wish to purchase land outright by means of an immediate full payment. Instead of a huge outlay immediately for the purchase of land, he or she prefers to work out a transaction whereby the seller agrees to permit the buyer to make payments for the land on a long-term basis. Assuming that ground rent payments fit into an adequate income pattern in this situation, such rents would be used to purchase the land as well as to produce an override of income.

The developer who wishes to purchase the land outright or by delayed payments over a long term will often also consider the greater flexibility in fixing prices of condominium leasehold units. The purchase price could be reduced so as to discount the absence of a land purchase. The combined costs of individual leasehold mortgage costs and ground rent to purchasers could be lower than the mortgage costs involved in a fee condominium. This may come about because fee mortgages tend to be amortized over fifteen to thirty years, whereas ground leases run for considerably longer periods, often between fifty and ninety-nine years. Therefore, the combination of a below-market ground lease and a leasehold mortgage could result in lowering the carrying charges to unit lessees. Of course, the discussion relates to possibilities and does not attempt to cover generalizations applicable to all cases.

During a recessionary period, those developers who are collecting ground rents are better able to weather the storm than those who do not enjoy such an annuity. Even during a seller's market, the landowner–developer may wish to maximize his or her profit by retaining land that he or she believes will continue to appreciate. If the land is sold subject to the leases in bulk several years later to an investor, the landowner may recognize capital gain on the sale, in lieu of ordinary income. Moreover, some developers of master-planned communities choose to lease the land as a way to maintain control over future development of parcels within the communities.

Market conditions that include a shortage of homes or the popularity of certain housing may lead the promoter to offer leasehold condominiums at prices and carrying costs equivalent to those of fee ownership. The developer may be interested in an annuity for his or her heirs, plus a reversionary interest at the end of the lease in a valuable building constructed with the funds of others. It should be noted, however, that there is authority under Internal Revenue Code Section 109 for stating that a lessor does not realize income from lessee improvements turned over to the lessor upon termination of the lease.

FRAGMENTED OR INDIVIDUAL UNIT LEASES

It is customary among larger institutional lenders on leasehold condominiums to require that each separate unit owner lease shall run directly to the landowner. Aside from the fact that there exist requirements for such a relationship under some state laws, as well as its being a prerequisite for FHA Section 234 financing, this attitude seems to be a wise one.

Fundamental to leasehold mortgages is the problem of guarding against the defeasance or wiping out of the lease by the landlord landowner or the intermediate lessee who subleases. Where one overall leasehold that is fragmented with respect to unit owner obligation exists, defeasance of the lease may be occasioned by acts or failures beyond the control of individual unit sublessees or lessee–assignees who are governed by a blanket lease. Whereas lenders tend to protect themselves by reserving the right to cure defaults on the lease, the degree of expenditures required of a unit lessee who is dependent on a blanket lease might be prohibitive enough to eliminate any real practical significance to his or her right to also cure, through his or her own efforts, defaults caused by others.

Individual leases provide institutional lenders with the means of spreading risk over a broader base, even if only one lender holds all of the mortgages on all of the unit leases. In the event of defeasance of one of many unit leases because of a default that was not cured by the mortgagee, the loss of security is far less than would be involved as a result of a default of a single overall lease that is entirely wiped out.

The occasional practice of sandwiching leases between landowner and condominium unit sublessee, or of otherwise fragmenting obligations under a single lease, presents substantial danger to condominium purchasers as well as to lending institutions and consequently necessitates maximum safeguards by statute in order to avoid excessive speculation, to provide for full disclosure to purchasers, and to assure adequate protection against wiping out the purchaser or lending position upon defeasance of the lease.

ATTORNMENT

If units are sold by a developer only in the form of sublease, purchasers should be protected by the same rights, including the right to notice of default with time to cure, as possessed by the primary lessee. This right to substitute a sublessee's position for a defaulting lessee, known generally as the right to *attornment,* would seem essential to anyone embarking on such a long-term sublessee position and should be tailored to the needs of fragmented interests. Such protection should also be made available to those who purchase unit leases on resale by way of subleasing arrangement.

ESCROW AND LEASEHOLD CONDOMINIUMS

A chief concern to unit lessees and sublessees should be the timely payment by the landowner and any intermediary lessees of property taxes, their own mortgage obligations, and ground rent, the default of which may cause defeasance of the condominium purchaser's ownership. For such reason, consideration should be given to direct payment for such obligations by the board of directors of the condominium (or impounded by the lender holding the leasehold or subleasehold mortgage) from amounts paid by condominium unit lessees in addition to common charges. In effect, the landowner would receive a net rent, as would any intermediary lessee.

Leasehold condominium mortgagees usually will require, at the minimum, that property taxes on the leasehold as well as hazard insurance premiums be paid into an escrow account maintained by the mortgagee, or that these amounts be escrowed by the condominium board with regular statements of account sent to the lender.

Most leasehold mortgagees, under existing American practice, insist on being given the right to timely notice to cure defaults by lessees, as well as the inclusion of a nondisturbance clause in any mortgages prior in right, in order to eliminate the chance of a fee mortgagee wiping out the basic security of the leasehold mortgage, the lease. In the latter case, the leasehold mortgagee would be given at least the right to receive adequate notice with time to cure defaults by the landowner with respect to the fee mortgage.

In addition, the leasehold mortgagee on unit leases usually will insist on insurance and condemnation provisions in the ground lease that will protect its financial position in case of the destruction of the property or the exercise of eminent domain.

TERMINATION OF THE LEASEHOLD CONDOMINIUM REGIME

When a fee condominium is terminated by vote of unit owners, land and other physical assets remain as a pool of security for fee unit mortgagees. However, upon such termination of a leasehold condominium regime, it must be expected that there will be much more disruption to security for leasehold mortgages. Mere clauses in leasehold mortgages that permit foreclosure in the event of a unit member or regime vote for termination hardly seem adequate protection for the mortgagee. And conditioning the finality of the vote on mortgagee approval may be inconsistent with some condominium statutes.

The safest situation for the mortgagee exists where the condominium statute conditions termination of the condominium regime upon the consent of the mortgagees. Mere imposition of monetary penalties on termination permitted by statute may not be adequate for leasehold lenders.

From the point of view of the unit lessee, the requirement that all mortgagees consent to termination may seriously affect his or her freedom of choice at some future date.

LEASEHOLDS—REAL OR PERSONAL PROPERTY

Quite often, an institutional lender will rely on the definitions set forth in a condominium-enabling statute in order to determine whether a leasehold condominium loan is authorized. An example of the confusion that can result from statutory drafting occurred in Florida. That statute spoke of condominium parcels as follows:

> A condominium parcel is a separate parcel of real property, the ownership of which may be in fee simple, or any other estate in real property recognized by law.

The argument, now largely academic because of new enactments, was made that a lease for years is personal property under Florida law and, thus, is not within the scope of the then Florida condominium law. Whether or not this position is justified, the importance of statutory clarification in all states of the intent to cover or not to cover leasehold condominiums is an important consideration to lenders, purchasers, and developers who are about to issue financing or organize under the provisions of the state condominium law.

Condominium-enabling legislation sometimes must be weighed against some state property laws that switch the characterization of long-term leases from personal property to real property if certain conditions are met. There are a few localities already providing for the direct assessment and taxation as real property of that part of ownership carved out in the form of long-term leases, even in the absence of submission of the leasehold to a condominium statute. What effect do such laws have on condominium statutes that do not expressly authorize leaseholds but cover real property? Some condominium statutes provide for separate taxation of unit leases only if the lease is a minimum term and requires the lessee to pay realty taxes, thereby confining the statute to only a segment of leaseholds.

LIABILITY OF PURCHASERS DURING CONSTRUCTION PERIOD

It is not unusual for a developer who enters into an initial construction lease to pay rent during the period of construction before the condominium is formed and individual leases issued or before assignments of the master lease are made on an independent basis. However, the developer may organize the condominium before construction, in order to place the burden of his or her own rental during construction on purchasers. Or he or she may obtain from the purchasers an agreement to contribute deposit money intended to represent the rental obligation of the purchaser even before the condominium exists. Starting on a lease before completion of the premises or before they are ready for occupancy should not be pursued by a purchaser without full legal counsel and a thorough explanation of rights involved.

FIXED OR VARIABLE RENTALS

Ground leases governing leasehold condominiums sometimes contain clauses providing for the escalation of rents after an initial period of the lease term has passed. Unfortunately, some of the clauses are so vague or are based on such a variety of unpredictable contingencies that the unit purchaser finds it unduly difficult to predict future rent liability. In addition, the market value of his or her lease may be seriously affected by an increased rental or the existence of the escalation clause.

In ordinary leasehold financing, it is not unusual to provide for periodic reappraisal of land market value (as if unimproved) for the purpose of fixing a rental based on some percentage formula such as 9 or 10 percent of appraised value. Such provision crops up in condominium ground leasehold arrangements as well, but in that case the rent would be set individually on some basis such as the percentage of common interest.

Another technique is to provide for the renegotiation of the rental after a number of years, with the matter to go to arbitration if no mutual agreement is reached. Because of the common use of separate leases, such an arrangement might provide for the condominium board's acting as the agent for the unit owners empowered to vote by majority on this issue. But such clause would violate the concept of separate, nondependent ground leases.

The simplest arrangements provide for specific increases in ground rent periodically. Sometimes the only escalation factor depends on an increase in real property taxes payable by the ground lessor.

The use of variable rentals removes somewhat the hedge against inflation and the opportunity for profit that ordinarily exists with respect to the fee condominium. However, the lending agencies in the secondary market usually will require the rents to be fixed for several years and then to be increased in accordance with a predetermined formula during at least the balance of the terms of the mortgages.

RESALE OF UNITS

Although not enough time has passed to gauge the experience of unit lessees trying to sell their interests, it may be expected that the passage of extensive periods after purchase will result in diminishing market resale prices. On the other hand, very long leases could be made more valuable by general economic inflationary conditions or by space shortages to such an extent that this problem will be hardly noticeable for a considerable period of time.

PURCHASING THE UNIT LEASE

Before signing a binding agreement the purchaser should be careful to obtain for review by his or her counsel at least the full text of the following documents:

1. The declaration.
2. The bylaws and house rules.

3. The ground lease (and any subleases and assignment agreements that govern his or her ownership).
4. The form of leasehold mortgage (and any fee mortgage that will remain in existence on the subject property).

A protective provision that adequate notice and time be given in the event of any curable default in the lease should be of primary importance to the purchaser–lessee. As noted previously, it is preferable from the purchaser's point of view to have a separate ground lease that runs directly from the landowner to the unit lease. It is also recommended that the governing condominium papers require that all ground rent leases must contain exactly the same language, with the exception of such individual matters as the names of unit lessees and the amount of the rental.

It is customary to set the unit lessee's share of the ground rent on the basis of the percentage of common interest assigned to the unit.

The most satisfactory title insurance policy for unit owners (if available) would insure against damages that result from the failure of the land title and the invalidity of the formation of the condominium under the law of the particular state.

The existence and extent of options granted to unit lessees to purchase the fee should be reviewed carefully. The option may require unanimous agreement by unit leaseholders, in order to convert to a fee condominium. This would avoid a patchwork situation that depreciates the value of the leasehold reversion to the landowner.

TWELVE

THE BROKER AND THE CONDOMINIUM

THE BROKER'S ROLE

It has been the interest and involvement of professional real estate brokers that has brought the final touches of confidence to purchasers in the condominium field. Brokers play a very important role in the resale of condominiums. The success and effectiveness of the resale market depends greatly on broker participation. While real estate moves more lethargically in resales than does the sale of listed securities with instant bid and offer prices, the mechanism of real estate brokerage gives a mobility that is essential to buyers of homes. After all, it is only reasonable to reflect about the possibilities for resale of a home being purchased. The consumer invests a large, if not the largest, portion of his or her wealth and credit in the purchase of a home and must, therefore, gauge the ease of liquidity in future years. The real estate broker is the recognized means of bringing buyer and seller together, of arranging financing, and of easing the negotiation on a practical level. The broker's commission, ordinarily payable by the seller, is his or her means of livelihood and depends on the consummation of the sale in most cases.

COMPETITION OF MANAGING AGENT

Few independent brokers handle resales in areas where the condominium format is relatively new. In such instances, the managing agent is the one who generally handles resales, using any of the following five methods:

1. The condominium bulletin board.
2. Newspaper advertising.
3. Storefront advertising at its nearby offices.
4. Discussions with home applicants who are initially interested in other forms of housing.
5. Discussions with applicants who make direct inquiries at the condominium offices.

It is not surprising that unit owners interested in selling tend to engage the managing agent to act as selling agent. The agent has access to the condominium books and records, is knowledgeable about its assets and method of operation, should have competent knowledge of going market prices, and will have the forms necessary for initial binders as well as brochures and other offering literature describing the premises.

The agent often is given the task (whether he or she is the broker in the transaction or not) of reviewing the background of the applicant in conformity with the right of first refusal lodged in the board. Of considerable importance, the agent must, in any event, arrange the details of moving in and out.

Where the agent also acts as broker, he or she must be licensed under state law and will probably engage his or her services at the prevailing rates charged by brokers in the area for the purchase of homes. The agent must also recognize that he or she is wearing two hats and avoid conflicts of interest wherever possible. The management business has become a natural loss leader to the brokerage business in California and some other states.

Where condominium ownership is more established, there has been a much greater influx of independent brokers into the condominium resale marketplace. In this case, the managing agent still retains a sizeable share of the market if he or she maintains a resident agent on the premises. If not, there is an equal likelihood that unit owners will seek out independent brokers for listing. Condominiums with smaller numbers of units that do not engage professional management are finding that unit resales regularly take place through independent brokers.

In states such as Florida, California, and Illinois, where the condominium has already taken on considerable significance, some brokers have veered toward condominiums as a specialty. Large brokerage firms may be expected more and more frequently to open condominium departments, as a considerable number have already done. Such activities have led to great competition in the management and original selling phase of the condominium.

NOTICE OF RESALES TO ASSOCIATION

Brokers too infrequently notify the condominium association of pending sales, perhaps because they are wary of any third party who could interfere with a prospective sale. The condominium association should have an effective means of receiving notice of prospective unit sales, so that it can clear up existing violations of the restrictions before close of the sale, and so that it can welcome the new homeowners and inform them of their obligations. Unfortunately, many associations do not learn of resales until months after they occur, often when the billings to the previous owner are returned unpaid.

Some jurisdictions (Maryland is an example) recognize what is known as the trust and lien-upon-sale technique to enforce assessment payments. The statutes of these jurisdictions require that upon any voluntary sale, all unpaid assessments must be paid either by the seller or by the purchaser. In jurisdictions where the trust and lien-upon-sale technique is not recognized, obtaining notice of resales can be difficult. Hence, notices of assessments creating liens and notices of noncompliance in architectural matters should be recorded as promptly as possible. To induce the purchaser to give the association notice of the resales, some projects' restrictions provide that the seller and the purchaser are jointly liable for the payment of assessments that accrued before the transfer.

One technique for obtaining prompt notice of resales is to request cooperation from local real estate brokers and escrow agents. Brokers and escrow agents may form the habit of furnishing information about pending sales to an association. Ultimately, the association may be able to maintain an undated index of new and pending purchasers as a service to the membership.

"FOR SALE" OR "FOR LEASE" SIGNS

The existence of many "for sale" and "for lease" signs in home windows or scattered around the common area can hamper the developer's continuing sales during the transition phase and can interfere with the smooth operation of the association after it has become independent. But it is difficult, if not illegal, to restrict the homeowner's ability to transfer his or her property. The enforceability of a restriction concerning the size, shape, color, and location of signs will be made easier if a reasonable alternative is available. Some associations have erected in the common area an aesthetically pleasing directory of homes available for sale or lease. The unit owners and local real estate brokers are then urged to utilize the directory instead of cluttering the common area with signs.

NEWSPAPER ADVERTISING TECHNIQUES

In the 1960s, one of the real difficulties encountered by condominium unit owners initially was finding a newspaper classified ad characterization in which to advertise a resale. At first, the tendency was to place the advertisement under the "homes for sale" classification if it was of the row house or townhouse type, and to place the advertisement under "apartments" or "cooperatives" if a highrise unit was involved. For such reason, newspapers in localities without heavy condominium concentrations are not too helpful in facilitating resales.

Now that the condominium form is well established, the classified sections generally contain headings such as "condominiums," "condominiums for sale," "community homes," "community homes–condominiums," or some similar descriptive headings.

Local real estate boards should continue to encourage newspapers to provide clarity in classification for this new form of ownership.

Typical language employed by brokers in condominium unit advertising is exemplified in catch phrases:

Don't pay the rent increase.
Privacy balconies, sun deck, sauna bath.
Maintenance costs and real estate taxes fully established.
Elevator condominium.
You can own a luxurious apartment home.
Almost new condominium.
Carefree living.
Freeze your own rent at—.
New and resale condominiums.
For sale or rent.
Tax deduction apartment.

An advertisement offering a unit both for sale and alternatively for rent often denotes a distress situation, although sometimes the owner merely wishes to learn of the income potential of renting. It is recommended that such units be advertised separately under condominiums for sale and apartments for rent, in order to avoid the immediate reader reaction that there is the probability of distress. Of course, some readers might feel that apparent distress guarantees a bargain.

If low down payments are required on resales, they are as much a selling feature as they are with other homes. In addition, the availability and terms of financing also might be emphasized, as is so often the case in condominium advertising.

Sometimes condominium advertisements read, "Lease with Option to Buy," or the equivalent. Such advertising belongs under "apartments" or "homes for lease." The broker should consider the commission in such cases, within the limits of local law, from the point of view of leasing and the possible sale. That is, the broker may wish to take the listing only on condition that he or she receive an additional commission on the resale.

Because of the growing mobility of the population, many brokers offering luxury units employ national media advertising in magazines or national newspapers. There is even a growing number of advertisements in Europe and South America in which foreigners seek second homes in the United States. Advertising in the United States for condominiums in such countries as France, Spain, Switzerland, and Israel is also not uncommon. Before advertising in a foreign country, it may be wise to employ the counsel of expert foreign brokers, unless the American brokerage firm employed maintains an international division.

A BASIC GUIDE FOR REAL ESTATE BROKERS

Assuming that a real estate broker has read the earlier material in this book, here is some additional material for his or her special use. First, it would be especially helpful for the broker or other reader to restudy the appraisal checklist shown in Chapter 4 from the point of view of a broker with whom a condominium home is being listed.

It is further suggested that the broker immediately obtain the following initial information for his or her file:

1. Both a graphic and a technical description of the unit and the specific percentage of common interest attached thereto.
2. The availability of a certificate of first refusal, or a waiver, from the board of managers.
3. The condition of the maintenance payment account on the unit (amount of charges, budgetary prospects for increases, method of collection, and initial escrow required of new owners).

4. Any mortgage outstanding on the unit offered for sale, with terms and conditions, especially the conditions for prepayment of principal, and the current payments to the mortgagee and constituent elements (taxes and insurance premiums, if included in the payments).

5. The number of units that are owner-occupied and the number of units leased or owned by the sponsor or his or her assignees.

6. Whether the condominium regime is in default, with respect to common elements, on any contract or obligation relating to construction, alteration, restoration, maintenance, or repair.

7. Whether the unit listed for sale or lease or the unit owner thereof is in default under the management documents.

8. The state of repair of recreational facilities such as swimming pools.

9. The names of all banks that have given condominium loans with respect to any units.

10. Any restrictions on residency (children, retirees, etc.).

11. Parking facilities.

12. Responsibility for internal and external maintenance.

13. The existence of any transfer fees on the sales of condominium association membership.

14. Responsibility for insurance of common areas and unit contents and exact line of demarcation.

Otherwise, the basic real estate information involved in offering a one-family home will be essentially similar.

WARNING TO BROKERS

To assure that the right of first refusal does not create any inconsistency with a broker's binder form, it is recommended that he or she add language similar to the following:

Binder for unit _____. This document is subject to conditions of sale set forth in the declaration and bylaws applicable to such unit.

THIRTEEN

THE STOCK COOPERATIVE—
HISTORICAL, SOCIAL,
AND FINANCIAL PERSPECTIVES

The most popular type of community housing in the United States in the period from 1945 through 1961 took the form of the cooperative housing corporations that issued stock and privileged proprietary leases to participants. In some states, the upsurge in popularity of this form of housing was dramatic. More than $100 million have been invested in Florida cooperatives alone since World War II. In New York City, generally considered to be truly America's co-op city, more than $1 billion was invested by purchasers of unsubsidized cooperative apartments by 1983. While there is evidence that the movement to new private cooperative construction was considerably curtailed in many previously active areas, such as Florida and Illinois, with the advent of the condominium, there has been a growing interest in the cooperative form in places as far apart as California and Massachusetts. The major conversion of rental apartment houses to cooperatives in Manhattan has been affected very little, thus far, by the condominium form. With few exceptions, existing rental units that were converted to resident ownership elsewhere in the United States before 1970 were changed also to cooperative rather than condominium status. An early example, the pioneer town laid out by the U.S. Resettlement Administration in 1935 to experiment with cluster housing in Greenbelt, Maryland, was later sold to tenants in cooperative form. After 1970, most conversions outside New York were made to condominiums. However, since 1980, a renewed interest in cooperatives has emerged.

The builder and the prospective resident, as well as government agencies charged with urban renewal responsibilities, still must often choose between the condominium and the cooperative, or between ordinary tenancy and cooperative, or between one-family homes and the cooperative apartment. In a few American localities, stringent shortages of apartments in central, high-rise locations have led to a major trend in conversions of existing apartment houses to cooperatives. There is movement to similarly convert waning hotels in good areas to cooperative ownership. Thousands of cooperative apartments are offered for resale each year, giving purchasers of resales this alternative form of housing in those communities containing substantial existing inventories, mainly large urban centers such as New York, Chicago, San Francisco, and Miami. Federal and state housing programs currently utilize the cooperative broadly and will support much of the new construction in this field.

Thus far this study has analyzed the condominium with only occasional mention of competitive forms, the chief reference being to its most important national alternative competition, full homeownership. Whereas such comparisons were usually without restriction regarding geographical location of condominium units, there are and will be major urban areas of the United States where the important competition to the condominium will be the rental apartment and the stock cooperative. And in a few situations the cooperative form is so well established that it will remain dominant for many years.

Some initial studies of the condominium were made by writers residing near major urban centers in which the cooperative had already been established. Because of the lack of both substantial experience and adequate economic and historical data for the condominium, the tendency was to emphasize comparisons with the cooperative, for which data (although limited) did exist. Subsequent writers tended to repeat such framework when discussing the condominium. The authors of this text have not followed that strategy. In contrast to such attitudes, they believe that the condominium should be presented on its own, as was attempted in earlier chapters of this book, because it is not derived from the cooperative and because the interested purchaser in most parts of the United States will not be judging the condominium in comparison with cooperatives.

The cooperative is a major form of housing that bears study on its own. The history and format of cooperatives may help the reader understand some of the basic underpinnings of community housing demands and solutions that dominated the first sixty-five years of this century in the United States.

HISTORICAL PERSPECTIVE—EUROPE

Cooperatives were not a significant factor in European housing development until the end of World War I and the ensuing housing and financing shortage. The period of greatest cooperative development followed World War II and resulted from similar conditions.

Scandinavian cooperatives, such as the Swedish HSB, have sought to eliminate the profit factor from new cooperative developments. There, the cooperative venture begins with building societies that manage fund raising and construction. These are the so-called mother cooperatives. The completed and operating housing cooperative, called a daughter, then functions separately under a protective alliance with the mother to provide for more effective management. The individual purchaser of the cooperative apartment owns shares in the development and is subject to a privileged lessee status that affords a great deal of independence. Similar types of cooperative organization exist in many other continental countries.

An interesting aspect of European cooperative housing societies has been the utilization of this device in a considerable number of cases for the purpose of creating outright individual ownership, rather than permanent cooperative tenancy. After the completion of construction, which is accomplished on a cooperative basis (and before which the eventual owner has purchased a certificate designating a number of cooperative shares), either individual or condominium form of ownership is conveyed, although this sometimes does not occur until the repayment by the purchaser of his or her share of the loan made to finance construction. In the latter case, the purchaser retains cooperative status while purchasing his or her home over a ten- or twenty-year period.

The typical French pre–World War II cooperative was organized exclusively to aid in outright home purchases. Only in 1947 did the Scandinavian form of permanent privileged tenancy come into use in France. By 1956, more than 80,000 homes in West Germany, which were built under cooperative auspices since the end of World War II, had been conveyed to purchasers as their individual property.

In many instances of such home purchases, the continual controls by the cooperative society resulted in a relationship that was more like a condominium than outright ownership. Resale was more often than not conditioned on cooperative board approval. Even after receiving his or her own home, the individual owner had to remain a member of the cooperative and was subject to some cooperative limitations on commonly used facilities. What was often characterized as full homeownership was actually title to and complete freedom within an individual apartment or home, with shared rights in the commonly used facilities. In countries where the populace has long equated the condominium with individual ownership, such remaining cooperative strings posed no problem to most purchasers.

European private lenders and government financing sources have readily financed nonprofit housing societies organized to develop housing units on a cooperative basis, both for permanent cooperative housing operation and even eventual individual ownership. Because of the expertise developed and the lower cost of production free from a private sponsor's profit motivation, many European countries were able to provide substantial numbers of new housing units at low and moderate cost to growing populations beset by housing shortages. In a few cases, there have been complaints of inefficiency and poor construction.

In Europe, private builders concerned with cooperative forms of housing have tended to concentrate on condominiums, financing the new construction on a private profit basis.

European cooperatives have been intended primarily as a means of solving acute shortages of housing for lower- and middle-income residents. This has been true particularly in Scandinavia, Germany, Italy, Austria, and Switzerland. The luxury cooperative is largely an American creation. Upper middle-class and luxury community apartments or homes in most European countries are typically condominium. The cooperative format dominates Soviet Russian housing and suffers from frantic consumer demand and poor construction.

SOME COMPARATIVE EUROPEAN FEATURES

An interesting feature of some European cooperatives is the allocation of a separate repair fund for each apartment, with an overall cooperative reserve fund set aside for emergencies. This feature has no real similarity to the American security deposit, since all repairs, from ordinary wear and tear to intentional abuse, are funded from the cooperator's own repair account. In the case of many Swedish cooperatives, such funds have been accumulated through monthly payments until 5 percent of the apartment's original value is reached. Cooperators who maintain their apartments in good repair can thus reduce their monthly payments. This method also removes some of the burden resulting from sudden assessments on residents to cover repairs in badly kept residences of others. The actual physical internal repairs are made by the cooperative but are paid for by the resident himself or herself through deductions from his or her own repair account, or by special assessments against him or her personally.

Another generally existing feature of importance is the widespread prohibition on speculation in apartments. This takes the form of limiting resale prices in order to assure a return of only the actual investment without additional profit. This approach has been a precursor of American attitudes toward middle- and lower-income publicly assisted cooperatives.

THE TWO FORMS OF AMERICAN COOPERATIVES

American cooperatives fall into two categories—conventional and publicly assisted. In the former, whether new construction, conversion, or rehabilitation of existing units, the promotion of housing is a private affair limited mainly by local zoning and building codes with prices fixed by the law of supply and demand. In the various approaches of the government-aided segment, there is a customary limited profit permitted to the private or organizational sponsor as a condition for the grant of government aid, which may be in such forms as direct financing (usually below market) or mortgage insurance, tax abatement, or direct subsidy to income groups sufficient to cover the purchase price or carrying charges, or both. Such programs involve federal, state, or local assistance, and often in combination.

Each type involves issuance of shares of stock to cooperators, who subject themselves to a tenancy status under a lease that defines their rights and obligations with respect to their apartments and commonly used facilities. In many instances, the lease is referred to as a proprietary lease because it is undertaken by a co-owner of the building.

Because these two forms of cooperatives are quite different in some important aspects, we must distinguish between them in our discussion. The limited number of publicly assisted condominium developments indicates that a principal choice alternative to a typical condominium purchaser will be the conventional, rather than subsidized, cooperative in the immediate future. Nevertheless, the prospect of future use of the condominium for government-subsidized housing looms large, and an understanding of the cooperative alternative is important.

FINANCING THE COOPERATIVE

In most conventional mortgage situations, the financing of the cooperative during both the development and take-out stage is more nearly like commercial real estate investment financing than it is financing of ordinary homeownership or condominium regimes. A single construction loan blankets the initial development, but the permanent loan usually is in the form of a single mortgage undertaken by the cooperative corporation.

Several important features stem from this relationship. The corporate loan eliminates an individual personal obligation to the lender. Its terms tend to equate with other commercial loans that carry high interest rates (interest rates paid by corporations are not limited by state usury laws in most cases), and frequently involve balloon payments at the end of three to ten years during which the borrower has made constant payments. Second mortgages are also common, because the ratio of first mortgage to total combined purchase price is, on the average, between 50 and 70 percent. Except for government programs, 80 or 90 percent cooperative mortgages are rare indeed.

Many purchasers of cooperatives, new and resale, do not pay adequate attention to the underlying financing arrangements. For example, there is too little concern that in three to ten years a large balloon payment is due, which, although its payment will be facilitated by an easy money climate, may be extremely difficult to handle if funds are tight. Of course, experience has shown that, in many actual cases of balloon maturity during tight money situations in the late 1970s, the lender holding the mortgage was forced into repeated refinancing where the alternative would have been foreclosure. In most cases, the lender is forced to refinance at an attractively increased interest rate. There is usually a much more rapid amortization of commercial mortgages, which start with a higher amortization formula than one-family home or condominium mortgages, so that a considerably reduced outstanding balance faces the cooperative at the time when the balloon comes due.

In the 1930s, balloon features led to the bankruptcy of many cooperative housing corporations in the United States. Such mortgages usually were standing mortgages, which did not provide for amortization until maturity. The problem of personal bankruptcy often accompanied these failures because of irrevocable proprietary leases that could not be abandoned without continuing liability by stockholder–tenants for nonpayment of charges that were insuperable because of defaults of others. The modern conventional proprietary lease in the active cooperative jurisdiction of New York generally permits the abandonment of premises and lease under terms that could at least avoid this personal liability. This tenant right is included in many leases written for publicly assisted housing cooperatives as well. In contrast, homeowners and condominium unit owners cannot merely walk away from their personal mortgage responsibility.

In effect, most cooperative mortgage loans carry only corporate (limited) liability. Because of the terms of the proprietary lease, there is really no personal responsibility for deficiencies in overall mortgage payments.

Whereas the homeowner or condominium unit owner can look forward to the benefits of refinancing his or her mortgage and a higher equity on resale, the cooperator is most often bound by management decisions applicable to the blanket mortgage condition. Unfortunately, a pro rata share of the corporate mortgage cannot be refinanced to provide cash for an emergency or the education of a child.

FINANCING THE DOWN PAYMENT

The commercial type of mortgage (with a lower loan-to-value ratio than other forms of housing) blanketing the conventional cooperative often necessitates a large cash investment by apartment purchasers in new construction. In conversions, the large underlying mortgage or mortgages can be used more flexibly to reduce the cash purchase price of units.

Generally, shares of cooperative stock entwined with a proprietary lease are not considered, for banking purposes, to be a form of real property capable of serving as security for a real estate mortgage loan. (See *State Tax Commission* v. *Shor,* 43 N.Y. 2d 151, decided by the New York Court of Appeals in 1977.) As an important result, special state enabling legislation is required for state-regulated institutions to make such loans. This has been done in some states, such as New York, Illinois, and California. Most federally chartered institutions can make loans secured by cooperative units, including federal savings and loan associations, that are allowed to make loans on terms similar to those secured by single-family homes. (See 12 C.F.R. Sections 541.10–4, 546.6–1[b].) New York savings associations in 1983 were allowed to make cooperative unit loans that are in the nature of alternative mortgage transactions.

Besides a note, security agreement, assignment of lease, and stock, the lender typically will also require a recognition agreement, signed by the cooperative apartment corporation, that indicates consent to the loan and sets the procedure to be followed on loan default. In addition, the institution should require basic, unchangeable clauses in a uniform proprietary lease that will tie a loan default, or lease default, to mutual action by the cooperative and the lender.

Some cooperative boards will not allow any pledge of stock, or they severely limit the percentage of appraisal value or purchase price that may be financed. This type of restriction, often said to be based on the need for individual fiscal responsibility, usually does not face the condominium buyer.

COST OF THE COOPERATIVE APARTMENT

Most purchasers of cooperatives relate the total cost of their apartments to the required cash investment, disregarding the pro rata share of the corporate mortgage that must be paid by each cooperator in the form of carrying charges.

On the other hand, the purchaser of a condominium or a one-family home relates the cost of the home to his or her cash investment plus the mortgage placed on the property.

For these reasons, cooperative apartments sometimes appear to be much more cheaply priced in advertising brochures and newspaper ads. When the cooperative mortgage is considered, a much more realistic comparison is made.

THE PRACTICALITY OF COOPERATIVES—LOCATION, ZONING, ACCEPTABILITY

Why should anyone make a substantial investment in order to become merely a tenant? That is the basic question asked by many who are faced with the choice between being an ordinary tenant and becoming a cooperator. The question is erroneous, because the cooperator has substantial ownership rights that far exceed those of the ordinary rental tenant, such as tenure, profitability, sharing in management, and income tax benefits. The answer is obvious in areas where no other housing can be obtained at affordable prices. In such situations the overriding benefit of housing availability puts most other considerations to rest. With few exceptions, there will be some competitive tenancy units in the same area, because the zoning that permits the cooperative will probably admit similar units designed for rentals. Many of the zoning problems applicable to condominiums also face cooperative developers, largely because reference to cooperatives rarely appears in zoning codes and the general use of the look-alike mystique guides so many local officials.

Throughout the United States, there is a greater tendency to permit the construction of condominiums in one-family house areas than there is to allow cooperative apartments to be so constructed. A continuation of this attitude may be expected because of the similarity of the direct tax burdens borne by homeowners and condominium unit owners. Even though the single real property and school tax placed on a highrise or lowrise cooperative corporation may be equated to the total sum of possible individual assessments on apartment owners, local homeowner bias works against the cooperative.

There has been a wider acceptance of cooperatives in one-family home neighborhoods when the price ranges of apartments are close to or higher than home prices. For example, in one luxury cooperative in a northeastern state, apartments, stacked two high, sold for prices considerably higher than many of the one-family homes in the adjoining area. The buildings jutted into a bay and were luxuriously furnished. Initial dissatisfaction on the part of some of the homeowner residents soon cooled when they realized that the assessments would bring badly needed taxes into the community and that most cooperative residents did not have primary-school-age children.

The cooperative form has provided middle- and low-income housing in some urban areas, but almost always housing has been constructed under public assistance programs, such as the Mitchell–Lama developments in New York and somewhat similar programs in Arkansas, California, Delaware, Florida, Illinois, Kansas, Massachusetts, New Jersey, Ohio, Pennsylvania, South Carolina, and Texas, or with the aid of mortgage insurance under FHA programs such as Section 213 of the National Housing Act. New programs are envisioned by Congress in legislation aimed at aiding low-income citizens in purchasing cooperatives who would not otherwise ever be able to own their residences. Developments already financed under local programs generally offer new housing with carrying charges below rentals of new apartment structures, although the gap that existed when most of these programs began lessened considerably with the passage of time. The two factors leading to the largest increase in carrying charges have been increased construction costs and higher interest rates on the housing bonds that must be liquidated by such charges in many programs. By increasing real estate tax abatement, some localities have alleviated some of the pressures of rising costs. Recent federal laws treat cooperative units as separate homes where authority exists for tax-exempt bonds to be issued by localities for the provision of below-market interest mortgages.

Because conventional cooperatives are accepted as luxury housing in a few localities, they appeal to community-living persons who are well able to afford rental apartments or even one-family homes in the surrounding area. For many wealthy residents, the cooperative offers very attactive living accommodations and not by any means a form of housing of last resort. Managing agents are well aware that the right to approve purchasers given to the board helps to foster and maintain snobbish economic and social status of the residents that many wealthy persons find attractive.

In the past several years, the private cooperative form has been used mainly in apartment conversions from rental status. In New York alone, more than 1000 buildings are so involved.

In 1981, a Model Real Estate Cooperative Act was proposed by the Uniform Laws Commissioners. Thus far, it has not been widely accepted.

PROFIT CONTROL

Proprietary leases typically run for the life of the conventional cooperative corporation. Technically, they generally have initial terms of twenty to fifty years but are either automatically renewable or can be extended at the will of the owners at the end of the lease term. Only in the cooperative where the corporation owns a long-term leasehold rather than full fee ownership must there be real concern about the eventual defeasance of ownership that will wipe out a valuable asset for a cooperator's heirs. Even in leasehold cooperatives, however, the standard term is typically so long a period as not to have much immediate significance, usually being fifty to ninety-nine years.

Long-term proprietary residence affords major protection against rent increases, which can usually be expected at the end of one to three years in ordinary leases. The profit factor is removed when the apartments are owned and operated by the self-owned cooperative corporation on a nonprofit basis.

To the extent that ownership is limited, as in the case of the leasehold cooperative, some aspects of landlord profiting may remain. Sometimes, initial ground rent is based on appraised value of the land (as if without the improvement) at the commencement of the leasehold term, with the rent ranging somewhere between 8 and 12 percent of such value. The lease may require periodic reappraisal of such land in order to fix a new rental. Some leasehold terms require escalation of rentals in the event that certain situations arise, such as increased real property taxes on the underlying land or the annual percentage increases of all costs to the cooperative other than rent.

Because of shorter terms underlying bank financing, readjustment of interest rates adds bank profit as another continued problem.

APPRECIATION IN VALUE

Subject to the approval of new owners by the cooperative board, the conventional cooperator may sell his or her apartment at the highest profit obtainable and retain such profit. Publicly assisted cooperatives generally prohibit such profits, as do many FHA-insured or subsidized developments that follow the European approach.

Tremendous profits have been made by many persons who bought cooperatives built at the end of World War II. These have more than offset the widespread pessimism engendered by the notoriety of tremendous losses experienced in the 1930s by cooperators in structures built before the Depression. Assuming a gradual rate of inflation, the owner of the conventional cooperative who makes a substantial investment can look forward to a potential profit in the same way as the homeowner does in this period of increasing population and prime land shortage. Looking to the future, the two chief factors of good location and good construction must be deliberated extensively, if the purchaser is interested in acquiring both a hedge against ordinary inflation and a protection against loss of value from an unsuspected decline in the economy.

However, there is no assurance that the price available for a particular cooperative unit must rise at all or by any point in time.

SHARING IN MANAGEMENT

Decoration and maintenance are subject to landlord control in ordinary tenancies, as is the determination of the adequacy of heating, snow removal, and play areas for children. In the case of the cooperative, the landlord's place will be assumed by the cooperative board of directors and its elected officers and committees, often operating through a managing agent under a one- to three-year contract. Because of his or her participation in the election of the board, the cooperator will have a voice in governing the cooperative, a factor lacking in ordinary tenancy. Some publicly assisted cooperatives are subject to government regulation that limits heavy expenditures without government approval. Sometimes the control is so great that management, although technically vested in a cooperative corporation, really has been placed in a government agency. In such cases, the cooperative eliminates the landlord's profit without assuming self-management. This procedure may help in overriding the difficulty of self-management arising in subsidized cooperatives, but many of the restrictions seem aimed at insulating government officials from the necessity of dealing with cooperators on management decisions and result in the prevention of any exercise of self-reliance on the part of lower-income groups. The security of housing bonds too often supersedes other considerations.

CAREFREE LIVING

One reason for the avoidance of homeownership by some persons is the desire not to assume the burdens of home maintenance, especially outside decoration and landscaping. Tenants often have been heard comparing their carefree status with homeowners who they contend spend an agonizing day each week in the summer doing gardening and cutting grass and many wintery days clearing snow. The cooperator usually eliminates such care by joint action in employing others. Vacations can be taken with less worry about the security of the home. Older residents possess a substantial degree of fixed living costs without the trials of heavy physical exertion. Cooperatively owned swimming pools and other recreational facilities sometimes exist in less urbanized areas, although to date most conventional cooperative developments possess a minimum of such facilities. These facilities have little attraction for city highrise cooperatives catering to the wealthy, who are more concerned with privacy and being surrounded by others of the same social status. The luxury resort cooperative that is actually a second home purchased exclusively for recreation presents an entirely different picture. Here, maintenance of expensive recreational facilities by management eliminates personal care and makes possible an arrangement whereby the cooperative can be kept ready for periodic visits.

MOBILITY

The apartment tenant undertakes a shorter-term lease than the average cooperator. Nevertheless, it is usually more difficult and slower, if possible at all, for the tenant to vacate the premises without continuing his or her liability for the payment of rent.

The cooperator usually can choose the time to sell his or her apartment. Presently, cooperative apartments are in great demand in many communities throughout the United States, and the means for resale have developed so that such transfers have been relatively easy. In general, the cooperator can look forward to greater mobility dependent only upon the decision to move. Such mobility reduces the danger of being saddled for long periods with unfriendly neighbors or of being tied to financial payments that prove to be beyond the cooperator's ability. Even if a loss must be sustained by the cooperator, he or she at least is relieved promptly of the responsibility for monthly charges.

On the opposite level, the trend toward apartment conversions lessens the freedom to move to other rental units. In future years, the only way to move will be to buy another apartment. Owning one beforehand enhances the ability to move by providing cash proceeds for the switch.

TAX BENEFITS TO COOPERATORS

Since 1913, homeowners have been allowed to deduct real property taxes and the interest paid on home mortgage obligations from their personal income taxes. During the early years of the income tax law, rates were too low to justify the conclusion that homeownership, as distinguished from apartment renting, carried a substantial financial boon. The flight to living accommodations that would provide the owner with income tax deductions has increased as the tax rates increased and rental costs rose. Under Section

216 of the Internal Revenue Code, these two deductions are allowed to co-operators.

The stories of thousands of cooperative apartment purchasers clearly demonstrates that an overwhelming majority considers the availability of tax deductions to be just as important as location and current carrying charges. Rarely is a cooperative sold today without a breakdown for the purchaser of available tax deductions. Such benefits did not come about easily, and it was not until 1954 that favorable deduction treatment was accorded to cooperative developments other than the previously covered apartment buildings given such benefits in 1942, so that now cluster and detached-unit cooperatives are also covered. In 1931, probably in recognition of the growing number of cooperatives, New York became the first American jurisdiction with an income tax statute granting cooperative dwellers the right to deduct interest and taxes applicable to their apartments. A restrictive provision of that law, requiring 100 percent occupancy of the building for dwelling purposes only, created a precedent that was carried over, though in less severe form, into federal law.

INTERNAL REVENUE CODE SECTION 216

The provisions of Section 216 of the Internal Revenue Code as set forth below describe the deductions of taxes, interest, and business depreciation that may be taken by cooperative housing corporation stockholder–tenants.

SECTION 216

Section 216(a). Allowance of Deduction. In the case of a tenant-stockholder (as defined in subsection (b) (2)), there shall be allowed as a deduction amounts (not otherwise deductible) paid or accrued to a cooperative housing corporation within the taxable year, but only to the extent that such amounts represent the tenant-stockholder's proportionate share of

1. the real estate taxes allowable as a deduction to the corporation under section 164 which are paid or incurred by the corporation on the houses or apartment building and on the land on which such houses (or building) are situated, or

2. the interest allowable as a deduction to the corporation under section 163 which is paid or incurred by the corporation on its indebtedness contracted

A. in the acquisition, construction, alteration, rehabilitation, or maintenance of the houses or apartment building, or

B. in the acquisition of the land on which the houses (or apartment building) are situated.

Section 216(b). Definitions.—For purposes of this section—

1. Cooperative Housing Corporation. The term "cooperative housing corporation" means a corporation

A. having one and only one class of stock outstanding,

B. each of the stockholders of which is entitled, solely by reason of his ownership of stock in the corporation, to occupy for dwelling purposes a house, or an apartment in a building, owned or leased by such corporation,

C. no stockholder of which is entitled (either conditionally or unconditionally) to receive any distribution not out of earnings and profits of the corporation except on a complete or partial liquidation of the corporation, and

D. 80 percent or more of the gross income of which for the taxable year in which the taxes and interest described in subsection (a) are paid or incurred is derived from tenant-stockholders.

2. Tenant-stockholder. The term "tenant-stockholder" means an individual who is a stockholder in a cooperative housing corporation, and whose stock is fully paid-up in an amount not less than an amount shown to the satisfaction of the Secretary as bearing a reasonable relationship to the portion of the value of the corporation's equity in the houses or apartment building and the land on which situated which is attributable to the house or apartment which such individual is entitled to occupy.

3. The term "tenant-stockholder's proportionate share" means that proportion which the stock of the cooperative housing corporation owned by the tenant-stockholder is of the total outstanding stock of the corporation (including any stock held by the corporation).

4. Stock owned by governmental units. For purposes of this subsection, in determining whether a corporation is a cooperative housing corporation, stock owned and apartments leased by the United States or any of its possessions, a State or any political subdivision thereof, or any agency or instrumentality of the foregoing empowered to acquire shares in a cooperative housing corporation for the purpose of providing housing facilities, shall not be taken into account.

5. Stock acquired through foreclosure by lending institution. If a bank or other lending institution acquires by foreclosure (or by instrument in lieu of foreclosure) the stock of a tenant-stockholder, and a lease or the right to occupy an apartment or house to which such stock is appurtenant, such bank or other lending institution shall be treated as a tenant-stockholder for a period not to exceed three years from the date of acquisition. The preceding sentence shall apply even though, by agreement with the cooperative housing corporation, the bank (or other lending institution) or its nominee may not occupy the house or apartment without the prior approval of such corporation.

6. Stock owned by person from whom the corporation acquired its property—

A. In General—If the original seller acquires any stock of the corporation from the corporation or by foreclosure, the original seller shall be treated as a tenant-stockholder for a period not to exceed 3 years from the date of the acquisition of such stock.

B.   Stock acquisition must take place not later than 1 year after transfer of dwelling units.—Except in the case of an acquisition of stock of a corporation by foreclosure, subparagraph (a) shall apply only if the acquisition of stock occurs not later than 1 year after the date on which the apartments or houses (or leaseholds therein) are transferred by the original seller to the corporation. For purposes of this subparagraph and subparagraph (a), the term "by foreclosure" means by foreclosure (or by instrument in lieu of foreclosure) of any purchase-money security interest in the stock held by the original seller.

C.   Original seller must have right to occupy apartment or house.—Subparagraph (A) shall apply with respect to any acquisition of stock only if, together with such acquisition, the original seller acquires the right to occupy an apartment or house to which such stock is appurtenant. For purposes of the preceding sentence, there shall not be taken into account the fact that, by agreement with the corporation, the original seller or its nominee may not occupy the house or apartment without the prior approval of the corporation.

D.   Original seller defined.—For purposes of this paragraph, the term "original seller" means the person from whom the corporation has acquired the apartments or houses (or leaseholds therein). The estate of an original seller shall succeed to, and take into account, the tax treatment of the original seller under this paragraph.

Section 216(c). Treatment as Property Subject to Depreciation.—So much of the stock of a tenant-stockholder in a cooperative housing cooperation as is allocable, under regulations prescribed by the Secretary, to a proprietary lease or right of tenancy in property subject to the allowance for depreciation under section 167(a) shall, to the extent such proprietary lease or right of tenancy is used by such tenant-stockholder in a trade or business or for the production of income, be treated as property subject to the allowance for depreciation under section 167(a). The preceding sentence shall not be construed to limit or deny a deduction for depreciation under 167(a) by a cooperative housing corporation with respect to property owned by such a corporation and leased to tenant-stockholders.

SAFEGUARDING RESIDENT–TENANT DEDUCTIONS

Eighty percent of the cooperative corporation's income must be derived from tenant–owner rentals, in order for the cooperators to be entitled to any deductions of proportionate shares of real property taxes and interest. Two thorny problems involve the identification of tenants as individuals entitled to dwelling residency and the computation of rentals as payment for ordinary residential occupancy rather than special services.

As occupants of the cooperative property, corporations, partnerships, or other business organizations may destroy entirely the deductions for tenant–owners if the premises that are commercially and professionally utilized contribute income that, when added to other tainted income, violates the 80 percent requirement. Such is the case whether or not the business or professional organization occupant is also a cooperator who has purchased stock and assumed a proprietary lease that permits the particular use of the premises.

In one case, the Treasury has ruled that the ownership of stock by a bank does not of itself violate the availability of deductions to resident individual tenants, even though the statute apparently requires that all tenant–owners be individuals who could use their apartments for residential occupancy. If the rentals from such tenants and other tainted sources raise nonresident owner income above 20 percent for the cooperative's taxable year, deductions for residents would not appear to be available. Cooperative corporation income from transfer fees and similar brokerlike transactions on resales of units would not appear to be tainted.

It is the current view that an individual making professional use of his or her cooperative unit may qualify as a tenant–stockholder if the following conditions are met:

1. The unit is part of an essentially residential building.
2. The unit could be altered, subject to favorable existing enabling laws and regulations, to become used as a self-contained housing unit (including kitchen, bathroom, and sleeping space).
3. The proprietary lease allows the unit owner the reasonably unobstructed freedom to convert to such residential use.

A conflict in the cases exists on treatment of mortgage amortization payment by tenant–shareholders. That part of cooperator rentals contributed for the purpose of amortizing the corporate mortgage was not considered as good gross income for the purpose of the 80–20 rule (but as an additional contribution of capital) in *Eckstein* v. *United States,* 452 F.2d 1036 (Ct. Claims 1971). But the contrary seems to have been the result in *Park Place, Inc.,* 57 T.C. 767 (Tax Ct. 1972).

Charges for garage space furnished by the corporation to cooperators qualify as income derived from tenant–stockholders, on the theory that such is a normal payment associated with occupancy of a dwelling. The Treasury has ruled (Revenue Ruling 68-387) that payment by cooperators to the corporation for furnishing maid services is income derived from tenant–stockholders that is attributable to their right to occupy a unit for dwelling purposes, thereby reversing a contrary 1966 ruling. Payments for commercially leased space bring tainted income to the corporation as far as determining compliance with the 80–20 rule is concerned. Personal secretarial services furnished to cooperators have been classified in the same 1968 ruling as a tenant service, thereby qualifying fees as rent derived from tenant–stockholders rather than business income.

In some cases, store tenants of cooperative corporations were continued at rentals considerably below market because of the danger to the cooperative from increasing rent that could jeopardize the 80 percent requirement. In some situations, the builder or other sponsor has taken an initial low-payment lease of commercial space and then subleased for his or her personal benefit at much higher levels to operating sublessees.

Condominium homeowners generally pay their own real estate taxes and interest on individual mortgages. Qualification for the deductions is clear, regardless of the consequences of commercial income to the regime. The corporate structure of the ordinary cooperative insulates tenant–stockholders from direct commercial income, although the 80–20 rule could far offset the benefits derived from the use of the corporate form.

Because the 80–20 computation is made at the end of the cooperative taxable year, a cooperator cannot take his or her deduction for a taxable year ending before that of the corporation. Preferably, the cooperative and all tenant–stockholders should use the same reporting period, presumably the calendar year. The cooperative should plan its budget year to end before such time, in order to have adequate time for needed adjustments.

TAX DEDUCTIONS AND LEASEHOLD COOPERATIVES

Real estate taxes that are deductible by cooperators must be the same as would be allowable as a deduction to the corporation. For this reason, tenant–stockholders cannot deduct realty taxes on land or building where the cooperative acquires the leasehold of an existing building. But where a corporation itself erects buildings under a long-term leasehold, it is ordinarily permitted a deduction of that part of the realty taxes that is applicable to the building. The tenant–stockholders in such cooperative may deduct their proportionate share of realty taxes levied on the value of the building.

Interest on indebtedness assumed by the cooperative corporation for the construction or acquisition of land or building is an allocable deduction for tenant–stockholders. Thus, interest paid by a cooperative on a leasehold mortgage made for the construction or acquisition of a building on leased land qualifies for cooperator deductions.

Most, but not all, leasehold cooperatives provide at least an interest deduction for tenant–stockholders. One cooperative venture involved an existing structure where all mortgage debt incurred in order to create the cooperative was undertaken by the promoting landowner, with the cooperative leasing corporation responsible only for rent. In that case, no deduction for realty taxes or interest was allowable to cooperators. The promoter took advantage of a major housing shortage to sell cooperative apartments strictly on the basis of location. While such financial arrangement is unusual, it emphasizes the need for adequate disclosure to prospective cooperative purchasers. Such disclosure is rare in most states. Many purchasers of condominiums retain counsel in contrast to cooperative buyers, where the percentage of those seeking legal assistance was about 50 percent lower, even when luxury-class residences were involved.

COMMERCIAL TENANT–STOCKHOLDERS

The doctor or other business or professional occupant gains considerable benefit from the purchase of a cooperative for use in his or her profession or trade. Not only may he or she deduct all ordinary and necessary business expenses, but he or she is allowed to depreciate the cost of stock (or amortize it, if it is a leasehold). The depreciation may be taken by any method the cooperative corporation would be allowed to take, even if a different method is actually used by such entity. Such deductions may be taken for taxable years commencing after December 31, 1961.

A stockholder who uses his or her apartment partly for business and partly for a residence would seem to be entitled to depreciate that part of the purchase price paid for the commercial space.

It should be noted that the stock purchase price includes cash investment as well as a proportionate share of the mortgage, giving a heavy cost basis to be depreciated.

In a mixed-use building, a cooperative apartment corporation that owns only a percentage of condominium units may still qualify under Section 216 (Revenue Ruling 78–31).

LOWER-INCOME COOPERATORS

Persons in low income brackets do not secure the benefit of tax and interest deductions as cooperators, if the standard deductions allowable exceed all itemized amounts. Private sponsors of government-subsidized cooperatives too often overemphasize tax benefits to prospective cooperative purchasers. The benefits may be nonexistent.

TAXING THE COOPERATIVE CORPORATION

The unrefunded overage of assessments received from tenant–stockholders in excess of taxable year requirements may be classified as taxable income to the cooperative corporation under Revenue Ruling 56-225. The cooperative corporation is in a better position than a condominium that incorporates management or common elements, because the cooperative has a large depreciation offset.

COOPERATIVES AND TAX-EXEMPT FINANCING

Section 103a of the Internal Revenue Code, as amended by the Tax Equity and Fiscal Responsibility Act of 1982, provides that cooperative units will be considered as single-family residences under Section 103a. The infusion of funds from this direction is still not fully clarified, and the overall concept may be changed by legislation in the years to come.

FEDERAL PROGRAMS FOR COOPERATIVES—SECTION 213

Three forms of construction loans insured under Section 213 are directed toward projects that will house tenant–stockholders seeking permanent cooperative residency and financing. These are loans made to (1) a management project (one organized as a nonprofit cooperative corporation or trust seeking to construct permanent cooperative housing for its stockholder participants), (2) a management conversion project (one organized as a nonprofit cooperative corporation or trust seeking to acquire and recast or rehabilitate existing rental housing structures for conversion to permanent cooperative ownership), and (3) an investor–sponsor project (one usually organized as a business profit corporation by its principals with the intention of selling the completed project to a nonprofit cooperative corporation or trust whose permanent financing is insured by FHA under Section 213).

Being motivated quite differently, the applicant for construction loan insurance under the sales project provision of Section 213 seeks construction of individual homes for its participants. Such loans are insured by FHA only when they involve new construction. The mortgagor during construction is a nonprofit housing corporation or trust created for the chief purpose of building private homes for its member–stockholders or trust beneficiaries. Each home is separately released from the overall construction loan when the project is satisfactorily completed, at which time individual financing is usually arranged under Section 213 pursuant to terms similar to ordinary homeownership programs of FHA. Frequently, the participants take a shareholder's interest in a cooperative homeowner association that owns and govern commonly used facilities, such as recreational centers.

The FHA also is authorized to issue mortgage insurance on loans that supplement mortgages already insured under any of the above programs.

In order for a mortgage to be eligible for insurance under FHA regulations, the ownership of the subject real estate must be held in one of several ways, namely:

1. In fee simple.
2. As the interest of the lessee under a lease for not less than ninety-nine years, which is renewable.
3. Under a lease executed by a government agency, provided that the term shall run for a period of not less than fifty years from the date the mortgage is executed.

To qualify for leasehold mortgages, the required form of leasehold agreement ordinarily includes a stipulation that the FHA (in addition to the mortgagee) be furnished copies of all notices, demands, and requests made by the ground landlord to the cooperative corporations. Such timely notice protects the FHA against defeasance that would result from the lack of sufficient opportunity to take steps to rectify defaults where they are practicable. Usually, the FHA also retains the right to acquire the leasehold under conditions set forth in the lease, with the additional privilege conferred on the FHA of exercising an option to purchase the fee title to the land once the leasehold is so acquired.

The FHA requires that an information bulletin and a copy of the bylaws be furnished to purchasers under the Section 213 program. Subscription agreements must also follow the model forms prescribed by the FHA. Usually, the purchaser is given ten days from the date of subscription to rescind the agreement. In New York and a few other states, the offering material must be delivered several days before the subscription. This procedure seems preferable because of the likelihood of subscribers reviewing the documents themselves or with counsel after signing the contract. Some bundles of FHA documents contain print so minuscule that magnification is needed even for normal eyes. In full disclosure states, the offering material and model forms must be bound in booklet form, must be in easily readable print, and must be preceded by a table of contents. Experience indicates that even fewer purchasers of FHA-insured cooperatives retain lawyers than do those who buy with conventional mortgage financing.

FEDERAL PROGRAMS FOR COOPERATIVES—OTHER SECTIONS

Cooperative housing receives rental housing status under Section 8 programs, created under the Housing and Community Development Act of 1974.

A unit in a cooperative conversion development may be financed under Section 203(n) if the FHA has insured the underlying blanket mortgage. However, administrative standards are set from time to time, such as notice number H 8083 (HUD), requiring that project rents before conversion be at or above 125 percent of the Section 8 levels for fair market returns (FMR) for the same location, size, and type of units. In addition, there has been litigation and conflict over the issue of consent by lenders to blanket mortgage assumption by the cooperative corporation.

There is also a viable cooperative program under Section 515 (enacted in 1962) for rural areas and small towns.

Depending on availability of renewed government interest, the reader is also referred to Sections 221(d)(3), 235, and 236 of the National Housing Acts.

REPORT OF THE PRESIDENT'S COMMISSION ON HOUSING

In April 1982, a presidential commission reported in part on condominium and cooperative housing, as follows.

Condominium and Cooperative Housing

The Commission recognizes the property rights of owners of rental housing and the substantial benefits to the individual and the community of homeownership opportunities created by conversion to condominium and cooperative ownership. The Commission has also considered the concerns of tenants affected by such conversion, including the needs of low-income elderly households. On the basis of this analysis, the Commission supports conversion to condominium or cooperative ownership and opposes undue restrictions thereon.

Conversion of multifamily units to cooperatives or condominiums enables many people to become homeowners who otherwise would not have this opportunity. The Commission believes that homeownership is beneficial not only for those who occupy the units, but also to the community as well. The substantial numbers of units that have been purchased under this form of ownership provides evidence of public awareness of the benefits. As the size and nature of households change, the attraction to condominiums and cooperatives is expected to grow.

There are, however, conflicting interests here. The Commission believes that potential homebuyers must continue to be served by the conversion option. Public policy must also protect the rights of apartment owners to dispose of their property. At the same time, the Commission recognizes that there may be important social consequences for those low-income tenants, particularly the elderly, who cannot afford homeownership and therefore must relocate. The Commission supports governmental policies that permit owners to convert while protecting tenants against undue disruption. Public policy should not interfere with free choice in the marketplace. The recommendations here are intended to allow conversions in response to market pressure.

Nationwide, 366,000 rental units were converted to condominiums and cooperatives during the 1970–79 period; 71 percent of these conversions (260,000) occurred during 1977–79. The number of condominiums and cooperatives increased annually through 1979, during which 135,000 units were converted. Compared to the entire rental stock, the number of conversions is relatively small (1.3 percent). Although concentrated in larger metropolitan areas, where conversions are roughly split evenly between the central cities and the suburbs, some evidence shows that the conversion phenomenon may be increasing in smaller metropolitan areas.

The benefits of conversion to the community as well as to homebuyers are considerable, but many demands have been made for imposition of government restrictions on conversions. One reason is the concern that rental housing is being removed, with adverse consequences to renters, who tend to be lower-income people. However, the mere number of gross conversions overstates the impact on the rental market. The conversion of rental units to ownership coincides with a movement of renters to ownership, which in large part is a voluntary movement. In addition, many units are purchased by investors and rerented. Therefore, some conversions do not represent reductions in the rental housing supply. In fact, the HUD report on condominium conversions indicated that the net impact of conversion—the reduction in the stock of rental housing relative to the number of remaining renters—is 5 units or less per 100 preconversion units.*

Although evidence indicates that most people moving from converted buildings experience little long-run hardship, the process of conversion can be stressful—especially for the elderly. Although great variation exists, tenants of converting buildings typically are given about 70-days notice to decide whether to buy. Nearly three-fourths of those who moved from converting buildings—but only one-fourth of those who remained—have stated that they felt pressure by the conversion experience.

In response to these concerns, by 1981 about one-half of the States had taken at least limited action to regulate conversions, and about one in five localities with conversions had adopted regulatory ordinances. Such regulations include those designed to protect tenants of converted buildings, those intended to protect buyer/owners of converted units, and those developed to preserve the supply of rental housing and/or housing for low- and moderate-income households. The most common regulations are those requiring advance notice to tenants and granting

---

* U.S. Department of Housing and Urban Development, Office of Policy Development and Research, "The Conversion of Rental Housing to Condominiums and Cooperatives," June 1980.

them the right to purchase before the units are offered to the public. Also common are provisions designed to protect tenants from disturbance during conversion, to protect buyers against possible unfair sales practices, and to provide assistance in moving if necessary.

Aside from the various procedural safeguards that might be afforded tenants during the conversion process, consideration has been given by some States—and should be given by all States—to relocation assistance or in-place financial assistance, in particular for the low-income elderly. Although the commission recognizes that equity considerations may require this form of compensation, State legislatures should determine the nature and amount of such assistance, provided that any such requirements do not unreasonably constrain the right of the owner to convert.

The Commission urges States to consider favorably the adoption of conversion procedures generally in accordance with those established in the Uniform Condominium Act, with comparable coverage for cooperatives.

The Commission finds that the model Uniform Condominium Act (UCA), developed by the National Conference of Commissioners on Uniform State Laws, attempts to balance the rights of owners to convert with the concerns of tenants about the hardships brought on by conversion. The development of the UCA involved extensive research, consultations with affected parties, and much debate, thus incorporating many diverse interests. It was adopted by the National Conference in 1977, approved by the American Bar Association in 1978, and transmitted to each State for consideration. To date four States have adopted the UCA; many others are considering its adoption.

Because the UCA covers certain aspects of the condominium form of ownership that are not of concern to the Commission, all aspects of the act are not endorsed. However, the Commission agrees with the principles embodied in the UCA, in particular the following:

- There should be advance notice of conversion to tenants, and advance notice of eviction.
- Tenants should have the right of first refusal for a reasonable period after conversion.
- Sale to a third party, at more favorable terms, should be prohibited for a specified period after notice of conversion.
- Buyer protections should include disclosures in a public offering of an engineer's report, outstanding building code violations, budget provisions, and legal documents.
- Buyer and tenant remedies should include provisions concerning unconscionable agreements or terms in contracts, punitive damages, and class actions.
- Provisions for express and implied warranties should be created.
- The buyer should have the right to cancel the contract of sale within 15 days of receipt of public offering or up to the time of sale, whichever is later.

While the UCA provides these protections to tenants, it also guarantees the owner the right to convert, without tenant approval. Furthermore, the UCA forbids local governments from using land-use regulations to prohibit condominiums or from imposing other restrictions that do not apply to identical, noncondominium developments. Thus the UCA represents a balancing of the interests of owners and tenants regarding the conversion process.

By using the term "undue" restrictions in the broad recommendations on conversion, the commission means to signal its opposition to requirements that would prevent landlords from undertaking conversion, except for those limited requirements contained in the UCA and, where necessary, reasonable provision for relocation of low-income elderly tenants. The Commission is firmly opposed to all other restrictions on conversion such as moratoria and requirements to obtain tenant approval.

No model code comparable to the UCA presently applies to conversions to cooperative homeownership, although the National Conference is in the process of developing one. The Commission believes that similar protections for tenants and rights of owners as found in the UCA are appropriate in the case of cooperative conversions.

The Commission considered taking a position on the question of insurance-backed warranties for conversion projects. The concern was with the converter who inadequately renovates or fails to disclose problem conditions. The Commission believes that an insurance-backed warranty system would impose little burden on the legitimate developer while protecting buyers (and the reputation of the industry) from the occasional "bad actor." However, the Commission believes that the concerns of adequate disclosure and liability will be sufficiently addressed under a law such as the UCA. As discussed above, the UCA requires an engineer's report, certain express or implied warranties, and other safeguards to the buyer.

In the sale or conversion of rental property, disincentives to the seller should be removed. The Commission further recommends that incentives be provided to facilitate sale of rental housing to tenants, particularly when a substantial portion are of low or moderate income. Restrictions on the types of income allowed cooperatives should also be relaxed to allow freer choice of this form of homeownership.
condominiums and cooperatives may offer the best opportunity for many renters to become homeowners, especially if tenants can accomplish the conversion themselves and cut down on their acquisition costs. However, elements in the Federal tax code and in federal regulations discourage owners from selling their rental units directly as condominium units. Other tax provisions and regulations cause impediments to the organization and operation of condominiums and cooperatives.

The Commission cites two examples of changes in tax regulations that could facilitate and encourage tenant conversions: (1) treatment of gain from direct sales to tenants, and (2) revision of the recapture provisions of the Internal Revenue Code.

The Code presently discourages owners from selling condominiums directly by taxing such sales as ordinary income, rather than at capital gains rates. In effect, owners are treated as "dealers" rather than investors, and as such do not qualify for capital gains treatment. The Code should be changed to permit capital gains treatment for conversions by owners, and remove this barrier.

Under current law, when an owner sells a rental building, the owner pays tax on the difference between the sale price and original cost less depreciation taken. At least part of the accelerated depreciation taken is taxed as ordinary income (recaptured), while the rest is subject to the lower capital gains tax rates. Providing owners with some reduction in the taxes due upon sale to tenants may encourage owners to consider tenant purchases of their buildings as an alternative to outside sale for developer-sponsored conversion, and selling a rental building to tenants may stop the cycle of rapid depreciation and tax loss on the converted building.

Another incentive for owners to sell to a tenant group is the "leasing partnership." In a leaseback agreement, owners enter into a partnership arrangement with a tenant group—either a cooperative or a condominium association—in which the partnership actually owns the property, receiving the depreciation deductions, and then leases the property to the tenant group, which acts as a co-managing or general managing partner. The limited partners have no management responsibilities but receive depreciation deductions. After a certain amount of time, the property is sold to the tenants at an agreed price.

A legal barrier exists, however, under current tax regulations. The Internal Revenue Service (IRS) considers that if a resale price is preset, the agreement is a financing mechanism and the building owner is functioning as a lender. Tenants would benefit from an agreed purchase price, without which they have no guarantee that the building would not be sold at the end of the lease. An IRS ruling that such an agreement would not impair the tax benefits to a partnership could facilitate tenant conversion and eventual purchase. Legislative authorization might be necessary.

The homeowner deduction section of the tax code for cooperative members (Section 216) restricts cooperatives by limiting to 20 percent the gross income that a cooperative corporation may receive from sources other than its tenant members, thus constraining the income that can be derived from renting commercial space to uses such as groceries, pharmacies, and day care centers. But such space provides both useful neighborhood services as well as potential income to reduce the effective housing costs for tenant shareholders. In some cases, tax law has caused cooperatives to rent out commercial space at below-market rents to avoid violation of the 20-percent rule. There does not appear to be a significant potential for tax abuse should 50 percent be allowed, but to eliminate any doubt, the IRS should adopt regulations to ensure that the interest and tax costs are properly allocated between residential and commercial facilities owned by the cooperative.

Section 277 of the tax code—which requires separation of membership and non-member income and expenses for social clubs and other membership organizations, including housing cooperatives—should be revised to permit interest income earned on required reserves to be classified as membership income for tax purposes. In some cases, cooperatives have removed reserve funds from interest bearing accounts to avoid the reporting difficulties under this requirement. This seems an unnecessary burden, particularly for low-income cooperatives.

Various impediments to the financing of cooperative purchase should be removed, such as (1) the lack of a secondary market for membership share loans; (2) the failure to implement FHA insurance on membership share loans; and (3) the 30-percent cap on housing loans by the National Consumer Cooperative Bank.

At present, neither the Federal National Mortgage Association (FNMA) nor the Federal Home Loan Mortgage Corporation (FHLMC) provides a secondary market for mortgage loans on individual cooperative shares, which considerably restricts the availability of such loans. In 1979, the Federal Home Loan Bank Board changed its regulations to permit savings and loan associations to issue loans for cooperative share purchase on the same basis as other real estate loans. Lenders have been slow to implement this change, in large part because of a lack of a secondary market for these loans.

Both FNMA and FHLMC provide secondary markets for loans on individual condominium units, but neither have implemented their authority to establish a secondary market for cooperative share loans. Within the past several months, FNMA has been considering the development of a program to purchase share loans, but current legislation prevents action by FHLMC without congressional action.

Section 203(n) is an FHA insurance program for cooperative share loans. Although passed by Congress in 1974, restrictions in the Department of Housing and Urban Development (HUD) regulations have limited its use. To facilitate acceptance of cooperative share loans in a secondary market, HUD should take the steps necessary to ensure full implementation of Section 203(n). In addition, the present statutory restriction of Section 203(n)—limiting coverage to cooperatives where FHA insures the blanket mortgage—should be removed. The financing of shares in all cooperatives should be eligible for FHA insurance, which should not be tied to the remaining term of the underlying mortgage, as is the case presently.

When the National Consumer Cooperative Bank was established by Congress in 1978, a cap of 30 percent (which becomes effective in 1985) was placed on the amount of the Bank's portfolio that could be held in housing loans. On January 1, 1982, the Bank became a private institution. The cap on its housing loan activity should be removed so that the Bank is free to operate in the marketplace like any other prudent lender, without requirements to limit its activity in any sector, and to meet the market demand for cooperative housing loans.

FOURTEEN

COOPERATIVES—OPERATIONS, LEGAL STRUCTURE, PURCHASES, AND SALES

WHY MOST CO-OPS ARE CORPORATIONS

General or limited partnerships or trusts are possible alternatives to the usual corporate form of cooperative. Nevertheless, the overwhelming choice has been the corporation, and for some good reasons.

Partnerships provide little insulation from taxation of the partners directly for income paid to the cooperative. General partners, and even their assignees, usually bear the heavy burden of personal liability for the acts of other general partners, making each partner a potential powder keg because of his or her apparent authority to act for the partnership. Limited partners would either have to relinquish the right to appoint, remove, and control management, or lose their status of limited liability. In a limited partnership, the few general partners would assume huge personal obligations for mortgage debt. It is dubious whether or not partners could convince lenders in many localities that the lenders should permit them the right to walk away from personal liability on the cooperative mortgage issued to the partnership. Partnerships involving large numbers of persons may find considerable difficulty in transferring title because of the need for many signatures.

In several states, the beneficiaries of trusts are still personally responsible on trust obligations. Moreover, banks often insist that mortgage obligations be imposed directly on trust beneficiaries, or that the trustees be given the right of recourse against the beneficial owners.

Use of the corporate form for cooperatives is widespread. It is a practical way to take title, to elect and control management, and to provide for centralized administration, while at the same time insulating cooperators from the direct personal liability for corporate obligations. Section 216 of the Internal Revenue Code preserves most homeowner benefits where the corporate form outlined therein is utilized.

Until recent years, many residential cooperatives were organized under state cooperative corporation laws that had originally been enacted to provide for farm cooperatives. This result came about because ordinary business corporation laws often did not permit restricted voting that limited each stockholder to one vote regardless of the number of shares held. In some cooperative ventures, such as those covered by Section 213 of the National Housing Act, limited voting rights were mandated.

Recently, revisions in business corporation laws in several states have begun to permit such restrictive voting rights in corporations that are organized under the state business corporation law. This trend has helped eradicate the silly business of a residential cooperative's having to submit to state dairy commissioners an annual form with many blank spaces provided for the purpose of recording milk, cream, and calf output.

Publicly assisted cooperatives are regularly chartered under specific enabling legislation rather than general business corporation laws. Specific legislation of this type customarily requires use of the corporate form.

Notably in California, some cooperatives have been organized as tenancies in common. Under this rather cumbersome procedure, each purchaser takes a deed to an undivided fractionalized share of the entire property, with a reservation of the exclusive use of his or her particular apartment or house. The tenancy-in-common format was an attempt by sponsors to add the deed as evidence that homeownership was really being conferred. The condominium may completely eliminate such a method because of the added statutory protections that are not available to tenancies in common.

CHECKLIST FOR A PROPRIETARY LEASE

A purchaser of a cooperative apartment should have some idea of the nature of the document providing for his or her occupancy of the unit—the proprietary lease. In reviewing a cooperative lease, it may be helpful to use a checklist in order to make certain that the usually cumbersome legal text does not contain objectionable matter. The need for the list is accentuated in all states where custom and law permit the delivery of a lease that lacks a table of contents, even though it may contain twenty to fifty pages in small print. Where a table of contents is included, important subjects may be hidden under topical headings that cloak the significance of the particular paragraph. The checklist that follows may provide some direction for prospective purchasers and professionals involved in this field.

Is the Lease Proprietary?

Some leases issued with cooperative stock, especially in publicly assisted housing, are in the form of short-term occupancy agreements covering two- or three-year periods and with the right of automatic renewal not being given to the cooperator. This short-term leasing method gives government-dominated cooperatives some flexibility in the provision of protection against exposure to possible cutoffs of government subsidies or below-market financing. Additionally, these cooperatives have better control over undesirable tenants as well as a policy regarding stockholder income limitations. Such leases are sometimes referred to as nonproprietary leases. The FHA occupancy agreement (FHA Form 3237) provides for a three-year occupancy but is renewable for the term of the mortgage at the option of the cooperator.

Are All Leases Uniform?

All tenant–stockholders should be subject to substantially the same form of lease agreement. Purchasers should be on guard against special consideration being given to sponsor-controlled apartments, especially such things as the lowering of payment obligations for carrying charges while apartments are vacant or subleased by the sponsor.

Who May Occupy the Apartment?

Many proprietary leases are made to specific persons as lessees or members. It is best to add that occupants may include their families as well, where children or grandchildren foreseeably must reside in the co-op. Leases abound with prohibitions against subletting or permitting boarders or permanent guests. Some permit families of lessees without defining the degree of relationship permitted.

Who Votes the Stock?

In most conventional cooperatives, voting rights are conferred in proportion to stock ownership. FHA's Section 213 and other publicly assisted cooperatives generally limit each stockholder to a single vote. It is through the exercise of this right to vote that the board of directors is elected. Corporate bylaws may specify the need for specific majorities to approve the yearly budget, terminate the cooperative, hire a new managing agent, and make other important decisions. If stock is owned jointly (as by a husband and wife), bylaws usually specify that one of the owners may vote the entire stock or that each possesses half a vote. The bylaws sometimes also require that voting may be done only by cooperators in actual residence for a specific period who are not in default in payments to the cooperative. It should, therefore, be remembered that the mere naming of a lessee in a proprietary lease, singly or jointly, does not assure the right to vote.

Inseparability from Stock, House Rules, and Bylaws

The lease should provide for its inseparability from cooperative stock. The stock issued to a cooperator should not be treated as if it were independent from the proprietary lease. No sale or abandonment of one without the other can be effected. The stock issued evidences ownership of the property in a syndicate of tenants, and the certificate itself usually bears the express legend of inseparability. The proprietary lease primarily details the legal obligations of the tenant and the corporation between themselves. Limitations and requirements applicable to the relationships among tenants themselves are also often described in the lease, although sometimes they are set forth in separately issued house rules. The government of the corporation is ruled by bylaws which sometimes may be used to actually alter or supersede lease terms, but usually only after a customary vote by stockholders controlling two-thirds of all stock in conventional cooperatives. Because the ownership of stock automatically carries the right to tenancy, under a specific lease format and interlocking bylaws that require operation for the sole benefit of tenants, the lease is proprietary in nature and certainly confers a preferred status as compared to that of an ordinary tenant.

How Was Stock Allocated?

The price of each apartment depends on the number of shares allocated to it, which should be specified in the lease. Not only is the initial price determined by the number of shares, but carrying charges and other important obligations and rights depend on the quantity of stock held. A purchaser should not sign a lease without first examining a schedule of stock allocations for all apartments, in order to assure himself or herself that the price of his or her prospective unit has been fairly determined. The purchaser should weigh such factors as the location of the apartment, the number of rooms, the number of bathrooms, and the rentals for apartments in comparable buildings in the particular neighborhood.

The Temporary Tenant

On occasion, a preliminiary tenancy status is undertaken by future cooperators who are eager to obtain residence before the cooperative plan has been declared effective upon the sale of a sufficient number of apartments. During such period, no part of any rentals paid is tax-deductible. The tenant gambles on the plan going into effect. It is suggested that in such cases great care be taken before the expenditure of substantial funds for decorating the apartment.

Carrying Charges and Direct Payments

One of the most misleading aspects of cooperative sales is the use of figures that represent expected carrying charges without spelling out exactly what is and what is not included in the amounts stated. Care should be exercised to learn if the carrying charges include gas and electricity, inside or outside painting, and maintenance and repair. In one case the advertised carrying charges did not include pro rata amounts necessary for the payment of amortization and interest on the cooperative mortgage. If payments must be made to reserve funds, the purchaser should find out what the purpose of such funds will be and if their use is circumscribed.

Initial carrying charges (whatever their coverage) are, at most, only a projection and are not accompanied by an operating history against which to check the accuracy of the projection. Deficits will be added to the next year's budget and will be collectible from carrying charges then. Unlike an ordinary lease for several years, the cooperative rental may not remain constant because of the possibility of erroneous projections and unforeseen expenses. Sometimes the permanent tax assessment is not made until after the cooperative has been sold on the basis of a substantially lower tax projection.

Stock is generally sold subject to a lien retained by the cooperative corporation for unpaid carrying charges.

Selling at a Profit

Generally, conventional cooperative leases and bylaws do not prohibit the resale of stock at a profit to the seller. In many FHA 213 cooperatives and publicly assisted ventures, the tenant–cooperator is not permitted to retain any amount received from resale over and above the book value of his or her stock. Book value is variously defined but often includes the amount of the original payment, charges directed to the reduction of mortgage debt, as well as any payment allocated to capital improvements.

The Mechanics of Resale, Subleasing, or Pledging

Most cooperative leases or bylaws require the approval by the board of directors of buyers and prospective sublessees. If the cooperative has been in existence for a considerable time, it may be possible to learn of its policies regarding transfers. The more luxurious the cooperative, the more difficult and trying may be the approval process.

A pledgee of stock and lease, or his or her designee, does not become a record stockholder with the right of occupancy unless approved by the board under usual bylaws. This is one reason why banks have hesitated to make loans secured by cooperative stock and lease without protection of an adequate recognition agreement signed by the board of directors. Condominium bylaws almost always authorize mortgagees to sell units on which mortgages have been foreclosed without being subject to board approval or the right of first refusal.

Management Services

It is important for a purchaser to learn whether or not the cooperative has engaged a resident maintenance employee and, if so, the actual extent of his or her obligations to tenants directly and to the corporation. Management by an experienced and well-known managing agent ordinarily should assure smoother operation of the cooperative.

Delivery of a Vacant Apartment

The prospective cooperator should require specification in the lease that his or her apartment will be delivered vacant, so as to avoid the necessity of paying carrying charges while fighting to oust the current resident. Some leases, in effect, merely assign to the lessees the rights of the corporation to evict anyone wrongfully in possession.

If painting or other decorations must attend delivery of the apartment, the purchaser should insist on specification of these requirements in the lease.

Examination of Books and Records of Cooperative

Better leases impose the obligation on the cooperative to maintain accurate and current books and records of account at a place convenient for examination by cooperators or their representatives during reasonable hours of inspection.

Enumeration of All Mortgages

It would seem to be good practice to have a listing of all current mortgages that are secured by the cooperative property, together with the amounts of debt outstanding, the interest rates, maturity dates, and a statement of whether or not they are self-liquidating. While this is almost never done, there is as much reason for such detailed specification as there is for listing a mortgage that is a direct personal obligation. The wide use of balloon-type mortgages, involving large principal amounts that suddenly become due, makes it urgent that the prospective cooperator know the essentials of the cooperative's financing.

If a leasehold cooperative is involved, there should be an itemized listing of the terms and duration of the ground lease, the terms of any mortgages secured by the underlying land or the leasehold, the degree of protection offered by notice from such possibilities as sudden foreclosures or termination of the leasehold by ground lessor and mortgagees, and the existence of any options to purchase the underlying land. If the cooperative is obligated to pay all costs arising out of the mortgage secured by the land, any limitations on refinancing should be stated.

Such additional detailed information would be furnished automatically in the few states requiring full disclosure.

Length of Term

The lease almost always will specify the duration of the term. Conditions necessary for its renewal usually are vaguely stated, or left out completely, and rarely are of concern to either the sponsor or the cooperator in a fee cooperative where a long period is covered. In a leasehold cooperative, the termination language is usually more specific, probably because of the interest of the sponsor in having the property revert back to his or her heirs.

The vague language existing in proprietary leases and other documents pertaining to the renewability of leases and the continuation of cooperative status should lead to much wrangling in the distant future.

Cooperative Obligations to Stockholders

The cooperative generally obligates itself to provide quiet enjoyment to the stockholder–lessee. The lease also should require that the cooperative obtain insurance against hazards and liability covering cooperative property, and that it will render annual financial reports that include tax deduction information for cooperators.

In the first few years of a conventional cooperative's life, most ill feelings and animosity tend to be directed against the sponsor or his or her selling agent. With the passage of three to four years, the cooperative will arrive at a point of true self-government, with the tenants responsible for their own decisions and aware that they will benefit from wise decisions and suffer from poor ones.

Important to stockholders are warranties and personal obligations of the sponsor with respect to the property and its maintenance. If any exist, the purchaser should become aware of such agreement on the part of the sponsor. Some rather horrendous exculpation clauses turn up in subscription agreements and proprietary leases that attempt to exonerate the sponsor, his or her agents, and his or her employees from every conceivable liability for negligence or even fraud. The prospective cooperative cooperator should be aware that such clauses cannot be written in certain states and are stricken at the insistence of competent counsel for purchasers in other localities.

Checklist Conclusion—The Need for Counsel

No one should purchase a cooperative apartment without representation by counsel.

In one case, a sponsor's attorney inadvertently failed to file a set of incorporation papers for a cooperative but nevertheless issued stock and proprietary leases to scores of purchasers who were not individually represented by counsel. Only after the would-be cooperative was in operation and had purportedly elected a board of directors was a discovery made of the failure to incorporate formally. All sorts of charges of lack of authority were hurled among residents, until all sides finally consented to an agreement.

Besides checking the title to the property and the incorporation of the cooperative, an attorney should review the subscription agreement, proprietary lease, bylaws, house rules, and all offering literature used, as well as the stock certificate issued. The attorney should avail himself or herself of all mortgage information and the text of any underlying ground leases. There is as much reason for retaining counsel when purchasing a co-op as when buying a one-family home or condominium or participating in a homeowner association.

INSURING THE COOPERATIVE AND STOCKHOLDERS

Cooperative corporations greatly adhere to the usual mortgagee requirements for hazard insurance and are best advised to place extended coverage for plate glass breakage, water damage, and damage to ornamental furniture that is not within the coverage of minimal policy specifications insisted upon by lenders. Commercial and professional tenants should be required to carry rent insurance that covers carrying charge obligations.

The cooperative is a separate corporate entity and, therefore, will insure its property in its own name as beneficiary. Stockholders wishing to insure their own personal property must obtain their own policies.

Liability policies also are placed in the corporate name for coverage of any injuries suffered within the corporation's obligation. Tenants must provide their own policies insuring against accidents in which they may possess direct responsibility, such as those caused by tenant negligence within their own apartments. In contrast to the condominium, personal liability for stockholders ordinarily will not extend to faulty maintenance of commonly used facilities. There is also less of a problem for a resident participant to sue management, which is a corporate entity, in the case of a cooperative than in the case of a condominium run on a noncorporate basis.

Managing agents have been vexed by the need for discernment of increased property values resulting from tenant decorations in luxury cooperatives. Enormously valuable additions to walls and ceilings may legally become part of the corporate real property, increasing both valuations and insurance costs to the cooperative. The same problem exists in luxury condominiums, but for a different reason. In the cooperative, all real property is owned by the corporation and must be insured under the blanket policy. In the condominium, although the skin of walls and ceiling usually remains the real property of the unit owner, it often may be covered by the condominium blanket policy that protects against hazards to the real property represented by the common elements as well as that portion of units fully owned.

Proprietary leases and cooperative policies quite frequently fail to clarify the responsibility for insurance covering tenant installations, thereby leaving the matter open to subsequent disputes.

Life insurance policies tailored to homeowner and condominium mortgage requirements are widely advertised and sold. Actually, these are only term policies with decreasing balances that can be issued independent of homeownership. Cooperators rarely purchase such policies, because death does not leave heirs with a direct personal obligation on a mortgage and certainly not one that can be liquidated individually. Yet the surviving family may wish to remain in residence if the carrying charges could be reduced.

Thought should be given by a cooperator to an additional insurance policy that will cover monthly charges and direct home-operating expenses during at least a year for the family of the tenant–stockholder.

EASE IN REMOVAL OF TENANTS

The popular notion that cooperators are safer than homeowners because obstructive and dissident neighbors can be removed readily pursuant to protective lease clauses has been widely accepted almost as an inviolate principle. Except for some publicly assisted cooperatives, a required high-percentage vote by assenting stockholders, usually the holders of two-thirds of corporate stock, somewhat restricts immediate implementation of clauses providing for such action.

A cooperative lease relationship does make for less arduous removal of undesirable neighbors than does the condominium form, and the greatest difficulty comes in ridding a neighborhood of disorderly, unclean, or otherwise disruptive persons when outright homeownership is the basis for occupancy. The law does not favor the problem tenant, but it does bend considerably in order not to disturb the obstructive owner holding title under a deed.

From the point of view of a sorely afflicted cooperative, the ease of tenant elimination may appear beneficial. Yet it is a boon that could also cause vexation to innocent parties against whom a majority acts arbitrarily and unfairly.

If the lease provides for the return of the investment upon such termination, the cooperative may have to find either substantial funds with which to buy the objectionable tenant's interest or someone willing to replace the wrongdoer. The condition of the apartment involved might cause delays while repairs are being made.

Wider nonconformity and the increased use of cooperatives for low-income residents could gradually weaken the strength of the cooperative lease club for nonconforming tenants.

Nonconformance with traditional mores seems to be a ritual with large numbers of younger people, with the result that a greater latitude of nonconformance will no doubt be generally acceptable in the future. In those cooperatives where publicly assisted tenants reside, the process of uplifting the poor must involve a sympathetic understanding of slowly changing patterns of living habits. Here, problems such as uncleanliness are dealt with more effectively by an initial educational program than by eviction under a technical lease clause.

INCREASED LABOR COSTS

Some cooperative promoters have projected initial budgets without making reference to known pending negotiations for new labor contracts. Industry-wide negotiations often are binding on a particular project that may interest prospective purchasers. Yet offering literature may adhere to existing contract costs. A purchaser should make certain that he or she discovers the duration of any building service employee contract that is industrywide, especially in buildings where maintenance employees constitute a heavy expense.

CHECKLIST FOR QUESTIONING A SELLING AGENT

It is extremely difficult to imagine what an apartment will look like in a building that is not yet constructed, especially if the new structure will not be similar to other buildings already visible. Astute observation is required when evaluating floor plans, brochures, and any room cutouts that may be available for examination at the selling agent's office. No one but the prospective purchaser himself or herself can determine what decor, room arrangement, outside appearance, and neighborhood facilities satisfy his or her individual tastes. Once there is an acceptance of either the present or future appearance as adequate, the next step should be a conference with the selling agent on cooperative particulars. That conference is essential whether or not there is a building in existence. Unfortunately, the average person who has never lived in a co-op may not be able to envision the areas of inquiry that are necessary before an informed decision can be made. The following list of questions covers a large number of essentials:

1. Which apartments are available, and what is the cash investment required?
2. Regarding the particular apartment that interests a prospective purchaser, what is the exact location of the apartment, the number of rooms, the number of baths, and the site with reference to the convenience and annoyance that could result from the placement of elevators, views, incinerator shafts, garages, roads, parking areas, bus stops, and recreational facilities?
3. What are the projected carrying charges, what do they include, how are they payable, and what conditions may result in increases?
4. Are copies of leases, bylaws, and offering plans available for a purchaser's lawyer to read before signing a subscription agreement?

5. Are there going to be income or social limitations (minimum or maximum earning requirements, restrictions on children, etc.)?

6. What about the existence and quality of schools, shopping facilities, open space, parks, playgrounds, and other recreational facilities? What is the distance to houses of worship?

7. What facilities are provided for washing machines and dryers, and, especially, what is their location if individual units are not permitted within apartments?

8. Will there be a managing agent and resident superintendent? If so, what will their duties be? Will tenants be free of outside mainte-nance responsibilities?

9. If there are to be stores or businesses in any parts of the premises, where will they be located, and what restrictions are there regarding the types of occupations permitted? What kinds of zoning restric-tions and local planning exist in the neighborhood and surrounding communities?

10. Will the apartment be delivered complete with any necessary paint-ing or decorations without additional charge? What discretion will the purchaser have in rearranging floor plans or wall decorations? May the purchaser make substantial apartment alterations once he or she takes ownership? Will the lease require all tenants to pur-chase wall-to-wall carpeting or other expensive items in order to make up for poor soundproofing?

11. What tax benefits will inure from cooperative ownership?

12. How many apartments have to be sold before the plan will be de-clared effective? Is there an outside date for abandonment of the plan, if such number has not been sold?

13. How much of a down payment is required when a subscription agreement is signed, and what are the conditions for its return be-fore the plan is declared effective and thereafter?

14. How long must the buyer wait for his or her apartment to be com-pleted?

15. Are there any limitations or restrictions on the resale of an apart-ment with reference to the choice of persons or profit? Is subletting permitted, with or without the approval of the board of directors?

16. With respect to parking, where do each tenant, guests, and delivery trucks park?

17. What is the amount and what are the terms of any mortgages that the cooperative will undertake? Will the tenant be personally re-sponsible for payment?

18. Are there conditions precedent to the tenants' taking control of their own affairs, such as full tenant occupancy or the issuance of a certificate of final acceptance by a government agency?

19. Will there be any interim period when the purchaser will be merely a tenant who is not entitled to tax deductions?

20. Has the sponsor placed any funds in trust as security for faulty construction or meeting specific obligations?

21. Are there any existing lawsuits instituted by tenants against the sponsor?

22. What is the business background of the sponsor? Are there buildings in existence which he or she built as cooperatives and which the prospective purchaser can visit?

The foregoing list includes many major problems to be discussed but cannot possibly cover every item of interest in specific cooperatives. Quite often, however, such an introductory list may lead to a conversation on other important topics. It does serve the purpose of preventing derailment of the conversation by glib salespeople from matters that should not be overlooked.

In the few states requiring full disclosure in cooperative offerings, such information would be contained in an offering brochure.

The sad experience of some purchasers proves that a purchaser should be on special guard against representations about adequate refrigerators and other appliances that do not designate the specific models to be included. The same goes for insulation, storm windows and screens, the heating and air-conditioning system, and the type and quality of landscaping.

As always, the most essential safety feature to look for will be the background, experience, and integrity of the sponsor and the building. A prudent buyer should never, as many persons do, rely merely on the fact that a bank or savings and loan association will lend substantial sums on the property. Their minimum standards may be much less than the purchaser's own requirements.

CONVERSION OF APARTMENT HOUSES TO COOPERATIVES

In a growing trend, many persons comfortably ensconced in rented apartments have been startled in the past few years to learn that the owner of the building where they reside as tenants has decided to convert their ordinary lease occupancy to a cooperative basis. There are two major reasons why dozens of occupied major buildings, several built more than two decades ago, have gone cooperative.

Owners of buildings in active conversion areas have been regularly receiving a higher total price on the resale of the building to a cooperative corporation than they would have obtained in the open market from other types of investors. Owners of apartment buildings have been tantalized by recent experiences of other owners who have converted comparable apartment buildings to cooperatives and have marked the going resale prices for cooperative apartments. The owner will formulate the pricing structure with the aid of professional selling agents and need not declare any plan effective unless he or she feels assured that the profit will be significantly in line with his or her projection. Unlike the builder of new construction who may tailor structures to cooperative residency, the owner of an occupied building has much more time and much less expense in testing the receptivity of the cooperative idea among current residents. Taxwise, the owner is selling his or her building to one purchaser, a cooperative corporation, and thus hopes to avoid the dealer tax status he or she would probably face if converting to a condominium. The capital gain aspect is sought by means of every possible protective device.

The second important reason for conversions is the prevailing housing shortage in certain urban areas, which effectively locks in long-time residents. Rarely is a conversion program accomplished efficiently in buildings housing short-term residents or transients. With many occupants fearing removal from rent control status under state and local law, thousands of New Yorkers living in Manhattan found themselves in the midst of a severe housing shortage in the upper- and middle-income range of rental apartments a few years ago. Almost at once, owners and sometimes recent speculative purchasers began converting the apartment tenancies to cooperatives. In the three years ending in September 1968, approximately $150 million was expended by resident tenants in purchasing their apartments. By 1983, some successful New York City single conversions brought in almost that amount. The $1 billion figure more appropriately describes this market.

Whereas conversion may calm and settle the occupant who is worried about being faced with a housing shortage, the price may involve a cash outlay impossible for him or her to meet or maintenance costs too steep for his or her income level. For that reason, some localities have enacted protective legislation.

ECONOMIC AND SOCIAL EFFECT OF MASSIVE CONVERSIONS ON HOUSING

Conversions tend to slow down resident turnover in neighborhoods that would ordinarily involve more mobility. Younger people and those experiencing changed economic status are circumscribed from prestige areas of a city. On the other side of the coin, many middle-income city residents would be forced to leave urban areas for the suburbs because of higher rentals and the lack of availability of adequate housing other than their converted apartments. The inadequate pace of private highrise residential construction may be expected to accelerate the movement to convert to cooperatives during the next five years.

Conversions of low-income public housing projects from rental to cooperative basis have taken place in some American localities. Obviously, the efforts are a valiant attempt at uplifting these income groups. The environment typical of public housing and the continuation of rigid government supervision, together with purchase price subsidies, have made it difficult to accomplish a substantial degree of pride of ownership. The same dislike of prohibitions against profits on resale for cooperators that was expressed when discussing condominiums for the poor is reiterated here.

THE TECHNIQUE OF CONVERTING TO COOPERATIVE

Conversions to cooperative usually originate in one of two ways, depending on the original initiator of the plan. In a small minority of situations, a group of tenants assembles for the purpose of convincing the owner of their building to convert the apartment house to a cooperative. This actually has come about in some cases when there has been fear of an impending sale by the landlord to a speculator and in other instances when tenants become fearful of sharp increases in rentals. Some old, well-kept buildings were about to be sold to developers who were considering ripping down the buildings to make way for commercial office structures or other nonresidential uses. Energetic and knowledgeable tenants were able in some cases to offer their landlords a more favorable price and sometimes were even able to achieve their desire to preserve their apartment homes at a purchase price below that offered by outsiders.

More commonly, the plan to convert originates strictly with the owner and is founded on high profit possibilities.

Probably no area of real estate exists in which rumors conjure up such imagined horrors in the minds of tenants as when there is talk of turning an apartment building into a cooperative. Too often, there is good reason for the fearfulness of tenants because of the callous, inconsiderate dealings of some owners. For example, some owners during a housing shortage waited until almost all leases on apartments had expired and then offered each tenant the option of either buying a cooperative apartment within two weeks or vacating his or her apartment. Through the efforts of the state attorney general in New York and a most effective cooperative statute, New Yorkers faced with a plan of conversion are generally given at least three months to decide whether to purchase or not, even if they are tenants presently residing without an existing lease.

In some states, leases for ordinary two- or three-year terms carry clauses to the effect that they are terminable at the will of the landlord if the tenant refuses to enter into a subscription agreement to purchase the apartment within a few days after the cooperative plan is announced.

Writers on real estate topics and others have commented in a few cases on the need for public protection in this field, with most favoring protection. Some states have assigned staff experienced in securities offerings to this task, and there is general belief that this form of protection comes under blue-sky commissioners because stocks are involved. While originally some laws may have provided an effective nail on which to hang justification for regulation, the regulation of cooperatives, as well as condominiums and homeowner associations, requires special skills and quite different attitudes from those pertaining to the mere protection of investors in securities. Purchasers of cooperatives and condominiums are really buying homes, not investing for income or short- or long-term capital gains.

Rarely will a plan to convert to cooperative be successful if a large number of current tenants refuse to become purchasers. For this reason, the prices that are first suggested for apartments may be bargained down by committees representing tenants, acting as if they were jointly jousting about price as investment purchasers. The condition of the building and the need for repairs often come up as urgent questions. Independent engineering reports and adequate reserve funds set aside from the purchase price for the new corporation are ways of handling this problem.

Conflicts regularly arise between the group of tenants eager to purchase apartments and the other group that wishes to battle such a plan with every shred of mettle available. One of the common bones of contention is the projected budget. Another is the allocation of stock to specific apartments that forms the basis for the determination of purchase prices and carrying charges.

In this most difficult aspect of cooperative promotion, prospective purchasers must attempt to gain a thorough understanding of the new method of ownership, with its legal, economic, and social variances from ordinary short-term tenancies. Competent legal counsel should be consulted in all cases.

BUYING OR SELLING A RESALE

Thousands of cooperative apartments change hands each year, but not with the same care that a buyer and seller usually demonstrate when a one-family home or condominium is resold. Part of the fault lies with real estate brokers and attorneys, who are called on to create procedures and documents without the benefit of the easy availability of standard forms published by title companies and broker organizations.

Unquestionably, a contract to sell the buyer's cooperative home requires the same degee of protective coverage as in the resale of other homes. In that connection, the checklist of subject matter for inclusion in such contract offered below can save anxiety and firm up the thinking of both sides on the vital questions involved:

1. The contract must contain an agreement to sell stock and assign and transfer the seller's proprietary lease. The stock should be all the stock owned by the seller and must be all that is allocated by the cooperative corporation to a particular apartment specifically designated by a number and lettering.

2. Articles of personal property owned by the seller and intended to be included in the sale are to be listed, and articles not to be sold may be stated to be excluded for emphasis and clarity. More than a seller's assurance is necessary to prove that the articles sold are the property of seller rather than of the cooperative corporation.

3. Terms of payment should divide the total obligation between the time of contract signing and the delivery of the apartment at the closing.

4. The contract ordinarily must be made subject to the approval of the board of directors and should set forth, as required action by buyer and seller, all steps required by the bylaws and the proprietary lease for board clearance of purchasers. For example, the buyer may have to furnish detailed references and financial information and may even have to appear for personal interviews, in addition to assuming the lease obligation in a specific manner. Provision for adjournment of the closing may be included, in order to cover delays in complying with corporate transfer rules.

5. The seller should append to the agreement a copy of the current budget, together with a copy of the last annual financial report and the most current tax deduction statement furnished by the apartment corporation. A purchaser may reasonably insist on being given copies of any notices of meetings for the purpose of increasing charges, or other notices applicable to increased charges. Contracts for resale must contain the seller's obligation to give written permission for the apartment corporation's furnishing confirmation of the accuracy of the aforesaid financial information, and whatever addi-

tional information is requested by the purchaser to which the seller is entitled upon due request. The seller should agree to obtain such information or confirmation in the event that the apartment corporation refused to furnish the same to the purchaser.

6. A well-drafted contract requires the seller expressly to provide the amount of yearly charges and the calendar for payment and also to list the expenditures covered by carrying charges.

7. Representations and warranties from the seller can be requested regarding full, unencumbered ownership of shares of stock and lease, the manner in which ownership of the apartment is recorded on the books of the corporation, and the assurance that all other property transferred is owned free and clear, with no debts or liens outstanding.

8. Representations by the seller about the condition of the property to be transferred depend upon the individual agreement, which may run the gamut from an "as is" clause to warranties of workability and condition at the time of closing.

9. If garage space is used by the seller under a separate agreement, he or she may be reasonably wary of assigning what may not be assignable because of the priority of the rights of other tenants. The contract should specify that the allocation of garage space will depend upon any individual agreement and its implementation by the board. If the purchaser conditions his or her purchase on definite garaging rights, this should be spelled out beyond any question.

10. The seller may agree to deliver the apartment in broom-clean and vacant condition by a certain date, if all prior conditions of the contract are met.

11. Responsibility for the payment of brokerage fees must be set forth, with an added statement of obligation for the payment of any special managing agent fees or corporation fees on transfer. These cause disputes because of their omission from contracts.

12. Prepayments, security deposits, and similar funds paid in advance must be apportioned at the closing.

13. At the closing, the buyer should insist that there be delivered a certificate of approval by the board of directors to the sale; the seller's stock certificate duly endorsed and in full compliance with local, state, or federal laws covering such transfers; an assignment of the lease, together with the seller's copy of the lease, in a form that meets the bylaw requirements of the apartment corporation; a statement from the managing agent that the seller is not in arrears in his or her payment of carrying charges and other required payments as

of a specific date; documents of title, usually a bill of sale, transferring title to items of personal property being sold; and keys to the apartment and entrances.

It is impossible for a listing such as this one to include a reference to each transaction in each state, but the above covers a wide range of key subjects that must be evaluated when formulating a mutually agreeable contract when an apartment is resold.

Not listed are two items that are almost always omitted, namely the mortgage details and the number of cooperators presently in default in their payments of carrying charges. Certainly, such information is of so great an importance as to become standard requirements.

Also be wary of building restrictions on nontenant occupants, visitors, pets, and related matters.

THE EFFECTIVE DATE

New apartment offerings, as well as conversions of rental housing to co-ops, ordinarily depend upon the success of sales in order for the cooperative plan to be declared effective, with the corporation obligated under a binding agreement to issue stock and lease. Too frequently, an outside date is not stipulated by which time the plan must be either declared effective or the deposits returned. Where sales are brisk, no problem exists in the rapid achievement of the effective date. A slow selling pace may create hardship for subscribers who have deposited substantial monies or have made temporary living arrangements and decoration plans without being aware of the long delay that is possible.

Usually, there are two key percentages that condition the plan's going into operation. The sponsor of a conventional co-op almost always reserves discretion to declare the plan effective after obtaining subscriptions to a small percentage of apartments, or stock, commonly 25 to 35 percent. Automatically, the plan may go into operation when a majority, often 65 percent, of such sales has taken place. Other factors also can block formal operation of the co-op. Mortgage commitments may not be finalized, or the mortgages themselves may be conditioned on a specific number of sales. In some cases, long delays ensued because complex legal documents had not been drafted, for the reason that the sponsor was avoiding the expense until he or she was certain of a successful sales program. New forms of reciprocal arrangements involving airspace or utilization of common areas by multiple-ownership structures can result in time-consuming legal and engineering delays.

SECURITIES REGULATION

In 1975, the Supreme Court ruled that stock sales in a housing cooperative were not securities under the definition in the Federal Securities Act (*United Housing Foundation* v. *Foreman,* 421 U.S. 837). Subsequent litigation has fairly well established that such ruling applies to subsidized housing cooperatives as well as conventional cooperative offerings. The Securities and Exchange Commission has issued guidelines on the applicability of the federal securities laws to condominiums and other forms of real estate development (Release 33-5347). Problems in the securities field probably will emerge if the offering is issued under an arrangement with emphasis on the economic benefit to be realized from the efforts of the promoter, if the offering involves participation by the offeree in a rental pool, or if the offering involves an arrangement whereby the purchaser must hold the unit available for rental for any part of the year, must use an exclusive rental agent, or is otherwise materially restricted regarding occupancy or rental of the particular unit.

New construction condominium offerings also may be subject to the Interstate Land Sales Act. The most usual exemption from the statute would involve units already completed or to be sold under a contract that obligates the developer to complete construction of the condominium regime fully within two years after the sales contract is executed.

The securities definitions above would likely apply as well to most states under blue-sky laws. Additionally, there are special local statutes that also may cover the offering of cooperative units within particular localities, such as retirement or subdivision laws.

BUILDING INSPECTION FOR COOPERATIVE CONVERSIONS

Below are excerpts from the New York State regulations that require a comprehensive description of a building subject to conversion. While the outline applies solely to offerings made in New York State, it is an excellent checklist for sponsors and purchasers involved in any cooperative conversion offering.

Section 18.7   Description of Property and Building Condition.

Each offering plan submitted pursuant to this Part must include a comprehensive narrative description of the building(s) and property included in the project. Emphasis should be on present condition of premises including deficiencies probably unknown to occupants, rather than description of material make-up visually obvious to each resident. The inspection of the property upon which the description is based must have taken place within 180 days prior to submission of the offering plan to the Department of Law. The Department of Law may in its discretion require a further inspection and report. The condition of all systems and materials must be fully described. Such report(s) shall disclose all defective conditions apparent upon inspection, and shall note any defective condition which is hazardous or which requires immediate repair to prevent further deterioration. Identify and describe all applicable items in the order listed below. Where an item is not specifically identifiable, it may be generally described, e.g. "two rows of deciduous trees" rather than "12 poplar and 12 maple trees in two lines." Where an item is not identifiable at all, a reason must be presented substantiating its unavailability.

(a) Location and use of property. State whether this property and proposed use will comply with all zoning and use requirements at closing. Include in discussion:

    (1) address;
    (2) block and lot number;
    (3) zoning; and
    (4) permissible use.

(b) Status of construction. State:

    (1) year built;
    (2) class of construction;
    (3) Certificate of Occupancy, type and number;
    (4) Alteration permit numbers and description of work done.

(c) Site. Discuss:

    (1) size;
    (2) number of buildings and use;
    (3) streets owned or maintained by the project:

        (i) paving (material and condition);
        (ii) curbing (material and condition);
        (iii) catch basins, drainage (location and condition);
        (iv) street lighting (material, type, location and condition).

    (4) drives, sidewalks and ramps:

        (i) paving (material and condition);
        (ii) curbing (material and condition);
        (iii) catch basins, drainage (location and condition);
        (iv) street lighting (material, type, location and condition).

(d) Utilities. Identify source or provider of each utility. Specifically identify which are public utilities or regulated companies and which are solely the obligation of the apartment corporation. Indicate whether water, sewer (or septic tank), gas, electric and telephone are metered individually, collectively or by any other method of billing.

(e) Sub-soil conditions. Describe (including water conditions):

    (1) whether uneven foundation movement or settling has occurred (cracking, mortar joint decay, etc.);

(2) whether there is any evidence of moisture or seepage or ground water infiltration and, if any, indicate whether corrective action is needed;

(3) whether there is any danger from flooding, either due to water table in area or overflow from other bodies of water. Note potential for mudslides or erosion and what preventive action is appropriate.

(f) Landscaping and enclosures. Describe:
    (1) grass cover (type, location);
    (2) plantings (type, location);
    (3) trees (location);
    (4) fencing (type, location);
    (5) gates (type, location);
    (6) garden walls (type, location);
    (7) retaining walls (type, location);
    (8) display pools and foundations (location, materials).

(g) Building size. Specify:
    (1) total height (approximate total feet from ground level to highest part of roof);
    (2) crawl spaces (floor to ceiling, height);
    (3) number of sub-cellars and cellars;
    (4) number of floors (actual including penthouses—give floor to ceiling height if not between 7½ and 8½ feet);
    (5) equipment rooms (location and use);
    (6) parapet (height above roof).

(h) Structural System. Decribe materials used, include type of foundation(s) and method of installation. Specify:
    (1) Exterior of Buildings:
        (i) Walls: List materials, type of construction, method of construction. For New York City builders, if Local Law 10 applies, state the results of the inspection. If Local Law 10 is inapplicable, so state. If such inspection is required but not performed specify as a violation. If insulted, describe material, type, size and insulating value where available.
        (ii) Windows: Specify type and materials in all parts of the building including sills, screens, window guards, lintels, storm sash, hardware, single or double glazing and caulking. Indicate whether lot line windows exist and describe any potential future problems.
    (2) Parapets and copings: State type of materials, how firmly secured in place and whether there is any indication of problems e.g. leakage, spalling, deterioration of mortar, cracking, etc.
    (3) Chimneys and caps: Indicate number, location and material of each chimney for boilers, incinerators, compactors and fireplaces. If fireplaces are not usable for wood fires, this fact must be conspicuously disclosed.
    (4) Balconies and terraces. Describe:

      (i)   Deck finish (material);

      (ii)   Balustrade (type, material);

      (iii) Railings (material);

      (iv) Copings (material);

      (v)   Soffits (material);

      (vi) Doors to Balconies and Terraces (type, material).

(5) Exterior entrances. Describe:

      (i)   Exterior doors and frames (material, type, lock);

      (ii)   Vestibule doors and frames (material, type, lock);

      (iii) Exterior stairs (material, location);

      (iv) Railings (material, location);

      (v)   Mail Boxes (type, location);

      (vi) Lighting (type, location).

(6) Service entrances. Describe:

      (i)   Doors and frames (material, type, lock);

      (ii)   Gates (material, type, lock);

      (iii) Exterior Stairs (material, location);

      (iv) Railings (materials, location).

(7) Roof and roof structures. Describe:

      (i)   Type roofs for all areas:

          (*a*) Material;

          (*b*) Insulation (size, type and insulating value if available);

          (*c*) Surface finish;

          (*d*) Bond or Guarantee;

          (*e*) Flashing materials including counter flashing.

      (ii)   Drains:

          (*a*) Location, material and type;

          (*b*) Gutters and Leaders (type, material).

      (iii) Skylights (location, type, material).

      (iv) Bulkheads:

          (*a*) Stairs (materials);

          (*b*) Elevator (materials);

          (*c*) Other.

      (v)   Metal Work at roof levels:

          (*a*) Exterior, metal stairs (materials);

          (*b*) Vertical ladders, including gooseneck (material);

          (*c*) Railings (material);

          (*d*) Hatches to roof (type, material);

          (*e*) Other.

      (vi) Rooftop facilities (describe in detail).

(8) Fire escapes. Describe at each floor and specify any unusual access situations:

      (i)   Location (describe how attached and supported);
      (ii)   Floors covered;
      (iii)   Drop ladder;
      (iv)   Type;
      (v)   Materials.

(9) Yard and courts. Describe each yard or court including front, rear and interior areas, listing methods of access:

      (i)   Paving (material);
      (ii)   Drainage (type and material);
      (iii)   Railings (material);
      (iv)   Stairs (material);
      (v)   Fencing (type and material);
      (vi)   Walls (type and material).

(10) Interior stairs. Describe:

      (i)   Number of stairs of each type;
      (ii)   Enclosure (construction and interior finishes);
      (iii)   Stair Construction (steel, concrete, wood);
      (iv)   Stringers (material);
      (v)   Treads (material);
      (vi)   Risers (material);
      (vii) Guard Rails (material);
      (viii) Balustrade (material).

(11) Interior doors and frames. Describe material, type, and location for each, and state whether fireproof or exceeds fire/safety standards:

      (i)   Unit entrance and interior doors and frames;
      (ii)   Corridor doors and frames;
      (iii)   Stair hall doors and frames;
      (iv)   Roof doors, basement doors and frames.

(12) Elevators. Describe.

      (i)   Number of passenger and service elevators;
      (ii)   Manufacturer, age of each and capacity (in lbs. and number of passengers);
      (iii)   Type of operation for each elevator by elevator number or location in building (for large numbers of elevators describe by class-passenger/freight);
      (iv)   Automatic (type of controls);
      (v)   Floors served;
      (vi)   Type (hydraulic; gearless);
      (vii) Doors (sliding, swinging, manual, automatic);
      (viii) Location of machine rooms;
      (ix)   DC to motor (manufacturer);
      (x)   AC to motor-generator set (manufacturer);
      (xi)   Other.

(13) Elevator cabs. Describe:

        (i)   Kind (manufacturer);

        (ii)   Floor (material);

        (iii) Walls (material);

        (iv) Ceiling (material);

        (v)   Lighting (describe);

        (vi) Alarm, Safety system.

(i) Auxiliary Facilities:

    (1) Laundry Rooms. Describe:

        (i)   Location and number of rooms;

        (ii)   Clothes washers, number and type (e.g. Heavy duty, coin operated, electric, gas);

        (iii)   Clothes dryer (number and type);

        (iv)   Room ventilation (method and final exhaust);

        (v)   Dryer ventilation (method and final exhaust).

    (2) Refuse Disposal. Describe, including:

        (i)   Incinerator(s) (number, location, capacity, type, manufacturer);

        (ii)   Compactor(s) (number, location, capacity, type, manufacturer);

        (iii)   Approvals by authority having jurisdiction (date of each approval);

        (iv)   Initial storage location (ultimate storage location);

        (v)   Pick-up schedule, and whether public or private provider.

(j) Plumbing and Drainage.

    (1) Water Supply. Describe system, pumps, storage and location.

    (2) Fire Protection System. Describe:

        (i)   Standpipes (material, size, location);

        (ii)   Hose racks, hoses and nozzles (location);

        (iii)   Sprinkler heads (type system, location);

        (iv)   Siamese connection (type, location).

    (3) Water Storage Tank(s) and Enclosures. Describe:

        (i)   Number, type, location of each;

        (ii)   Material (interior, exterior and roof of tank);

        (iii)   Access to tank (e.g. vertical gooseneck ladder);

        (iv)   Capacity (total gallons);

        (v)   Capacity (fire reserve).

    (4) Water Pressure and How Maintained.

    (5) Sanitary Sewage System. Describe, including:

        (i)   Sewage Piping (materials);

        (ii)   Sewage Pumps (if any);

        (iii)   Sewage Disposal (public/private; treatment; drainfield; sewer).

    (6) Permit(s) Required. List and include date(s) obtained.

    (7) Storm Drainage System. Describe system, adequacy method of disposal and materials including:

        (i)   Catch basins (location);

      (ii)   Yard and Roof Drains (location);

      (iii) Piping (materials);

      (iv) Eject or sump pumps (describe in detail and describe conditions requiring pumps).

(k) Heating. Describe (including space heating and domestic hot water heating):

    (1) Describe heating and distribution of domestic hot water and whether capable of providing peak required services. Describe heating system's ability to maintain legally required conditions under anticipated weather conditions, specifying internal temperature and ambient temperature used in calculations.

    (2) Number of boilers and description;

    (3) Manufacturer and age of boiler(s) (model, capacity—alternatively give type, approximate age and approximate remaining useful life);

    (4) Manufacturer and age of burners (model—alternatively give type and approximate remaining useful life);

    (5) Type of controls;

    (6) Radiators, piping, insulation, valves, pumps;

    (7) Fuel (for oil give type and grade);

    (8) Location of oil tank, materials, enclosure;

    (9) Capacity of oil tank;

   (10) For gas (details on type and supply system).

(l) Gas supply (if not described above). Describe:

    (1) Type;

    (2) Meters;

    (3) Piping.

(m) Air conditioning. Describe cooling system's adequacy to maintain comfortable conditions under anticipated weather conditions, specifying internal temperature and base ambient temperature used in calculations. Describe:

    (1) Type of system;

    (2) Central system (give manufacturer, model and capacity);

    (3) Cooling towers, condensers (roof top, self-contained units, including number, location and description);

    (4) Individual units covered by the offer (window/sleeve—specify number, capacity, amperage and efficiency).

(n) Ventilation. Describe system in kitchens, fireplaces and all windowless areas such as corridors, garages, laundries, baths, etc.

(o) Electrical system. Specify:

    (1) Service from main service switchgear (amperes, voltage, phases, wire, protective equipment);

    (2) Service to individual units (risers, etc.);

    (3) Compartment switch gear (location and floor of sectional meter boards and transformers supplying power to the meter boards);

    (4) Unit service (ratings of main fuses, circuit breakers or fuses to units and ratings);

    (5) Adequacy

       (i)   Service—average number of circuits per apartment and capacity to handle modern appliances—specifically air conditioners, dishwashers and electric dryers;

       (ii)   Lighting and fixtures;

       (iii) Convenience outlets, appliance outlets.

  (6)   Intercommunication and/or door signal systems.

(p)   Television reception facilities (Master antennae, cable TV, antennae by tenants, security closed circuit TV).

(q)   Public Area Lighting. Describe and state adequacy (Entrances, halls and stairs, corridors, basements, courts and yards).

(r)   Garages and parking areas. Describe:

  (1)   Location of garages (description of facility);

  (2)   Location of parking areas (number of spaces in each);

  (3)   Surfaces (materials used, lighting, fencing, etc.);

  (4)   Parking (attended or not attended);

  (5)   Garage ventilation (method and equipment);

  (6)   Garage fire protection (method and equipment);

  (7)   Drainage.

(s)   Swimming Pool(s). Describe in detail:

       (i)   Type (concrete, material composition) and location on property;

       (ii)   Size, including length, width, depth, and approximate number of bathers permitted at any time;

       (iii) Enclosure (material including roof);

       (iv) Pumping and filter system (describe material);

       (v)   Water heating equipment, or usage of building's hot water (feed or heat exchangers);

       (vi) If on building roof, specify structural support system.

(t)   Tennis Courts, Playgrounds and Recreation Facilities.

  (1)   Tennis Courts. Describe:

       (i)   Type (clay, macadam, turf);

       (ii)   Number and size;

       (iii) Lighting (number and type);

       (iv) Fencing or enclosure (including distance between fence or enclosure and all sides of court).

  (2)   Playgrounds. Describe location and size(s) of playground(s), fencing (if any), equipment types, and sand bed or safety padding.

  (3)   Other Recreation Facilities. Describe any beach or lake front, boating facilities, golf course(s), handball, basketball or other game courts.

(u)   Permits and Certificates. List all applicable permits which must be obtained and inspections which are to be done. List type of inspection, authority inspecting and duration of approval once obtained, include all compactors, incinerators, boilers, oil storage, tanks, elevators, etc. In New York City include Department of Air Resources, Elevator Safety, Boiler Safety, Fire Department and Buildings Department permits.

(v)   Violations. List all violations outstanding as the date of this report and the agency imposing the violation, the condition involved, the date violation issued, and work required by violation notice to cure. If no violations are outstanding, so state.

(w)   Unit Information. Specify the number of units inspected. Specify the unit designations for each typical unit or line of units, including the number and type of rooms. Give criteria for calculations. For lofts give useable residential space in square feet. Describe (include foyers, living rooms, dining areas, kitchen, bedrooms, bathrooms, etc.):

(1)   Type and grade of finish material used in each type of unit and the number of coverings given. Include paint, wall and floor coverings, as well as specifying the type of flooring, walls and ceiling used.

(2)   Describe presence, type and condition of all bathroom fixtures.

(3)   Describe presence, type and condition of kitchen and laundry equipment.

(i)   if data is substantially the same for all units a single narrative may be substituted for this schedule.

(ii)   if any equipment or fixtures described are not included in the offering price, or the offering price is conditioned on the equipment and fixtures selected, such fact must be conspicuously noted in the body of the plan.

(x)   Finish Schedule of Spaces Other Than Units. The following is a form of schedule to be given for each floor.

Room   Floor   Walls   Ceiling   Remarks

(1)   Show all common rooms and spaces including but not limited to: Sub-sub cellar, sub-cellar, basement, first floor, penthouse floor, public and service halls, corridors, lobbies.

(y)   Safety and Warning Devices. Describe any fire or smoke safety devices installed in units and common areas. State what devices are required by law, and whether any required devices have not been installed.

(z)   Additional information required. Include the following in the Description of Property Section of the Plan:

(1)   A site plan showing roads, the outside dimensions of the building and clearly designated common areas, including recreation and refuse disposal areas, if more than one building is being offered;

(2)   An area map showing the location of the cooperative with respect to its surroundings, if the cooperative is not located in a highly urban area.

CONDOMINIUM AND COOPERATIVE ABUSE RELIEF ACT OF 1980

After much study and debate, Congress finally enacted the above law (15 USC Section 3601 and following) in order to safeguard purchasers from certain extreme promoter activities. The provisions of the statute follow.

CONDOMINIUM AND COOPERATIVE
ABUSE RELIEF ACT OF 1980

(15 USC §§ 3601 *et seq.*)

CHAPTER 62—CONDOMINIUM AND COOPERATIVE
CONVERSION PROTECTION AND ABUSE RELIEF

§3601.   Congressional findings and purpose

(a) The Congress finds and declares that—

(1) there is a shortage of adequate and affordable housing throughout the Nation, especially for low- and moderate-income and elderly and handicapped persons;

(2) the number of conversions of rental housing to condominiums and cooperatives is accelerating, which in some communities may restrict the shelter options of low- and moderate-income and elderly and handicapped persons;

(3) certain long-term leasing arrangements for recreation and other condominium- or cooperative-related facilities which have been used in the formation of cooperative and condominium projects may be unconscionable; in certain situations State governments are unable to provide appropriate relief; as a result of these leases, economic and social hardships may have been imposed upon cooperative and condominium owners, which may threaten the continued use and acceptability of these forms of ownership and interfere with the interstate sale of cooperatives and condominiums; appropriate relief from these abuses requires Federal action; and

(4) there is a Federal involvement with the cooperative and condominium housing markets through the operation of Federal tax, housing, and community development laws, through the operation of federally chartered and insured financial institutions, and through other Federal activities; that the creation of many condominiums and cooperatives is undertaken by entities operating on an interstate basis.

(b) The purposes of this chapter are to seek to minimize the adverse impacts of condominium and cooperative conversions particularly on the housing opportunities of low- and moderate-income and elderly and handicapped persons, to assure fair and equitable principles are followed in the establishment of condominium and cooperative opportunities, and to provide appropriate relief where long-term leases of recreation and other cooperative- and condominium-related facilities are determined to be unconscionable.

§ 3602.   Conversion lending

It is the sense of the Congress that lending by federally insured lending institutions for the conversion of rental housing to condominiums and cooperative housing should be discouraged where there are adverse impacts on housing opportunities of the low- and moderate-income and elderly and handicapped tenants involved.

§ 3603.   Definitions

For the purpose of this chapter—

(1) "affiliate of a developer" means any person who controls, is controlled by, or is under common control with a developer. A person "controls" a developer if the person (A) is a general partner, officer, director, or employer of the developer, (B) directly or indirectly or acting in concert with one or more other persons, or

through one or more subsidiaries, owns, controls, holds with power to vote, or holds proxies representing, more than 20 per centum of the voting interests of the developer, (C) controls in any manner the election of a majority of the directors of the developer, or (D) has contributed more than 20 per centum of the capital of the developer. A person "is controlled by" a developer if the developer (i) is a general partner, officer, director or employer of the person, (ii) directly or indirectly or acting in concert with one or more other persons, or through one or more subsidiaries, owns, controls, holds with power to vote, or holds proxies representing, more than 20 per centum of the voting interests of the person, (iii) controls in any manner the election of a majority of the directors, or (iv) has contributed more than 20 per centum of the capital of the person;

(2) "automatic rent increase clause" means a provision in a lease permitting periodic increases in the fee under the lease which is effective automatically or at the sole option of the lessor, and which provides that the fee shall increase at the rate of an economic, commodity, or consumer price index or at a percentage rate such that the actual increases in the rental payment over the lease term cannot be established with specificity at the time the lease is entered into;

(3) "common elements" means all portions of the cooperative or condominium project, other than the units designated for separate ownership or for exclusive possession or use;

(4) "condominium association" means the organization, whose membership consists exclusively of all the unit owners in the condominium project, which is, or will be responsible for the operation, administration, and management of the condominium project;

(5) "condominium project" means real estate (A) which has five or more residential condominium units, in each residential structure, and the remaining portions of the real estate are designated for common ownership solely by the owners of those units, each owner having an undivided interest in the common elements, and (B) where such units are or have been offered for sale or sold, directly or indirectly, through the use of any means or instruments of transportation or communication of interstate commerce, or the mails;

(6) "condominium unit" means a portion of a condominium project designated for separate ownership;

(7) "conversion project" means a project, which has five or more residential units, which was used primarily for residential rental purposes immediately prior to being converted to a condominium or cooperative project;

(8) "convey or conveyance" means (A) a transfer to a purchaser of legal title in a unit at settlement, other than as security for an obligation, or (B) the acquisition by a purchaser of a leasehold interest for more than five years;

(9) "cooperative association" means an organization that owns the record interest in the residential cooperative property or a leasehold of the residential property of a cooperative project and that is responsible for the operation of the cooperative project;

(10) "cooperative project" means real estate (A) which has five or more residential cooperative units, in each residential structure, subject to separate use and possession by one or more individual cooperative unit owners whose interest in

such units and in the undivided assets of the cooperative association which are appurtenant to the unit are evidenced by a membership or share interest in a cooperative association and a lease or other muniment of title or possession granted by the cooperative association as the owner of all the cooperative property, and (B) an interest in which is or has been offered for sale or lease or sold, or leased directly or indirectly, through use of any means or instruments of transportation or communication in interstate commerce or of the mails;

(11) "cooperative property" means the real estate and personal property subject to cooperative ownership and all other property owned by the cooperative association;

(12) "cooperative unit" means a part of the cooperative property which is subject to exclusive use and possession by a cooperative unit owner. A unit may be improvements, land, or land and improvements together, as specified in the cooperative documents;

(13) "cooperative unit owner" means the person having a membership or share interest in the cooperative association and holding a lease, or other muniment of title or possession, of a cooperative unit that is granted by the cooperative association as the owner of the cooperative property;

(14) "developer" means (A) any person who offers to sell or sells his interest in a cooperative or condominium unit not previously conveyed, or (B) any successor of such person who offers to sell or sells his interests in units in a cooperative or condominium project and who has the authority to exercise special developer control in the project including the right to: add, convert, or withdraw real estate from the cooperative or condominium project, and maintain sales offices, management offices and rental units; exercise easements through common elements for the purpose of making improvements within the cooperative or condominium; or exercise control of the owners' association;

(15) "interstate commerce" means trade, traffic, transportation, communication, or exchange among the States, or between any foreign country and a State, or any transaction which affects such trade, traffic, transportation, communication, or exchange;

(16) "lease" includes any agreement or arrangement containing a condominium or cooperative unit owner's obligation, individually, collectively, or through an association to make payments for a leasehold interest or for other rights to use or possess real estate, or personal property (which rights may include the right to receive services with respect to such real estate or personal property), except a lease does not include mortgages or other such agreements for the purchase of real estate;

(17) "person" means a natural person, corporation, partnership, association, trust or other entity, or any combination thereof;

(18) "purchaser" means any person, other than a developer, who by means of a voluntary transfer acquires a legal or equitable interest in a unit other than (A) a leasehold interest (including renewal options) of less than five years, or (B) as security for an obligation;

(19) "real estate" means any leasehold or other estate or interest in, over or under land, including structures, fixtures, and other improvements and interests which by custom, usage, or law pass with a conveyance of land though not de-

scribed in the contract of sale or instrument of conveyance. "Real estate" includes parcels with or without upper or lower boundaries, and spaces that may be filled with air or water;

(20) "residential" means used as a dwelling;

(21) "sale," "sale of a cooperative unit" or "sale of a condominium unit" means any obligation or arrangement for consideration for conveyance to a purchaser of a cooperative or condominium unit, excluding options or reservations not binding on the purchaser;

(22) "special developer control" means any right arising under State law, cooperative or condominium instruments, the association's bylaws, charter or articles of association or incorporation, or power of attorney or similar agreement, through which the developer may control or direct the unit owners' association or its executive board. A developer's right to exercise the voting share allocated to any condominium or cooperative unit which he owns is not deemed a right of special developer control if the voting share allocated to that condominium or cooperative unit is the same voting share as would be allocated to the same condominium or cooperative unit were that unit owned by any other unit owner at that time;

(23) "State" includes the several States, the District of Columbia, the Commonwealth of Puerto Rico, and the territories and possessions of the United States; and

(24) "tenants' organization" means a bona fide organization of tenants who represent a majority of the occupied rental units in a rental housing project.

§ 3604. Exemptions

The provisions of this chapter shall not apply to—

(1) a cooperative or condominium unit sold or offered for sale by the Federal Government, by any State or local government, by any corporate instrumentality of the United States, or by any agency thereof;

(2) a cooperative or condominium project in which all units are restricted to nonresidential purposes or uses; or

(3) any lease or portion thereof—

(A) which establishes any leasehold or other estate or interest in, over or under land on or in which one or more residential condominium or cooperative units are located, the termination of which will terminate the condominium or cooperative project, or reduce the number of units in such project, or

(B) which establishes a leasehold interest in, or other rights to use, possess, or gain access to, a condominium or cooperative unit.

§ 3605. Notice of conversion and opportunity to purchase; responsibility of State and local governments

It is the sense of the Congress that, when multifamily rental housing projects are converted to condominium or cooperative use, tenants in those projects are entitled to adequate notice of the pending conversion and to receive the first opportunity to purchase units in the converted projects and that State and local governments which have not already provided for such notice and opportunity for purchase should move toward that end. The Congress believes it is the responsibility of State and local governments to provide for such notice and opportunity to purchase in a prompt manner. The Congress has decided not to intervene and therefore leaves this responsibility to State and local governments to be carried out.

§ 3606.   Federal Housing Administration mortgage or loan insurance; expedition of application process and decision

Where an application for mortgage or loan insurance in connection with a conversion or purchase of a rental housing project being undertaken by a tenants' organization is submitted, the Secretary of Housing and Urban Development shall expedite the processing of the application in every way and shall make a final decision on such application at the earliest practicable time.

§ 3607.   Termination of self-dealing contracts

Operation, maintenance, and management contracts; penalty

(a) Any contract or portion thereof which is entered into after October 8, 1980, and which—

(1) provides for operation, maintenance, or management of a condominium or cooperative association in a conversion project, or of property serving the condominium or cooperative unit owners in such project;

(2) is between such unit owners or such association and the developer or an affiliate of the developer;

(3) was entered into while such association was controlled by the developer through special developer control or because the developer held a majority of the votes in such association; and

(4) is for a period of more than three years, including any automatic renewal provisions which are exercisable at the sole option of the developer or an affiliate of the developer.

may be terminated without penalty by such unit owners or such association.

Time of termination

(b) Any termination under this section may occur only during the two-year period beginning on the date on which—

(1) special developer control over the association is terminated; or

(2) the developer owns 25 per centum or less of the units in the conversion project,

whichever occurs first.

Vote of owners of units

(c) A termination under this section shall be by a vote of owners of not less than two-thirds of the units other than the units owned by the developer or an affiliate of the developer.

Effective date of termination

(d) Following the unit owners' vote, the termination shall be effective ninety days after hand delivering notice or mailing notice by prepaid United States mail to the parties to the contract.

§ 3608. Judicial determinations respecting unconscionable leases

Lease characteristics; authorization by unit owners; conditions precedent to action

(a) Cooperative and condominium unit owners through the unit owners' association may bring an action seeking a judicial determination that a lease or leases, or portions thereof, were unconscionable at the time they were made. An action may be brought under this section if each such lease has all of the following characteristics:

(1) it was made in connection with a cooperative or condominium project;

(2) it was entered into while the cooperative or condominum owners' association was controlled by the developer either through special developer control or because the developer had a majority of the votes in the owners' association;

(3) it had to be accepted or ratified by purchasers or through the unit owners' association as a condition of purchase or a unit in the cooperative or condominium project;

(4) it is for a period of more than twenty-one years or is for a period of less than twenty-one years but contains automatic renewal provisions for a period of more than twenty-one years;

(5) it contains an automatic rent increase clause; and

(6) it was entered into prior to June 4, 1975.

Such action must be authorized by the cooperative or condominium unit owners through a vote of not less than two-thirds of the owners of the units other than units owned by the developer or an affiliate of the developer, and may be brought by the cooperative or condominium unit owners through the units owners' association. Prior to instituting such action, the cooperative or condominium unit owners must, through a vote of not less than two-thirds of the owners of the units other than units owned by the developer or an affiliate of the developer, agree to enter into negotiation with the lessor and must seek through such negotiation to eliminate or modify any lease terms that are alleged to be unconscionable; if an agreement is not reached in ninety days from the date on which the authorizing vote was taken, the unit owners may authorize an action after following the procedure specified in the preceding sentence.

Presumption of unconscionability; rebuttal

(b) A rebuttable presumption of unconscionability exists if it is established that, in addition to the characteristics set forth in subsection (a) of this section, the lease—

(1) creates a lien subjecting any unit to foreclosure for failure to make payments;

(2) contains provisions requiring either the cooperative or condominium unit owners or the cooperative or condominium association as lessees to assume all or

substantially all obligations and liabilities associated with the maintenance, management and use of the lease property, in addition to the obligation to make lease payments;

(3) contains an automatic rent increase clause without establishing a specific maximum lease payment; and

(4) requires an annual rental which exceeds 25 percentum of the appraised value of the leased property as improved: *Provided,* That, for purposes of this paragraph "annual rental" means the amount due during the first twelve months of the lease for all units, regardless of whether such units were occupied or sold during that period, and "appraised value" means the appraised value placed upon the leased property the first tax year after the sale of a unit in the condominium or after the sale of a membership or share interest in the cooperative association to a party who is not an affiliate of the developer.

Once the rebuttal presumption is established, the court, in making its finding, shall consider the lease or portion of the lease to be unconscionable unless proven otherwise by the preponderance of the evidence to the contrary.

Presentation of evidence after finding of unconscionability

(c) Whenever it is claimed, or appears to the court, that a lease or any portion thereof is, or may have been, unconscionable at the time it was made, the parties shall be afforded a reasonable opportunity to present evidence at least as to—

(1) the commercial setting of the negotiations;

(2) whether a party has knowingly taken advantage of the inability of the other party reasonably to protect his interests;

(3) the effect and purpose of the lease or portion thereof, including its relationship to other contracts between the association, the unit owners and the developer or an affiliate of the developer; and

(4) the disparity between the amount charged under the lease and the value of the real estate subject to the lease measured by the price at which similar real estate was readily obtainable in similar transactions.

Remedial relief; matters considered; attorneys' fees

(d) Upon finding that any lease, or portion thereof, is unconscionable, the court shall exercise its authority to grant remedial relief as necessary to avoid an unconscionable result, taking into consideration the economic value of the lease. Such relief may include, but shall not be limited to rescission, reformation, restitution, the award of damages and reasonable attorney fees and court costs. A defendant may recover reasonable attorneys' fees if the court determines that the cause of action filed by the plaintiff is frivolous, malicious, or lacking in substantial merit.

Actions allowed after termination of special developer control

(e) Nothing in this section may be construed to authorize the bringing of an action by cooperative and condominium unit owners' association, seeking a judicial determination that a lease or leases, or portions thereof, are unconscionable, where such unit owners or a unit owners' association representing them has, after the termination of special developer control, reached an agreement with a holder of such lease or leases which either—

(1) sets forth the terms and conditions under which such lease or leases is or shall be purchased by such unit owners or associations; or

(2) reforms any clause in the lease which contained an automatic rent increase clause, unless such agreement was entered into when the leaseholder or his affiliate held a majority of the votes in the owners' association.

§ 3609. Void lease or contract provisions

Any provision in any lease or contract requiring unit owners or the owners' association, in any conversion project involving a contract meeting the requirements of section 3607 of this title or in any project involving a lease meeting the requirements of section 3608 of this title, to reimburse, regardless of outcome, the developer, his successor, or affiliate of the developer for attorneys' fees or money judgments, in a suit between unit owners or the owners' association and the developer arising under the lease or agreement, is against public policy and void.

§ 3610. Relationship of statutory provisions to State and local laws

Nothing in this chapter may be construed to prevent or limit the authority of any State or local government to enact and enforce any law, ordinance, or code with regard to any condominium, cooperative, or conversion project, if such law, ordinance, or code does not abridge, deny, or contravene any standard for consumer protection established under this chapter. Notwithstanding the preceding sentence, the provisions of this chapter, except for the application of section 3608 of this title and the prohibition included in section 3609 of this title as it relates to a lease with respect to which a cause of action may be established under section 3608 of this title, shall not apply in the case of any State or local government which has the authority to enact and enforce such a law, ordinance or code, if, during the three-year period following October 8, 1980, such State or local government enacts a law, ordinance, or code, or amendments thereto, stating in substance that such provisions of this chapter shall not apply in that State or local government jurisdiction.

§ 3611. Additional remedies

Suits at law or equity

(a) Unless otherwise limited as in section 3607 or 3608 of this title, any person aggrieved by a violation of this chapter may sue at law or in equity.

Recovery of actual damages

(b) In any action authorized by this section for a violation of section 3607 or 3609 of this title where actual damages have been suffered, such damages may be awarded or such other relief granted as deemed fair, just, and equitable.

Contribution

(c) Every person who becomes liable to make any payment under this section may recover contributions from any person who if sued separately, would have been liable to make the same payment.

Amounts recoverable; defendant's attorneys' fees

(d) The amounts recoverable under this section may include interest paid, reasonable attorneys' fees, independent engineer and appraisers' fees, and court costs. A defendant may recover reasonable attorneys' fees if the court determines that the cause of action filed by the plaintiff is frivolous, malicious, or lacking in substantial merit.

§ 3612.   Concurrent State and Federal jurisdiction; venue; removal of cases

The district courts of the United States, the United States courts of any territory, and the United States District Court for the District of Columbia shall have jurisdiction under this chapter and, concurrent with State courts, of actions at law or in equity brought under this chapter without regard to the amount in controversy. Any such action may be brought in the district wherein the defendant is found or is an inhabitant or transacts business, or in the district where the sale took place, and process in such cases may be served in other districts of which the defendant is an inhabitant or wherever the defendant may be found. No case arising under this chapter and brought in any State court of competent jurisdiction shall be removed to any court of the United States, except where any officer or employee of the United States in his official capacity is a party.

§ 3613.   Limitation of actions

No action shall be maintained to enforce any right or liability created by this chapter unless brought within six years after such cause of action accrued, except that an action pursuant to section 3608 of this title must be brought within four years after October 8, 1980.

§ 3614.   Waiver of rights as void

Any condition, stipulation, or provision binding any person to waive compliance with any provisions of this chapter shall be void.

§ 3615.   Nonexclusion of other statutory rights and remedies

The rights and remedies provided by this chapter shall be in addition to any and all other rights and remedies that may exist under Federal or State law.

§ 3616.   Separability

If any provisions of this chapter or the application thereof to any person or circumstance is held invalid, the remainder of this chapter shall not be affected thereby.

FIFTEEN

HOMEOWNER ASSOCIATIONS AND NEW TOWNS

THE PURPOSE OF ASSOCIATIONS

Before the advent of the condominium in the 1960s, owners of detached and attached single-family homes who shared community facilities usually did so by the use of a homeowner association in which members owned participating shares. Legal relationships were rather loose until recent years, when broker organizations and conservationists who were interested both in cluster housing and in safeguarding open space funded programs for the purpose of developing appropriate organizational machinery and management techniques. An older form of relationship, called a homeowner association, typified by the trite and largely disregarded contents of reservations and covenants in tract development deeds, placed on purchasers of homes mutual restrictions and obligations relative to such matters as signs, fencing, and the transfer of ownership (sometimes with racial overtones that have been continually rendered ineffective by the courts). Sometimes these reservations were important, as when they covered sewage disposal, utility easements, and water rights, especially when local or state laws and ordinances were silent on such subjects. In most of these last instances of neighborhood associations, community ownership of property was not a principal feature. Our discussion will concentrate on homeowner associations that involve community ownership for the bona fide purpose of sharing common facilities, a type of relationship that has won the support of bank and insurance company financing.

Typical homeowner associations (or planned-unit developments, as they are called in some states) are found throughout the United States in developments of detached, semidetached, and row housing—and in their modern setting homeowner associations usually encompass common ownership of recreational centers and green areas.

The planners and developers of the growing number of American "new towns" have groped for legal machinery with which to protect the dependent and reciprocal relationships among citizens and between citizens and industry. There the homeowner association format has been attempted in new ways that will be explored on succeeding pages in an effort to ascertain its validity and its usefulness in future programs.

THE RATIONALE FOR COMMUNITY LIVING

The homeowner association may formalize a needed community relationship concerning limited matters, such as the government of swatches of common greens; or its scope may stretch out in entirely new directions in the future. Most homeowners fool themselves if they downgrade forms of community living because they do not wish to experience a dilution of their ownership rights. If such critics looked about them with an eye to the truth, they might conclude that community relationships imposed by statute or judge-made law deeply affect the control of their everyday exercise of homeowner rights. Party walls, drainage, garbage disposal, school construction and maintenance, tree islands dividing streets, common recreation, common fencing or hedges, tree branches overhanging property lines, and a myriad of other matters depend on mutual rights and interests. If grass stretches in a continuous carpet between two houses, use of the same gardener and same-day cuttings may be essential. A neighbor's failure to maintain the exterior of his or her home may seriously damage a neighborhood.

In California, legislation was passed in 1980 to limit real property taxes, and similar legislation has been introduced in other states. As a consequence of this legislation, cities and counties are increasingly conditioning their approvals of new developments on the creation of homeowners associations to maintain properties the municipality has previously maintained. These "public" functions include the maintenance of slopes, parks, parkways, monuments, bus benches, public streets, and the like. This trend will probably continue into the foreseeable future.

Unlike those who predict confusion and lawsuits from the continued advances made in new forms of community living, we feel that the legal proceedings, the ill feelings among neighbors, and the decay of housing will be considerably lessened by wise and effective housing strategies carried out on a community basis.

Government is a primary form of community association. In recent times some local governing bodies have sought to create attributes of single homeowner associations for an entire population, as an example, a town or village swimming and recreational club maintained after its construction by membership dues. Tax money builds the enterprise, even if some residents do not become members.

A greater degree of protective personal ownership and control over important community relations should exist if the formalization of a homeowner association, cooperative, or condominium is effectively instituted. Party walls come under written rules and regulations; grass maintenance is required to be uniform; and housing exteriors are governed by a painting schedule. Less depends on the whims or pride of neighbors than in the case of single-family homeownership even if it is possible that they may be exercised to a bothersome degree.

The rationale for community living by associations should be based on orderliness, convenience, and protection with respect to all relationships that are dependent on neighbor or community action, as well as on the beneficial extension of the organization to provide facilities and comfort which would not otherwise be available.

LEGAL PREREQUISITES FOR HOMEOWNER ASSOCIATIONS

Three fundamental steps are essential for the creation of a workable homeowner association. First, a nonprofit group organization, usually in corporate form, is created pursuant to state law which authorizes the issuance of membership or shareholder evidences of interest. Second, the commonly used land and improvements that are to be owned by the development residents have to be conveyed to the association by the developer. Third, the title to each individual home is subjected to covenants tying the homeowner's and all succeeding owners' responsibility for the association's maintenance and operations to individual homeownership.

The FHA, in its *Land Planning Bulletin No. 6,* has described the legal foundation that is required in connection with approval by that agency of a planned-unit development established by means of a homeowner association. Listed in the bulletin are the following seven components, which must be present if the recorded documents are to be considered adequate for the purpose intended, and all of which will be seen to fall within the above three categories. The documents must:

1. Legally create an automatic membership nonprofit homes association
2. Place title to the common property in the homes association, or give definite assurance that it automatically will be so placed within a reasonable, definite time

3. Appropriately limit the uses of the common property
4. Give each lot owner the right to the use and enjoyment of the common property
5. Place responsibility for operation and maintenance of the common property in the homes association
6. Place an association charge on each lot in a manner which will assure sufficient association funds and provide adequate safeguards for the lot owners against undesirably high charges
7. Give each lot owner voting rights in the association

FHA insurance for cluster developments utilizing an association is possible under Section 203(b), Section 213 project sales, and provisions for experimental housing. The Section 235 low-income purchaser, mortgage assistance, and insurance program presumably would also qualify. It would seem that in most cases like this the land underlying each home must be owned in fee entirely by the individual homeowner, although such separate ownership may be by a long-term ground lease.

The governing authority for cementing an association to homeownership may be one or more recorded documents. Various names have been used for the papers recorded, including land subdivision plat and protective covenants; master deed; declaration of covenants, restrictions, easements, charges, and liens; deed, agreement, and declaration; and deed of dedication. A subdivision plat sometimes may merely refer to, and incorporate by reference, the terms of a separately recorded dedication of the common areas to a homeowner association. Such dedication, regardless of the number of recorded documents used, usually sets forth the conditions and commitment for the conveyance by the developer of the common areas. In addition, such action removes any cloud of implied public dedication.

Many dedications include specific management and administration rules which are ordinarily found in bylaws in condominiums and cooperatives, such as voting rights, easements of enjoyment, restrictions on use resulting from infractions of rules or failure to pay assessments. Quite often the fundamental rights of ownership that are implicit in full title are emphasized so as to remove any doubts on certain rights of the association, such as financing based on the security of common areas. Also found in these documents is the contract between developer and purchaser, which spells out the time and conditions for construction and the transfer of the common areas and facilities, as well as the period during which the builder will retain actual control of the common areas after the homes are sold.

In some of the more extensive and sophisticated situations (e.g., some new towns), a special set of bylaws is initially drafted for each association that governs its administration and connective linkage with other segments of the residential and industrial community.

BENEFITS OF HOMEOWNER ASSOCIATIONS

Builders have often selected the association form of community ownership in preference to a condominium or a total cooperative because it is easier to sell a development as a group of ordinary individual homes. The homeowner on resale has less explanation to give buyers about common responsibilities, perhaps thereby smoothing the sales processing.

One sales method used by some builders is to give the association a name suggestive of a country club or swimming association. This might well be a questionable practice for homeowner associations that may assess the homeowners for all exterior painting and repairs made on all houses, that may retain the responsibility for the maintenance of all landscaping, snow removal, and parking areas, and that will administer pools and playgrounds.

Section 528 of Internal Revenue Code covers homeowner associations as well as condominium associations. See Chapter 10.

The association form is clearly preferable where minimal community ownership is involved. If, for example, a small parking area adjoining a group of detached homes is used for guest and business visitors, there would hardly be any need to form a condominium or total cooperative. It is a serious question in some states as to whether or not a valid condominium could be formed for such purpose, because of the express or implied statutory requirement that all underlying land be owned in common.

Condominiums and total cooperatives generally require full home or apartment owner participation in common area maintenance. Some homeowner associations permit residents an option of belonging. In other cases minimum charges are assessed, but additional payments depend on voluntary subscription to use recreational or other common facilities. It would seem more protective of the group interest to make full cost assessments mandatory on all residents, as is the almost universal case with respect to condominiums and total cooperatives.

THE EFFECTIVENESS OF ASSOCIATIONS

In the past, homeowner associations were usually limited in size and facilities to small developments catering to upper-income residents, whether they were located in the country or in urban areas. Studies of their possible effectiveness in future housing programs aimed at achieving broader economic and social goals must evaluate past practices, owner attitudes, and the basic flexibility of this form of ownership as compared with the condominium and total cooperative. An association that in reality governs large areas of land and improvements should be founded on a solid legal basis. Unlike the statutory condominium, the association rarely can refer to a specific statute as a guide to the solution of unanswered or novel questions and problems resulting from its expanded usage.

Changes in the homeowner association form are necessary if this method of community living is to be used beyond its present provincial function. Most of the several thousand associations in the United States have involved limited developments by current standards both as to size and scope of community ownership and control. We might question the wisdom of relying on their relative success when contemplating more complicated and larger enterprises where common ownership and responsibilities range far beyond past efforts.

One factor delaying the surrounding community's acceptance of cluster housing has been fear that a homeowner association may sell off land, especially open spaces. This has rarely occurred, but the practice of the developer in deeding an open space easement to local government may be adequately reassuring. If not, outright deeding of title to government may be prerequisite. In the comparative condominium form, the interests in common areas are indivisible from unit ownership by statutory mandate, and the chances of the feared eventuality ever materializing are drastically reduced without the lurking shadow of government abuse of an easement or title. Moreover, the condominium's master declaration often conditions complete or partial dissolution on consent of one or more mortgagees.

OWNERSHIP OF COMMON AREAS

An association may hold full fee title to community land and facilities that are specified in underlying documents. It is just as possible to have various lease arrangements involving the developer or the developer's controlled entities as lessor, whether for the entire common areas or segmented portions. Occasionally, the developer only leases recreational facilities, such as a swimming pool, but the homeowner association is saddled with the responsibility for its maintenance, repair, and replacement as well as for the payment of rent under the lease. This practice is most prevalent in the State of Florida. Some institutional lenders who have issued loans backed by homes sharing in an association have not adequately absolved themselves from the necessity of contributing to leasehold rentals on foreclosure, even though the facilities after the passage of some years may be worn or abandoned. Moreover, the authors have noted few occasions when lending institutions have imposed voting controls over major homeowner association decisions in the form that is common in the case of condominiums. Recorded covenants occasionally require unanimous mortgagor approval for the dissolution of the association or for the sale of common facilities. Yet, other uncontrolled decisions, such as the right to encumber community land by a first mortgage, may critically affect the appraised value of the individual homes that may be mortgaged to other lenders.

A recent innovation is the deeding by the developer of community areas to a perpetual trustee (institution or foundation) and the granting of architectural and other controls to the trustee. Residents have little or no voting power for countermanding trustee decisions.

CONTINGENCIES SURROUNDING SALES

Homes are often sold with a mere precatory statement about the possibility and desirability of conveying land and constructing a recreation or other center for the residents if enough homes are sold. Another contingency found during our study pertained to local approval of plans to be filed in the future. Prospective homeowners are rarely given detailed plans, although more reliable builders do make some effort in this direction. Some common facilities are planned for an offsite location, without much information regarding the surrounding area being given to prospective purchasers, such as the exact location and the type of construction planned for the encircling land. The time limit for erecting common facilities usually is not specified.

Sales agents of many association developments emphasize that membership contributions are limited to modest initial amounts, and perhaps some small additional annual fee. This may be reassuring, but it can also lead to the deterioration of facilities for lack of expenditure. Because in some cases the maximum charge is restricted by covenants running with the land, it is almost impossible to increase charges without the consent of the developer, most of the current owners, and possibly most of the mortgagees on all homes and common areas, if so required by the governing documents. For this reason, it would seem preferable to have association charges set by separate bylaws that may be modified by a large percentage of homeowners, without the aid of the original developer.

Covenants limiting the use of space can effectively prevent expansion in the form of cabanas, sauna baths, or other uses that could be self-supporting or might even turn a profit that could be used to offset other expenses. In a luxury development, such additions may be made in response to the will of the majority despite increased costs.

Builders of some of the larger developments have adopted covenants granting to themselves almost unlimited authorization to extend the home-owner association to new developments, thereby increasing the use and traffic without any need to expand community areas. This technique may cut expenses, but it also reduces community exclusiveness and individuality. These changes are effected when the builder reserves the exclusive right to record a supplemental bundle of new or amended covenants and thus enable new communities to utilize the identical facilities.

TITLE INSURANCE

Homeowners are rarely able to obtain title insurance covering both the ownership of their individual home and their interest in the homeowner association. Sometimes the association itself will seek out title insurance, but this practice is not at all as general as it ought to be. Frequently this expenditure is foregone because of pressures to keep maintenance charges low for the first year. The greatest danger exists in the failure to obtain title insurance where the common facilities are not mortgaged initially, so that a situation exists in which no reputable lender is known to have checked or insured the title.

INSURANCE

We have already noted the customary statutory provisions that require the rebuilding of damaged condominium units. On the other hand, if one of a cluster of homes in a homeowner association is gutted by fire, there is much less likelihood of community action to reconstruct, because hazard policies for such purpose are rarely carried by associations themselves. There is no question that condominium statutes give much greater protection to a community's appearance than do series of typical documents that have contributed to the traditional concepts of homeowner associations. However, the VA, FHA, FNMA and FHLMC recently have begun to encourage the associations to carry such blanket insurance, so its use will probably become more widespread. In states where banks and other lenders must relinquish, in favor of rebuilding, their usual right to liquidate loans if condominium units are destroyed, this presents another factor that favors blanket insurance and that tends to override the psychological freedom of ownership attending associations.

It is customary to include in covenants the minimum requirements for public liability insurance covering common association areas. In our experience, the same cannot be said for the regularity of hazard insurance.

A total cooperative almost invariably insures the required percentage of full property value because the usual corporation is the sole owner of the entire premises which are maintained on a cooperative basis. Most condominiums carry single hazard policies covering all units as well as the commonly used property. In both of those situations, the selling prices give guideposts that help in formulating the amount of hazard insurance which should be carried in the overall policies. But the homeowner association faces a serious dilemma in determining the proper amount of hazard insurance to be carried. The builder has not charged separately for those areas, so the insurance should be related to replacement cost. At most, a great deal of conjecture is necessary in establishing the value when common areas are separated from the rest of the development. Difficulties in settling claims may be greater than they are in condominiums and cooperatives.

HOMEOWNER ASSOCIATIONS AND NEW TOWNS

Giant strides have been taken in use of the association form since 1960, when a radical concept in U.S. housing began to take shape that has come to be known as the "new town." Whereas the concept probably germinated as the result of prior British government innovations in total community development, the U.S. communities today are largely sponsored by huge publicly held private corporations whose principal business is not the production of housing.

A new town is generally considered to be a huge area of contiguous acreage on which is created a residential, commercial, industrial, and recreational "total community." One of the most important characteristics that sets these developments apart from other housing enterprises is the fact that each constitutes a self-contained source of employment for a large number of residents. The more rural the setting, the more local employment opportunities must be created in the new town. Few new communities exist without an inflow and outflow of labor, even though some larger communities are capable of absorbing a majority of residents into their own industries.

The homeowner association has been used in two different ways in these new cities. The old form of community group organization is often employed in order to cope with small clusters of residential areas where some degree of independence and self-government is felt to be desirable. Frequently superimposed on such associations, or on condominiums and cooperatives existing separately within the overall areas, is a master homeowner association to which all residential areas are linked by obligations, assessments, and architectural controls. It is this latter feature that presents the novel use of associations in new towns. See Chapter 16 for a discussion of mixed-use developments using vertical subdivisions in new towns.

One is justified in arguing that it is inaccurate to refer to the master association as one that is representative only of homeowners. These associations quite often include resident tenants and cooperators, as well as condominium unit-owners and ordinary homeowners. Voting in that event depends on the particular lot occupied rather than ownership in fee simple.

Many master associations provide independent design controls that are not subject to change by the board of directors. These controls take the form of requirements set by a board of three or four architects intended to limit substantial exterior alterations, additions, or replacements; to provide for periodic inspection of interior and exterior maintenance, uses, and changes; to restrict the planting, removal, or pruning of trees and shrubs; and to control time schedules for grass cutting and watering. The architectural committee governing such matters is not subject to direct removal by a vote of residents, although this provision is sometimes modified by granting the developer exclusive appointive and removal power during the initial sales period. In effect, the committee serves as a private zoning board. Their power appears absolute in certain new towns and may seriously impede the power of self-determination and the authority of group associations, condominiums, and cooperatives with the new community. However, courts in some states are holding that the members of architectural committees owe fiduciary duties of fairness to the property owners whom they represent.

The most urgent problem faced by developers of new towns has been inadequate financing during the long wait between the time that construction has been completed and the time that the comprehensive city begins to produce income. This crisis led to a virtual monopoly of promotions by large industrial giants, who have been able to handle planning and construction without worrying about the sources of continued financing. Unfortunately, because of this difficulty some idealistic and imaginative builders have had to assign their interests in such ventures to large corporations. Government support was needed to bring economic and social balance to new towns, but this support was only scantily forthcoming until the Housing and Urban Development Act of 1968. Title IV of this act was well intended, but it failed for numerous reasons.

TITLE X PROGRAM

The FHA Title X Land Development Program provides unsubsidized mortgage insurance for loans made to developers to refinance or purchase, and develop medium to large tracts of land. In order to qualify for a Title X loan, a project must be primarily residential, but FHA has administratively determined that the site may contain up to 25 percent of the acreage for retail, commercial, and light industrial uses. According to the Program Summary for Sponsors, there are no prescribed maximum limitations on the price range or rental rates for the residential units to be completed on the site.

A Title X loan is *nonrecourse,* and may be made for a term of up to ten years, with an interest rate not to exceed the current FHA Title X maximum interest rate. Backed by the FHA loan insurance, the financing will be funded by a private lender with yields that are commensurate with the marketplace at the time the loan is funded. However, because of the FHA insurance, the yields typically required by private lending sources are considerably below conventional financing alternatives.

For larger tracts of land, a Title X loan may utilize a "land bank" approach. In some cases, the loan will cover the cost to acquire or refinance the entire acreage, and the loan will also cover the development costs associated with the land improvements on an initial phase of development. The initial phase of development may not exceed three years in duration, and during that initial phase the Title X loan itself will cover the financing expense and interest carry of the project.

Future phases, including interest carry after the completion of the initial phase, may be financed with subsequent Title X loans covering those individual phases. This legislation serves to give recognition to the need for government assistance in carrying out massive solutions to housing and other community problems based on the development of new communities, by means of a guarantee of investment so as to enlist large amounts of private capital.

GUARANTEE AUTHORITY

Regulations dealing with the Title X Land Development Program were amended in 1979. Under Title X, FHA will insure a loan amount calculated as the lesser of the following three criteria:

1. Ninety percent of the Commissioner's estimate of the development cost plus 80 percent of the Commissioner's estimate of the value of the land before development; or

   2. The total of:
  - **a.** The Commissioner's estimate of the development cost, plus
  - **b.** The greater of acquisition cost or all outstanding indebtedness secured by the land, plus
  - **c.** Fifty percent of the difference between the applicable amount in item "2" and the Commissioner's estimate of the value of the land before development; or
   3. Eighty-five percent of the Commissioner's estimated value of the property after the completion of the development.

The term *acquisition cost* refers to the cost of the land plus all costs associated with acquiring the title, closing costs, zoning, holding costs, and so on. *Indebtedness* is all indebtedness that is secured by the land. Indebtedness incurred within two years of the date of the SAMA application may not be treated as indebtedness for the purpose of determining the maximum mortgage amount except as approved by the Commissioner.

The Title X loan is funded in two segments. An interim loan, with a term equal to the time allocated for completion of the initial phase of development (typically one to three years), is funded in a manner consistent with typical construction financing procedures. To the extent available, funds may be advanced at initial closing to cover the greater of the acquisition cost of land or the allowable existing land indebtedness, but not to exceed 80 percent of the Commissioner's estimate of the "as is" value of the land. Additionally, funds may be drawn to cover required financing costs and other loan closing expenses. Thereafter, during the remaining term of the interim loan, advances will be made monthly on the basis of draw requests against the percentage of work completed for all line item costs, plus interest charges.

On completion of the initial phase of development, a "permanent" loan closing occurs, at which time any loan proceeds not previously advanced will be disbursed to the borrower.

CREATIVITY IN THE FUTURE

The emergence of the condominium, the wide experience with stock cooperatives and homeowner associations, and the added potential of new towns should help the country attain many long-sought housing goals. The next decades will call for flexibility in housing solutions, and the forms of community housing discussed in this book should help to supply the answers, or to provoke them.

SIXTEEN

MIXED-USE CONDOMINIUMS

Some commentators have suggested that a mixed-use development occurs when the restrictions for a restricted-use project fail. While this may be the case in some projects, the mixed-use developments focused on here are those that were designed at the outset to accommodate a mixture of residential and office or retail uses. However, some of the following considerations will apply to mixtures of office, retail, and light industrial uses with no residential use.

With the long-term trend of the cost of fuel increasing and with the country continuing on an inflationary bias, there are some signs of a movement of businesses and residents back to the inner city. Cities and counties, finding themselves short on funds, will continue to exact large fees as a condition to the development of virgin land. Some developers are turning to the mixed-use development to maximize efficiency of land, particularly parking areas that tend to be used by the businesses at times when they are not used heavily by residents. Hence, there are some signs of regression to the Middle Ages, and the Old World project in Huntington Beach, California, illustrates this trend. In this mixed-use project, each unit in the two-story attached structures consists of two physically separated areas designed and restricted for different uses—a trade–retail establishment on the lower level and a residential unit for the retail owner located above the business establishment. Other prominent mixed-use projects include the Water Tower Place and Hancock Buildings in Chicago and the Diamond Center in New York.

The differences between residential and commercial projects, as well as between for-sale and for-lease developments, must be kept clearly in mind at each stage of the planning, development, and operational stages of the project. For an excellent discussion of the unique factors that distinguish a pure residential condominium from a pure business condominium, see *The Business Condominium* (John Wiley & Sons, 1973). In the balance of this chapter, some of the principal areas of the development process that may cause problems in creating a mixed-use co-ownership project will be highlighted.

REGULATION OF PROJECT

Anyone who is considering the development of a mixed-use, co-ownership project must check local zoning codes to ensure that the mix of uses contemplated is authorized. If a conversion is planned, the converter must check local ordinances to determine whether there are provisions governing tenant protections (such as relocation rights, rights of first refusal, etc.) that would apply to the conversion of the mixed-use project. The risk of rent control and conversion moratoria is higher in a mixed-use project than in a purely commercial project. Such requirements usually are adopted to protect tenants in residential projects, and the protections can spill over into a mixed-use project.

Most cities and counties are more cooperative in approving commercial conversions than residential conversions, because residential tenants collectively have a louder political voice than commercial tenants. Federal and state agencies that have been created to protect purchasers from fraud in the sale of property tend to scrutinize residential offerings more than commercial offerings. There is a belief that a business purchaser is better off financially than a residential consumer and that the business unit purchaser can afford to hire professional consultants to protect himself or herself.

The restrictions that are usually imposed by regulatory agencies as conditions for issuing their approvals for the residential sales could unduly interfere with the successful leasing or selling of space in the commercial buildings. For example, the offices of Interstate Land Sales Registration of HUD will count commercial and residential lots or condominiums under a common promotional scheme to satisfy their jurisdictional requirements for registration of the offering. In addition, government securities agencies are generally more restrictive in reviewing residential investment contracts than commercial investment contracts in determining whether the offering provides adequate disclosure or is fair, just, and equitable, so mixed-use contracts tend to be scrutinized more than pure commercial contracts. These agencies tend to review the commercial aspects of the development to assure that the residential purchasers are adequately protected before issuing their approvals for the sale of residential units. In most states, after the jurisdictional minimum number of residential units has been reached (usually five to ten residential units), the laws and regulations apply, regardless of the number of residential units or the ratio of residential units to units of other uses.

OPERATION OF THE PROJECT

Separation of Incompatible Uses

As a general rule, one should attempt to separate both physically and legally the operations of incompatible uses, and a residential use is usually incompatible with both office and retail use of space. A mixed-use association has a better chance of survival if areas of potential conflict are addressed at the design stage as well as in the legal documents. For instance, it is usually advisable to provide separate access (capable of being secured) to the residential portion of the building from the public access to the commercial portion of the building. However, there are some cases where certain common areas can be shared and services can be combined. For example, one exterior window-washing apparatus has successfully served the Olympia Towers in New York, a mixed-use project with residential and office space under one roof. In addition, office users tend to experience peak parking demands during times when the parking needs of the residents are relatively low, and vice versa.

Regardless of the few exceptions to the general rule of separation, one should assume that there will be general animosity or apathy between the occupants of the residential space and the occupants of the commercial space. The tendency on the part of the developer is to place a greater burden on the commercial owners so as to satisfy concerns of the regulatory agencies that the residential purchasers will be protected. The result is that the commercial property may no longer be attractive as either a for-sale or for-lease product.

One developer of a mixed-use (residential and retail) project attempted to burden the commercial portion of the project with approximately 16 percent of the expenses of the owners' association but furnished the owner of the commercial space with only about 8 percent of the services of the association. The sale of units in the commercial portion of the building was not feasible under this arrangement. Further, the developer could not rent the space because he could not economically pass along the high association assessment costs to the prospective commercial tenants. The inevitable result was that the owner of the commercial space filed a lawsuit to legally partition the commercial project from the residential project, so that the two portions of the building could be operated separately under separate cost centers. Similar problems can be foreseen when the developer attempts to place undue burdens on the residential sector, but the state agencies usually take steps to protect the homeowners.

Commercial occupants will demand some services that will not be required by residential occupants (such as weekly window washing). Also, residents will demand some services that may not be required by commercial occupants (such as maintenance of swimming pools or separate security on floors and in certain elevators). Hence, separate cost centers should be established for the residential and commercial areas, with some control in owners from areas using unique services. Of course, general assessments for office and administrative costs can be paid equally by all owners within the project. The management costs of a mixed-use association will be considerably greater than the management costs for a single-use association.

An equitable manner of apportioning the voting power between the commercial owners and the residential owners must be established in the documents. The documents may require at least one director to be elected from each of the different use areas to help assure balanced thinking on the board. In any event, whenever separate cost centers have been created under one association, some control should be given to the owners in the commercial and the residential areas to control the budgets for their respective cost centers. Moreover, the owners within the residential and the commercial areas should have some influence over the rules promulgated to govern the respective areas. Where both commercial and residential owners are members of the same association, there is usually considerably more voting power residing in either the commercial or the residential members, depending upon the design of the project. All of the differences between residential for-sale and commercial for-sale developments must be reconciled if only one association is created. For example, the residential members may wish to meet in the evening while the commercial members may prefer to meet during working hours, and this conflict may be hard to reconcile.

At first blush, one may assume that the use restrictions for the commercial area should be totally separate from the use restrictions for the residential area, and that the commercial and residential owners should have autonomous control over the enforcement and amendment of their respective restrictions. However, there are some restrictions (such as waste removal) that may apply to both the commercial and the residential areas. Moreover, the residential owners may wish to veto certain changes in the commercial uses. For example, if the owner of a restaurant in a highrise, mixed-use development wishes to convert its use to a disco, or if the owner of a hair-dressing salon wishes to convert its use to an adult bookstore with the approval of the local government, the residents may have a legitimate objection to such proposed changes in use. Hence, the documentation should be drafted with these possibilities in mind.

In the area of damage, destruction, and condemnation, some losses may not affect the residential uses but will affect the viability of businesses being conducted in a commercial unit (and vice versa). Thus, the documentation for a mixed-use project located in one building must be drafted very carefully in these areas of concern to take into account the inherent differences.

If a mixed-use association is created to operate a residential and commercial project, then it may not qualify under Section 528 of the Internal Revenue Code to elect to have its member income exempt from taxation. If at least 85 percent of the space is residential and if other criteria are satisfied, then the association may not lose this option. In some jurisdictions (such as New York), stock cooperative–condominiums are used to avoid negative income tax consequences of mixed-use developments. See Chapter 10 concerning condominium income tax factors.

Two-Tier Association Concept

For very large planned communities, it is usually desirable to create a two-tier association concept. The diverse interests of the various uses can be blended into a master association that would be responsible for uniform architectural and landscape control, general use restriction enforcement, and the maintenance of any communitywide areas and facilities. Then, supplemental declarations can be recorded to authorize the creation of separately incorporated subassociations to govern separate residential and commercial projects under the umbrella of the master association. This structure allows the owners of properties with incompatible uses to share facilities that they commonly use and to work together on common problems. At the same time, the owners of properties with similar uses can control their neighborhood areas with relative freedom.

There is a very large, mixed-use, planned community south of Denver, Colorado, which incorporates the two-tier association concept. That project is planned to eventually cover approximately 11,000 acres with several thousand homes and several acres of commercial properties. The commercial owners are given no automatic right to use the recreational facilities. A novel delegate voting system has been incorporated into the documents, whereby the entire community is divided into delegate districts consisting of approximately 200 homes each as a designated acreage of commercial property. The property owners in each delegate district elect one person to cast all of the votes as a form of proxy on behalf of the owners of property located in the respective districts.

As an alternative to creating a two-tier association structure, separate commercial and residential condominium associations may be created to govern their respective buildings (or portions of buildings). The members of the respective associations can be given cross-easements in accordance with joint use and maintenance agreements that contain formulas for sharing expenses of maintenance of the property. There will probably be higher administrative costs involved in running a two-tier association concept than in running separate associations for each different use area without a master association, but one must be extremely careful in creating the easements and agreements between the associations where the two-tier association concept is not utilized.

Vertical Planned Unit Development Condominium

Conventional planned developments involve the creation of separate lots around each building, the ownership of which would (theoretically) extend down to the center of the earth and up to the sky above. Unfortunately, relatively uniform building codes, which have been adopted by many cities throughout the United States, require that adjoining lots be separated by fire walls, where they are involved in closed, connecting space designed for human occupancy. Such a requirement would severely interfere with the operation of a large project with highrise, mixed-use buildings and a subterranean parking garage extending under the buildings.

A novel concept for mixed-use developments involves the creation of a three-dimensional or vertical planned unit development condominium. In some jurisdictions, the developer may create a vertical planned development to preserve flexibility to periodically change the project designs, proposed uses, and forms of ownership to meet changing laws, technology, and market desires. This concept involves the creation of three-dimensional lots on a subdivision or plat map. Each lot would be described in terms of its upper and lower dimensions, so that the subdivision would resemble a condominium plan (unit location map) with several airspace cube–lots. The lot lines must be very carefully drawn to satisfy the fire wall requirements of the city or county as may be contained in its building code.

By creating a vertical planned unit development, the developer could retain the flexibility to sell one or more of the lots to other persons. A planned development association could be created for the purposes of owning and maintaining master common areas (landscaping, driveways, walkways, certain exterior lighting, etc.) to ensure overall architectural control within the project and to enforce rules and regulations formed to benefit and protect the entire project. The master common areas could consist of several three-dimensional lots outside the building envelope–lots beginning at the roof of the subterranean parking structure and extending an unlimited distance upward. Each owner of a lot would contribute to the cost of operating the association through some equitable formula. By creating separate lots, the master developer would retain the ability to legally phase the development of the project so that each lot or group of lots would constitute a separate phase of development.

The most significant advantage of the vertical subdivision is that it allows the developer the flexibility to further subdivide any or all of the lots into condominium projects governed by subassociations under the master planned development association. This flexibility would permit the master developer to condominiumize any or all of the office buildings and residential buildings and the garage parcel. If none of the lots is ever condominiumized, the project would be operated through only one planned development association. However, if a building is further subdivided, the master legal documentation could be prepared to accept a two-tier association concept described above. Each unit owner in a condominiumized building would become a member of both the master planned development association and the subassociation that would be formed to manage that building.

If a residential building is eventually subdivided into a condominium project, the two-tier association concept would be particularly attractive. The two-tier concept legally separates the operation of the commercial use areas from the residential use areas more than does the single association concept, and this separation is important for the reasons previously discussed in this chapter. In addition, the favorable income tax status of the residential subassociation (under Section 528 of the Internal Revenue Code) would not be jeopardized by the commercial properties if the two-tier association concept is implemented. This structure allows the developer maximal flexibility to plan for the income tax consequences of the subassociation, while not locking himself or herself into a particular form of ownership, product design, or use.

HUD LEGAL POLICIES

APPENDIX 24

HUD LEGAL POLICIES. The attached policy statements will serve to assist attorneys certifying that legal documents meet HUD's objectives. Legal documents submitted to HUD for project approval must be accompanied by certification from the mortgagee's attorney or other attorney that the documents comply with State and local condominium laws, HUD regulations and with the HUD policy statements attached.

NOTE: HUD will accept legal documents that have been accepted by FNMA, FHLMC, and/or VA. Evidence shall be submitted that the documents have been approved.

October, 1980

REVISED LEGAL POLICIES*

1. TYPES OF CONDOMINIUMS

The following types of basic ownership arrangements are generally acceptable provided they are established in compliance with the applicable condominium law of the jurisdiction(s) in which the condominium is located:

(a) Ownership of units by individual owners coupled with an undivided interest in all common elements.

(b) Ownership of units by individual owners coupled with an undivided interest in general common elements and specified limited common elements.

The agencies and corporations will consider for approval, on an individual case basis, an arrangement involving ownership of units by individual owners coupled with an undivided interest in the general common elements and/or limited common elements, with title to additional property for common use vested in an association of unit owners, where such a configuration of ownership is not precluded by the applicable condominium law. As to this type of ownership arrangement, in addition to compliance with the requirements of the organizations' respective condominium

---

* The Revised Legal Policies set forth herein provide a listing of those general policies agreed to by HUD, VA, FNMA, and FHLMC with respect to provisions of legal significance usually contained in the constituent legal documentation for a condominium project. The applicable regulations and related publications of the Department of Housing and Urban Development and the Veterans Administration and the basic contracts and guides of the Federal National Mortgage Association (FNMA) and the Federal Home Loan Mortgage Corporation (FHLMC) should be consulted for a complete statement of the respective legal policies and requirements of each Task Force member organization governing their approval of condominiums or unit mortgages.
** Not applicable to conventionally financed existing condominium projects.

programs, there must be compliance with the applicable requirements of the organizations' respective planned unit development (PUD) programs.

The above descriptions of types of ownership arrangements are not intended to exclude other variations. Other forms of ownership may be acceptable, on an individual case basis, to any or all of the agencies and corporations.

2. ESTATE OF UNIT OWNER

The legal estate of each unit owner must generally be held in fee simple or acceptable leasehold estate. The acceptability of leasehold estates varies among the agencies and corporations.

The declaration or equivalent document shall allocate an undivided interest in the common elements to each unit. Such interest may be allocated equally to each unit, may be proportionate to that unit's relative size or value, or may be allocated according to any other specified criteria provided that the method chosen is equitable and reasonable for that condominium.

3. CONDOMINIUM DOCUMENTATION

(a) *Compliance with applicable law.* The declaration, by-laws and other enabling documentation shall conform to the laws governing the establishment and maintenance of condominium regimes within the jurisdiction in which the condominium is located, and to all other laws which apply to the condominium.

(b) *Recordation.* The declaration and all amendments or modifications thereof shall be placed of record in the manner prescribed by the appropriate jurisdiction. If recording of plats, plans, or by-laws or equivalent documents and all amendments or modifications thereof is the prevailing practice or is required by law within the jurisdiction where the project is located, then such documents shall be placed of record. If the by-laws are not recorded, then convenants, restrictions and other matters requiring record notice should be contained in the declaration or equivalent document.

(c) *Availability.* The owners association shall be required to make available to unit owners, lenders and the holders and insurers of the first mortgage on any unit, current copies of the declaration, by-laws and other rules governing the condominium, and other books, records and financial statements of the owners association. The owners association also shall be required to make available to prospective purchasers current copies of the declaration, by-laws, other rules governing the condominium, and the most recent annual audited financial statement, if such is prepared. "Available" shall at least mean available for inspection upon request, during normal business hours or under other reasonable circumstances.

The declaration, or its equivalent, shall provide that upon written request from any of the agencies or corporations which has an interest or prospective interest in the condominium, the owners association shall be required to prepare and furnish within a reasonable time an audited financial statement of the owners association for the immediately preceding fiscal year.

4. REAL PROPERTY DESCRIPTION

(a) *Property Description.* The description of the units, common elements, any recreational facilities and other related amenities, and any limited common elements shall be clear and in conformity with the law of the jurisdiction where the project is located.

Responsibility for maintenance and repair of all portions of the condominium shall be clearly set forth.

** (b) *Developmental Plan.* The declaration or other legally enforceable and binding document must state in a reasonable manner the overall development plan of the condominium, including building types, architectural style and the size of the units. Under the applicable provisions of the declaration or such other legally enforceable and binding document, the development of the condominium must be consistent with the overall plan, except that the declarant may reserve the right to change the overall plan or decide not to construct planned units or improvements to the common elements if the declaration sets forth the conditions required to be satisfied prior to the exercise of that right, the time within which the right may be exercised, and any other limitations and criteria that would be necessary or appropriate under the particular circumstances. Such conditions, time restraints and other limitations must be reasonable in light of the overall plan for the condominium.

5. DECLARANT'S RIGHTS AND RESTRICTIONS

(a) *Disclosure and Reasonableness of Reserved Rights.* Any right reserved by the declarant must be reasonable and set forth in the declaration.

(b) *Examples of Acts and Reserved Rights Which are Usually Unacceptable.* The following action on the part of the declarant, the developer, an affiliate of the declarant, the sponsor of a project, or any other party, (collectively referred to as "declarant") usually would be unacceptable.

Binding the owners association either directly or indirectly to any of the following agreements unless the owners association shall have a right of termination thereof which is exercisable without penalty at any time after transfer of control, upon not more than 90 days' notice to the other party thereto:

(i) Any management contract, employment contract or lease of recreational or parking areas or facilities;

(ii) Any contract or lease, including franchises and licenses, to which a declarant is a party.

The requirements of (i) and (ii) of this subparagraph do not apply to acceptable ground leases.

As used in this section, "affiliate of a declarant" shall mean any person or entity which controls, is controlled by, or is under common control with, a declarant. A person or entity shall be deemed to control a declarant if that person or entity (i) is a general partner, officer, director, or employee of the declarant; (ii) directly or indirectly or acting in concert with one or more persons, or through one or more subsidiaries, owns, controls, or holds with power to vote, or holds proxies representing, more than 20 percent of the voting shares of the declarant; (iii) controls in any manner the election of a majority of the directors of the declarant; or (iv) has contributed more than 20 percent of the capital of the declarant. A person or entity shall be deemed to be controlled by a declarant if the declarant (i) is a general partner, officer, director, or employee of that person or entity; (ii) directly or indirectly or acting in concert with one or more persons or through one or more subsidiaries, owns, controls, or holds with power to vote, or holds proxies representing, more than 20 percent of the voting share of that person or entity; (iii) controls in any manner the election of a majority of the directors of that person or entity; or (iv) has contributed more than 20 percent of the capital of that person or entity.

(c) *Examples of Reserved Rights Which are Usually Acceptable.* The following rights in the common elements may usually be reserved by the declarant for a reasonable period of time, subject to a concomitant obligation to restore:

   (1) Easement over and upon the common elements and upon lands appurtenant to the condominium for the purpose of completing improvements for which provision is made in the declaration, but only if access thereto is otherwise not reasonably available.

   (2) Easement over and upon the common elements for the purpose of making repairs required pursuant to the declaration or contracts of sale made with unit purchasers.

   (3) Right to maintain facilities in the common areas which are identified in the declaration and which are reasonably necessary to market the units. These may include sales and management offices, model units, parking areas, and advertising signs.

6. TRANSFER OF CONTROL

(a) The declarant shall relinquish all special rights, expressed or implied, through which the declarant may directly or indirectly control, direct, modify, or veto any action of the owners association, its executive board, or a majority of unit owners, and control of the owners association shall pass to the owners of units within the project, not later than the earlier of the following:

**   (1) 120 days after the date by which 75 percent of the units have been conveyed to unit purchasers, or

** (2) The last date of a specified period of time following the first conveyance to a unit purchaser, such period of time to be reasonable for the
particular project and to be subject to approval in each instance by
the agency or corporation concerned. The maximum acceptable
period usually will be from three to five years for single phased condominium regimes and five to seven years for expandable condominiums.

(b) The foregoing requirements shall not affect the declarant's rights, as a unit
owner, to exercise the votes allocated to units which it owns.

** (c) Declarants should provide for and foster early participation of unit owners
in the management of the project.

** (d) FNMA and FHLMC will consider on a case basis possible modifications or
variations of the requirements in subparagraph (a) above particularly in
circumstances involving very large condominium developments.

7. OWNERS ASSOCIATION'S RIGHTS AND RESTRICTIONS

(a) *Right of Entry Upon Units and Limited Common Elements.* The owners association shall be granted a right of entry upon unit premises and any limited common elements to effect emergency repairs, and a reasonable right
of entry thereupon to effect other repairs, improvements, replacement or
maintenance deemed necessary.

(b) *Power to Grant Rights and Restrictions in Common Elements.* The owners
association should be granted other rights, such as the right to grant utility
easements under, through or over the common elements, which are reasonably necessary to the ongoing development and operation of the
project.

(c) *Responsibility for Damage to Common Elements and Units.* A provision
may be made in the declaration or by-laws for allocation of responsibility
for damages resulting from the exercise of any of the above rights.

(d) *Assessments.*

(1) *Levy and collection.* The declaration or its equivalent shall describe
the authority of the owners association to levy and enforce the collection of general and special assessments for common expenses and
shall describe adequate remedies for failure to pay such common expenses. The common expenses assessed against any unit, with interest,
costs and reasonable attorney's fees shall be a lien upon such unit in
accordance with applicable law. Each such assessment, together with
interest, costs, and attorney's fees shall also be the personal obligation
of the person who was the owner of such unit at the time the assessment fell due. The personal obligation for delinquent assessments
shall not pass to successors in title or interest unless assumed by them,
or required by applicable law.

Common expenses as used in this Statement of Policies shall mean
expenditures made or liabilities incurred by or on behalf of the

owners association, together with any assessments for the creation and maintenance of reserves.

(2) *Reserves and Working Capital.* There shall be established an adequate reserve fund for the periodic maintenance, repair and replacement of the common elements, which fund shall be maintained out of regular assessments for common expenses. Additionally, a working capital fund must be established for the initial months of the project operations equal to at least a two months' estimated common area charge for each unit.

(3) *Priority of Lien.* To the extent permitted by applicable law, HUD, VA, FNMA and FHLMC require that the declaration shall provide any lien of the owners association for common expense charges and assessments becoming payable on or after the date of recordation of the first mortgage, shall be subordinate to the first mortgage on the unit. Such a lien for common expense charges and assessments shall not be affected by any sale or transfer of a unit, except that a sale or transfer of a unit pursuant to a foreclosure of a first mortgage shall extinguish a subordinate lien for common expense charges and assessments which become payable prior to such sale or transfer. Any such sale or transfer pursuant to a foreclosure shall not relieve the purchaser or transferee of a unit from liability for, nor the unit so sold or transferred from the lien of, any common expense charges thereafter becoming due.

8.   UNIT OWNERS' RIGHTS AND RESTRICTIONS

(a) *Obligation to pay espenses.* The declaration or equivalent document shall establish a duty on each unit owner, including the declarant, to pay a proportionate share of common expenses upon being assessed therefor by the owners association. Such share may be allocated equally to each unit, may be proportionate to that unit's common element interest, relative size or value, or may be allocated according to any other specified criteria provided that the method chosen is equitable and reasonable for that condominium.

(b) *Voting Rights.* The declaration or equivalent document shall allocate a portion of the votes in the association to each unit. Such portion may be allocated equally to each unit, may be proportionate to that unit's common expense liability, common element interest, relative size or value, or may be allocated according to any other specified criteria provided that the method is equitable and reasonable for that condominium. The declaration may provide different criteria for allocations of votes to the units on particular specified matters and may also provide different percentages of required unit owner approvals for such particular specified matters.

(c) *Ingress and Egress of Unit Owners.* There may not be any restriction upon any unit owner's right of ingress and egress to his or her unit. It is recommended that the declaration affirmatively provide for the right of ingress to and egress from such unit, with such right being perpetual and appurtenant to the unit ownership.

(d) *Easements for Encroachments—Units and Common Elements.* In the event any portion of the common elements encroaches upon any unit or any unit encroaches upon the common elements or another unit as a result of the construction, reconstruction, repair, shifting, settlement, or movement of any portion of the improvements, a valid easement for the encroachment and for the maintenance of the same shall exist so long as the encroachment exists. The declaration may provide, however, reasonable limits on the extent of any easement created by the overlap of units, common elements, and limited common elements resulting from such encroachments.

(e) *Right of First Refusal.* The right of a unit owner to sell, transfer, or otherwise convey his or her unit in a condominium shall not be subject to any right of first refusal or similar restriction. It is recommended that the declaration affirmatively provide that a unit owner may transfer his or her unit free of any such restriction.

(f) *Leasing Restrictions.* (1) All leases should be in writing and be subject to the declaration and by-laws. (2) FNMA, HUD and VA agree that unit owners should be prohibited from leasing their units for an initial term of less than 30 days. The three organizations would not object to a requirement that leases have a minimum initial term of up to six months; however, they agree that no prohibition related to the term of a lease shall apply to a lease having an initial term exceeding six months. While FHLMC does not have any requirements regarding minimum lease terms, it would not object to documents meeting the requirements of the other organizations.

9. FIRST LIEN HOLDERS' RIGHTS

(a) *Notices of Action.* A holder, insurer or guarantor of a first mortgage, upon written request to the owners association, (such request to state the name and address of such holder, insurer or guarantor and the unit number), will be entitled to timely written notice of:

(1) Any proposed amendment of the condominium instruments effecting a change in (i) the boundaries of any unit or the exclusive easement rights appertaining thereto, (ii) the interests in the general or limited common elements appertaining to any unit or the liability for common expenses appertaining thereto, (iii) the numer of votes in the owners association appertaining to any unit or (iv) the purpose to which any unit or the common elements are restricted;

(2) Any proposed termination of the condominium regime;

(3) Any condemnation loss or any casualty loss which affects a material portion of the condominium or which affects any unit on which there is a first mortgage held, insured or guaranteed by such eligible holder;

(4) Any delinquency in the payment of assessments or charges owed by an owner of a unit subject to the mortgage of such eligible holder, insurer or guarantor, where such delinquency has continued for a period of 60 days;

(5) Any lapse, cancellation or material modification of any insurance policy maintained by the owners association pursuant to paragraph 14(a)(i) and (ii).

(b) *Other Provisions for First Lien Holders.* To the extent possible under applicable law, the following protections for the benefit of first mortgage holders must be legally binding with respect to the condominium by virtue of the constituent documents, applicable law or otherwise:

(1) Any restoration or repair of the condominium after a partial condemnation or damage due to an insurable hazard shall be substantially in accordance with the declaration and the original plans and specifications unless the approval of the eligible holders of first mortgages on units to which at least 51% of the votes of units subject to mortgages held by such eligible holders are allocated, is obtained.

(2) Any election to terminate the condominium regime after substantial destruction or a substantial taking in condemnation of the condominium property must require the approval of the eligible holders of first mortgages on units to which at least 51% of the votes of units subject to mortgages held by such eligible holders are allocated.

(3) Unless the formula for reallocation of interests in the common elements after a partial condemnation or partial destruction of the condominium project is fixed in advance by the declaration or by applicable law, no reallocation of interests in the common elements resulting from a partial condemnation or partial destruction of the condominium project may be effected without the approval of the eligible holders of first mortgages on units to which at least 51% of the votes of units subject to mortgages held by such eligible holders are allocated.

NOTE: As used in this section, the term "eligible holder, insurer or guarantor" shall mean a holder, insurer or guarantor of a first mortgage on a unit in a condominium which has requested notice in accordance with the provisions of Section 9(a) above.

10. AMENDMENT TO DOCUMENTS

The following provisions do not apply to amendments to the constituent documents or termination of the condominium regime made as a result of destruction, damage or condemnation pursuant to Section 9 above, or to a reallocation of interests in the common elements which might occur pursuant to any plan of expansion or phased development previously approved by the agencies and corporations, to the extent such approval was required under the applicable condominium programs of the agencies and corporations. VA will accept, but does not require, the provisions of this Section 10.

(a) The consent of owners of units to which at least 67 percent of the votes in the owners association are allocated and the approval of the eligible holders of first mortgages on units to which at least 67 percent of the votes of units subject to a mortgage appertain, shall be required to terminate the condominium regime.

(b) The consent of owners of units to which at least 67 percent of the votes in the owners association are allocated and the approval of eligible holders of first mortgages on units to which at least 51 percent of the votes of units subject to a mortgage appertain, shall be required to materially amend any provisions of the declaration, by-laws or equivalent documents of the condominium, or to add any material provisions thereto, which establish, provide for, govern or regulate any of the following:

(1) Voting;

(2) Assessments, assessment liens or subordination of such liens;

(3) Reserves for maintenance, repair and replacement of the common elements;

(4) Insurance or Fidelity Bonds;

(5) Rights to use of the common elements;

(6) Responsibility for maintenance and repair of the several portions of the condominium;

(7) Expansion or contraction of the condominium regime or the addition, annexation or withdrawal of property to or from the regime;

(8) Boundaries of any unit;

(9) The interests in the general or limited common elements;

(10) Convertibility of units into common elements or of common elements into units;

(11) Leasing of units;

(12) Imposition of any right of first refusal or similar restriction on the right of a unit owner to sell, transfer, or otherwise convey his or her unit in the condominium;

(13) Establishment of self-management by the condominium association where professional management has been required by any of the agencies or corporations.

(c) The consent of owners of units to which at least 67 percent of the votes in the owners association are allocated and the approval of eligible holders of first mortgages on units to which at least 51 percent of the votes of units subject to a mortgage appertain, shall be required to amend any provisions included in the declaration, by-laws or equivalent documents of the condominium which are for the express benefit of holders or insurers of first mortgages on units in the condominium.

(d)   For first mortgagees to be eligible holders under Section 10, they must request notice in accordance with the provisions of Section 9(a).

11.   RIGHTS OF ACTION

The owners association and any aggrieved unit owner shall be granted a right of action against unit owners for failure to comply with the provisions of the declaration, by-laws, or equivalent documents, or with decisions of the owners association which are made pursuant to authority granted the owners association in such documents. Unit owners shall have similar rights of action against the owners association.

**12.   FLEXIBLE CONDOMINIUMS

(a)   *Expandable Condominiums.* The following policies apply to condominium regimes which may be increased in size by the declarant.

   (1)   The declarant's right to expand the regime must be fully described in the declaration. The declaration must contain provisions adequate to ensure that future improvements to the condominium will be consistent with initial improvements in terms of quality of construction.

   (2)   The reservation of a right to expand the condominium regime, the method of expansion and the result of an expansion must not affect the statutory validity of the condominium regime or the validity of title to the units.

   (3)   The declaration or equivalent document must contain provisions satisfactory to HUD, VA and FNMA, requiring that no additional property may be added to the existing condominium without the prior written consent of each of them that holds, insures or guarantees any mortgage in such existing condominium at the time such property is to be added. Such consent will not be withheld if the property to be added substantially conforms to a plan of expansion which has been fully described in the declaration or equivalent document and the other requirements of these policies have been met.

   (4)   The declaration must provide that all improvements on the property to be added shall be substantially completed before such property is added to the existing condominium.

   (5)   Liens arising in connection with the declarant's ownership of, and construction of improvements upon, the property to be added must not adversely affect the rights of existing unit owners, or the priority of first mortgages on units in the existing condominium property. All taxes and other assessments relating to such property, covering any period prior to the addition of the property, must be paid or otherwise satisfactorily provided for by the declarant.

   If FNMA holds any mortgage in the existing condominium at the time additional property is to be added, FNMA must be furnished with title evidence, in a form satisfactory to it, which discloses any lien, easement or other encumbrance affecting the property to be added or which will affect the existing condominium property after such addition.

(6) The declarant's right to expand the condominium must be for a reasonable period of time with a specific ending date. The maximum acceptable period usually will be from five to seven years after the date of recording the declaration.

(7) The declaration or equivalent document shall clearly set forth the basis for reallocation of unit owners' ownership interests, common expense liabilities and voting rights in the event the number of units in the condominium is increased. Such reallocation shall be according to the applicable criteria set forth in Sections 2, 8(a) and 8(b) of these policies.

** (b) *Other Flexible Condominiums.* Condominiums containing withdrawable real estate (contractable condominiums) and condominiums containing convertible real estate (portions of the condominium within which additional units or limited common elements, or both, may be created) will be considered by the agencies and corporations on an individual case basis.

13. POLICIES FOR BY-LAWS

The by-laws of the condominium should be sufficiently detailed for the successful governance of the condominium by unit owners. Among other things, such documents should contain adequate provisions for the election and removal of directors and officers.

14. INSURANCE AND RELATED REQUIREMENTS

The following provisions of (a) and (b) contain the requirements of HUD, FNMA and FHLMC regarding insurance of condominiums. VA suggests that the insurance requirements of HUD, FNMA and FHLMC in (a) and (b) be followed. VA insurance requirements are governed by Sections 36.4326 and 36.4359(e) of Title 38 of the Code of Federal Regulations. The provisions in (c) relating to "Qualifications of Insurance Carriers" are applicable only to FNMA and FHLMC; HUD and VA take no position with respect to these provisions. Paragraph (d) of this section contains requirements regarding condemnation and total or partial loss or destruction of the condominium property, which requirements are applicable only to FNMA. FHLMC, HUD and VA have no specific requirements related to condemnation and loss or destruction to the condominium property, but would accept a project which is in conformity therewith. In addition to the following provisions the owners association must maintain any insurance coverage requirement by law, such as workmen's compensation insurance. Without limiting or diminishing the responsibilities of the mortgagee under the HUD mortgage insurance contract to obtain and maintain insurance in an amount sufficient to protect the security against the risks or hazards to which the property may be subjected, HUD agrees that the owners association must be required to maintain adequate blanket property insurance, liability insurance, flood insurance, fidelity bond coverage and workmen's compensation insurance by virtue of provisions in the declaration or equivalent document or by applicable law in accordance with the requirements in (a) and (b) of Section 14 hereof.

(a) *Type and Scope of Insurance Coverage Required*

(i) *Insurance for Fire and Other Perils*

The owners association must be required either by the terms of the declaration (or other appropriate constituent document of the condominium) or by applicable law, to obtain, maintain, and pay the premiums upon, as a common expense, a "master" or "blanket" type policy of property insurance covering all of the common elements and limited common elements, (except land, foundation, excavation and other items normally excluded from coverage) including fixtures, to the extent that they are part of the common elements of the condominium, building service equipment and supplies, and other common personal property belonging to the owners association. All references herein to a "master" or "blanket" type policy of property insurance, are intended to denote single entity condominium insurance coverage. In addition, any fixtures, equipment or other property within the units which are to be financed by a mortgage to be purchased by FNMA or FHLMC (regardless of whether or not such property is a part of the common elements) must, by the terms of the declaration or equivalent document, be required to be covered in such "blanket" or "master" policy. The declaration or other appropriate constituent document of the condominium must contain a clear delineation of all property which is to be covered by such policy. For the purposes hereof, the term "limited common elements" shall have the meaning described by any applicable law of the jurisdiction or as defined in the declaration or other constituent document of the condominium.

Such policy must be consistent with state and local insurance laws and at least equal to such coverage as is commonly required by prudent institutional mortgage investors in the area in which the condominium is located. The policy shall be in an amount equal to 100% of current replacement cost of the condominium exclusive of land, foundation, excavation and other items normally excluded from coverage.

The name of the insured under such policies must be set forth therein substantially as follows:

"Association of Owners of the _____ Condominium for use and benefit of the individual owners (designated by name if required by law)."

The policies may also be issued in the name of an authorized representative of the owners association, including any insurance trustee with whom the association has entered into an Insurance Trust Agreement, or any successor trustee, as insured, for the use and benefit of the individual owners. Loss payable shall be in favor of the owners association (or Insurance Trustee), as a trustee, for each unit owner and each such owner's mortgagee. The owners association or insurance trustee, if any, must be required to hold any proceeds of insurance in trust for unit owners and their first mortgage holders, as their interests may appear. Each unit owner and each unit owner's mortgagee, if any, shall be beneficiaries of the policy in the percentage of common ownership or in an amount determined pursuant to a reasonable formula prescribed in the declaration or appropriate exhibit thereto. Certificates of insurance shall be issued to each unit owner and mortgagee upon request.

Such policies shall contain the standard mortgage clause, or equivalent endorsement (without contribution), which is commonly accepted by private institutional mortgage investors in the area in which the property is located and which appropriately names FNMA and FHLMC if such corporations are holders of first mortgages on units within the condominium. Such policies must also provide that they may not be cancelled or substantially modified, without at least 10 days' prior written notice to the owners association and to each holder of a first mortgage listed as a scheduled holder of a first mortgage in the policies.

Policies are unacceptable where: (i) under the terms of the insurance carrier's charter, by-laws, or policy, contributions or assessments may be made against borrowers, FNMA, FHLMC, or the designee of FNMA or FHLMC; or (ii) by the terms of the carrier's charter, by-laws or policy, loss payments are contingent upon action by the carrier's board of directors, policyholders, or members, or (iii) the policy includes any limiting clauses (other than insurance conditions) which could prevent FNMA, FHLMC, or the borrowers from collecting insurance proceeds.

The policies must also provide for the following: recognition of any Insurance Trust Agreement; a waiver of the right of subrogation against unit owners individually; that the insurance is not prejudiced by any act or neglect of individual unit owners which is not in the control of such owners collectively; and that the policy is primary in the event the unit owner has other insurance covering the same loss. The requirements stated in this paragraph are generally provided by the insurer in the form of a "Special Condominium Endorsement" or its equivalent.

The insurance policy shall afford, as a minimum, protection against the following:

(1) loss or damage by fire and other perils normally covered by the standard extended coverage endorsement;

(2) in the event the condominium contains a steam boiler, loss or damage resulting from steam boiler equipment accidents in an amount not less than $50,000 per accident per location (or such greater amount as deemed prudent based on the nature of the property);

(3) all other perils which are customarily covered with respect to condominiums similar in construction, location and use, including all

perils normally covered by the standard "all-risk" endorsement, where such is available.

** In addition, FNMA requires that such policies include an "Agreed Amount Endorsement" and, if available, an "Inflation Guard Endorsement". FHLMC requires the foregoing endorsements only if they are available and are commonly required by prudent institutional mortgage investors in the area in which the condominium is located.

FNMA and FHLMC may also require, on an individual case basis, construction code endorsements (such as a Demolition Cost Endorsement, a Contingent Liability from Operation of Building Laws Endorsement and an Increased Cost of Construction Endorsement) if the condominium is subject to a construction code provision which would become operative and require changes to undamaged portions of the building(s), thereby imposing significant costs in the event of partial destruction of the condominium by an insured hazard.

(ii) *Liability Insurance*

The owners association must be required either by the terms of the declaration (or other appropriate constituent document of the condominium) or by applicable law, to maintain comprehensive general liability insurance coverage covering all of the common elements, commercial space owned and leased by the owners association, and public ways of the condominium project. Coverage limits shall be in amounts generally required by private institutional mortgage investors for projects similar in construction, location, and use. However, such coverage shall be for at least $1,000,000 for bodily injury, including deaths of persons and property damage arising out of a single occurrence, with the exception that FHLMC does not require coverage in such amount if the condominium consists of 30 or fewer units. Coverage under this policy shall include, without limitation, legal liability of the insureds for property damage, bodily injuries and deaths of persons in connection with the operation, maintenance or use of the common elements, and legal liability arising out of lawsuits related to employment contracts of the owners association. Such policies must provide that they may not be cancelled or substantially modified, by any party, without at least 10 days' prior written notice to the owner's association and to each holder of a first mortgage on any unit in the condominium which is listed as a scheduled holder of a first mortgage in the insurance policy. FNMA and FHLMC may also require such coverage to include protection against such other risks as are customarily covered with respect to condominiums similar in construction, location and use, including, but not limited to, host liquor liability, employers liability insurance, contractual and all-written contract insurance, and comprehensive automobile liability insurance.

(iii) *Flood Insurance*

FNMA and FHLMC will not purchase any mortgage secured by a condominium property located in an area which has been identified by the

Secretary of Housing and Urban Development as having special flood hazards (by publication in the Federal Register of a Flood Insurance Boundary Map or Insurance Rate Map) for which flood insurance is not available because the community in which the condominium is located is ineligible for participation in the National Flood Insurance Program, except for any mortgage which was closed prior to July 1, 1975 or is closed within one year following the publication of the Flood Hazard Boundary Map, whichever is later.

Where the condominium is located within an area which has been officially identified by the Secretary of Housing and Urban Development as having special flood hazards and for which flood insurance has been made available under the National Flood Insurance Program (NFIP), the owners association must be required by the terms of the declaration or other appropriate constituent document of the condominium to obtain and pay the premiums upon, as a common expense, a "master" or "blanket" policy of flood insurance on the buildings and any other property covered by the required form of policy (herein insurable property), in an amount deemed appropriate by the owners association, but not less than the following:

The lesser of: (a) the maximum coverage available under the NFIP for all buildings and other insurable property within the condominium to the extent that such buildings and other insurable property are within an area having special flood hazards; or (b) 100% of current "replacement cost" of all such buildings and other insurable property within such area.

Such policy shall be in a form which meets the criteria set forth in the most current Guidelines on the subject issued by the Federal Insurance Administrator.

(iv) *Fidelity Bonds*

By the terms of the declaration or other appropriate constituent document of the condominium, blanket fidelity bonds shall be required to be maintained by the owners association for all officers, directors, and employees of the owners association and all other persons handling, or responsible for, funds of or administered by the owners association. Where the management agent has the responsibility for handling or administering funds of the owners association, the management agent shall be required to maintain fidelity bond coverage for its officers, employees and agents handling or responsible for funds of, or administered on behalf of, the owners association. Such fidelity bonds shall name the owners association as an obligee and shall not be less than the estimated maximum of funds, including reserve funds, in the custody of the owners association or the management agent, as the case may be, at any given time during the term of each bond. However, in n o event may the aggregate amount of such bonds be less than a sum equal to 3 months' aggregate assessments on all units plus reserved funds. The bonds shall contain waivers by the issuers of the bonds of all defenses based upon the exclusion of persons serving without compensation from the definition of "employees", or similar terms or expressions. The premiums on all bonds required herein, except those maintained by the management agent, shall be paid by the owners association as a common expense. The bonds shall provide that they may not be cancelled or substantially modified (including cancellation for non-payment of premium) without at least 10 days' prior witten notice to the owners association or Insurance Trustee. The Federal National Mortgage Association also requires, as a condition to approval of condominium projects, that such bonds provide that the FNMA Servicer, on behalf of FNMA, also receive such notice of cancellation or modification. Fidelity bond coverage is not required for condominiums consisting of 30 or fewer units.

(b) *Insurance Trustees; Power of Attorney.* The declaration or other appropriate constituent document of the condominium shall provide that, notwithstanding any of the foregoing provisions and requirements relating to property or liability insurance, there may be named as an insured, on behalf of the owners association, the owners association's authorized representative, including any trustee with whom such owners association may enter into any Insurance Trust Agreement or any successor to such trustee (each of whom shall be referred to herein as the "Insurance Trustee"), who shall have exclusive authority to negotiate losses under any policy providing such property or liability insurance and to perform such other functions as are necessary to accomplish this purpose.

Where appropriate under applicable law, the declaration shall contain a provision whereby each unit owner appoints the owners association, or any Insurance Trustee or substitute Insurance Trustee designated by the owners association, as attorney-in-fact for the purpose of purchasing and maintaining such insurance, including: the collection and appropriate disposition of the proceeds thereof; the negotiation of losses and execution of releases of liability; the execution of all documents; and the performance of all other acts necessary to accomplish such purpose.

(c) *Qualifications of Insurance Carriers.* FNMA and FHLMC reserve the right to set standards and qualifications for insurance carriers. The declaration shall require the owners association to use generally acceptable insurance carriers. Reference should be made to the FNMA Conventional Home Mortgage Selling Contract Supplement and the FHLMC Sellers Guide for specific requirements regarding the qualifications of insurance carriers.

(d) *Condemnation and Total or Partial Loss or Destruction.* The following provisions contain the requirements of FNMA regarding condemnation and total or partial loss or destruction of the condominium property.

The owners association shall represent the unit owners in the condemnation proceedings or in negotiations, settlements and agreements with the condemning authority for acquisition of the common elements, or part thereof, by the condemning authority. Where appropriate under applicable law, the declaration should contain a provision whereby each unit owner appoints the owners association as attorney-in-fact for such purpose.

The declaration may provide for the appointment of a Trustee to act on behalf of the unit owners, in carrying out the above functions, in lieu of the owners association.

In the event of a taking or acquisition of part or all of the common elements by a condemning authority, the award or proceeds of settlement shall be payable to the owners association, or any Trustee, to be held in trust for unit owners and their first mortgage holders as their interests may appear.

A reasonable method for dealing with any total or partial loss or destruction of the condominium property, and with any total or partial condemnation of such property, must be provided in the declaration or other appropriate constituent document of the condominium or by applicable law.

MODEL FOR CONDOMINIUM BYLAWS—CALIFORNIA

---

* *Note:* This appendix is intended as a model for instruction purposes only, rather than for actual use in any particular transaction, for which counsel should be consulted in your jurisdiction.

BYLAWS

OF

_____

TABLE OF CONTENTS
FOR BYLAWS
OF

BYLAWS
OF

_____

ARTICLE I
PLAN OF CONDOMINIUM OWNERSHIP

Section 1.01. *Name.* The name of the corporation is _____, hereinafter referred to as the "Association." The principal office of the Association shall be located in _____ County, California.

Section 1.02. *Application.* The provisions of these Bylaws are applicable to the residential condominium project known as _____, located in the County of _____, California. All present and future Owners and their tenants, future tenants, employees, and any other person who might use the facilities of the Project in any manner, are subject to the regulations set forth in the Bylaws and in the Declaration of Covenants, Conditions and Restrictions, and Reservation of Easements for _____ (the "Declaration" herein) Recorded or to be Recorded in the Office of the _____ County Recorder and applicable to the Project. The mere acquisition or rental of any Condominium in the Project or the mere act of occupancy of any Condominium will signify that these Bylaws are accepted, ratified, and will be complied with.

Section 1.03. *Meaning of Terms.* Unless otherwise specifically provided herein, the capitalized terms in these Bylaws shall have the same meanings as are given to such terms in the Declaration.

ARTICLE II
VOTING BY ASSOCIATION MEMBERSHIP

Section 2.01. *Voting Rights.* The Association shall have two (2) classes of voting Membership, as further provided in the Declaration.

Class A. Class A Members shall be those Owners with the exception of Grantor for so long as there exists a Class B Membership. Class A Members shall be entitled to one (1) vote for each Condominium owned which is subject to assessment, as further provided in the Declaration.

Class B. The Class B Member shall be Grantor. The Class B Member shall be entitled to three (3) votes for each Condominium owned by Grantor, provided that the Class B Membership shall cease and be converted to Class A Membership on the happening of the earliest to occur of the following events:

(1) When the total votes outstanding in the Class A Membership equal the total votes outstanding in the Class B Membership;

(2) The second anniversary of the original issuance of the most recently issued Final Subdivision Public Report for a Phase of Development; or

(3) The fourth anniversary of the original issuance of the Final Subdivision Public Report for Phase 1.

Except as provided in Section 14.02 of the Declaration and Section 4.08 of these Bylaws, as long as there exists a Class B Membership, any provision of these Bylaws which expressly requires a vote or written consent of a specified percentage of the voting power of the Association before being undertaken shall require the approval of such specified percentage of the voting power of each class of membership. Except as provided in Section 14.02 of the Declaration and Section 4.08 of these Bylaws, upon termination of the Class B Membership, any provision of these Bylaws which expressly requires a vote or written consent of Owners representing a specified percentage of the voting power of the Association shall then require the vote or written consent of Owners representing such specified percentage of both the total voting power of the Association and the voting power of the Association residing in Owners other than Grantor.

Section 2.02. *Majority of Quorum.* Unless otherwise expressly provided in these Bylaws or the Declaration, any action which may be taken by the Association may be taken by a majority of a quorum of the Members of the Association.

Section 2.03. *Quorum.* Except as otherwise provided in these Bylaws, the presence in person or by proxy of at least a majority of the voting power of the Membership of the Association shall constitute a quorum of the Membership. The members present at a duly called or held meeting at which a quorum is present may continue to do business until adjournment, notwithstanding the withdrawal of enough Members to leave less than a quorum.

Section 2.04. *Proxies.* Votes may be case in person or by proxy and all proxies must be in writing. Every proxy shall be revocable and shall automatically cease after completion of the meeting for which the proxy was filed.

ARTICLE III
ADMINISTRATION

Section 3.01. *Association Responsibilities.* In accordance with the provisions of the Declaration, the Association shall have the responsibility of administering the Property, approving the annual Budget, establishing and collecting all assessments applicable to the Property, and arranging for overall architectural control of the Property.

Section 3.02. *Place of Meetings of Members.* Meetings of the Members shall be held on the Property, or such other suitable place as proximate thereto as practicable, in _____ County, convenient to the Owners, as may be designated by the Board of Directors.

Section 3.03. *Annual Meetings of Members.* The first annual meeting of Members shall be held within forty-five (45) days after Close of Escrow for the sale of fifty-one percent (51%) of the Condominiums in Phase 1 or within six (6) months after the Close of Escrow for the sale of the first Condominium in phase 1, whichever occurs first. Thereafter, the annual meetings of the Members shall be held on or about the anniversary date of the first annual meeting. At each annual meeting there shall be elected by ballot of the Members a Board of Directors of the Association, in accordance with the requirements of Article IV, Section 4.05 of these Bylaws. The Members may also transact such other business of the Association as may properly come before them. Each first Mortgagee of a Condominium in the Project may designate a representative to attend all annual meetings of the Members.

Section 3.04. *Special Meetings of Members.* It shall be the duty of the Board to call a special meeting of the Members, as directed by resolution of a majority of a quorum of the Board of Directors, or upon receipt by the Secretary of a petition signed by Members representing at least five percent (5%) of the total voting power of the Association. The notice of any special meeting shall be given within twenty (20) days after adoption of such resolution or receipt of such petition and shall state the time and place of such meeting and the purpose thereof. The special meeting shall be held not less than thirty-five (35) days nor more than ninety (90) days after adoption of such resolution or receipt of such petition. No business shall be transacted at a special meeting except as stated in the notice. Each first Mortgagee of a Condominium in the Project may designate a representative to attend all special meetings of the Members.

Section 3.05. *Notice of Meetings to Members.* It shall be the duty of the Secretary to send a notice of each annual or special meeting by first-class mail, at least ten (10) but not more than thirty (30) days prior to such meeting, stating the purpose thereof as well as the day, hour and place where it is to be held, to each Member of record, and to each first Mortgagee of a Condominium, which Mortgagee has filed a written request for notice with the Secretary. The notice may set forth time limits for speakers and nominating procedures for the meeting. The notice of any meeting at which Directors are to be elected shall include the names of all those who are nominees at the time the notice is given to the Members. The mailing of a notice, postage prepaid, in the manner provided in this Section, shall be considered notice served, forty-eight (48) hours after said notice has been deposited in a regular depository of the United States mail. Such notice shall be posted in a conspicuous place on the Common Property, and such notice shall be deemed served upon a Member upon posting if no address for such Member has been then furnished the Secretary. The Board of Directors may fix a date in the future as a record date for the determination of the Members entitled to notice of any meeting of Members. The record date so fixed shall be not less than ten (10) days nor more than sixty (60) days prior to the date of the meeting. Only Members who on the record date for notice of the meeting are entitled to vote thereat, shall be entitled to notice of the meeting, notwithstanding any transfer of or issuance of Membership certificates on the books of the Association after the record date.

Section 3.06. *Adjourned Meetings.* If any meeting of Members cannot be organized because a quorum is not present, a majority of the Members who are present, either in person or by proxy, may adjourn the meeting to a time not less than five (5) days nor more than thirty (30) days from the time the original meeting was called, at which meeting the quorum requirement shall be the presence in person or by proxy of the Members holding at least twenty-five percent (25%) of the voting power of the Association. Such an adjourned meeting may be held without notice thereof as provided in this Article III, provided that notice is given by announcement at the meeting at which such adjournment is taken. If, however, such an adjourned meeting is actually attended, in person or by proxy, by Members having less than one-third (1/3rd) of the voting power of the Association, notwithstanding the presence of a quorum, no matter may be voted upon except such matters notice of the general nature of which was given pursuant to Section 3.05 hereof.

Section 3.07. *Order of Business.* The order of business at all meetings of the Members shall be as follows: (a) roll call to determine the voting power represented at the meeting; (b) proof of notice of meeting or waiver of notice; (c) reading of Minutes of preceding meeting; (d) reports of officers; (e) reports of committees; (f) election of inspector of elections (at annual meetings or special meetings held for such purpose); (g) election of Directors (at annual meetings or special meetings held for such purpose); (h) unfinished business; and (i) new business.

Section 3.08. *Action Without Meeting.* Any action, which may be taken at a meeting of the Members (except for the election of Directors) may be taken without a meeting by written ballot of the Members. Ballots shall be solicited in the same manner as provided in Section 3.05 for the giving of notice of meetings of Members. Such solicitations shall specify (a) the number of responses needed to meet the quorum requirements, (b) the percentage of approvals necessary to approve the action, and (c) the time by which ballots must be received in order to be counted. The form of written ballot shall afford an opportunity to specify a choice between approval and disapproval of such matter and shall provide that, where the Member specifies a choice, the vote shall be cast in accordance therewith. Receipt within the time period specified in the solicitation of a number of ballots which equals or exceeds the quorum which would be required for approval if the action were taken at a meeting and a number of approvals which equals or exceeds the number of votes which would be required for approval if the action were taken at a meeting at which the total number of votes cast was the same as the total number of ballots cast shall constitute approval by written ballot.

Section 3.09. *Consent of Absentees.* The transactions of any meeting of Members, either annual or special, however called and noticed, shall be as valid as though had at a meeting duly held after regular call and notice, if a quorum be present either in person or by proxy, and if, either before or after the meeting, each of the Members not present in person or by proxy, signs a written waiver of notice, or a consent to the holding of such meeting, or an approval of the Minutes thereof. All such waivers, consents or approvals shall be filed with the corporate records or made a part of the Minutes of the Meeting.

Section 3.10.   *Minutes, Presumption of Notice.* Minutes or a similar record of the proceedings of meetings of Members, when signed by the President or Secretary, shall be presumed truthfully to evidence the matters set forth therein. A recitation in the Minutes of any such meeting that notice of the meeting was properly given shall be prima facie evidence that such notice was given.

ARTICLE IV
BOARD OF DIRECTORS

Section 4.01.   *Number and Qualification.* The affairs of the Association shall be governed and managed by a Board of Directors composed of _____ (   ) Persons, each of whom, except for those appointed and serving as first Directors, must either be an Owner or an agent of Grantor for so long as Grantor owns a Condominium in the Project. The authorized number of Directors may be changed by a duly adopted amendment to the Bylaws. Directors and officers shall not receive any salary or compensation for their services as Directors and officers unless such compensation is approved by the vote or written consent of Members representing at least a majority of both the Class A and Class B voting power; provided, however, that (1) nothing herein contained shall be construed to preclude any Director from serving the Association in some other capacity and receiving compensation therefor, and (2) any Director or officer may be reimbursed for his actual expenses incurred in the performance of his duties.

Section 4.02.   *Powers and Duties.* The Board of Directors has the powers and duties necessary for the administration of the affairs of the Association and may do all such acts and things as are not by law or by these Bylaws directed to be exercised and done by the Members. The Board of Directors shall not enter into any contract for a term in excess of one (1) year, without the vote or written consent of the Members representing at least a majority of the voting power of the Association, except for (1) any contract of a minimum term with a public utility company regulated by the Public Utilities Commission which requires a term in excess of one (1) year, (2) a management contract the terms of which have been approved by the Veterans Administration or the Federal Housing Administration, (3) prepaid casualty or liability insurance policies of not to exceed three (3) years' duration, provided that the policies permit short term cancellation by the Association, and (4) lease agreements for laundry room fixtures and equipment of not to exceed five (5) years duration provided that the lessor under any such agreement is not an entity in which Grantor has a direct or indirect ownership interest of ten percent (10%) or more.

Section 4.03.   *Special Powers and Duties.* Without prejudice to such foregoing general powers and duties and such powers and duties as are set forth in the Declaration, the Board of Directors is vested with, and responsible for, the following powers and duties:

(a) The power and duty to select, appoint, and remove all officers, agents and employees of the Association, to prescribe such powers and duties for them as may be consistent with law, the Articles of Incorporation, the Declaration and these Bylaws; to fix their compensation and to require from them security for faithful service when deemed advisable by the Board.

(b) The power and duty to conduct, manage and control the affairs and business of the Association, and to make and enforce such rules and regulations therefor consistent with law, the Articles of Incorporation, the Declaration and these Bylaws, as the Board may deem necessary or advisable.

(c) The power but not the duty to change the principal office for the transaction of the business of the Association from one location to another within the County of _____, as provided in Article I hereof; to designate any place within said County for the holding of any annual or special meeting or meetings of Members consistent with the provisions of Article III, Section 3.02 hereof; and to adopt and use a corporate seal and to alter the form of such seal from time to time, as the Board, in its sole judgment, may deem best, provided that such seal shall at all times comply with the provisions of law.

(d) With the approval of Members representing at least two-thirds (2/3rds) of the voting power of the Association, the power but not the duty to borrow money and to incur indebtedness for the purposes of the Association, and to cause to be executed and delivered therefor, in the Association's name, promissory notes, bonds, debentures, deeds of trust, mortgages, pledges, hypothecations or other evidences of debt and securities therefor.

(e) The power and duty to fix and levy from time to time Annual Assessments, Special Assessments, and Reconstruction Assessments upon Members, as provided in the Declaration; to fix and levy from time to time in any Fiscal Year Capital Improvement Assessments applicable to that year only for capital improvements; to determine and fix the due date for the payment of such assessments, and the date upon which the same shall become delinquent; provided, however, that such assessments shall be fixed and levied only to provide for the payment of the Common Expenses of the Association and of taxes and assessments upon real or personal property owned, leased, controlled or occupied by the Association, or for the payment of expenses for labor rendered or materials or supplies used and consumed, or equipment and appliances furnished for the maintenance, improvement or development of such property or for the payment of any and all obligations in relation thereto, or in performing or causing to be performed any of the purposes of the Association for the general benefit and welfare of its Members, in accordance with the provisions of the Declaration. The Board of Directors is hereby authorized to incur any and all such expenditures for any of the foregoing purposes and to provide, or cause to be provided, adequate reserves for replacements as it shall deem to be necessary or advisable in the interest of the Association or welfare of its Members. The funds collected by the Board of Directors from the Members, attributable to replacement reserves, for maintenance costs which cannot normally be expected to occur on an annual basis and for capital improvements, shall at all times be held in trust for the Members. Disbursements from such trust reserve fund shall be made only in accordance with the provisions of the Declaration. Such Annual Assessments, Reconstruction Assessments, Special Assessments and Capital Improvement Assessments shall be fixed in accordance with the provisions of the Declaration. Should any Member fail to pay such assessments before delinquency, the Board of Directors in its discretion is authorized to enforce the payment of such delinquent assessments as provided in the Declaration.

(f) The power and duty to enforce the provisions of the Declaration, these Bylaws or other agreements of the Association.

(g) The power and duty to contract for and pay for, as reasonably necessary, fire, casualty, blanket liability, malicious mischief, vandalism, errors and omissions, liquor liability and other insurance, insuring the Members, the Association, the Board of Directors and other interested parties, in accordance with the provisions of the Declaration, covering and protecting against such damages or injuries as the Board deems advisable (which may include without limitation, medical expenses of persons injured on the Common Property).

(h) The power and duty to contract for and pay for maintenance, legal, accounting, gardening, and common utilities services, and for materials and supplies and other Common Expenses relating to the Common Property, and relating to the Units only to the extent not separately metered or charged, and to employ personnel necessary for the operation of the Property, including legal and accounting services, and to contract for and pay for Improvements on the Common Property.

(i) The power but not the duty to delegate its powers according to law, and subject to the approval of the Members, to adopt these Bylaws.

(j) The power but not the duty to grant easements where necessary for utility and other purposes over the Common Property for the benefit of the Members of the Association.

(k) The power and duty to adopt such Rules and Regulations as the Board may deem necessary for the management of the Project, which Rules and Regulations shall become effective and binding after (1) they are adopted by a majority of the board at a meeting called for that purpose, or by the written consent of the Board in accordance with Section 4.13, and (2) they are posted in a conspicuous place in the Common Property. Such Rules and Regulations may concern, without limitation, use of the Common Property; signs; collection and disposal of refuse; minimum standards of property maintenance consistent with the Declaration and the procedures of the Architectural Committee; and any other matter within the jurisdiction of the Association as provided in the Declaration; provided, however, that such Rules and Regulations shall be enforceable only to the extent that they are consistent with the Declaration, the Articles of Incorporation and these Bylaws, and the Rules and Regulations may not be used to amend any of said documents.

(l) The power and duty to keep, or cause to be kept, a complete record of all acts and corporate affairs of the Association and to present a statement thereof to the Members at the annual meeting of the Members and at any other time that such statement is requested by at least ten percent (10%) of the Members who are entitled to vote.

(m) The power but not the duty to appoint a Membership Committee composed of at least one (1) Director and at least one (1) Association Member at large. The Membership Committee shall be responsible for contacting all purchasers of Condominiums in the Project as soon as any transfer of title to a Condominium is discovered. The Membership Committee shall further attempt to establish initial contact with all Members who are delinquent in the payment of any assessments or other charges due the Association.

(n) The power but not the duty to sell property of the Association; provided, however, that the prior vote or written approval of the Members representing at least a majority of the voting power of the Association must be obtained to sell during any Fiscal Year any property of the Association having an aggregate fair market value greater than five percent (5%) of the budgeted gross expenses of the Association for that Fiscal Year.

Section 4.04. *Management Agent.* The Board of Directors may engage for the Association a professional management agent at a compensation established by the Board to perform such duties and services as the Board shall authorize. Such agreement, and any other contract providing for services by Declarant, must provide for termination by either party for cause upon no more than thirty (30) days' written notice, and without cause nor payment of a termination fee, upon no more than ninety (90) days' prior written notice.

Section 4.05. *Election and Term of Office.*

(a) Directors shall be elected by secret written ballot of the Members. At the first annual meeting of the Members, new Directors shall be elected by the Members as provided in these Bylaws, and all positions on the Board of Directors shall be filled at that election. In the event that an annual meeting is not held, or the Board is not elected thereat, the Board may be elected at any special meeting of the Members held for that purpose. Each Director shall hold office until his successor has been elected or until his death, resignation, removal or judicial adjudication of mental incompetence. The term of office of each Director elected at the first annual meeting and the term of office of each Director elected to fill a vacancy created by the expiration of the term of office of the respective past Director shall be one (1) year. The term of office of each Director elected to fill a vacancy created by the resignation, death or removal of his predecessor shall be the balance of the unserved term of his predecessor. Any person serving as a Director may be re-elected, and there shall be no limitation on the number of terms during which he may serve. Cumulative voting shall be used in the election of Directors for any election in which more than two (2) Directors are to be selected, subject only to the procedural prerequisites to cumulative voting in the following sentence. A member may cumulate his votes for any candidate for the Board if the candidate's name has been placed in nomination prior to the voting and if such Member, or any other Member, has given notice at the meeting prior to the voting of such Member's intention to cumulate votes. If a Member cumulates his votes, such Member may cast a number of votes equal to the Member's share of the voting power as set forth in the Declaration, multiplied by the number of Directors to be elected.

(b) Notwithstanding the foregoing, whenever (1) notice is given for an election of Directors of the Board and (2) upon such date the Members other than Grantor do not have a sufficient percentage of the voting power of the Association to elect at least one (1) Director through the foregoing cumulative voting procedure, such notice shall also provide for the following special election procedure. Election of one (1) Director shall be apportioned entirely to the Members other than Grantor. Any person shall be an eligible candidate for the special election upon receipt by the Secretary of a Declaration of Candidacy, signed by the candidate, at any time prior to the election. Such election shall be by secret ballot unless a majority of the Members other than Grantor determine otherwise. The person receiving a majority of the votes cast by the Members other than Grantor shall be elected a Member of the Board in a co-equal capacity with all other Directors. The remaining Directors of the Board shall be elected through the customatry cumulative voting procedure outlined above.

Section 4.06. *Books, Audit.* The Board of Directors shall cause to be maintained a full set of books and records showing the financial condition of the affairs of the Association in a manner consistent with generally accepterd accounting principles. A pro forma operating statement (Budget) for each Fiscal Year shall be distributed to the members not less than sixty (60) days before the beginning of the Fiscal Year. A balance sheet and an operating (income) statement for the Association shall be prepared as of an accounting date which shall be the last day of the month closest in time to six (6) months following the date of the first Close of Escrow for the sale of a Condominium to a Member, and shall be distributed to each Member (and to any institutional first Mortgagee of a Condominium in the Project upon request), within sixty (60) days of such accounting date. Such operating statement shall include a schedule of assessments received or receivable itemized by Unit number and by the name of the person or entity assessed. Thereafter, the Board shall prepare and distribute to each Member (and to any institutional first Mortgagee of a Condominium in the Project upon request), within ninety (90) days of the last day of the Association's Fiscal Year, an annual report as provided in the Declaration.

All books, records and papers of the Association shall be made available for inspection and copying by any Member, prospective purchaser of a Condominium in the project, and any Beneficiary, insurer, and guarantor of a first Mortgage, or their duly appointed representatives at the principal office of the Association or at such other place within the Property as the Board may prescribe. The Board shall establish reasonable rules with respect to (1) notice to be given to the custodian of the records by the Member desiring to make the inspection, (2) hours and days of the week when such an inspection may be made and (3) payment of the cost of reproducing copies of documents requested by a Member. Every Director shall have the absolute right at any reasonable time to inspect all books, records and documents of the Association, and the physical properties owned or controlled by the Association. The right of the inspection by a Director shall include the right to make extracts and copies of documents.

Section 4.07. *Vacancies.* Vacancies in the Board of Directors caused by any reason other than the removal of a Director by a vote of the Members of the Association shall be filled by vote of the majority of the remaining Directors, even though they may constitute less than a quorum. Any vacancy caused by the removal of a Director may be filled by the vote of the majority of the remaining Directors but only with the approval, by vote or written consent, of a majority of the voting power of the Association residing in Members other than Grantor. Each person so elected shall be a Director until a successor is elected at the next annual meeting of the Members of the Association, or at a special meeting of the Members called for that purpose. A vacancy or vacancies shall be deemed to exist in case of death, resignation, removal or judicial adjudication of mental incompetence of any Director, or in case the Members fail to elect the full number of authorized Directors at any meeting at which such election is to take place. Any vacancy not filled by the Directors may be filled by vote of the Members at a special meeting of the Members called for such purpose.

Section 4.08. *Removal of Directors.* At any regular or special meeting of the Members duly called, any one individual Director or the entire Board may be removed prior to the expiration of their terms of office with or without cause

by the vote of Members representing a majority of the voting power of the Association (including votes attributable to Grantor).

by the vote of Members representing a majority of a quorum of Members.

as follows: (i) for so long as fewer than fifty (50) Condominiums are included within the Project, by the vote of Members representing a majority of the total voting power of the Association (including votes attributable to Grantor), and (ii) once fifty (50) or more Condominiums are included within the Project, by the vote of Members representing a majority of a quorum of Members.

Notwithstanding the foregoing, if the entire Board of Directors is not removed as a group pursuant to a single vote, no individual Director shall be removed if the number of votes cast against his removal would be sufficient to elect such Director if voted cumulatively at an election at which the same total number of votes were cast and the entire number of Directors authorized at the time of the Director's most recent election were then being elected. Any Director whose removal has been proposed by the Members shall be given an opportunity to be heard at the meeting. If any or all of the Directors are so removed at a meeting, new Directors may be elected at the same meeting. Notwithstanding the foregoing, any Director who has been elected to office solely by the votes of Members other than Grantor pursuant to Section 4.05 of this Article IV may be removed from office prior to the expiration of his term of office only by the vote of at least a simple majority of the voting power residing in Members other than Grantor.

Section 4.09. *Organization Meeting of Board.* The first regular ("organization") meeting of a newly elected Board of Directors shall be held within ten (10) days of election of the board, at such place as shall be fixed and announced by the Directors at the meeting at which such Directors were elected, for the purpose of organization, election of officers and the transaction of other business. No notice shall be necessary to the newly elected Directors in order legally to constitute such meeting; provided that (1) a majority of the whole Board shall be present when the time and place are announced at the membership meeting and (2) the meeting is held on the same day and at the same place as the meeting of the Members at which the newly constituted Board was elected.

Section 4.10. *Regular Meetings of Board.* Regular meetings of the Board of Directors shall be open to all Members, provided that members who are not Directors may not participate in any deliberation or discussion at such regular meetings unless expressly so authorized by a vote of a majority of a quorum of the Board of Directors. Regular meetings may be held at such time and place within the Project as shall be determined, from time to time, by a resolution adopted by a majority of a quorum of the Directors; provided, however, that such meetings shall be held no less frequently than quarterly. Notice of the time and place of regular meetings of the Board of Directors shall be given to each Director, personally or by mail, telephone or telegraph, and posted at a prominent place or places within the Common Property at least four (4) days prior to the date named for such meeting.

Section 4.11. *Special Meetings of Board.* Special meetings of the Board of Directors shall be open to all Members, provided that Members who are not Directors may not participate in any deliberation or discussion at such special meetings, unless expressly so authorized by a vote of a majority of a quorum of the Board of Directors. Special meetings may be called by the President or by any two (2) Directors. At least four (4) days' notice shall be given to each Director, personally or by mail, telephone or telegraph, which notice shall state the time, place (as hereinabove provided) and the purpose of the meeting, and shall be posted at a prominent place or places within the Common Property in the same manner as prescribed for regular meetings. If served by mail, each such notice shall be sent, postage prepaid, to the address of each Director reflected on the records of the Association, and shall be deemed given, if not actually received earlier, at 5:00 o'clock p.m. on the second day after it is deposited in a regular depository of the United States mail as provided herein. Whenever any Director has been absent from any special meeting of the Board, an entry in the Minutes to the effect that notice has been duly given shall be conclusive and incontrovertible evidence that due notice of such meeting was given to such Director, as required by law and as provided herein.

Section 4.12. *Waiver of Notice.* Before or at any meeting of the Board of Directors, any Director may, in writing, waive personal notice of such meeting and such waiver shall be deemed equivalent to the giving of such notice to such Director. Attendance by a Director at any meeting of the Board shall be a waiver by him of personal notice of the time and place thereof. If all the Directors are present at any meeting of the Board, no notice to Directors shall be required and any business may be transacted at such meeting. The transactions of any meeting of the Board, however called and noticed or wherever held, shall be as valid as though had at a meeting duly held after regular call and notice, if (1) a quorum be present, (2) notice to the Members of such meeting was posted as provided in Section 4.10 of this Article IV, and (3) either before or after the meeting, each of the Directors not present signs a written waiver of notice, a consent to holding such meeting, or an approval of the Minutes thereof. All such waivers, consents and approvals shall be filed with the records of the Association or made a part of the Minutes of the meeting.

Section 4.13. *Action Without Meeting.* Any action required or permitted to be taken by the Board may be taken without a meeting, if all directors individually or collectively consent in writing to such action. Such written consent or consents shall be filed with the Minutes of the proceedings of the Board. Such action by written consent shall have the same force and effect as a unanimous vote of such Directors. An explanation of any actiion taken by unanimous written consent without a meeting shall be posted by the Board in a prominent place or places in the Common Property within three (3) days after the written consents of all Directors have been obtained.

Section 4.14. *Quorum and Adjournment.* Except as otherwise expressly provided herein, at all meetings of the Board of Directors, a majority of the Directors shall constitute a quorum for the transaction of business, and the acts of the majority of the Directors present at a meeting at which a quorum is present shall be the acts of the Board of Directors. If at any meeting of the Board of Directors, there is less than a quorum present, the majority of those present may adjourn the meeting from time to time. At any such adjourned meeting, any business which might have been transacted at the meeting as originally called may be transacted without further notice.

The Board of Directors may, with the approval of a majority of a quorum of the Directors, adjourn a meeting and reconvene in executive session to discuss and vote upon personnel matters, litigation in which the Association is or may become involved and orders of business of a similar nature. The nature of any and all business to be considered in executive session shall first be announced in open session.

Section 4.15. *Fidelity Bonds.* The Board of Directors may require that all officers and employees of the Association handling or responsible for Association funds shall furnish adequate fidelity bonds. The premiums on such bonds shall be paid by the Association.

Section 4.16. *Committees.* The Board of Directors, by resolutiion, may from time to time designate such committees as it shall desire, and may establish the purposes and powers of each such committee created. The resolution designating and establishing the committee shall provide for the appointment of its members, as well as a chairman, shall state the purposes of the committee, and shall provide for reports, termination, and other administrative matters as deemed approporiate by the Board.

ARTICLE V
OFFICERS

Section 5.01. *Designation.* The principal officers of the Association shall be a President, a Vice President, a Secretary, and a Treasurer, all of whom shall be elected by the Board of Directors. The Board of Directors may appoint an Assistant Treasurer, and an Assistant Secretary, and such other officers as in their judgment may be necessary. Officers other than the President need not be Directors. One Person may hold more than one office.

Section 5.02. *Election of Officers.* The officers of the Association shall be elected annually by the Board of Directors at the organization meeting of each new Board of Directors, and each officer shall hold his office at the pleasure of the Board of Directors, until he shall resign or be removed or otherwise disqualified to serve or his successor shall be elected and qualified to serve.

Section 5.03. *Removal of Officers.* Upon an affirmative vote of a majority of the entire Board of Directors, any officer may be removed, either with or without cause, and his successor elected at any regular meeting of the Board of Directors, or at any special meeting of the Board of Directors called for such purpose. Any officer may resign at any time by giving written notice to the Board or to the President or Secretary of the Association. Any such resignation shall take effect at the date of receipt of such notice or at any later time specified therein; and unless otherwise specified in said notice, acceptance of such resignation by the Board shall not be necessary to make it effective.

Section 5.04. *Compensation.* Officers, agents, and employees shall receive such reasonable compensation for their services as may be authorized or ratified by the Board; provided, however, that no officer shall receive any compensation for services performed in the conduct of the Association's business unless such compensation is approved by the vote or written consent of Members representing at least a majority of the voting power of the Association; and provided further, that (1) nothing herein contained shall be construed to preclude any officer from serving the Association in some other capacity and receiving compensation therefor, and (2) any officer may be reimbursed for his actual expenses incurred in the performance of his duties. Appointment of any officer, agent, or employee shall not of itself create contractual rights of compensation for services performed by such officer, agent, or employee. Notwithstanding the foregoing, no officer, employee or director of Grantor or any affiliate of Grantor may receive any compensation.

Section 5.05. *President.* The President shall be the chief executive officer of the Association. He shall preside at all meetings of the Association and of the Board of Directors. He shall have all of the general powers and duties which are usually vested in the office of the President of an Association, including but not limited to the power, subject to the provisions of Article IV, Section 4.16, to appoint committees from among the Members from time to time as he may in his discretion decide is appropriate to assist in the conduct of the affairs of the Association. The President shall, subject to the control of the Board of Directors, have general supervision, direction and control of the business of the Association. The President shall be ex officio a member of all standing committees, and shall have such other powers and duties as may be prescribed by the Board of Directors or these Bylaws of the Association.

Section 5.06. *Vice President.* The Vice President shall take the place of the President and perform his duties whenever the President shall be absent or disabled or whenever the President refuses or is unable to act. If neither the President nor the Vice President is able to act, the Board of Directors shall appoint some other member of the Board to do so on an interim basis. The Vice President shall also perform such other duties as shall from time to time be imposed upon him by the Board of Directors or these Bylaws of the Association.

Section 5.07. *Secretary.* The Secretary shall keep the Minutes of all meetings of the Board of Directors and the Minutes of all meetings of the Association at the principal office of the Association or at such other place as the Board of Directors may order. The Secretary shall keep the seal of the Association in safe custody and shall have charge of such books and papers as the Board of Directors may direct; and the Secretary shall, in general, perform all of the duties incident to the office of Secretary. The Secretary shall give, or cause to be given, notices of meetings of the Members of the Association and of the Board of Directors required by these Bylaws or by law to be given. The Secretary shall maintain a record book of Owners, listing the names and addresses of Owners, as furnished to the Association, and such books shall be changed only at such time as satisfactory evidence of a change in ownership of a Condominium is presented to the Secretary. The Secretary shall perform such other duties as may be prescribed by the Board of Directors or these Bylaws.

Section 5.08. *Treasurer.* The Treasurer shall be the chief financial officer of the Association and shall have responsibility for Association funds and securities and shall be responsible for keeping, or causing to be kept, full and accurate accounts, tax records and business transactions of the Association, including accounts of all assets, liabilities, receipts and disbursements in books belonging to the Association. The Treasurer shall be responsible for the deposit of all monies and other valuable effects in the name, and to the credit, of the Association in such depositories as may from time to time be designated by the Board of Directors. The Treasurer shall disburse the funds of the Association as may be ordered by the Board of Directors, in accordance with the Declaration, shall render to the President and Directors, upon request, an account of all of his transactions as Treasurer and of the financial conditions of the Association, and shall have such other powers and perform such other duties as may be prescribed by the Board of Directors or these Bylaws.

ARTICLE VI
OBLIGATIONS OF THE MEMBERS

Section 6.01. *Assessments.*

(a) All members are obligated to pay, in accordance with the provisions of the Declaration, all assessments imposed by the Association, to meet all expenses of the Association.

(b) All delinquent assessments shall be enforced, collected or foreclosed in the manner provided in the Declaration.

Section 6.02. *Maintenance and Repair.*

(a) Every Member must perform promptly, at his sole cost and expense, such maintenance and repair work within his own Residence, as required under the provisions of the Declaration. As further provided in the Declaration, all plans for alterations and repair of structural or utility bearing portions of the buildings housing and Units must receive the prior written consent of the Architectural Committee. The Architectural Committee shall establish reasonable procedures for the granting of such approval, in accordance with the Declaration.

(b) As further provided in the Declaration, each Member shall reimburse the Association for any expenditures incurred in repairing or replacing any portion of the Common Property, which is damaged through ther fault of such Member or his family, guests, tenants or invitees. Such expenditures shall include all court costs and reasonable attorneys' fees incurred in enforcing any provision of these Bylaws or the Declaration.

ARTICLE VII
AMENDMENTS TO BYLAWS

These Bylaws may be amended by the Association by the vote or written consent of Members, representing at least (1) a majority of the voting power of each class of the Members, and (2) a majority of the voting power of the Association residing in members other than Grantor; provided that the specified percentage of each class of the Members necessary to amend a specific Section or provision of these Bylaws shall not be less than the percentage of affirmative votes prescribed for action to be taken under that Section or provision. The prior written approval of Beneficiaries of seventy-five percent (75%) of all first Mortgages on Condominiums in the Project must be secured before any amendment to the provisions of these Bylaws affecting matters delineated in Article XII and Section 13.02 of the Declaration may take effect, and this sentence may not be amended without such prior written approval. Notwithstanding the foregoing, if a first Mortgagee who receives a written request from the Board to approve a proposed amendment or amendments to the Bylaws does not deliver a negative response to the Board within thirty (30) days of the mailing of such request by the Board, such first Mortgagee shall be deemed to have approved the proposed amendment or amendments.

ARTICLE VIII
MORTGAGEES

Section 8.01. *Notice to Association.* Every Member who mortgages his Condominium shall notify the Association through the Manager, or through the Secretary in the event there is no Manager, of the name and address of his Mortgagee; and the Association shall maintain such information in a book entitled "Mortgagees of Condominiums." Upon request, any such Member shall likewise notify the Association as to the release or discharge of any such Mortgage.

Section 8.02. *Notice of Unpaid Assessments.* The Board of Directors of the Association shall at the Request of a Mortgagee of a Condominium, report any unpaid assessments due from the Unit Owner of such Condominium, in accordance with the provisions of the Declaration.

ARTICLE IX
CONFLICTING PROVISIONS

In case any of these Bylaws conflict with any provisions of the laws of the State of California, such conflicting Bylaws shall be null and void upon final court determination to such effect, but all other Bylaws shall remain in full force and effect. In case of any conflict between the Articles of Incorporation and these Bylaws, the Articles of Incorporation shall control; and in the case of any conflict between the Declaration and these Bylaws, the Declaration shall control.

ARTICLE X
INDEMNIFICATION OF DIRECTORS AND OFFICERS

The Board may authorize the Association to pay expenses incurred by, or to satisfy a judgment or fine levied against, any present or former Director, officer, employee, or agent of the Association to the extent and under the circumstances provided in the Declaration.

ARTICLE XI
MISCELLANEOUS

Section 11.01. *Checks, Drafts and Documents.* All checks, drafts or other orders for payment of money, notes or other evidences of indebtedness, issued in the name of or payable to the Association, shall be signed or endorsed by such person or persons, and in such manner as, from time to time, shall be determined by resolution of the Board of Directors.

Section 11.02. *Execution of Documents.* The Board of Directors may authorize any officer or officers, agent or agents, to enter into any contract or execute any instrument in the name and on behalf of the Association, and such authority may be general or confined to specific instances; and unless so authorized by the Board of Directors, no officer, agent, or employee shall have any power or authority to bind the Association by any contract or engagement or to pledge its credit or to render it liable for any purpose or in any amount.

Section 11.03. *Inspection of Bylaws.* The Association shall keep in its office for the transaction of business the original or a copy of these Bylaws as amended or otherwise altered to date, certified by the Secretary, which shall be open to inspection by the Members and all Beneficiaries, insurers and guarantors of first Mortgages in accordance with Article IV, Section 4.06 hereof.

Section 11.04. *Fiscal Year.* The Fiscal Year of the Association shall be determined by the Board of Directors, and having been so determined, is subject to change from time to time as the Board of Directors shall determine.

Section 11.05. *Membership Book.* The Association shall keep and maintain in its office for the transaction of business a book containing the name and address of each Member. Termination or transfer of membership shall be recorded in the book, together with the date on which membership ceased or was transferred, in accordance with the provisions of the Declaration.

ARTICLE XII
NOTICE AND HEARING PROCEDURE

Section 12.01. *Suspension of Privileges.* In the event of an alleged violation of the Declaration, these Bylaws or the Rules and Regulations of the Association, and after written notice of such alleged failure is delivered personally or mailed to the Member or any agent of the Member ("respondent") alleged to be in default in the manner herein provided, by first-class mail or by certified mail return receipt requested, or both, the Board of Directors shall have the right, after affording the respondent an opportunity for an appropriate hearing as hereinafter provided, and upon an affirmative vote of a majority of all Directors on the Board, to take any one (1) or more of the following actions: (1) levy a Special Assessment as provided in the Declaration; (2) suspend or condition the right of said Member to use any recreational facilities owned, operated or maintained by the Association; (3) suspend said Member's voting privileges as a Member, as further provided in the Declaration; or (4) record a notice of noncompliance encumbering the Condominium of the respondent. Any such suspension shall be for a period of not more than thirty (30) days for any noncontinuing infraction, but in the case of a continuing infraction (including nonpayment of any assessment after the same becomes delinquent) may be imposed for so long as the violation continues. The failure of the Board to enforce the Rules and Regulations of the Association, these Bylaws or the Declaration shall not constitute a waiver of the right to enforce the same thereafter. The remedies set forth above and otherwise provided by these Bylaws shall be cumulative and none shall be exclusive. However, any individual Member must exhaust all available internal remedies of the Association prescribed by these Bylaws, or by the Rules and Regulations of the Association, before that Member may resort to a court of law for relief with respect to any alleged violation of the Declaration, these Bylaws or the Rules and Regulations of the Association by another Member, provided that the foregoing limitation pertaining to exhausting administrative remedies shall not apply to the Board or to any Member where the complaint alleges nonpayment of Annual Assessments, Special Assessments, Capital Improvement Assessments or Reconstruction Assessments.

Section 12.02. *Written Complaint.* A hearing to determine whether a right or privilege of the respondent under the Declaration or these Bylaws should be suspended or conditioned, or whether a Special Assessment should be levied, shall be initiated by the filing of a written Complaint by any Member or by any officer or member of the Board of Directors with the President of the Association or other presiding member of the Board. The Complaint shall constitute a written statement of charges which shall set forth in ordinary and concise language the acts or omissions with which the respondent is charged, and a reference to the specific provisions of the Declaration, these Bylaws or the Rules and Regulations of the Association which the respondent is alleged to have violated. A copy of the Complaint shall be delivered to the respondent in accordance with the notice procedures set forth in the Declaration, together with a statement which shall be substantially in the following form:

"Unless a written request for a hearing signed by or on behalf of the person named as respondent in the accompanying Complaint is delivered or mailed to the Board of Directors within fifteen (15) days after the Complaint, the Board of Directors may proceed upon the Complaint without a hearing, and you will have thus waived your right to a hearing. The request for a hearing may be made by delivering or mailing the enclosed form entitled 'Notice of Defense' to the Board of Directors at the following address:

_____.

You may, but need not, be represented by counsel at any or all stages of these proceedings. If you desire the names and addresses of witnesses or an opportunity to inspect any relevant writings or items on file in connection with this matter in the possession, custody or control of the Board of Directors, you may contact _____

_____

_____."

The respondent shall be entitled to a hearing on the merits of the matter if the Notice of Defense is timely filed with the Board of Directors. The respondent may file a separate statement by way of mitigation, even if he does not file a Notice of Defense.

Section 12.03. *Notice of Hearing.* The Board shall serve a notice of hearing, as provided herein, on all parties at least ten (10) days prior to the hearing, if such hearing is requested by the respondent. The hearing shall be held no sooner than thirty (30) days after the complaint is mailed or delivered to the respondent as provided in Section 12.02 of this Article XII. The notice to the respondent shall be substantially in the following form but may include other information:

"You are hereby notified that a hearing will be held before the Board of Directors of the _____ Association at _____

_____

_____ on the _____ day of _____, 19___, at the hour of _____, upon the charges made in the Complaint served upon you. You may be present at the hearing, may but need not be represented by counsel, may present any relevant evidence, and will be given full opportunity to cross-examine all witnesses testifying against you. You are entitled to request the attendance of witnesses and the production of books, documents or other items by applying to the Board of Directors of the Association."

Section 12.04. *Hearing.* The hearing shall be held before the Board in executive session pursuant to this notice affording the Member a reasonable opportunity to be heard. Prior to the effectiveness of any sanction hereunder, proof of notice, and the invitation to be heard shall be placed in the minutes of the meeting. Such proof shall be deemed adequate if a copy of the notice together with a statement of the date and manner of delivery is entered by the officer or Director who mailed or delivered such notice. The notice requirement shall be deemed satisfied if a violator appears at the meeting. The minutes of the meeting shall contain a written statement of the results of the hearing and the sanction, if any, imposed. No action against the Member arising from the alleged violation shall take effect prior to the expiration of (a) fifteen (15) days after the Member's receipt of the notice of hearing, and (b) five (5) days after the hearing required herein.

CERTIFICATE OF SECRETARY

I, the undersigned, do hereby certify that:

1. I am the duly elected and acting Secretary of _____ ASSOCIATION, a California nonprofit corporation ("Association"); and

2. The foregoing Bylaws comprising 20 pages including this page constitute the Bylaws of the Association duly adopted at a special meeting of the Board of Directors of the Association held on _____, 19__ .

IN WITNESS WHEREOF, I have hereunto subscribed my hand and affixed the seal of the Association this ____ day of _____, 19__ .

_____
                                                           Secretary

(SEAL)

SYNOPSIS OF COOPERATIVE LEGAL MANAGEMENT DOCUMENTATION—CALIFORNIA

Note: This appendix is intended as a model for instruction purposes only, rather than for actual use in any particular transaction, for which counsel should be consulted in your jurisdiction.

SYNOPSIS OF COOPERATIVE LEGAL MANAGEMENT DOCUMENTATION

1. Master Proprietary Lease. The Master Proprietary Lease is the recorded document which entitles each member to the exclusive use of his unit, restricted common area parking space and the nonexclusive use of the remaining facilities of the project. The rights and obligations under the Master Lease will be assigned to each member pursuant to the Assignment and Assumption of Existing Proprietary Lease (item no. 5 below).

2. Association Bylaws. The Bylaws of the cooperative homeowners association contain the majority of the substantive provisions governing the operation, maintenance, use, enjoyment, repair and replacement of the project and the relative rights of the members with respect to these items. The Bylaws contain provisions normally found in the CC&Rs for a condominium project. The association Bylaws are attached to and incorporated into the Master Lease as Exhibit "ONE."

3. Association Articles of Incorporation. The articles of incorporation are the basic charter of the corporate homeowners association and are filed with the Office of the Secretary of State. The articles authorize the association to own and administer the cooperative project, subject to the provisions of the Bylaws, and are attached to the Bylaws as Exhibit "A."

4. Cooperative Plan. The cooperative plan discloses the relative locations of the various units in the project, enabling the title company and the owners to identify which units and parking spaces have been leased to which owners. The cooperative plan is attached to the Bylaws as Exhibit "B" and to the Master Lease as Exhibit "TWO." Each owner of a membership certificate will be entitled to lease a specific unit, as described in Exhibit "B" to the association Bylaws.

5. Assignment and Assumption of Existing Proprietary Lease. The Assignment is the recorded instrument which reflects the transfer to a buyer of a leasehold interest in a specified unit under the Master Lease. This document is the substantive equivalent of a deed and is signed by both buyer and seller. The form of the Memorandum of Assignment is attached to the association Bylaws as Exhibit "C-2."

6. Association Trust Deed Securing Assessments. The association trust deed is prepared on a title company form, with an attached addendum, and creates a lien in favor of the homeowners association to secure the payment of each member's assessment. One such trust deed will be recorded against the leasehold interest in *each unit* in the project. The association trust deeds will all be executed by the sponsor, as the original lessee under the Master Lease, prior to the close of any escrows in the project. The form of the associatiion trust deed securing assessments is attached to the Master Lease as Exhibit "THREE."

7. Grant Deed of Project. The grant deed of project is the instrument conveying fee title to the project to the cooperative homeowners association. The Grant Deed will be recorded first, followed by the Master Lease, leasing all of the units back to the sponsor. Thereafter, individual assignments of leases will be recorded, reflecting the transfer of leasehold interests under the Master Lease to the various buyers for their respective units.

BUYERS' GUIDE TO COOPERATIVE OWNERSHIP—CALIFORNIA

Note: This appendix is intended as a model for instruction purposes only, rather than for actual use in any particular transaction, for which counsel should be consulted in your jurisdiction.

ASPECTS OF COOPERATIVE OWNERSHIP

1. Will I Own My Unit? Cooperative "Owners" do not own their Units in the traditional sense. Rather, they own a Membership in the Cooperative Association which owns the entire Project, including the Units, subject to each Owner's exclusive right to occupy his respective Unit during the term of a 99 year lease. The lease term will commence shortly before the sale of the first cooperative interest to a member of the public. Under the terms of each Owner's lease, the Owner shall be entitled to the exclusive use, occupancy and control of the interior of his Unit, as well as the non-exclusive use and enjoyment of the "common" facilities of the Project.

2. What Happens to the Project When the Leases Expire in 99 Years? When all leases expire in 99 years the Owners may vote to authorize new leases with all Owners or to have the Project sold and the proceeds divided among the Owners (and their mortgagees) based upon the relative fair market valuations of their respective Units.

3. Am I Responsible for My Neighbor's Defaults in Association Assessments or Mortgage Payments? The cooperative Owners are jointly responsible *only* for the costs of physical maintenance of the Project and unsegregated real property taxes assessed against the Project. The Cooperative Association is required to allocate Owners' assessments first to payment of unsegregated taxes, thereby reducing the possibility that unsegregated taxes on the Project would become delinquent. Under recently enacted Section 2188.7 of the California Revenue and Taxation Code, the Cooperative Association may apply for the segregation of property taxes on the Project. Tax segregation can become effective as early as the Cooperative Association's second year of operations and, following segregation, each Owner will receive his own tax bill and will no longer be responsible for any tax delinquencies associated with other Units in the Project.

Each Owner will have an individual loan for financing the purchase of his cooperative interest. Any one Owner's failure to pay this loan will not affect any other Owner in the Project.

4. How Is the Association Asssured That Owners Will Pay Their Share of Maintenance Costs? Each Owner's cooperative interest will be subject to a trust deed in favor of the Association, securing the payment of Association assessments. If an Owner fails to pay his assessments, the Association may foreclose its lien. Foreclosure of the Association's Assessment Lien is the only manner in which the Association may prematurely terminate an individual Owner's interest in the Project. An Owner's first trust deed lender is exempt from Association assessments which become delinquent prior to the foreclosure of the first trust deed.

5. Must the Association Approve Resales? Each Owner's interest in his cooperative Unit is freely transferable without the prior consent of the Association. The Association is merely entitled to assure itself that the transferred cooperative interest remains subject to the Association's lien rights for delinquent assessments and that the Owner of the cooperative interest has not caused any mechanic's lien to be filed against the entire Project.

6. Am I Entitled to Income Tax Deductions for My Mortgage Interest? Since each Owner must obtain his own individual loan for financing the purchase of his cooperative Unit, interest payments on this loan are deductible in the same manner as any other home loan.

7. Other Tax Benefits. At this time there are certain apparent discrepancies between the laws and regulations of the State of California governing the sale of cooperatives and certain provisions of the U.S. Internal Revenue Code and the California Revenue and Taxation Code governing the availability of certain income tax benefits to cooperative Owners. Until these discrepancies are resolved, it cannot be determined whether the cooperative Owners will be entitled to certain income tax benefits generally available to homeowners, including the right to direct deduction of the portion of the association assessments which are allocated to the payment of unsegregated real property taxes on the Project, the one time exclusion from gross income of up to $125,000 following the sale of a principal residence, and the deferred recognition of income following a qualifying sale of a principal residence. If the cooperative Owners avail themselves of these tax benefits, there is some degree of risk that Federal or State taxing authorities may later disallow these deductions or other tax benefits.

8. Who Is Responsible for Maintaining the Project? It is the responsibility of the Association to maintain and manage the entire Project, except for the interiors of the Units leased to the various cooperative Owners. Maintenance responsibilities of the Association include the upkeep of all private driveways, recreation facilities, parking areas, walkways, structural elements of the buildings and all commonly metered utilities serving the Project. The Association is also responsible for maintaining liability and structural casualty insurance on the Project.

Each cooperative Owner is responsible for maintaining and replacing the interior living elements of his respectively leased Unit, including all windows and the interior surfaces of the walls, ceilings, floors, floor coverings, doors, cabinets and permanent fixtures. Owners are also responsible for maintaining liability and contents insurance for the interiors of their Units.

9. Is My Use of the Project Facilities and Units Subject to Restrictions? Use and enjoyment of the Project facilities, including the Owner's Unit, is subject to compliance with the restrictions contained in the Owner's lease and the Association Bylaws. These provisions include, in part, restrictions on the age of persons residing in the Project, restrictions on parking and vehicular uses, restrictions on commercial uses, signs, animals, exterior installations and similar activities. Breach of these restrictions may be remedied by legal proceedings initiated by the Association or an Owner and may result in the imposition of a fine by the cooperative Association. The restrictions as contained in the leases and Bylaws, may not be amended except upon the vote of the cooperative Owners. However, the Association is authorized to adopt implementing rules and regulations, provided that these rules are not inconsistent with the restrictions contained in the leases and Bylaws.

10. Who Controls the Association? The Association is governed by a board of directors elected by the cooperative Owners. Each Owner is entitled to one vote for each Unit which is leased to him. The developer is also entitled to one vote for each Unit leased to the developer. However, special voting procedures set forth in the Association Bylaws provide that certain actions may not be undertaken by the Association or its members without first receiving the approval of a specified percentage of the voting power of the Association residing in both the developer and nondeveloper Owners. These special voting procedures will remain in effect for a specified period of time following the first sale of a cooperative interest.

SELECTED AMERICAN CASES

CONTENTS

1. ASSESSMENTS

Association of Unit Owners v. Gruenfeld, 277 Or. 259 (1977).

Beech Mountain Property Owners' Ass'n, Inc. v. Current, 35 N.C. App. 135, 240 S.E.2d 503 (1978).

Beech Mountain Property Owners' Ass'n, Inc. v. Seifart, 48 N.C. App. 286 (1980).

Bellemeade Condominium Ass'n, Inc. v. Williamson, C.A. No. 78A-7170 (State Ct. Cobb Co., Ga. 1979).

Bellemeade Condominium Ass'n, Inc. v. Sherrill, C.A. No. 79A-2874, (State Ct. Cobb Co., Ga. 1980).

Bessemer v. Gersten, 381 So. 2d 1344 (Fla. 1980).

Board of Managers, Artist Lake Condominium v. Berlin, New York Law Journal, May 30, 1980, page 13, column 4 (Sup. Ct. Nassau County).

Board of Managers, Colony West Townhomes Owners Ass'n v. Bucalo, 69 Ill. App. 3d 287 (1979).

Board of Managers of General Apartment Corporation Condominium v. Gans, 72 Misc. 2d 726, 340 N.Y.S.2d 826 (1972).

Bodily v. Parkmount Village Green Homeowners Ass'n, Inc., 104 Cal. App. 3d 348 (1980).

Boyle v. Lake Forest Property Owners Ass'n, Inc., 538 F. Supp. 765 (So. Dist. Ala. 1982).

Brooks v. Palm Bay Towers Condominium Ass'n, Inc., 275 So. 2d 348 (Fla. 1979).

Casita de Castillian, Inc. v. Kamrath, 129 Ariz. 146 (App. 1981).

Century 21 Commodore Plaza, Inc. v. Commodore Plaza at 21 Condominium Ass'n, Inc., 340 So. 2d 945 (Fla. App. 1976).

Chimney Hill Owners' Ass'n, Inc. v. Antignani, 136 Vt. 446 (1978).

Cole v. Angora Enterprises, Inc., 403 So. 2d 1010 (Fla. 4th D.C.A. 1981).

Cromwell Condominium Ass'n v. Lawler, Case No. 29295, Sup. Ct., Middlesex Jud. Dist. (Conn. 1982).

D'Elia v. Ass'n of Apartment Owners of Fairview Manor, 632 P.2d 296 (Haw. App. 1981).

Dorset House Ass'n, Inc. v. Dorset, Inc., 371 So. 2d 541 (Fla. D.C.A. 1979).

Duffy v. Sunburst Farms East Mutual Water and Agricultural Company, Inc., 124 Ariz. 425 (App. 1979), *vacated* 124 Ariz. 413 (1979).

Guinee, Trustee v. Prager, et al., Case No. 81-00323-A, Adv. Proc. No. 81-0130-A, U.S. Bankruptcy Ct. for E. Dist. of Va. (1982).

Hur v. Saul J. Morgan Enterprises, Inc., 325 So. 2d 446 (Fla. 3rd D.C.A. 1976).

Indian Mountain Lake Civic Ass'n v. Coyle, 283 Pa. Super. 545 (1981).

Johnson v. Pistakee Highlands Community Ass'n, 72 Ill. App. 3d 402 (1979).

Lynnhill Condominium Council of Homeowners v. Hudley, Law 85, 819 (Cir. Ct. Prince George's Co., Md. 1981).

Margate Village Condominium Ass'n, Inc. v. Wilfred, Inc., 350 So. 2d 16 (Fla. 4th D.C.A. 1977).

Marside, Inc. v. Moseley, 29 Md. App. 366 (1975).

Martin's Landing Foundation, Inc. v. Landing Lake Associates, C.A. No. B-80-1126A (N.D. Ga. 1981).

Mittleman v. Reston Homeowners Ass'n, C.A. No. 39748 (Cir. Ct. Fairfax Co., Va. 1977).

Montgomery v. Board of Directors, Cir. Ct. Arlington Co., Va., at law No. 23832 (Apr. 12, 1983), allowing association to levy special assessment without owner consent.

Mountain Home Properties, Inc. v. Pine Mountain Lake Ass'n, 135 Cal. App. 3d 959 (1982).

Munroe v. Dulles Park Homeowners Ass'n, C.A. No. 55107 (Cir. Ct. Fairfax Co., Va. 1977).

Mushket v. Pickawillany Condominium Unit Owners' Ass'n, No. 80AP-765 (Franklin City, Ohio, App. Ct., 1981).

Occidental Land, Inc., v. Superior Court of Orange County, 18 Cal. 3d 355 (1976). Good lowballing class action case.

Old Virginia Ass'n v. Rivers (Sup. Ct. Fulton Co., Ga. 1977).

Owens v. Tiber Island Condominium Ass'n, 373 A.2d 890 (D.C. App. 1977).

Palm Beach Leisureville Community Ass'n, Inc. v. Raines et al., 398 So. 2d 471 (Fla. 4th D.C.A. 1981).

Papalexiou v. Tower West Condominium, 167 N.J. Super. 516 (1979).

Pine Island Ridge Condominium "F" Ass'n, Inc., et al. v. Waters, et ux., 374 So. 2d 1033 (Fla. 4th D.C.A. 1979).

Propes v. Stonington Home Owners Ass'n, Inc., 149 Ga. App. 135 (1979).

Raines v. Palm Beach Leisure Community Ass'n, 317 So. 2d 814 (Fla. 4th D.C.A. 1975).

Raintree Corporation v. Rowe, 38 N.C. App. 664 (1978).

Raleigh Square Condominium Ass'n, Inc. v. Womack, C.A. No. C-34427 (Sup. Ct. Fulton Co., Ga. 1979).

Raybin v. Boxer, C.A. No. 3112/77 (N.Y.S.C. Westchester Co., 1977).

Shannon Villas Condominium Ass'n, Inc. v. Kelly, C.A. No. 597093 (State Ct. Fulton Ca., Ga. 1976).

Streams Sports Club Ltd. v. Richmond, 440 N.E.2d 1264 (Ill. Ct. App., 1982).

Thiess v. Island House Ass'n, Inc., 311 A.2d 142 (Pa. 1975).

Town of Redington Shores v. Redington Towers, Inc., 354 So. 2d 942 (Fla. 2nd D.C.A. 1978).

Trafalgar Towers Ass'n No. 2, Inc. v. Zimet, 314 So. 2d 595 (Fla. 4th D.C.A. 1975).

Twin Lakes Golf and Country Club v. King County, 87 Wash. 2d 1 (1976).

Washington Federal Savings and Loan Ass'n v. Schneider, 408 N.Y.S.2d 588 (1978).

Waterford Point Condominium Apartments, Inc. v. Fass, 402 So. 2d 1327 (Fla. 4th D.C.A. 1981).

Westchester House Ass'n v. McPherson, C.A. No. 76-2564 (Cir. Ct. 17th Cir. Fla. 1977).

Windham Creek Owners Ass'n v. Lacey, C.A. No. 596388 (State Ct. Fulton Co., Ga. 1977).

Wisconsin Avenue Associates, Inc. v. 2720 Wisconsin Avenue Cooperative Ass'n, 385 A.2d 20 (D.C. App. 1978).

2. DOCUMENTS, CONTRACTS, AMBIGUITIES

Adams v. Lindberg, 125 Ariz. 441 (App. 1980).

Baltimore Humane Impartial Society and Aged Men's and Women's Home v. Pierce, 100 Md. 520 (1905).

Barber v. Chalfonte Dev. Corp., 369 So. 2d 983 (Fla. 4th D.C.A. 1979).

Barclay v. Deveau, 415 N.E.2d 239 (Mass. App. 1981).

Bay Management, Inc. v. Beau Monde, Inc., 366 So. 2d 788 (Fla. 4th D.C.A. 1979).

Beech Mountain Property Owners' Ass'n, Inc. v. Seifart, 48 N.C. App. 286 (1980).

Blakely v. The Housing Authority of the County of King, 8 Wash. App. 204 (1973).

Calvin v. Limco Ltd., 587 P.2d 1216 (Haw. 1978).

Candib v. Carver, 344 So. 2d 1312 (Fla. 3rd D.C.A. 1977).

Carrigan & Boland, Inc. v. Worrock, 402 So. 2d 514 (Fla. 5th D.C.A. 1981).

Conyers v. Malloy, 50 Ill. App. 3d 17 (1977).

D'Elia v. Ass'n of Apartment Owners of Fairview Manor, 632 P.2d 296 (Haw. App. 1981).

Dickey v. Barnes, 268 Or. 226 (1974).

Discount Drugs, Inc. v. Tulip Realty Co., 396 So. 2d 764 (Fla. 4th D.C.A. 1981).

Dulaney Towers Maintenance Corporation v. O'Brey, 46 Md. App. 464 (1980).

F.D.I.C. v. James T. Barry Co., Inc., 453 F. Supp. 81 (E.D. Wisc. 1978).

Felice v. Clausen, 22 Wash. App. 608 (1979).

Flamingo Ranch Estates, Inc. v. Sunshine Ranches Homeowners, Inc., 303 So. 2d 665 (Fla. 4th D.C.A. 1974).

Fountainview Ass'n, Inc., No. 4 v. Bell, 203 So. 2d 657 (Fla. 3rd D.C.A. 1967).

Gilmer v. Beauchamp, C.A. No. 19073 (Gwinnet Co., Ga. 1977); *aff'd Selby v. Gilmer,* 240 Ga. 241 (1977).

Holmes v. Worthey, 159 Ga. App. 262 (1981).

Kaufman v. Shere, 347 So. 2d 626 (Fla. 3rd D.C.A. 1977).

Lenhoff v. Birch Bay Real Estate, Inc., 22 Wash. App. 70 (1978).

Logan v. 3750 North Lake Shore Drive, Inc., 17 Ill. App. 3d 584 (1974).

Makeever v. Lyle, 125 Ariz. 384 (App. 1980).

Maurice River Company v. Roscott, C.A. No. C-854-76 (Sup. Ct. Cumberland Co., N.J. 1978).

Mayo v. Andress, 373 So. 2d 620 (Ala. 1979).

McCown v. Heidler, 527 F.2d 204 (10th Cir. 1975).

Metius v. Julio, 27 Md. App. 491 (1974).

Norris v. Peck, 381 So. 2d 353 (Fla. 5th D.C.A. 1980).

O'Quinn, et al. v. Beach Associates, 272 S.C. 95 (1978).

Pawgan v. Silverstein, 265 F. Supp. 898 (S.D. N.Y. 1967).

Peck Plaza Condominium v. Div. of Florida Land Sales and Condominiums, 371 So. 2d 152 (Fla. 1st D.C.A. 1979).

Pepe v. Whispering Sands Condominium Ass'n, Inc., 351 So. 2d 755 (Fla. 2nd D.C.A. 1977).

Petersen v. Hubschman Construction Co., Inc., 53 Ill. App. 3d 626 (1977), *aff'd* 76 Ill. 2d 31 (1979).

Pico Development Corporation v. Edwards, 367 So. 2d 698 (Fla. 2nd D.C.A. 1979).

Piechowski v. Case, 255 N.W.2d 72 (S.D. 1977).

Pittman v. Cohn Communities, Inc., 240 Ga. 106 (1977).

Point East Management Corp. v. Point East One Condominium Corp., Inc., 282 So. 2d 628 (Fla. 1973).

Realty Growth Investors v. Council of Unit Owners, Delaware Sup. Ct., 26 (Oct., 1982).

Reibel v. Rolling Green Condominium, Inc., 311 So. 2d 156 (Fla. 3rd D.C.A. 1975).

Reider v. P-48, Inc., 362 So. 2d 105 (Fla. 1st D.C.A. 1978).

Rodruck v. Sand Point Maintenance Commission, 48 Wash. 2d 565 (1956).

Schulz v. Zoeller, 568 S.W.2d 677 (Tx. Civ. App. 1978).

Stuewe v. Lauletta, 93 Ill. App. 3d 1029 (1981).

Swaggerty v. Petersen, 280 Or. 739 (1977).

Timmreck v. Munn, 433 F. Supp. 396 (N.D. Ill. 1977).

Tucson-North Town Home Apartments Homeowners Ass'n v. Robb, 123 Ariz. 4 (App., 1979).

Twenty East Cedar Condominium Ass'n v. Luster, 39 Ill. App. 3d 532 (1976).

Village Gate Homeowners Ass'n v. Hales, 219 Va. 321 (1978).

Vogel, et al. v. Vandiver, 373 So. 2d 366 (Fla. 2nd D.C.A. 1979).

Ware v. Scott, 220 Va. 317 (1979).

Wash and Dry, Inc. v. Bay Colony Club Condominium, Inc., 368 So.2d 50 (Fla. 4th D.C.A. 1979).

White Egret Condominium, Inc. v. Franklin, 379 So. 2d 346 (Fla. 1979).

Winslette v. Keeler, 220 Ga. 100 (1964).

Wisconsin Avenue Associates, Inc. v. 2720 Wisconsin Avenue Cooperative Association, 385 A. 2d 20 (D.C. App. 1978).

3. SALES AND LEASE RESTRICTIONS

Avila South Condominium Ass'n, Inc., et al. v. Kappa Corporation, et al., 347 So. 2d 599 (Fla. 1977).

Bachleda v. Ocone, NO. 166254 (Sup. Ct. Jd. Dist. New Haven, Conn. 1980).

Backus v. Smith, 364 So. 2d 786 (Fla. 1st D.C.A. 1978).

Barber v. Chalfonte Development Corporation, 369 So. 2d 983 (Fla. 4th D.C.A. 1979).

Berkley Condominium Ass'n, Inc. v. Berkley Condominium Residences, Inc., 448 A.2d 510 (Sup. Ct. N.J. 1982), denying developer's exercise of right of first refusal on resale.

Blakely v. The Housing Authority of the County of King, 8 Wash. App. 204 (1973).

Board of Managers of Surf East Condominium v. Cohn, 396 N.Y.S.2d 999 (1977).

Board of Managers of Village House v. Frazier, 439 N.Y.S.2d 360 (1981).

Breene, et al. v. Plaza Tower Ass'n, 310 N.W.2d 730, Sup. Ct. N.D. (1981), leasing restrictions may not be applied retroactively.

Chianese v. Culley, 397 F. Supp. 1344 (S.D. Fla. 1975).

Coquina Club, Inc., v. Mantz, 342 So. 2d 112 (Fla. 2nd D.C.A. 1977).

Coventry Square Condominium Ass'n v. Halpern, No. 905-165 (Monmouth County, D.C., N.J. 1981).

Day v. Miramar Holding Corp., 362 So.2d 305 (Fla. 3rd D.C.A., 1978).

Dayenian v. American National Bank and Trust Co., 91 Ill. App. 3d 622 (1980).

Duffy v. Sunburst Farms East Mutual Water and Agricultural Company, Inc., 124 Ariz. 425 (App. 1979), *vacated* 124 Ariz. 413 (1979).

Eastman Community Ass'n and Controlled Environment Corporation v. Savitz, C.A. No. 8169 (Sup. Ct. N.H. 1976).

F.D.I.C. v. James T. Barry Co., 453 F. Supp. 81 (E.D. Wisc. 1978)

Felice v. Clausen, 22 Wash. App. 608 (1979).

Fifth Morrings Condominiums, Inc. v. Shere, 81 F.R.D. 712 (S.D. Fla. 1979).

Fleeman v. Case, 342 So. 2d 815 (Fla. 1976).

Gentry v. Northeast Management Co., Inc., 472 F. Supp. 1248 (N.D. Tx. 1979).

Glenvale Condominium v. Driscoll, C.A. No. 53418 (Cir. Ct. Fairfax Co., Va. 1977).

Goldenberg v. Dome Condominium Ass'n, Inc., 376 So. 2d 37 (Fla. 3d. D.C.A. 1979).

Gundlach v. Marine Tower Condominium, Inc. 338 So. 2d 1099 (Fla. 4th D.C.A. 1976).

Holiday Out in America at St. Lucie, Inc., v. Bowes, 285 So. 2d 63 (Fla. 4th D.C.A. 1973).

Hudson Oil Co. v. Shortstop, 111 Cal. App. 3d 488 (1980).

Jayno Heights Landowners Ass'n v. Preston, 85 Mich. App. 443 (1978).

Johnson v. Nationwide Industries, 450 F. Supp. 948 (N.D. Ill. 1978).

Kroop v. Caravelle Condominium, Inc., 323 So. 2d 307 (Fla. 3rd D.C.A. 1975).

Laguna Royale Owners Ass'n v. Darger, 119 Cal. App. 3d 670 (1981).

LeFebvre v. Osterndorf, 87 Wisc. 3d 525 (1979).

Logan v. 3750 North Lake Shore Drive, Inc., 17 Ill. App. 3d 584 (1974).

Lowery v. Ford Hill Investment Co., 37 Colo. App. 260 (1975), *rev'd* 192 Colo. 125 (1976).

Lyons v. Council of Co-Owners of 4600 Connecticut Avenue, et al., C.A. 398077 (Sup. Ct. Wash. D.C. 1977).

Lyons v. King, 397 So. 2d 964 (Fla. 4th D.C.A. 1981).

Maloney v. Atlantique Condominium Complex, Inc., 399 So. 2d 1111 (Fla. 5th D.C.A. 1981).

Marina Point Ltd. v. Wolfson, 30 Cal. 3d 721 (1982).

Martin v. Villa Roma, Inc., 131 Cal. App. 3d 632 (1982).

Moskowitz v. Saul J. Morgan Enterprises, Inc., C.A. No. 74-570, Civ-WMA (S.D. Fla. 1979).

Palm-Aire Country Club Condominium Ass'n, No. 2, Inc., et al. v. F.P.A. Corp., 357 So. 2d 249 (Fla. 4th D.C.A. 1978).

Phillips v. Butler, No. 80C3823 (N.D. Ill. 1981).

Phillips v. Hunters Trails Community Ass'n, 685 F.2d 184 (7th Cir., 1982), denying association's transfer of right of first refusal.

Ritchey v. Villa Nueva Condominium Ass'n, 81 Cal. App. 3d 688 (1978).

Royal Bahamian Ass'n, Inc., v. Morgan, 338 So. 2d 876 (Fla. 3rd D.C.A. 1976).

Ryan, et al. v. Grasso, et al., C.A. No. H77-59 (D. Conn. 1977).

Samuelson National v. Kaiser Aetna, 99 Cal. App. 3d 523 (1979).

Savitz v. Savitz, C.A. No. 8169 (Sup. Ct. N.J. 1976).

Schlytter v. Baker, 580 F.2d 848 (5th Cir. 1978).

Seagate Condominium Ass'n, Inc., 330 So. 2d 484 (Fla. 4th D.C.A. 1976).

Seashore Club of Atlantic City v. Seashore Club Condominium Ass'n, Inc., 180 N.J. Super. 81 (1981).

Southhampton Civic Club v. Foxworth, 550 S.W.3d 152 (Tx. Civ. App. 1977).

Twenty East Cedar Condominium Ass'n v. Luster, 39 Ill. App. 3d 532 (1976).

Vogel, et al, v. Vandiver, 373 So. 2d 366 (Fla. 2nd D.C.A. 1979).

Ware v. Scott, 220 Va. 317 (1979).

Welch v. Point of Americas Condominium Apartments, Inc., 373 So. 2d 60 (Fla. 4th D.C.A. 1979).

Wiggins v. Apanas, Law No. 79C2584 (E.D. Ill. 1981).

Zaid v. Island House Condominium Ass'n, 170 N.J. Super. 206 (1979).

4. RESTRICTIONS AND BOARD RULES

A. Architectural Control

Cohen v. Kite Hill Community Ass'n, 142 C.A.3d 642 (1983).

Conrad v. Dunn, 92 Cal. App. 3d 236 (1979).

Davis v. Huey, 608 S.W.2d 944 (Tx. Civ. App. 1980).

Edgewater Apartments, Inc. v. Freedman, New York Law Journal, page 7 (Sup. Ct. N.Y. Co. 1980).

Fifty-Six Sixty Collins Avenue Condominium, Inc. v. Dawson, 354 So.2d 432 (Fla. 3rd D.C.A. 1978).

Forstmann v. Joray Holding Co., 244 N.Y. 22 (1926).

Fountains of Palm Beach Condominium, Inc., No. 5 v. Farkas, 355 So.2d 163 (Fla. 4th D.C.A. 1978).

Friedberg, et al. v. Riverpoint Building Committee, 218 Va. 659 (1977).

Heritage Heights Home Owners Ass'n v. Esser, 115 Ariz. 330 (App. 1977).

Highbaugh Enterprises, Inc. v. Deatrick, 554 S.W.2d 878 (Ky. 1977).

Ladner v. Plaza Del Prado Condominium Ass'n, Inc., XXX S.2d XXX (3d D.C. App., Fla., 1982).

Lake Forest, Inc. v. Drury (4th Cir. Ct. App., La., 1977).

Lenhoff v. Birch Bay Real Estate, Inc., 22 Wash. App. 70 (1978).

Makeever v. Lyle, 125 Ariz. 384 (App. 1980).

Martin v. Moore, 562 S.W.2d 274 (Tx. Civ. App. 1978).

Maurice River Co. v. Roscott, C-854-76, (Sup. Ct., Cumberland Co., N.J. 1978).

Nugent v. Lake Village Homeowners Ass'n, Inc., C.A. No. 8288 (Dist. Ct. Douglas Co., Nev. 1978).

Plaza Del Prado Condominium Ass'n, Inc. v. Richman, 345 So. 2d 851 (Fla. 3rd D.C.A. 1977).

Prestwick Landowners' Ass'n v. Underhill, 69 Ohio App. 2d 45 (1980)

Saypal v. Mannes, C.A. No. 76-7912 (17th Jud. Cir. Fla. 1977).

Seligman v. Tucker, 6 Cal. App. 3d 691 (1970).

Skinner v. Henderson, 556 S.W.2d 730 (Mo. App. 1977).

Sterling Village Condominium, Inc. v. Breitenbach, 251 So. 2d 685 (Fla. 4th D.C.A. 1971).

Tate v. Moran, 264 Pa. Super. 540 (1979).

Trails Homeowners Ass'n, Inc. v. Linden, 7th Jud. Cir. Volusia Co., Fla., Case No. 814393-CA-01 (Jun., 1982).

Tucson-North Town Home Apartments Homeowners Ass'n v. Robb, 123 Ariz. 4 (App. 1979).

Ventura v. Hunter Barrett & Co., 552 S.W.2d 918 (Tx. Civ. App. 1977).

Village Gate Homeowners Ass'n v. Hales, 219 Va. 321 (1978).

Village Greens Residents Ass'n, Inc. v. Karolewicz, 83 A.D.2d 550 (N.Y. App. 1981).

Vinick v. Taylor, 270 So. 2d 413 (Fla. 4th D.C.A. 1972).

Wright v. Cypress Shores Development Co., Inc., 413 So. 2d 1115 (Ala. 1982).

Wright v. Dorfman, 116 Cal. App. 3d 892 (1981).

B. Covenant Enforcement—General

Adams v. Lindberg, 125 Ariz. 441 (App. 1980).

Allen v. Forbes, 345 So. 2d 950 (La. App. 1977).

Amoruso v. Board of Managers of Westchester Hills Condominium, 330 N.Y.S.2d 107 (1972).

Antill v. Sigman, 240 Ga. 511 (1978).

Bachleda v. Ocone, No. 166254 (Sup. Ct., Jud. Dist. New Haven, Conn. 1980).

Bellarmine Hills Ass'n v. Residential Systems Company, 84 Mich. App. 554 (1978).

Board of Managers of New City Condominiums II v. Birch, Index No. 1291/76 (Sup. Ct. Rockland Co., N.Y. 1976).

Board of Managers of Surf East Condominium v. Cohn, 396 N.Y.S.2d 999 9 (1977).

Candib v. Carver, 344 So. 2d 1312 (Fla. 3rd D.C.A. 1977).

Cheatham v. Taylor, et al., 148 Va. 26 (1925).

Chelmsford Community Ass'n v. Zane, Sup. Ct. N.J. App. Div. (A-2435-80T3), March, 1983

Chevy Chase Village V. Jaggers, 261 Md. 309 (1971).

Cinnamon Creek Homes Ass'n v. Roberts, Chancery No. 43443 (19th Jud. Cir., Va. 1975).

Colonia Verde Homeowners Ass'n v. Kaufman, 122 Az. 574 (App. 1979).

Conrad v. Dunn, 92 Cal. App. 3d 236 (1979).

Coquina Club, Inc. v. Mantz, 342 So. 2d 112 (Fla. 2nd D.C.A. 1977).

Country Club Estates Ass'n v. Gronick, C.A. No. 77-8523 C.Z. (Mich. 1978).

Dickstein v. Williams, 93 Nev. 605 (1977).

Dulaney Towers Maintenance Corporation v. O'Brey, 46 Md. App. 464 (1980).

Ezer v. Fuchsloch, 99 Cal. App. 3d 849 (1979).

Fairwood Greens HOA, Inc. v. Young, 26 Wash. App. 758 (1980).

Fifty-Six Sixty Collins Avenue Condominium, Inc. v. Dawson, 354 So. 2d 432 (Fla. 3rd D.C.A. 1978).

Guilford Ass'n, Inc. v. Beasley, 29 Md. App. 694 (1976).

Harpst v. Presley of Southern California, et al., C.A. No. 29-48-50 (Orange Co., Ca. 1978).

Hidden Harbour Estates, Inc. v. Basso, 393 So. 2d 637 (Fla. 4th D.C.A. 1981).

Hidden Harbour Estates, Inc. v. Norman, 3Q9 So. 2d 180 (Fla. 4th D.C.A. 1975).

Hilltop Village Cooperative No. 4, Inc. v. Goldstein, 244 N.Y.S.2d 454 (1963), *rev'd* 252 N.Y.S.2d 7 (1964), *aff'd* 258 N.Y.S.2d 348 (1965).

Holleman v. Mission Tract Homeowners Ass'n, 556 S.W.2d 632 (Tx. Civ. App. 1977).

Huey v. Davis, 556 S.W.2d 860 (Tx. Civ. App. 1977).

Jayno Heights Landowners Ass'n v. Preston, 85 Mich. App. 443 (1978).

Johnson v. Keith, 368 Mass. 316 (1975).

Knolls Cooperative Section No. II, Inc. v. Cashman, 243 N.Y.S.2d 182 (1963), *aff'd* 14 N.Y.2d 579 (1964).

Knox v. Streatfield, 79 Cal. App. 3d 565 (1978).

Laguna Royale Owners Ass'n v. Darger, 119 Cal. App. 3d 670 (1981).

Lake Arbor Homeowners' Ass'n v. Harris, C.A. No. 48020, Div. 4, (Dist. Ct. Jefferson Co., Colo., 1976).

Leland Acres Home Owners Ass'n, Inc. v. R.T. Partnership, 106 Mich. App. 790 (1981).

Lenhoff v. Birch Bay Real Estate, Inc., 22 Wash. App. 70 (1978).

Luna Park Housing Corp. v. Besser, 329 N.Y.S.2d 332 (1972).

MacDonald Properties, Inc. v. Bel-Air Country Club, 72 Cal. App. 3d 693 (1977).

Malcolm v. Shamie, 95 Mich. App. 132 (1980).

Marina Point Ltd. v. Wolfson, 30 Cal. 3d 721 (1982).

Martin v. Moore, 562 S.W.2d 274 (Tx. Civ. App., 1978).

Maurice River Co. v. Roscott, C-854-76 (Sup. Ct., Cumberland Co., N.J. 1978).

Mavrakis v. Playa Del Sol Ass'n, Inc., C.A. No. 77-6049 (Fla. 1978).

Mid-State Equipment Company, Inc. v. Bell, 217 Va. 133 (1976).

Millbridge Apartments v. Linden, 5 HDR 170 (1977).

Mock v. Shulman, 226 Cal. App. 2d 263 (1964).

Mulberry Ass'n, Inc. v. Richards, 369 So. 2d 185 (La. App. 1979).

Northcrest Homeowners' Ass'n v. Friedman, C.A. No. 966677 (Sup. Ct. DeKalb Co., Ga. 1977).

O'Connor v. Village Green Homeowners Ass'n, 123 Cal. App. 3d 789 (1981).

100 South Doheny Condominium Ass'n, Inc., v. Starling, LASC C349471 (1981).

Parnell Woods Condominium Ass'n, Inc., v. Schneider, 156-639 Cir. Ct., Milwaukee Co., Wisc. (1982).

Piechowski v. Case, 255 N.W.2d 72 (S.D. 1977).

Pilafian v. Cherry, 355 So. 2d 847 (Fla. 3rd D.C.A. 1978).

Pinewood Greens Homeowners' Ass'n v. Murtha, C.A. No. 48301 (Cir. Ct. Fairfax Co., Va. 1976).

Plaza Del Prado Condominium Ass'n, Inc. v. Richman, 345 So. 2d 851 (Fla. 3rd D.C.A. 1977).

Raintree Corporation v. Rowe, 38 N.C. App. 664 (1978).

Rego v. Bentley Woods Condominium Ass'n, Inc., C.A. No. 79-2015 (Sup. Ct. Cobb Co., Ca. 1979).

Riley v. Stoves, 22 Az. App. 223 (1974).

Riordan v. Hale, 215 Va. 638 (1975).

Ritchey v. Villa Neuva Condominium Ass'n, 81 Cal. App. 3rd 688 (1978).

Romak v. Naples Mobile Estates Community Ass'n, Inc., 373 So. 2d 693 (Fla. 2nd D.C.A. 1979).

Sain v. Silvestre, 78 Cal. App. 3d 461 (1978).

Sauder v. Harbour Club Condominium No. Three, Inc., 346 So. 2d 556 (Fla. 2nd D.C.A. 1977).

Schulz v. Zoeller, 568 S.W.2d 677 (Tx. 1978).

Seaton v. Clifford, 24 Cal. App. 3d 46 (1972).

Shapiro v. Levin, 223 Pa. Super. 535 (1973).

Smith v. Rasqui, 176 Cal. App. 2d 514 (1959).

Southampton Civic Club v. Foxworth, 550 S.W.3d 152 (Tx. Civ. App. 1977).

Sterling Village Condominium, Inc. v. Breitenbach, 251 So. 2d 685 (Fla. 4th D.C.A. 1971).

Sterner v. Saugatuck Harbor Yacht Club, Inc., 450 A.2d 369 (Conn. 1982).

Styers v. Mara, 631 P.2d 1138 (Colo. 1981).

Swaggerty v. Petersen, 280 Or. 739 (1977).

Tate v. Moran, 264 Pa. Super. 540 (1979).

Taylor v. Dobrey, No. 880 (Ct. of Spec. App., Md. 1981).

Terry v. James, 72 Cal. App. 3d 438 (1977).

Trahms v. Starrett, 34 Cal. App. 3d 766 (1973).

Village Gate Homeowners Ass'n v. Hales, 219 Va. 321 (1978).

Vinick v. Taylor, 270 So. 2d 413 (Fla. 4th D.C.A. 1972).

Werner v. Graham, 181 C. 174 (1973).

Westgate Terrace Community Associates, Inc. v. Burger King Corp., 66 Ill. App. 3d 721 (1978).

Wethersfield Cluster Ass'n v. Gulf Reston, Inc., et al., C.A. No. 53027 (Cir. Ct. Fairfax Co., Va. 1977).

White Egret Condominium, Inc. v. Franklin, 379 So. 2d 346 (Fla., 1979).

Wilshire Condominium Ass'n, Inc. v. Kohlbrand, 368 So. 2d 629 (Fla. 4th D.C.A. 1979).

Winslette v. Keller, 220 Ga. 100 (1964).

Winston Towers 200 Ass'n, Inc. v. Saverio, 360 So. 2d 470 (Fla. 3rd D.C.A. 1978!.

C. Use Restrictions

Adams v. Lindberg, 125 Ariz. 441 (App. 1980).

Bellarmine Hills Ass'n v. Residential Systems Company, 84 Mich. App. 554 (1978).

Biagini v. Hyde, 3 Cal. App. 3d 877 (1970), strictly construing residential use against beautician.

Bomer v. Echols, 6 HDR 44 (June 12, 1978).

City of Chula Vista v. Pagard, 97 Cal. App. 3d 627 (1979), vacated 115 Cal. App. 3d 785 (1981).

Dobry v. Taylor, No. A-7913 (Cir. Ct. St. Mary's Co., Md. 1980).

Feeley v. Birenbaum, 554 S.W.2d 432 (Mo. App. 1977).

Hidden Harbour Estates, Inc. v. Norman, 309 So. 2d 180 (Fla. 4th D.C.A. 1975).

Hudson Oil Co. v. Shortstop, 111 Cal. App. 3d 488 (1980).

Jayno Heights Landowners Ass'n v. Preston, 85 Mich. App. 443 (1978).

Joslin v. Pine River Development Corp., 116 N.H. 814 (1976).

Kessler v. Stough, 361 So. 2d 1048 (Ala., 1978).

Leland Acres Home Owners Ass'n, Inc. v. R. T. Partnership, 106 Mich. App. 790 (1981).

Malcolm v. Shamie, 95 Mich. App. 132 (1980).

Mulberry Ass'n, Inc. v. Richards, 369 So. 2d 185 (Fla. App. 1979).

Nonnenmann v. Lucky Stores, Inc., 53 Ill. App. 3d 509 (1977).

O'Connor v. Village Green Homeowners Ass'n, 33 Cal. 3d 790 (1983), holding that age restrictions in condominium violate Unruh Civil Rights Act.

Riley v. Bear Creek Planning Commission, 17 Cal. 3d 500 (1976), holding that restrictions must be incorporated by reference into first deed.

Samuelson National v. Kaiser Aetna, 99 Cal. App. 3d 553 (1979), upholding noncompetition restriction.

Sissel v. Smith, 242 Ga. 595 (1978).

Southampton Civic Club v. Foxworth, 550 S.W.2d 152 (Tx. Civ. App. 1977).

Star Lake North Commodore Ass'n, Inc. v. Parker, 3d D.C.A. Fla. (1982), upholding age restrictions.

Welsch v. Goswick, 130 Cal. App. 3d 398 (1982).

White Egret Condominium, Inc. v. Franklin, 379 So. 2d 346 (Fla. 1979), upholding age restrictions.

5. CONVERSIONS

California Coastal Commission v. Quanta Investment Corp., 113 Cal. App. 3d 579 (1980).

Claridge House One, Inc. v. Borough of Verona, 490 F. Supp. 706 (D.N.J. 1980) *aff'd* 633 F.2d 209 (3rd Cir. 1980).

Collins v. City of Los Angeles, 116 Cal. App. 3d 463 (1981).

Dayenian v. American National Bank & Trust Co., 91 Ill. App. 3d 622 (1980).

Fishman v. Pollack, 165 N.J. Sup. 235 (1979).

Hampshire House Sponsor Corp. v. Borough of Fort Lee, 172 N.J. Sup. 426 (1979).

Johnson v. Nationwide Industries, 450 F. Supp. 948 (N.D. Ill. 1978).

Jones v. Eagle II, 424 N.E.2d 1253 (Ill. App. 1981).

Krater v. City of Los Angeles, 130 Cal. App. 3d 839 (1982).

100 South Doheny Condominium Ass'n, Inc. v. Starling, LASC C349471 (1981).

People v. Grundy County National Bank, 422 N.E.2d 648 (Ill. 1981).

Santa Monica Pines Ltd. v. Rent Control Board, 132 Cal App. 3d 301 (1982).

Wisconsin Avenue Associates, Inc., v. 2720 Wisconsin Avenue Cooperative Ass'n, 385 A.2d 20 (D.C. App. 1978).

6. COOPERATIVES

Berman v. Watergate West, Inc., 391 A.2d 1351 (D.C. App., 1978).

California Coastal Commission v. Quanta Investment Corp., 113 Cal. App. 3d 579 (1980).

Earl W. Jimerson Housing Co., Inc. v. Butler, 412 N.Y.S. 2d 560 (1978).

Edgewater Apartments, Inc. v. Freedman, New York Law Journal, page 7 (N.Y. Co. Sup. St. 1980).

Hilltop Village Cooperative No. 4, Inc. v. Goldstein, 244 N.Y.S.2d 454 (1963), *rev'd* 252 N.Y.S.2d 7 (1964), *aff'd* 258 N.Y.S.2d 348 (1965).

LeFebvre v. Osterndorf, 87 Wisc. 3d 525 (1979).

Luna Park Housing Corp. v. Besser, 329 N.Y.S.2d 332 (1972).

Martin V. Villa Roma, Inc., 131 Cal. App. 3d 632 (1982).

Northridge Co-op Section No. 1, Inc. v. 32nd Ave. Construction Corp., 2 N.Y.2d 514 (1957).

Shelter Creek Development Corp. v. City of Oxnard, 132 Cal. App. 3d 240 (1982).

Shore Terrace Co-op, Inc., v. Roche, 268 N.Y.S.2d 278 (1966).

Suarez v. Rivercross Tenants' Corp., 438 N.Y.S.2d 164 (1981).

United Housing Foundation, Inc. v. Forman, 421 U.S. 837 (1975).

Wisconsin Avenue Associates, Inc. v. 2720 Wisconsin Avenue Cooperative Ass'n, 385 A.2d 20 (D.C. App. 1978).

7. TIMESHARES

Cal-Am Corp. v. D.R.E., 104 Cal. App. 3d 453 (1980).

Laguna Royale Owners Ass'n v. Darger, 119 Cal. App. 3d 670 (1981).

Royal Aloha Partners v. Real Estate Division, 651 P.2d 1350 (Ct. App. Ore., 1982).

State of Nevada, Dept. of Commerce, Division of Real Estate v. Carriage House Associates, 94 Nev. 707 (1978).

8. DEVELOPMENTAL RIGHTS

Allen v. City & County of Honolulu, 58 Haw. 432 (1977).

Arnel Development Co. v. City of Costa Mesa, 28 Cal. 3d 511 (1980).

Avco Community Development, Inc. v. South Coast Regional Commission, 17 Cal. 3d 785 (1976), *cert. denied* 429 U.S. 1083 (1977).

Barber v. Chalfonte Development Corp., 369 So. 2d 983 (Fla. 4th D.C.A. 1979).

Barclay v. Deveau, 415 N.E.2d 239 (Mass. App. 1981).

Bryant v. Lake Highlands Development Co., 618 S.W.2d 921 (Tex. Civ. App., 1981).

California Coastal Commission v. Quanta Investment Corp., 113 Cal. App. 3d 579 (1980).

City of Alexandria v. West Alexandria Properties, Inc. (Cir. Ct. Alexandria, Va. 1979).

Dawe v. City of Scottsdale, 119 Ariz. 493 (App. 1978), *vacated* 119 Ariz. 486 (1978).

Hargroder v. City of Eunice, et al., 341 So. 2d 463 (La. App. 1976).

Horn v. County of Ventura, 24 Cal. 3d 605 (1979).

Kelber v. City of Upland, 155 Cal. App. 2d 631 (1957).

Laurel Hills Homeowners Ass'n v. Los Angeles, 83 Cal. App. 3d 515 (1978).

Norris v. Peck, 381 So. 3d 353 (Fla. 5th D.C.A. 1980).

Oceanic California, Inc. v. North Central Coast Regional Commission, 63 Cal. App. 3d 57 (1976).

Pardee Construction Company v. California Coastal Commission, 95 Cal. 3d 471 (1979).

Piechowski v. Case, 255 N.W.2d 72 (S.D. 1977).

Pittmann v. Cohn Communities, Inc. 240 Ga. 106 (1977).

Robert Mueller Associates v. Zoning Hearing Board of Buffalo Township, 30 Pa. Cmwlth, 386 (1977).

Samuelson National v. Kaiser Aetna, 99 Cal. App. 3d 553 (1979).

In re San Clemente Estates, 5 B.R. 605 (1980).

Seashore Club of Atlantic City v. Seashore Club Condominium Ass'n, Inc., 180 N.J. Sup. 81 (1981).

Welch v. Point of Americas Condominiums Apartments, Inc., 373 So. 2d 60 (Fla. 4th D.C.A. 1979).

9. DEVELOPER-DIRECTOR LIABILITY, RISKS, FIDUCIARY DUTY

Armetta, et al. v. Clevetrust Realty Investors, et al., 359 So. 2d 540 (Fla. 4th D.C.A. 1978).

Avilia South Condominium Ass'n, Inc. v. Kappa Corporation, 347 So. 2d 599 (Fla. 1977).

B&J Holding Corporation v. Weiss, 353 So. 2d 141 (Fla. 3rd D.C.A. 1978).

Barber v. Chalfonte Development Corp., 369 So. 2d 983 (Fla. 4th D.C.A. 1979).

Bay Colony Club Condominium, Inc. v. Drexel Properties, Inc., C.A. No. 76-1967 (Cir. Ct. Broward Co., Fla. 1979).

Beri, Inc. v. Salishan Properties, Inc., 282 Or. 569 (1978).

Berman v. Watergate West, Inc., 391 A.2d 1351 (D.C. App. 1978).

Bodily v. Parkmount Village Green Homeowners Ass'n, Inc., 104 Cal. App. 3d 348 (1980).

Bradler v. Craig, 274 Cal. App. 2d 466 (1969).

Brandman v. Coronado Cay Company, C.A. No. 394178 (Sup. Ct. San Diego Co., Cal., 1978).

Burleigh House Condominium, Inc. v. Buch, 368 So. 2d 1316 (Fla. 3rd D.C.A. 1976).

Burleigh House Condominium, Inc. v. Buchwald, 533 F.2d 934 (5th Cir. 1976).

Callaizakis v. Astor Development Co., 4 Ill. App. 3d 163 (1972).

Chandler v. Bunick, 279 Or. 353 (1977).

Chotka v. Fidelco Growth Investors, 383 So. 2d 1169 (Fla. 2nd D.C.A. 1980).

Cohen v. Commodore Plaza at Century 21 Condominium Ass'n, Inc., 368 So. 2d 613 (Fla. 3rd D.C.A. 1979).

Cohen Kite Hill Community Ass'n, 142 Cal. App. 3d 642 (1983), extending fiduciary duties to homeowner directors and to architectural committee members.

Connor v. The Great Western Savings & Loan Ass'n, 69 Cal. 2d 850 (1968).

Cook v. Salishan Properties, Inc., 279 Or. 333 (1977).

Cooper v. Jevne, 56 Cal. App. 3d 860 (1976).

Costa Viva Homeowners Ass'n v. Johns-Manville Corporation, et al., San Diego Sup. Ct., Cal. (1982).

Council of Co-Owners of Place One Condominium v. Union Bank, Law No. 5342 (Cir. Ct. Alexandria, Va. 1979).

Country Club Estates Ass'n v. Gronick, No. 77-8523CZ (Mich. 1978).

Crawford v. Shepherd, 86 Wisc. 2d 362 (1978).

David v. B&J Holding Corporation, 349 So. 676 (Fla. 3rd D.C.A. 1977).

Deal v. 999 Lakeshore Ass'n, 94 Nev. 301 (1978).

Del Mar Beach Club v. Imperial Contracting, 123 Cal. App. 3d 898 (1981).

DePinto v. United States, 407 F. Supp. 1 (D. Az. 1975).

Dickey v. Barnes, 268 Or. 226 (1974).

Dunson v. Stockton, Whatley, Davin & Co., 346 So. 2d 603 (Fla. 1st D.C.A. 1977).

Edenfield v. Woodlawn Manor, Inc., 62 Tenn. App. 280 (1970).

First Wisconsin National Bank v. Roose, 348 So. 2d 610 (Fla. 4th D.C.A. 1977).

Foster v. West Alexandria Properties, Inc., C.A. No. 79-764-A (E.D. Va. 1980).

Fountainview Ass'n, Inc., No. 4 v. Bell, 203 So. 2d 657, *aff'd* 214 So. 2d 609 (Fla. 3rd D.C.A. 1967).

Friendly Village Community Ass'n, Inc. v. Silva & Hill Construction Co., 31 Cal. App. 3d 220 (1973).

Governors Grove Condominium Ass'n, Inc. v. Hill Development Corp., 36 Conn. Sup. 145 (1980).

Gravely v. Providence Partnership, 549 F.2d 958 (4th Cir. 1977).

Greenburg v. Johnston, 367 So. 2d 229 (Fla. 2nd D.C.A. 1979).

Hartley v. Ballou, 20 N.C. App. 493 (1974), *rev'd* 286 N.C. 51 (1974).

Hillcrest East No. 23, Inc. v. Hollywood Beach Hotel Co., Inc., 359 So. 2d 546 (Fla. 4th D.C.A. 1978).

Holmes v. Worthey, 159 Ga. App. 262 (1981).

Hur v. Saul J. Morgan Enterprises, Inc., 325 So. 2d 446 (Fla. 3rd D.C.A. 1976).

Imperial Point Colonnades Condominium, Inc., v. Mangurian, 549 F.2d 1029 (5th Cir. 1977).

Ireland, et al. v. Wynkoop, et al., 36 Colo. App. 205 (1975).

Isaacs v. Trustees of Riverview Condominium Trust, Sup. Ct., Cambridge, Mass. (Oct. 8, 1980).

Johnson v. Nationwide Industries, 450 F. Supp. 948 (N.D. Ill. 1978).

Kleinman v. High Point of Hartsdale I Condominium, 438 N.Y.S. 2d 47 (1979).

Klos v. Gockel, 87 Wash. 2d 567 (1976).

Krol v. York Terrace Bldg., Inc., 35 Md. App. 321 (1977).

Lake Mabel Development Corp. v. Bird, 99 Fla. 253 (1930).

Loyola Federal Savings & Loan v. Galanes, 33 Mo. App. 359 (1976).

Luster v. Jones, 7 HDR 1126 (1979).

Margate Village Condominium Ass'n, Inc. v. Wilfred, Inc., 350 So. 2d 16 (Fla. 4th D.C.A. 1977).

Mayo v. Andress, 373 So. 2d 620 (Ala. 1979).

McCown v. Heidler, 527 F.2d 204 (10th Cir. 1975).

McDonald v. Mobley, 555 S.W.2d 916 (Tx. Civ. App. 1977).

Miller v. Granados, 529 F.2d 393 (5th Cir. 1976).

Mitchell Gardens No. 3 Co-ops Corp. v. Third BN Assoc., Inc., 162 N.Y.S. 2d 152 (1957).

Northridge Co-op Section No. 1, Inc. v. 32nd Ave. Construction Corp., 2 N.Y. 2d 514 (1957).

Occidental Land, Inc. v. Superior Court of Orange County, 18 Cal. 3d 355 (1976).

O'Dell v. Custom Builders Corporation, 560 S.W. 2d 862 (Mo. 1978).

Oliver v. City Builders, Inc., et al., 303 So. 2d 466 (Miss. 1974).

O'Quinn v. Beach Associates, 272 S.C. 95 (1978).

Palma Sola Harbour Condominium, Inc. v. Huber, 374 So. 2d 1135 (Fla. 2nd D.C.A. 1979).

Patitucci v. Drelich, 153 N.J. Super. 177 (1977).

People v. Kaufman & Broad Homes of Long Island, 378 N.Y.S. 2d 258 (1975).

Pittman v. Cohn Communities, Inc., 240 Ga. 106 (1977).

Polland v. Saxe & Yalles Development Company, 12 Cal. 3d 374 (1974).

Raven's Cove Townhomes, Inc. v. Knuppe Development Company, Inc., et al., 114 Cal. App. 3d 783 (1981).

Reider v. P-48, Inc., 362 So. 2d 105 (Fla. 1st D.C.A. 1978).

Rice v. First Federal Savings & Loan Ass'n, 207 So. 2d 22 (Fla. 2d D.C.A. 1968), *cert. denied* 212 So. 2d 879 (Fla. 1968).

Riviera Condominium Apartments, Inc. v. Weinberger, 231 So. 2d 850 (Fla. 3rd D.C.A. 1970).

Sauder v. Harbour Club Condominium No. Three, Inc., 346 So. 2d 556 (Fla. 2nd D.C.A. 1977).

Shore Terrace Co-op, Inc. v. Roche, 268 N.Y.S.2d 278 (1966).

Siller, et al. v. Hartz Mountain Associates, Docket No. C-969-80 (Sup. Ct., Chancery Div. N.J. 1981).

Sprecher v. Adamson Companies, 114 Cal. App. 3d 414 (1981), hearing granted.

Stern v. Lucy Webb Hayes National Training School for Deaconesses and Missionaries, 381 F. Supp. 1003 (D.C. D.C. 1974).

Stoney Ridge Hill Condominium Owners Ass'n v. Auerbach, 64 Ohio App. 2d 40 (1979).

Strathmore Riverside Condominium Ass'n, Inc. v. Paver Development Corp., 6 H.D.R. 1033 (1979).

Suarez v. Rivercross Tenants' Corp., 438 N.Y.S.2d 164 (1981).

Summerhouse Condominium Ass'n, Inc. v. Majestic Savings & Loan Ass'n, 615 P.2d 71 (Colo. App. 1980).

Tallmadge v. Skyline Construction, Inc., 86 Wisc. 2d 356 (1978).

Tassan v. United Development Co., 88 Ill. App. 3d 581 (1980).

Terlinde v. Neely, 271 S.E.2d 768 (S.C. 1980).

Tillman v. Wheaton-Haven Recreation Ass'n, Inc. 517 F.2d 1141 (4th Cir. 1975).

Timmreck v. Munn, 433 F. Supp. 396 (N.D. Ill. 1977).

Troy v. Village Green Owners Ass'n, LASC 369312 (1982).

United States v. Western Resort Properties, C.A. No. 3789456-G (N.D. Tx. 1978).

Waggoner v. Midwestern Development, Inc., 83 S.D. 57 (1967).

Walters v. Greengrade Villas Homeowners Ass'n, Inc., 399 So. 2d 538 (Fla. 1981).

Waterford Condominium Ass'n, Inc. v. Dunbar Corp., 432 N.E.2d 1009 (Ill. App. 1982).

Wayne V. Unigard Mutual, Inc., 316 So. 2d 581 (Fla. 3rd D.C.A. 1975).

Welch v. Point of Americas Condominium Apartments, Inc., 373 So. 2d 60 (Fla. 4th D.C.A. 1979).

Westborough Hills Condominium Ass'n v. Loews Corporation, et al., San Mateo Co. Sup. Ct., Ca. 1980.

Wittington Condominium Apartments, Inc. v. Braemer Corp., 313 So. 2d 463 (Fla. 4th D.C.A. 1975).

10. WARRANTIES

Air Heaters, Inc. v. Johnson Electric, Inc., 258 N.W.2d 649 (N.D. 1977).

Amos v. McDonald, 123 Ga. App. 509 (1971).

B&J Holding Corporation v. Weiss, 353 So. 2d 141 (Fla. 3rd D.C.A. 1978).

Barnes v. Mac Brown & Company, Inc., 264 Ind. 227 (1976).

Beri, Inc. v. Salishan Properties, Inc., 282 Or. 569 (1978).

Berman v. Watergate West, Inc., 391 A.2d 1351 (D.C. App. 1978).

Bruce Farms, Inc. v. Coupe, 219 Va. 287 (1978).

Casavant v. Campopiano, 114 R.I. 24 (1974).

Chandler v. Bunick, 279 Or. 353 (1977).

Chotka v. Fidelco Growth Investors, 383 So. 2d 1169 (Fla. 2nd D.C.A. 1980).

Conyers v. Mallory, 50 Ill. App. 3d 17 (1977).

Cook v. Salishan Properties, Inc., 279 Or. 333 (1977).

David v. B&J Holding Corporation, 349 So. 2d 676 (Fla. 3rd D.C.A. 1977).

Dean v. Rutherford, 49 Ill. App. 3d 768 (1977).

Drexel Properties, Inc. v. Bay Colony Club Condominium, 406 So. 2d 515 (Fla. 4th D.C.A., 1981).

Duncan v. Schuster-Graham Homes, Inc., 39 Colo. App. 921 (1977), *rev'd* 194 Colo. 441 (1978).

East Hilton Drive Homeowners' Ass'n v. Western Real Estate Exchange, Inc., 136 Cal. App. 3d 630 (1982), successor-seller not liable under strict liability or implied warranty.

Elmore v. Blume, 31 Ill. App. 3d 643 (1975).

Equitable Life Assurance Soc. of the U.S. v. Tinsley Mill Village, 249 Ga. 769 (1982).

Gable v. Silver, 258 So. 2d 11 (Fla. 4th D.C.A. 1972), *aff'd* 264 So. 2d 418 (Fla. 1972).

Gallegos v. Graff, 32 Colo. App. 213 (1973).

Goggin v. Fox Valley Construction Corporation, 48 Ill. App. 3d 103 (1977).

Golden v. Conway, 55 Cal. App. 3d 948, 128 Cal. Rptr. 69 (1976).

Governors Grove Condominium Ass'n, Inc. v. Hill Development Corp., 36 Conn. Sup. 145 (1980).

Greenburg v. Johnston, 367 So. 2d 229 (Fla. 2nd D.C.A. 1979).

Hartley v. Ballou, 20 N.C. App. 493 (1974), *rev'd* 286 N.C. 51 (1974).

Herlihy v. Dunbar Builders Corp., 92 Ill. App. 3d 310 (1980).

Holmes v. Worthey, 159 Ga. App. 262 (1981).

Klos v. Gockel, 87 Wash. 2d 567 (1976).

Krol v. York Terrace Bldg., Inc., 35 Md. App. 321 (1977).

Matulunas v. Baker, 569 S.W.2d 791 (Mo. App. 1978).

Mayo v. Andress, 373 So. 2d 620 (Ala. 1979).

Mazurek v. Nielsen, 42 Colo. App. 386 (1979).

McDonald v. Mianecki, 159 N.J. Super. 1 (1978), *aff'd* 79 N.J. 275 (1979).

McDonald v. Mobley, 555 S.W.2d 916 (Tx. Civ. App. 1977).

Millbridge Apartments v. Linden, 151 N.J. Super. 168 (1977).

Navajo Circle, Inc. v. Development Concepts Corporation, 373 So. 2d 689 (Fla. 2d D.C.A. 1979).

Newman v. Tualatin Development Co., Inc., 287 Ore. 47 (1979).

Norton v. Burleaud, 115 N.H. 435 (1975).

O'Dell v. Custom Builders Corporation, 560 S.W.2d 862 (Mo. 1978).

Oliver v. City Builders, Inc. et al., 303 So. 2d 466 (Miss. 1974).

Patitucci v. Drelich, 153 N.J. Super. 177 (1977).

Petersen v. Hubschman Construction Co., Inc., 53 Ill. App. 3d 626 (1977), *aff'd* 76 Ill. 2d 31 (1979).

Polland v. Saxe & Yalles Development Company, 12 Cal. 3d 374 (1974).

Sousa v. Albino, 388 A.2d 804 (R.I. 1978).

Suarez v. Rivercross Tenants Corp., 438 N.Y.S.2d 164 (1981).

Tassan v. United Development Co., 88 Ill. App. 3d 581 (1980).

Terlinde v. Neely, 271 S.E.2d 768 (S.C. 1980).

Vantage View, Inc. v. Bali East Development Corporation, et al., 4th Dist. Ct. App., Florida No. 81-289 (1982), loss not required to collect under breach of implied warranty.

Waggoner v. Midwestern Development, Inc., 835 S.D. 57 (1967).

Waterford Condominium Ass'n, Inc. v. Dunbar Corp., 432 N.E. 2d 1009 (Ill. App. 1982).

Witty v. Schramm, 62 Ill. App. 3d 185 (1978).

11. RECREATION LEASES

Avilia South Condominium Ass'n, Inc. v. Kappa Corporation, 347 So. 2d 599 (Fla. 1977).

Bay Management, Inc. v. Beau Monde, Inc., 366 So. 2d 788 (Fla. 2nd D.C.A. 1979).

Buckley Towers Condominium, Inc. v. Buchwald, 533 F.2d 934 (5th Cir. 1976).

Burleigh House Condominium, Inc. v. Buchwald 328 So. 2d 554 (Fla. 3rd D.C.A. 1976).

Burleigh House Condominium, Inc. v. Buchwald 368 So. 2d 1316 (Fla. 3rd D.C.A. 1979).

Century Village, Inc. v. Wellington E, F, K, L, H, M, & G Condominium Ass'n, 370 So. 2d 1244 (Fla. 4th D.C.A. 1979).

Chatham Condominium Ass'n v. Century Village, Inc., 597 F. 2d 1002 (5th Cir. 1979).

Cole v. Angora Enterprises, Inc., 403 So. 2d 1010 (Fla. 4th D.C.A. 1981).

Fifth Morrings Condominiums, Inc. v. Shere, 81 F.R.D. 712 (S.D. Fla. 1979).

Goldenberg v. Dome Condominium Ass'n, Inc., 376 So. 2d 37 (Fla. 3d D.C.A. 1979).

Imperial Point Colonnades Condominium, Inc. v. Mangurian, 549 F.2d 1029 (5th Cir. 1977).

King Mountain Condominium Ass'n v. Grundloch, File No. 78-9175 (Cir. Ct. Broward Co., Fla. 1980).

Margate Village Condominium Ass'n, Inc. v. Wilfred, Inc., 350 So. 2d 16 (Fla. 4th D.C.A. 1977).

Maskowitz v. Saul J. Morgan Enterprises, Inc., C.A. No. 74-570 Civ-WMA (S.D. Fla. 1979).

Royal Bahamian Ass'n, Inc. v. Morgan, 338 So. 2d 876 (Fla. 3rd D.C.A. 1976).

Sachs v. Plaza Del Prado Condominium Ass'n, Inc., C.A. No. 79-2250 (11th Cir. Fla. 1979), *appeal dismissed* 374 So. 2d 109 (Fla. 3rd D.C.A. 1979).

Shaughnessy v. Rec. Centers, Inc., 361 So. 2d 807 (Fla. 4th D.C.A. 1978).

Urbanek v. Candell, Case No. 75-524-CAA (Fla.).

Waterford Point Condominium Apartments, Inc., v. Fass, 402 So. 2d 1327 (Fla. 4th D.C.A. 1981).

Westchester House Ass'n v. McPhearson, C.A. No. 76-2564 (Cir. Ct. 17th Cir. Fla. 1977).

12. ANTITRUST

Buckley Towers Condominium, Inc. v. Buchwald, 533 F.2d 934 (5th Cir. 1976).

Burleigh House Condominium v. Buchwald, 546 F.2d 57 (5th Cir. 1977).

Chatham Condominium Ass'n v. Century Village, Inc., 597 F.2d 1002 (5th Cir. 1979).

Cohen v. Commodore Plaze at Century 21 Condominium Ass'n, Inc., 368 So. 2d 613 (Fla. 3rd D.C.A. 1979).

Fifth Morrings Condominiums, Inc., v. Shere, 81 F.R.D. 712 (S.D. Fla. 1979).

Green Belt Homes, Inc. v. Nyman Realty, Inc. 48 Md. App. 42 (1981).

Imperial Point Colonnades Condominium, Inc. v. Mangurian, 549 F.2d 1029 (5th Cir. 1977).

Johnson v. Nationwide Industries, 450 F. Supp. 948 (N.D. Ill. 1978).

Maskowitz v. Saul J. Morgan Enterprises, Inc., C.A. No. 74-570 Civ-WMA (S.D. Fla. 1979).

Miller v. Granados, 529 F.2d 393 (5th Cir. 1976).

Stern v. Lucy Webb Hayes National Training School for Deaconesses and Missionaries, 381 F. Supp. 1003 (D.C. D.C. 1974).

13. MECHANIC'S LIENS

Bessemer v. Gersten, 381 So. 2d 1344 (Fla. 1980).

Dean v. Rutherford, 49 Ill. App. 3d 768 (1977).

Johnson v. Pistakee Highlands Community Ass'n, 72 Ill. App. 3d 402 (1979).

Papa v. Greenwich Green, Inc., 177 Conn. 295 (1979).

Ramsey v. DiSabatino, 347 A.2d 650 (Del. Sup. Ct. 1975).

Roundhouse Construction Corp. v. Telesco Masons Supplies Co., 168 Conn. 371 (1975), *vacated* 423 U.S. 809 (1975).

Sukut-Coulson, Inc. v. Allied Canon Co., 85 Cal. App. 3d 648 (1978).

Superior Lumber Co. v. Sutro, 92 Cal. App. 2d 954 (1979).

14. PLATS AND MAPS

Beechler v. Winkel, 59 Ohio App. 2d 65 (1978).

Benny v. City of Alameda, 105 Cal. App. 3d 1006 (1980).

Broward County v. Narco Realty, 359 So. 2d 509 (Fla. 4th D.C.A. 1978).

Carmel Valley View, Ltd. v. Maggini, 91 Cal. App. 3d 318 (1979).

Dawe v. City of Scottsdale, 119 Ariz. 493 (App. 1978), *vacated* 119 Ariz. 486 (1978).

Horn v. County of Ventura, 24 Cal. 3d 605 (1979).

Kelber v. City of Upland, 155 Cal. App. 2d 631 (1957).

Palma Sola Harbour Condominium, Inc. v. Huber, 374 So. 2d 1135 (Fla. 2nd D.C.A. 1979).

Piechowski v. Case, 255 N.W.2d 72 (S.D. 1977).

Pioneer Trust and Savings Bank v. Village of Mt. Prospect, 22 Ill. 2d 375 (1961).

St. Francis Court's Condominium Ass'n v. Investor's Real Estate, 432 N.E.2d 1274 (Ill. App. 1982).

Wes Linn Land Co. v. Bd. of Co. Commissioners, Linn Co., 36 Or. App. 39 (1978).

Young v. Stillwater County Commission, 177 Mont. 488 (1978).

Youngblood v. Board of Supervisors, 22 Cal. 3d 644 (1978).

15. MUNICIPAL RELATIONS, ZONING, VOTING TAX

Allen v. City and County of Honolulu, 58 Haw. 432 (1977).

Andrews v. City of Greenbelt, 441 Atl. 2d 106-4 (Md. Ct. App., 1982), allowing unit owner to recover consequential charges upon condemnation of common elements.

Apartment Ass'n of Los Angeles County, Inc. v. City of Los Angeles, Inc., 75 Cal. App. 3d 13 (1977).

Arlington Heights v. Metropolitan Housing Development Corporation, 429 U.S. 252 (1977).

Arnel Development Co. v. City of Costa Mesa, 28 Cal. 3d 511 (1980).

Avco Community Development, Inc. v. South Coast Regional Commission, 17 Cal. 3d 785 (1976), *cert. denied* 429 U.S. 1083 (1977).

Ball v. James, 451 U.S. 355 (1981).

Beckett Ridge Ass'n No. I v. Butler County Board, 1 Ohio St. 3d (Ohio Supreme Ct. 1982).

Benny v. City of Alameda, 105 Cal. App. 3d 1006 (1980).

Blakely v. Housing Authority of King Co., 8 Wash. App. 204 (1973).

Board of County Commissioners of Pasco City v. Hesse, 351 So. 2d 1124 (Fla. 1977).

California Coastal Commission v. Quanta Investment Corp., 113 Cal. App. 3d 579 (1980).

Call v. Feher, 93 Cal. App. 3d 434 (1979).

City of Chula Vista v. Pagard, 97 Cal. App. 3d 627 (1979), *vacated* 115 Cal. App. 3d 785 (1981).

Claridge House One, Inc. v. Borough of Verona, 490 F. Supp. 706 (D.N.J. 1980) *aff'd* 633 F.2d 209 (3rd Cir. 1980).

Collins v. City of Los Angeles, 116 Cal. App. 3d 463 (1981).

DePinto v. United States, 407 F. Supp. 1 (D. Az. 1975).

Fish v. City of New Smyrna Beach, 382 So. 2d 307 (Fla. 1st D.C.A. 1979), *quashed* 384 So. 2d 1272 (Fla. 1980).

Garden State Farms, Inc. v. Bay, 77 N.J. 439 (1978).

Hampshire House Sponsor Corp. v. Borough of Fort Lee, 172 N.J. Super. 426 (1979).

Hargroder v. City of Eunice, et al., 341 So. 2d 463 (La. App. 1976).

Horn v. County of Ventura, 24 Cal. 3d 605 (1979).

Horst v. Derry Township Board of Supervisors, 97 Dauph. 131, *rev'd* 21 Pa. Cmwlth. 556 (1975).

J&B Development Company, Inc., v. King County, 621 Pac. 2d 1002 (Ct. App. Wash., 1981).

Kelber v. City of Upland, 155 Cal. App. 2d 631 (1957).

Krater v. City of Los Angeles, 130 Cal. App. 3d 839 (1982).

Laurel Hills Homeowners Ass'n v. Los Angeles, 83 Cal. App. 3d 515 (1978).

Markley v. Los Angeles City Council, 131 Cal. App. 3d 656 (1982).

Matter of Rothman v. Bd. of Assessors of Nassau Co., Index No. 9884-69 (Sup. Ct. Nassau Co., N.Y. 1977).

Mittleman v. Reston Homeowners Ass'n, C.A. No. 39748 (Cir. Ct. Fairfax Co., Va. 1977).

Moore v. City of East Cleveland, 431 U.S. 494 (1977).

Moscowitz v. Saul J. Morgan Enterprises, Inc., C.A. No. 74-570 Civ-WMH (S.D. Fla. 1979).

Myers, et al. v. Hamilton, Inc., 51 Pa. Cmwlth. 504 (1980).)

Nonnenman v. Lucky Stores, Inc., 53 Ill. App. 3d 509 (1977).

Oceanic California, Inc. v. North Central Coast Regional Commission, 63 Cal. App. 3d 57 (1976).

Okemo Trailside Condominiums, Inc. v. Blais, 135 Vt. 500 (1977).

Owens v. Tiber Island Condominiums, 373 A.2d 890 (D.C. App. 1977).

Pardee Construction Co. v. California Coastal Commission, 95 Cal. App. 3d 471 (1979).

Peck Plaza Condominium v. Div. of Florida Land Sales & Condominiums, 371 So. 2d 152 (Fla. 1st D.C.A. 1979).

The Pines v. City of Santa Monica, 29 Cal. 3d 656 (1981).

Pioneer Trust and Savings Bank v. Village of Mt. Prospect, 22 Ill. 2d 375 (1961).

Public Service Commission v. Howard Research & Development Corp., 271 Md. 141 (1974).

Residents of Beverly Glen, Inc. v. City of Los Angeles, 34 Cal. App. 3d 117 (1973).

Reston Homeowners Ass'n v. Board of Supervisors of Fairfax County, Va., et al., Case No. 811097, Supreme Court Va. (1982).

Robert Mueller Associates v. Zoning Hearing Bd., 30 Pa. Cmwlth. 386 (1977).

Rutland Environmental Protection Ass'n v. Kane County, 31 Ill. App. 3d 82 (1975).

Sayler Land Company v. Tulare Lake Basin Water Storage District, 410 U.S. 719 (1973).

State of Nevada, Dept. of Commerce, Div. of Real Estate v. Carriage House Associates, 94 Nev. 707 (1978).

Swaggerty v. Petersen, 280 Or. 739 (1977).

Sweetwater Properties, SBC v. Alta, 622 P.2d 1178 (Utah 1981).

Topanga Ass'n, etc. v. County of Los Angeles, 11 Cal. 3d 506 (1974).

Town of Redington Shores v. Redington Towers, Inc., 354 So. 2d 942 (Fla. 2nd D.C.A. 1978).

Trianon Park Condominium Ass'n, Inc. v. City of Hialeah, 3rd Dist. Ct. App. (Case No. 81-1626, Fla., 1982).

Twin Lakes Golf and Country Club v. King County, 87 Wash. 2d 1 (1976).

Village of Belle Terre v. Boraas, 416 U.S. 1 (1974).

Waterville Estates Ass'n v. Town of Campton, C.A. No. E-80-243 (Sup. Ct. N.H. 1981).

Wes Linn Land Co. v. Bd. of County Commissioners, Linn Co., 36 Or. App. 39 (1978).

Westgate Terrace Community Associates, Inc., v. Burger King Corp., 66 Ill. App. 3d 721 (1978).

Wildwood Condominium Phase I Owners Ass'n v. City of Fairfield, Ohio, Case No. CA 7901-0100 (12th App. Dist., Ohio 1981).

Youngblood v. Board of Supervisors, 22 Cal. 3d 644 (1978).

16. COMMERCIAL AND INDUSTRIAL PROJECTS

Allen v. Forbes, 345 So. 2d 950 (La. App. 1977).

Barclay v. Deveau, 415 N.E.2d 239 (Mass. App. 1981).

Hargroder v. City of Eunice, et al., 341 So. 2d 463 (La. App. 1976).

Hudson Oil Co. v. Shortstop, 111 Cal. App. 3d 488 (1980).

Nonnenmann v. Lucky Stores, Inc., 53 Ill. App. 3d 509 (1977).

Norris v. Peck, 381 So. 2d 353 (Fla. 5th D.C.A. 1980).

Pawgan v. Silverstein, 265 F. Supp. 898 (S.D. N.Y. 1967).

Peck Plaza Condominiums v. Div. of Fla. Land Sales & Condominiums, 371 So. 2d 152 (Fla. 1st D.C.A. 1979).

Piechowski v. Case, 255 N.W. 2d 72 (S.D. 1977).

Samuelson National v. Kaiser Aetna, 99 Cal. App. 3d 553 (1979).

Sissel v. Smith, 242 Ga. 595 (1978).

Unit Owners of Buildamerica-1, A Condominium v. Gillman, 223 Va. XXX (1982).

Westgate Terrace Community Associates, Inc. v. Burger King Corp., 66 Ill. App. 3d 721 (1978).

17. ASSOCIATION OPERATIONS AND MISCELLANEOUS PROBLEMS

Ashanazi v. Winston Towers 300 Ass'n, C.A. No. C-2505-76 (1979).

Axler v. First Newport Realty Investments, 106 Montgomery Co. Law Rptr. 86 (1979).

B & J Holding Corporation v. Weiss, 353 So. 2d 141 (Fla. 3rd D.C.A. 1978).

Backus v. Smith, 364 So. 2d 786 (Fla. 1st D.C.A. 1978).

Barber v. Chalfonte Dev. Corp., 369 So. 2d 983 (Fla. 4th D.C.A. 1979).

Bauer, et al. v. Harn, et al., 223 Va. (Sup. Ct. Va., 1982).

Bay Management, Inc. v. Beau Monde, Inc., 366 So. 2d 788 (Fla. 2nd D.C.A. 1979).

Bellemeade Condominium Ass'n, Inc. v. Sherrill, C.A. No. 79A-2874 (St. Ct. Cobb Co., Ga. 1980).

Board of Directors v. Sondock, Case No. 2358 cv Tx. Ct. App., 13th District, Aug. 26, 1982, pertaining to modification of use of common elements.

Board of Managers of General Apartment Corporation Condominium v. Gans, 340 N.Y.S.2d 826 (1972).

Board of Managers of Woodgate Village Condominium v. Kaufman & Broad Homes of Long Island, Inc. (Sup. Ct. Suffolk Co., N.Y. 1976).

Brandman v. Coronado Cay Co., C.A. No. 394178 (Sup. Ct. San Diego Co., Ca. 1977).

Buckley Towers Condominium, Inc. v. Buchwald, 533 F.2d 934 (5th Cir. 1976).

Chimney Hill Owners' Ass'n, Inc. v. Antignani, 136 Vt. 446 (1978).

Country Club Estates Ass'n v. Gronick, C.A. No. 77-8523 CZ (March 1978).

Crest Builders, Inc. v. Willow Falls Improvement Ass'n, 74 Ill. App. 3d 420 (1979).

d'Elia v. Ass'n of Apartment Owners of Fairview Manor, 632 P.2d 296 (Haw. App. 1981).

Del Mar Beach Club v. Imperial Contracting, 123 Cal. App. 3d 898 (1981).

Duffy v. Sunburst Farms East Mutual Water and Agricultural Company, Inc., 124 Ariz. 425 (App. 1979), *vacated* 124 Ariz. 413 (1979).

Dulaney Towers Maintenance Corporation v. O'Brey, 46 Md. App. 464 (1980).

Dutcher v. Owens, Tx. Sup. Ct. (C-1473) March 23, 1983, holding that condominium owners are only liable *pro rata* for torts committed on common areas.

Enright v. Sea Towers Owners' Ass'n, Inc., 370 So. 2d 28 (Fla. 2nd D.C.A. 1979).

Ferrari v. Gillespie, C.A. No. 388310 (Sup. Ct., Santa Clara Co., Ca. 1977).

Fifth Moorings Condominium, Inc., v. Shere, 81 F.R.D. (S.D. Fla. 1979).

Friendly Village Community Ass'n, Inc. v. Silva & Hill Construction Co., 31 Cal. App. 3d 220 (1973).

Gentry v. Northeast Management Company, Inc., 472 F. Supp. 1248 (N.D. Tx. 1979).

Guibord v. Gatehouse Condominium Homeowner's Ass'n, C.A. No. 330998 (Sup. Ct. Santa Clara Co., Ca. 1975).

Hargroder v. City of Eunice, et al., 341 So. 2d 463 (La. App. 1976).

Harpst v. Presley of California, et al., C.A. No. 29-48-50 (Sup. Ct. Orange Co., Ca. 1978).

Hemispheres Condominium Ass'n, Inc. v. Corbin, 357 So. 2d 1074 (Fla. 3rd D.C.A. 1978).

Hendler v. Rogers House Condominium, Inc., 234 So. 2d 128 (Fla. 4th D.C.A. 1970).

Homeowners Ass'n of Big Canoe Corporation, C.A. No. C-65248 (Sup. Ct. Fulton Co., Ga. 1980).

Illinois Migrant Council v. Campbell Soup Co., 438 F. Supp. 222 (N.D. Ill. 1977).

Iram Enterprises v. Veditz, 126 Cal. App. 3d 603 (1981).

Isaacs v. Trustees of Riverview Condominium Trust, Sup. Ct., Cambridge, Mass. (1980).

Johnson v. Pistakee Highlands Community Ass'n, 72 Ill. App. 3d 402 (1979).

Juno by the Sea Condominium Ass'n, Inc. v. Manfredonia, 397 So. 2d 297 (Fla. 4th D.C.A. 1980).

King v. Ilikai, 632 P.2d 657 (Haw. App. 1981).

La Costa Beach Homeowners Ass'n v. Wayne, 89 Cal. App. 3d 327 (1979).

Laguna Royale Owners Ass'n v. Darger, 119 Cal. App. 3d 670 (1981).

Makeever v. Lyle, 125 Ariz. 384 (App. 1980).

Matter of Rothman, No. 9884-69 (N.Y. Sup. Ct. 1977).

Mitchell v. Stetson Management Company, Inc., Case No. 79M31493 (3d Munic. Dist. Cook Co., Ill. 1980).

1000 Grandview Ass'n, Inc., v. Mt. Washington Associates, 434 A.2d 796 (Pa. 1981).

Palma Sola Harbour Condominium v. Huber, 374 So. 2d 1135 (Fla. 2nd D.C.A. 1979).

Papalexiou v. Tower West Condominium, 167 N.J. Super. 516 (1979).

Patitucci v. Drelich, 153 N.J. Super. 177 (1977).

Pepe v. Whispering Sands Condominium Ass'n, Inc., 351 So. 2d 755 (Fla. 2nd D.C.A. 1977).

Phillips v. Butler, No. 80C3823 (N.D. Ill. 1981).

Raven's Cove Townhomes, Inc. v. Knuppe Development Company, Inc., et al., 114 Cal. App. 3d 783 (1981).

Rego v. Bentley Woods Condominium Ass'n, Inc., C.A. No. 79-2015 (Sup. Ct. Cobb Co., Ga. 1979).

Rodruck v. Sand Point Maintenance Commission, 48 Wash. 2d 565 (1956).

Ryan v. Baptiste, 565 S.W.2d 196 (Mo. App. 1978).

Sachs, et al. v. Plaza del Prado Condominium Ass'n, Inc., C.A. No. 79-2250 (Cir. Ct. 11th Jud. Dist. Dade Co., Fla. 1979).

St. Francis Court's Condominium Ass'n v. Investor's Real Estate, 432 N.E.2d 1274 (Ill. App. 1982).

Salyer Land Co. v. Tulare Lake Basin Water Storage Dist., 410 U.S. 719 (1973).

Slatnick, et al. v. Leadership Housing Systems of Florida, Inc., et al., 368 So. 2d 78 (Fla. 4th D.C.A. 1978).

Stewart v. Parish School Bd. of Parish of St. Charles, 310 F. Supp. 1172 (E.D. La. 1970).

Summerhouse Condominium Ass'n, Inc. v. Majestic Savings & Loan Ass'n, 615 P.2d 71 (Colo. App. 1980).

30 Sutter Place Corporation, 240 NLRB 94.

Tillman v. Wheaton-Haven Recreation Ass'n, Inc., 517 F.2d 1141 (4th Cir. 1975).

Tower Forty-One Ass'n v. Levitt, XXX S.E.2d XXX (Fla. 3d D. Ct. App. 1983), holding that association may not violate its own bylaws.

Tower House Condominium, Inc. v. Millman, Case No. 80-1468 (Fla. 3rd D.C.A. 1981).

Village Management, Inc. v. Waltham Condominium Ass'n, C.A. No. 75-474-CA(L)01-A (Cir. Ct. Palm Beach Co., Fla., 1979).

Westgate Terrace Community Associates, Inc., v. Burger King Corp., 66 Ill. App. 3d 721 (1978).

White v. Cox, 17 Cal. App. 3d 824 (1971).

Wiggins v. Apanas, Law No. 79C2 584 (N.D. Ill. 1979).

Winston Towers 300 Ass'n, Inc., et al., v. Centex Homes of New Jersey, Inc., et al., C.A. No. C-1971-77 (Sup. Ct. N.J. 1978).

Winter v. Plaza del Sol, Inc., 353 So. 2d 598 (Fla. 4th D.C.A. 1977).

Woodham Estates v. Sartori, C.A. No. 388310, (Sup. Ct. N.M. 1977).

Yorkland Development Company, Inc., et al. v. Royal Park Condominium Ass'n, C.A. No. 76-963655 (Ct. Common Pleas Cuyahoga Co., Ohio 1980).

Zaid v. Island House Condominium Ass'n, 170 N.J. Super. 206 (1979).

INDEX